ARCTIC OCEAN

Barrow

BEAUFORT SEA

ARCTIC AND WESTERN ALASKA
Pages 218–235

EASTERN INTERIOR ALASKA
Pages 180–201

ARCTIC AND WESTERN ALASKA

CANADA

Eagle

Fairbanks

EASTERN INTERIOR ALASKA

WESTERN INTERIOR ALASKA

Tok

WESTERN INTERIOR ALASKA
Pages 156–179

ANCHORAGE   Valdez

SOUTHWEST ALASKA

Seward   Cordova

PRINCE WILLIAM SOUND

Dillingham

THE KENAI PENINSULA

Juneau

GULF OF ALASKA

Kodiak

Sitka

SOUTHEAST ALASKA

Ketchikan

SOUTHEAST ALASKA
Pages 124–155

PACIFIC OCEAN

EYEWITNESS TRAVEL

ALASKA

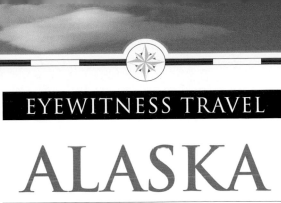

EYEWITNESS TRAVEL

ALASKA

MAIN CONTRIBUTOR: DEANNA SWANEY

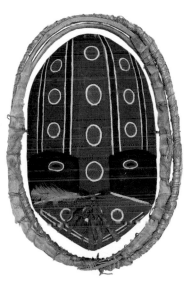

LONDON, NEW YORK,
MELBOURNE, MUNICH AND DELHI
www.dk.com

MANAGING EDITOR Aruna Ghose
ART EDITOR Priyanka Thakur
PROJECT EDITOR Ankita Awasthi
PROJECT DESIGNER Mathew Kurien
EDITOR Arundhti Bhanot
DESIGNER Baishakhee Sengupta
SENIOR CARTOGRAPHER Uma Bhattacharya
CARTOGRAPHER Alok Pathak
SENIOR PICTURE RESEARCHER Taiyaba Khatoon
PICTURE RESEARCHER Sumita Khatwani
DTP COORDINATOR Shailesh Sharma
DTP DESIGNERS Vinod Harish, Azeem Siddiqui

CONTRIBUTORS
Deanna Swaney, Eric Amrine

PHOTOGRAPHERS
Nigel Hicks, Andrew Holligan

ILLUSTRATORS
Arun Pottirayil, Madhav Raman, T. Gautam Trivedi

Reproduced in Singapore by Colourscan
Printed in China by L.Rex Printing Company Limited.

First American Edition, 2006
10 11 12 13 10 9 8 7 6 5 4 3 2 1

Published in the United States by DK Publishing, Inc.,
375 Hudson Street, New York, New York 10014

Reprinted with revisions 2008, 2010

Copyright © 2006, 2010 Dorling Kindersley Limited, London
A Penguin Company

Published in Great Britain by Dorling Kindersley Limited.

A CATALOG RECORD FOR THIS BOOK IS AVAILABLE FROM
THE LIBRARY OF CONGRESS.

ISSN 1542-1554
ISBN: 978-0-75666-199-1

Front cover main image: Hubbard Glacier, Yakutat Bay

MIX
Paper from
responsible sources
FSC
www.fsc.org   FSC™ C018179

**The information in this
DK Eyewitness Travel Guide is checked regularly.**
Every effort has been made to ensure that this book is as up-to-date
as possible at the time of going to press. Some details, however,
such as telephone numbers, opening hours, prices, gallery hanging
arrangements and travel information are liable to change. The
publishers cannot accept responsibility for any consequences arising
from the use of this book, nor for any material on third party
websites, and cannot guarantee that any website address in this book
will be a suitable source of travel information. We value the views
and suggestions of our readers very highly. Please write to: Publisher,
DK Eyewitness Travel Guides, Dorling Kindersley, 80 Strand,
London, WC2R 0RL, Great Britain, or email: travelguides@dk.com.

◁ Lily pond along the Seward Highway, Chugach National Forest

Brown bear roaming the tundra
of Denali National Park

CONTENTS

INTRODUCING
ALASKA

DISCOVERING
ALASKA **8**

PUTTING ALASKA
ON THE MAP **12**

A PORTRAIT
OF ALASKA **14**

ALASKA THROUGH
THE YEAR **42**

THE HISTORY
OF ALASKA **48**

St. Innocent Russian Orthodox
Cathedral, Anchorage

ALASKA AREA BY AREA

ALASKA AT A
GLANCE **60**

ANCHORAGE **62**

THE KENAI
PENINSULA **92**

PRINCE WILLIAM
SOUND **112**

The day's catch of halibut displayed
at the waterfront, Seward

SOUTHEAST
ALASKA **124**

WESTERN INTERIOR
ALASKA **156**

EASTERN INTERIOR
ALASKA **180**

SOUTHWEST
ALASKA **202**

ARCTIC AND WESTERN
ALASKA **218**

Handwoven
Aleut basket

TRAVELERS' NEEDS

WHERE TO STAY **238**

WHERE TO EAT **252**

CRUISING IN
ALASKA **264**

OUTDOOR
ACTIVITIES **272**

Kayaking in the calm waters off
Whittier, Prince William Sound

SURVIVAL GUIDE

PRACTICAL
INFORMATION **278**

TRAVEL
INFORMATION **288**

GENERAL INDEX **300**

ACKNOWLEDGMENTS
310

Cocktail bar at Aurora Ice Museum,
Chena Hot Springs

Kennicott *(see pp188–9)*

INTRODUCING
ALASKA

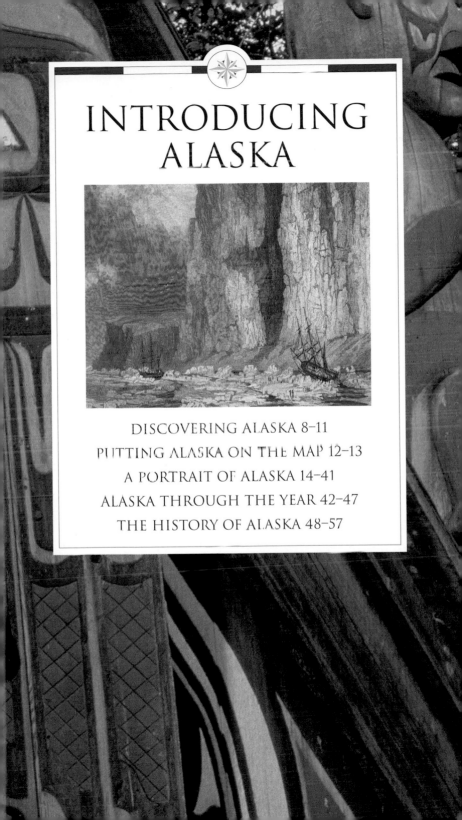

DISCOVERING ALASKA 8–11

PUTTING ALASKA ON THE MAP 12–13

A PORTRAIT OF ALASKA 14–41

ALASKA THROUGH THE YEAR 42–47

THE HISTORY OF ALASKA 48–57

DISCOVERING ALASKA

Alaska can be roughly divided into eight main regions. The largest city, Anchorage, brings a taste of urban life to the wilderness, while to the south, the Kenai Peninsula offers a range of outdoor activities. Prince William Sound, a spectacular bay on the south coast, features superb scenery and wildlife-viewing. Southeast Alaska, an archipelago of stunning islands, boasts the state capital Juneau, and a host of charming towns. The vast Interior, bisected by the Alaska Range, contains Fairbanks, the state's second city, and Alaska's portion of the Klondike goldfields. Southwest Alaska combines stark volcanic landscapes with fine fishing grounds, while Arctic and Western Alaska is a pristine wilderness. Below is an overview of each of these diverse regions.

Aerial view of Anchorage with the Chugach Range in the background

ANCHORAGE

- **Ample shopping**
- **Anchorage Museum**
- **Alaska Native Heritage Center**
- **The backyard wilderness of Chugach State Park**

Alaska's largest city, busy and sprawling Anchorage makes a great introduction to the state. Dotted with pleasant green areas and flanked by Turnagain and Knik Arms, it enjoys a striking location and offers plenty of opportunities for outdoor adventure on its doorstep.

The downtown **Anchorage Museum** (see pp68–9), with its extensive displays, is a must-see sight. The **Alaska Native Heritage Center** (see pp72–3), which provides an introduction to Alaska's diverse Native cultures, merits at least half a day. An afternoon can be spent shopping for

gifts (see pp88–9), watching the floatplanes at Lake Hood/Lake Spenard, the country's busiest floatplane complex, or exploring the scenic **Tony Knowles Coastal Trail** (see pp74–5).

A full day can be spent in the incredibly attractive **Chugach State Park** (see pp78–9), perhaps including a hike from the Eagle River Nature Center. Alternatively, a day can be spent driving the beautiful route along **Turnagain Arm** (see pp80–81) to Portage

Glacier. With more time, it is worth visiting the **Matanuska-Susitna Valley** (see pp84–5), known for its giant vegetables.

THE KENAI PENINSULA

- **World-class fishing**
- **Excellent hiking**
- **Whale-watching in Kenai Fjords National Park**
- **Free-spirited Homer**

With glaciated peaks, forests, and fjords in the east and excellent fishing and views of the Aleutian volcanoes in the west, the Kenai Peninsula is among the state's most scenic and diverse regions. Often referred to as Alaska's Playground, it offers countless recreational opportunities.

The amount of time needed to explore this region will depend on individual interests. Keen anglers would do well with at least three days: a day of halibut fishing in Resurrection Bay off **Seward** (see pp98–9) or **Homer** (see pp110–11) and two on the **Kenai River** (see p96). Avid hikers should allow about

Humpback whale diving in Aialik Bay, Kenai Fjords National Park

◁ Vividly painted façade of the Raven Clan House at Totem Bight State Park, Ketchikan

Cruise ship sailing past the glaciers of College Fjord, Prince William Sound

five days to hike the popular **Resurrection Pass Trail** *(see p97)*. The Seward Highway from Anchorage to Seward makes a pleasant drive. A morning at Seward's **Alaska SeaLife Center** *(see pp100–1)* and an evening glacier- and whale-watching cruise in **Kenai Fjords National Park** *(see pp104–105)* are particularly recommended. Also worthwhile is the leisurely drive on the Sterling Highway to Homer, stopping at Skilak Lake and historic **Kenai** *(see pp106–107)*, or at the Russian village of **Nikolaevsk** *(see p108)*. An additional day might include a cruise out of Homer or a hike in **Kachemak Bay State Park** *(see p111)*.

PRINCE WILLIAM SOUND

- **Sea kayaking**
- **Close-up glacier viewing**
- **Atmospheric Cordova**
- **Childs Glacier**

The sheltered waters of Prince William Sound open up Alaska's greatest concentration of tidewater glaciers, as well as excellent opportunities for cruising, kayaking, and viewing marine wildlife. To see the best of the area will require at least three days. Fortunately, travel connections are good, with regular Marine Highway ferries between Whittier, Cordova, and Valdez. Visitors to **Whittier** *(see p116)* can either hire kayaks or hop aboard a cruise to **College Fjord** *(see p117)* for an

exhilarating trip. **Valdez** *(see pp118–19)*, with world-class heli-skiing and the Alyeska Pipeline Terminal, is the unofficial capital of the region. From here, a drive to **Worthington Glacier** and the tumbling waterfalls of **Keystone Canyon** *(see p119)* is a good option. From the quiet little town of **Cordova** *(see p122)*, a popular activity is to drive out along the beautiful **Copper River Highway** *(see p123)* to view the always-calving **Childs Glacier**.

SOUTHEAST ALASKA

- **Cruising the Inside Passage**
- **Charming Sitka**
- **Glacier Bay National Park**
- **Historic Skagway**

Dotted with friendly port communities, this spectacular island-studded landscape of forested mountains and deep fjords serves as an introduction to the state for many visitors. Bustling **Ketchikan**

(see pp128–9) merits at least two days, and is also the gateway for trips into the atmospheric **Misty Fiords National Monument** *(see p130)* or visiting authentic **Prince of Wales Island** *(see pp132–3)*. A ferry ride to the north are the towns of **Wrangell** *(see pp134–5)*, offering bear viewing at Anan Creek, and Norwegian-influenced **Petersburg** *(see p138)*. Farther north, compact **Sitka** *(see pp140–41)* merits a full day to explore its impressive Russian and Tlingit heritage. Visitors to Alaska's capital, **Juneau** *(see pp142–5)*, will need at least two days to explore its historic buildings and museums. The city is also the jumping-off point for UNESCO World Heritage Site, **Glacier Bay National Park** *(see pp146–7)*. From **Skagway** *(see pp150–51)* visitors can retrace the **Gold Rush Routes** *(see pp152–3)* used by early stampeders, including the world-famous hike along the Chilkoot Trail.

Totem Square and the boat harbor, Sitka

Denali National Park Road winding through tundra with Mount McKinley in the distance

WESTERN INTERIOR ALASKA

- Denali National Park
- Viewing the aurora borealis
- Fairbanks
- Relaxing hot springs

Covered with boreal forests and lakes and enjoying the state's best summer weather, the vast Western Interior attracts visitors with the renowned **Denali National Park** *(see pp166–9)*, abundant wildlife, and the bright lights of Fairbanks. From September through March, the region also offers some of Alaska's best aurora viewing.

Denali National Park is the region's biggest draw, with spectacular scenery and wildlife viewing. Those on organized tours can see the best of the park in a day, but individual visitors must allow at least two days to handle logistics, ride the shuttle bus to Wonder Lake, and perhaps take a rafting trip on the **Nenana River** *(see p172)*. Nearby **Denali State Park** *(see p164)* offers great hiking and some of the finest views of Mount McKinley.

Fairbanks, Alaska's second city *(see pp174–7)*, offers a host of attractions, including the Morris Thompson Cultural and Visitor Center and the University of Alaska Museum of the North. The Riverboat Discovery Cruise will take most of a day, while a third day will suffice to hike through the Chena

River State Recreation Area and soak in the relaxing Chena Hot Springs. Add two more days to reach Manley Hot Springs on the **Elliott Highway** *(see p178)* or drive the **Steese Highway** *(see p179)* to the village of Circle on the Yukon River.

EASTERN INTERIOR ALASKA

- **Wrangell-St. Elias National Park**
- **Historical Kennicott**
- **Yukon River cruises**
- **Gold Rush remnants**

The heart of Alaska's Klondike, the Eastern Interior takes in vast swathes of landscape, the peaks of the Wrangell-St. Elias Mountains, and the broad **Yukon River** *(see pp198–9)*, which offers adventure around every

Historic Kennicott within Wrangell-St. Elias National Park

bend. A UNESCO World Heritage Site, **Wrangell-St. Elias National Park** *(see pp192–3)* is appearing on a growing number of itineraries. **Kennicott** *(see pp188–9)*, the most popular destination within the park, is accessed via the **Edgerton Highway/McCarthy Road** *(see p187)* from near **Copper Center** *(see pp184–5)*. Kennicott merits a whole day to fully explore the fascinating ruins of the mine, especially for those who wish to try a glacier walk along Kennicott Glacier, hike to Bonanza Mine, or take a flightseeing trip over the spectacular surroundings.

After a stop at the pleasant **Tok River State Recreation Site** *(see pp194–5)*, it is worth driving down the Alaska Highway to view trumpeter swans at the **Tetlin National Wildlife Refuge** *(see p195)*. Alternatively, head north on the Taylor Highway. After a stop in the quirky Gold Rush village of **Chicken** *(see p196)*, travelers can decide whether to continue north to the charming town of **Eagle** *(see p197)* or head east along the Top of the World Highway into Canada to the Gold Rush town of **Dawson City** *(see pp200–1)*, whose attractions are worth a stay of two or even three days. With some extra time, it is possible to cruise the Yukon River between Dawson and Circle through **Yukon-Charley Rivers National Preserve** *(see p196)*.

SOUTHWEST ALASKA

- **Russian and Alutiiq culture in Kodiak**
- **The world's best brown bear viewing**
- **The Aleutian Islands**
- **The wildlife-rich Pribilofs**

Alaska's remote Southwest attracts adventurous visitors with its wild volcanic landscapes, exceptional wildlife viewing opportunities, and Russian and Native heritage. Visits will need more planning than to mainland areas on the highway system, as the region is accessible only by air or ferry. Wildlife and angling aficionados visiting the Island of **Kodiak** *(see pp206–207)* will need two or three days for wilderness trips into Kodiak National Wildlife Refuge. Kodiak town, which highlights the island's Alutiiq and Russian cultures, will provide an enjoyable day of exploring at the Baranov and Alutiiq Museums and the Holy Resurrection Russian Orthodox Church.

Two days are essential for **Katmai National Park** *(see pp210–11)*, with its unsurpassed bear viewing at Brooks Falls and fabulous volcanic scenery. Permit lottery winners can also view

bears in the McNeil River State Game Sanctuary.

The graceful volcanic arc of the Aleutian Islands is most easily visited at **Dutch Harbor/Unalaska** *(see pp214–15)*, which has an airport and ferry terminal. With great hiking around Summer Bay and the wonderful Museum of the Aleutians, the island merits at least two days. The remote **Pribilof Islands** *(see pp216–17)* offer fantastic bird-watching and fur seal rookeries and require two days or more to explore thoroughly.

Also in the Southwest, visitors can experience the **Walrus Islands State Game Sanctuary** *(see p208)*, the immense **Wood-Tikchik State Park** *(see p209)*, and the caldera at **Aniakchak National Monument** *(see p212)*.

ARCTIC AND WESTERN ALASKA

- **Driving the Dalton Highway**
- **Intriguing Native cultures**
- **The icy Arctic Ocean**
- **Superb bird-watching**

Alaska's lonely Arctic and Western regions are characterized by seemingly endless expanses of tundra slashed by wild mountain ranges and

Musk oxen on the snowy tundra plains of the North Slope

untamed rivers. This is the land of the Yup'ik and Inupiat who have thrived in this harsh environment for thousands of years. Apart from places along the Dalton Highway, Arctic and Western Alaska is accessible only by air and most visitors usually opt to visit only one part of this vast region that stretches from the Canadian border to the Bering Sea.

For those with a car or RV, the **Dalton Highway** *(see pp222–3)* opens up some of the finest landscape in the region, including the scenic corridor through the Brooks Range to the Prudhoe Bay oilfields at the coast of the **Arctic Ocean** *(see p224)*. It is wise to allow at least five days for the long and rugged round trip from Fairbanks.

Barrow *(see pp226–7)* and **Kotzebue** *(see p230)* provide close-up Arctic Ocean views, as well as excellent introductions to Alaska's Inupiat culture. **Nome** *(see pp233–5)* recalls its rollicking Gold Rush days, but also boasts three quite distinct wilderness routes – the Council, Teller, and Kougarok Roads – to explore the diverse faces of the lonely and scenic Seward Peninsula. In this area, birders will find some of the world's best bird-watching, as well as the picturesque Last Train to Nowhere.

Visits to far-flung national parks and wildlife refuges can be commercially or privately organized and take from three days to three weeks.

Sow bear and yearling cubs at Naknek Lake, Katmai National Park

Putting Alaska on the Map

Flanked by the Arctic and Pacific Oceans, separated
from Russia by the Bering Strait, and bordered by
Canada in the east, Alaska lies across the Arctic Circle.
Covering over 586,400 sq miles (1.5 million sq km)
and with just 650,000 people, it is the largest and least
densely populated US state. Almost half of all
Alaskans live in Anchorage, while the rest are concentrated around Fairbanks, Southeast Alaska, the Mat-Su
Valley, and the Kenai Peninsula. The spectacular landscape, dotted with national parks, is dominated by
glaciers, rugged mountain ranges, island chains,
broad river valleys, and wide coastal plains.

Barrow
Wainwright

Point Lay

Umiat
Colville

Arctic Circle

Point Hope

Kivalina
Anaktuvuk Pass

Noatak
Wiseman

Kotzebue Kiana Ambler Coldfoot
Arctic Circle Bettles

Shishmaref A L A S

RUSSIA

Wales Deering
Teller Kougarok
Koyukuk Huslia
Council
Koyukuk Tanana Yukon
Nome Galena Ruby Manley H
Springs
Gambell
Savoonga Shaktoolik Poorman
Unalakleet

BERING SEA Stebbins
Der
Villa

Sheldon Kotlik Ophir
Point Anvik McGrath

KEY

✈ International airport

☒ Airstrip Hooper Bay Holy Cross Iditarod Talkeetr

⛴ Ferry terminal Newtok Aniak Stony River Wasilla
Anchorag
▬ Alaska Highway Mekoryuk Bethel Kashegelok

▬ Highway Kwigillingok Kenai
Soldotna
═ Minor road Kipnuk Quinhagak Ninilchik

▪▪ International border Aleknagik Iliamna Kakhonak Hom
Platinum Togiak
— Railroad Dillingham Naknek

Egegik King Salmon

St. Paul Pilot Point Port Lions Kodiak
Pribilof
Islands St. George Akhiok Old Harbor

Port Heiden

Port Moller Chignik

Cold Bay King Sand
Cove Point
Unalaska/Dutch Akutan
Harbor

Aleutian Islands

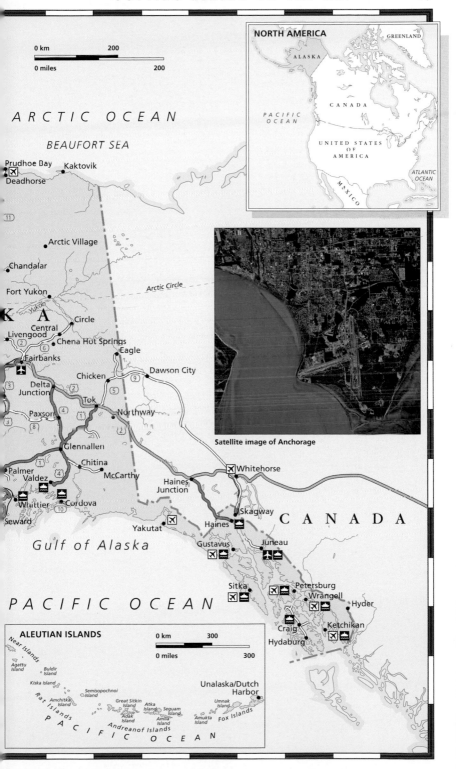

GREENLAND

ALASKA

PACIFIC
OCEAN

CANADA

UNITED STATES
OF
AMERICA

ATLANTIC
OCEAN

MEXICO

0 km   200

0 miles   200

ARCTIC OCEAN

BEAUFORT SEA

Prudhoe Bay   Kaktovik
Deadhorse

11

Arctic Village

Chandalar

Fort Yukon

Arctic Circle

K   A

Yukon   Circle
Central
Livengood
2   Chena Hot Springs
6   Eagle
Fairbanks   Dawson City
Chicken
3   2
Delta   Tok   5
Junction   9
Paxson   4   1
3   8   Northway
2

Glennallen

Chitina
Palmer   McCarthy
Valdez
1   Haines
4   Junction   Whitehorse
Whittier   Cordova
Seward   10   Skagway

Gulf of Alaska   Yakutat   Haines   **C A N A D A**

Gustavus   Juneau

Sitka   Petersburg
Wrangell   Hyder

PACIFIC OCEAN   Craig   Ketchikan
Hydaburg

Satellite image of Anchorage

ALEUTIAN ISLANDS   0 km   300

0 miles   300

Near Islands
Agattu
Island   *Buldir*
Island
Kiska Island   *Semisopochnoi*   *Unalaska/Dutch*
Island   *Harbor*
Rat Islands   *Amchitka*   *Great Sitkin*   *Umnak*
Island   *Island*   *Atka*   *Seguam*   *Island*
Adak   *Amlia*   *Island*
Island   *Island*   *Amukta*   *Fox Islands*
Andreanof Islands   *Island*
PACIFIC   O C E A N

A PORTRAIT OF ALASKA

Dominated by thundering glaciers, vast forests, wild rivers, and island-studded seas and fjords, Alaska is undoubtedly one of America's most scenic states. The magnificence of the land, wildlife viewing opportunities, an almost unmatched range of outdoor activities, and the chance to explore the state's Russian and Native heritage, all combine to draw visitors to Alaska.

Detached from the rest of the country by Canada's Yukon Territory and British Columbia, Alaska is the largest state in the US. While its monumental size can at times seem overwhelming, no one could fail to appreciate the sheer grandeur of the land.

Totem, Saxman Totem Park

Evidence of Alaska's Native heritage abounds in many towns and rural villages, where many indigenous groups keep their age-old traditions alive. Museums across the state are filled with Native artifacts and ceremonial objects, but the best place for an overview of these diverse cultures is the Alaska Native Heritage Center in Anchorage.

Remnants of Alaska's Russian past are also still in evidence. In the 18th century, Russian Orthodox clergy followed Russian trappers to Alaska and converted many locals. Several large communities have at least one Russian Orthodox church, and Kodiak, Sitka, and Unalaska retain especially strong Russian influences.

The state offers an incredible variety of outdoor activities, including whitewater rafting and wildlife viewing in the summer, and skiing and dogsledding in the winter. It is also one of the top cruise destinations in the world, with spectacular trips in the Gulf of Alaska and through the quiet channels of the Inside Passage.

Traditional crosses and domes of St. Innocent Russian Orthodox Cathedral in Anchorage

◁ **Mountains flanking the Resurrection River along the border of Kenai Fjords National Park**

Serene landscape of the Chugach National Forest along the Seward Highway

THE LAND AND ECOLOGY

Alaska's wilderness landscapes and diverse wildlife have long provided both resources and inspiration for those fortunate enough to experience them. The impact of humans reaches back many thousands of years to when the first Native peoples are said to have arrived via the Bering land bridge. Roaming across the landscape in search of resources, these semi-nomadic hunter-gatherers lived largely in harmony with the environment.

When the Russians arrived in the 18th century, however, their interest in sea otter and seal pelts sparked drastic declines in populations of those marine mammals, which have only recently begun to return in large numbers. The Russians were followed by Gold Rush prospectors, who trailed the Interior rivers in search of gold. Large-scale dredging along these water-courses left mountains of tailings, or mining residue, that remain as unsightly scars across the landscape.

After the discovery of oil on the North Slope in the 1970s, the Trans-Alaska Pipeline was built amid widespread concern that it would alter the ecology along its corridor. As a result of extensive environmental impact studies, the pipeline was designed to allow caribou to migrate freely beneath it or over it, and drilling companies were required to follow strict drilling and cleanup guidelines.

Today, Alaska has the largest population of bears, moose, wolves, and bald eagles in the US, and also supports species, such as musk oxen and caribou, that are found in no other US state. The prolific wildlife is due not only to Alaska's relative remoteness, but also to the fact that it has more protected or semi-protected habitat than any other state.

However, Alaska faces several prominent ecological issues, from the possibility that an enormous gold mine will be developed on the Bristol Bay Watershed to the aerial hunting of

Caribou on the autumn tundra, Denali National Park

wolves. Global warming also ignites passions. Scientists report that human-created greenhouse gases, especially in Arctic regions, have caused rapid changes. Alaska faces dramatic changes as rising sea levels erode coastal villages, glaciers continue to recede, ocean acidification threatens fish and crab populations, and insect infestations and forest fires become more devastating. Polar bears and walruses also face a bleak future as the sea ice melts.

THE ECONOMY

Historically, Alaska's economy revolved around timber, fishing, and mining, but that changed in the 1960s when oil was discovered at Prudhoe Bay. Even with the closure of most sawmills, commercial fishing and seafood processing remain viable industries. The most prominent export is salmon, and Alaska provides one of the world's last wild stocks of salmon. However, competition with cheaper farmed salmon from Chile, Norway, Scotland, and other places led to declines in the market in the 1990s. More recently, prices have rebounded as consumers have come to appreciate the advantages of wild Alaskan salmon over farmed fish. On the mining front, the zinc mine near Kotzebue and a

Alaska Pipeline with the backdrop of the Alaska Range

large gold mine near Fairbanks are also proving profitable. In addition, both tourism and government agencies provide major sources of employment.

GOVERNMENT AND POLITICS

In general, Alaskan politics tend to be more conservative than most other US states. Due to its small population of around 650,000, Alaska is represented in the US Congress by the usual two senators but only one representative. It also has a state governor, lieutenant governor, and a bicameral legislature. Unlike other states, Alaska has no county governments, but is instead

Cruise ship *Carnival Spirit* docked at the marina in Seward

Yup'ik dancer performing at the Anchorage Native Heritage Center

organized into boroughs and municipalities.

Alaska's position as the crossroads between North America and Asia makes it a militarily strategic site for the US. During World War II, the Aleutian Islands were attacked by Japanese forces and even today, Alaska is considered a first line of defense against potential troubles from the west. Anchorage and Fairbanks have army and air force bases, and there are military installations across the state.

Politically, the most sensitive issues involve resource exploitation. One very vocal group of mostly younger people view the land as a wilderness

Colorful buildings in downtown Juneau in Southeast Alaska

to be preserved, while others who arrived in the earlier, more rough-and-ready days can be opportunists who see vast wealth to exploit. Conflicts between these two groups frequently escalate into national debate.

PEOPLE AND SOCIETY

On the whole, Alaskans are friendly and genuinely welcome visitors with great pride in their home state. While typically American in most respects, Alaskans are usually younger and live a somewhat more rugged life. Beyond the major cities, most people are accustomed to the remoteness, extreme cold, and high retail prices. Alaska has more hunting licenses per capita and more subsistence hunters living off the land than any other state. More Alaskans own snow-machines (the local term for snowmobiles) and all-terrain vehicles than other Americans, and about one in 50 residents is a private pilot.

All but about 30 percent of Alaskans are

transplanted from elsewhere and are in the state by choice. Many have come for economic opportunities or with the military, but a majority have moved here because of a perceived sense of individual freedom that is becoming increasingly rare in most of the Lower 48 (the contiguous US states).

Demographically, about 16 percent of Alaskans are of Native heritage, while the rest are mainly of European descent. Around 10 percent of the population is African-American, Hispanic, Asian, or Pacific Islander, but minority numbers are increasing, especially in Anchorage. Most of the Native population lives in rural Alaska off the road system, while other minorities live primarily in Juneau, Anchorage, Fairbanks, and other large towns. Significant numbers of Asians, mainly Koreans and Filipinos, work as temporary laborers on fishing boats and in canneries along the Gulf of Alaska, and every summer, the cruising and tourist industry employs hundreds of seasonal workers.

Most Alaskans tend to hole up during the cold, dark months of winter, preferring to work on indoor projects and plan for the summer, although this hibernation is usually

Kayaking in glacial waters in Southeast Alaska

broken up by forays into the outdoors to ski, ice fish, buzz around on snow-machines, or go mushing (dog-sledding). In the endless daylight of summer, however, Alaskans go into overdrive, packing in as many activities as possible before the season winds down, the days shorten and winter returns. While summer visitors would be forgiven for assuming that all Alaskans are hyperactive, there is so much to see and do that it is almost impossible not to join them in their infectious round-the-clock summer spirit.

Fly fishing in the clear blue waters of the Kenai River

Alaska's Native Cultures

Alaska's Native peoples have long enjoyed rich cultures based upon deep spiritual values derived from their relationships to the plants, animals, and climates of their natural environments. There is no single "Native" culture or way of life, as each group has its own traditions and arts that were initially linked to the environment they lived in and the available resources *(see pp22–3)*. While few Natives now strictly follow traditional ways, many have a renewed interest in preserving their heritage, both through material arts and the revival of Native languages. Evidence of this resurgence is seen in Native villages and cultural centers, where visitors can meet Native Alaskans and explore their traditions, art, and crafts.

Summer visitors to Kotzebue participating in a blanket toss

Traditional housing *included Aleut semi-subterranean shelters, such as this* ulax *replica at the Alaska Native Heritage Center* (see pp72–3).

The raven is honored in the colorful stylized motif that graces the front of this clan house.

The colors used were significant. Red represented valor, blue stood for the sea and sky, and white signified space and peace.

CLAN HOUSES

These community dwellings, such as this Tlingit Raven clan house in Totem Bight State Historical Park *(see p129)*, housed up to 50 people in one large room. Each family had its own space, but shared a single fireplace and stored its belongings beneath the planked flooring.

Doorways were small to conserve heat, and those passing through needed to stoop down to enter.

Igloos *(structures constructed of blocks of ice) were historically built by Inuit hunters and mountain climbers as temporary shelters. The word itself simply means "house."*

Whaling *is an annual springtime event for Inupiat and St. Lawrence Island Yup'ik peoples, who set out in traditional sealskin boats called* umiaqs *as soon as ice conditions permit. Skins need to be changed every other year to remain watertight.*

Dancing, *as in this Inupiat performance, is usually accompanied by chanting and drumming and is used to celebrate festive events and ceremonial rituals.*

Drumming *and drum-making, using caribou hide or sealskin, are spiritually-rooted Inupiat traditions. Here, a Kotzebue elder beats a drum while chanting in the Inupiat language.*

The main house pole shows Duk-toothl, a legendary man of the Raven clan, who wears a weasel skin hat.

Totem pole raisings *are festive events for the Tlingit, Haida, and Tsimshian peoples of Southeast Alaska. Historically, such events were commemorated by potlatches, or gifting feasts. Here, Tsimshian celebrants lift a pole into place at a gathering of three clans in Metlakatla.*

Soapstone carving *is prominent among the Inupiat and Yup'ik, who use soft black soapstone to create figurines of hunters, dancers, and animals. They also make scrimshaw, intricate designs carved on ivory or whalebone.*

Each eye of the raven in this design has been expanded to depict a complete face.

Aleut baskets, *such as this one at the Anchorage Museum of History and Art, are tightly woven of Aleutian Island grasses.*

Athabaskan beaded boots *are traditionally worn by women for dancing on festive occasions. The designs are usually intricate and demonstrate great skill.*

Tlingit masks *feature human-like visages, depicting interaction between humans and supernatural beings, or animals, representing individual clans, such as Beaver or Wolf.*

NATIVE ART AND CRAFTS

Every Native group celebrates its cultural heritage in arts and crafts that utilize locally available media. Thus, the Inupiat used walrus ivory for scrimshaw, while Aleuts are skilled at basket-weaving. Historically, all Native art either had a practical or ceremonial use. Today, while much of the art still serves traditional purposes, works are also sold in shops across Alaska. They may also be purchased directly from the artists.

Native Peoples of Alaska

Some anthropologists believe that the first Native peoples migrated to Alaska 30,000 to 12,000 years ago during the Ice Age that lowered sea levels and created a land bridge across the Bering Strait. These hunter-gatherers, ancestors of modern-day Indian peoples, were followed by the Inuit and Aleut peoples, who arrived by boat starting around 8,000 years ago, after the disappearance of the land bridge. There are, however, other theories that dispute this. Today, about 16 percent of Alaska's population claims Native descent. The Inuit or Eskimo include the Inupiat, Alutiiq, Aleut, Yup'ik, while the Indians include the Tsimshian, Athabaskan, Eyak, Tlingit, and Haida. While the term "Eskimo" ("eaters of raw meat" in Athabaskan) is generally not considered offensive in Alaska, Native Alaskans usually refer to themselves as members of a particular group, or collectively as Natives.

KEY

☐	Athabaskan
☐	Tlingit
■	Haida
■	Tsimshian
☐	Inupiat
☐	Yup'ik
☐	Aleut and Alutiiq

ATHABASKAN

Historically, the Athabaskans occupied the vast taiga forests of the Interior, which are characterized by a harsh climate. Largely a hunting and gathering society, the Athabaskans spent summers in riverside tent camps, collecting and drying fish and game for the cold season. In winter, they lived in houses made of sod and wood. Their clothing was made primarily of caribou or moose hide, colorfully decorated with porcupine quills and, after the arrival of the Europeans, with traded goods such as beads. Modern Athabaskans live mainly in the Interior, many in Fairbanks, where they enjoy an urban lifestyle but also make efforts to demonstrate their traditional ways to visitors.

Athabaskan family with pelts from the winter catch

TLINGIT

Alaska's Tlingit (pronounced KLINK-it), a Northwest Coast culture, have long inhabited Southeast Alaska. Historically, the Tlingit were a seafaring people, and their traders traveled as far as present-day Washington State in huge ocean-going canoes hewn from single cedar logs. Traditional Tlingit society had no central government, but each village had a stratified society that included high-ranking families, commoners, and slaves captured from neighboring tribes. Like the Haida, Tsimshian, and other Northwest Coast cultures, the Tlingit carved totem poles *(see p129)* to commemorate the culture unique to their respective clans. Pole-raisings and memorial ceremonies were accompanied by grand feasts called potlatches. Currently, the art of totem carving is re-emerging across Southeast Alaska, and other Tlingit arts are enjoying widespread popularity.

Tlingit dancer dressed in traditional style

HAIDA

The Haida share many cultural traditions with the Tlingit, including clan structures and totem pole carving. Expert sailors, they were known for their decorative ceremonial canoes. They traditionally depended on salmon and sea mammals for their subsistence. In the late 19th century, as many as 10,000 Haida lived in far southern Alaska, but by the 1890s, their numbers had been decimated by diseases brought in by Western explorers. Today, the Alaskan Haida population is about 2,000, but many more claim partial Haida descent. While they are now centered on Hydaburg on Prince of Wales Island, people of Haida descent live across southern Alaska.

Haida man in a bark hat and button cloak

TSIMSHIAN

Alaska's Tsimshian are descendants of 823 people who left Canada with Anglican missionary, Father Duncan, after local authorities denied their land claims. Settling in an abandoned Tlingit settlement on Annette Island, which they named Metlakatla after their village in British Columbia, they set up a model Protestant Christian community of white houses and well-appointed churches. The Tsimshian were the only Alaskan Native group that rejected the Alaska Native Claims Settlement Act of 1971 *(see p56)*. As a result, they are the only Native group to retain sovereignty over their land, with Annette Island being Alaska's only official Indian Reservation.

Tsimshian drummers at a ceremony

Inupiat men returning with a caribou caught in Kobuk Valley National Park

INUPIAT

The Inupiat (plural Inupiaq) mainly occupy areas along the Arctic Ocean coast and on the North Slope. Prior to European contact and influence, distinct Inupiat groups of extended families occupied home territories between Norton Sound on the Bering Strait and the Canadian border. Some groups were settled, but others traveled great distances to cooperatively hunt seals, whales, caribou, and other game animals. The Inupiat had no chiefs, but each family was headed by an *umialik*, who managed food and other family needs. Women were responsible for gathering plants and berries, skinning animals, drying *muktuk* (whale blubber), meat, and fish, and preparing food. While conflicts existed between groups, peaceful interaction did occur, especially during trade fairs at the end of each hunting season, which drew participants from as far away as Siberia. While some Inupiat today work for Native corporations or government agencies, many rural residents still make a livelihood from subsistence hunting, fishing, and gathering.

YUP'IK

The Yup'ik traditionally lived on the broad, marshy plains of the Yukon-Kuskokwim Delta, as well as on the Bering Sea coast and parts of the Seward Peninsula. Due to the milder and more vegetated environment, the Yup'ik made more use of wood, vegetables, and land animals than the Inupiat. With summer hunting camps, they also had permanent villages, where men lived in *qasgiqs*, or communal houses, and women and children in sod dwellings called *enet*. Lacking the resources Europeans wanted, the Yup'ik first encountered Westerners much later than the Aleut, Alutiiq, and Inupiat. In recent years, many Yup'ik have moved to towns, especially Bethel, but some still practice subsistence hunting or spend the summers working in family fish camps.

Yup'ik family beneath an *umiaq*, a traditional skin boat

Alutiiq woman in a beaded headdress

ALEUT AND ALUTIIQ

Both the Aleut and Alutiiq live in Southwest Alaska, the former in the Aleutian Islands and the latter from Prince William Sound to Kodiak Island and the Alaska Peninsula. The difference in their languages, however, suggests that they have entirely separate origins. Despite Southwest Alaska's stormy climate, both groups had a maritime hunting culture, using *baidarkas* (skin boats) to chase seals, otters, and whales. Early Russian otter hunters often killed or enslaved them and also introduced foreign diseases. The Russian Orthodox clergy that followed converted large numbers to the church, which remains a strong spiritual force for both groups. During World War II, entire villages were transferred to evacuation centers in Southeast Alaska to keep them from being taken prisoner by the Japanese. Today, associations in Kodiak and Unalaska are reviving both cultures and their languages.

Volcanoes and Earthquakes

Alaska lies on the geologically active Pacific Ring of Fire, where tectonic shifts can result in earthquakes and volcanic eruptions. One of the earth's tectonic plates is sliding under another, causing major geological changes. The entire southern Alaskan region is geologically dynamic; it is the site of about 8 percent of all the world's earthquakes and boasts dozens of active volcanoes. The second strongest earthquake in recorded history struck Southcentral Alaska in 1964, and in 1912, Novarupta exploded in what was the second most powerful eruption ever recorded.

LOCATOR MAP

— Aleutian Megathrust

— Subduction zone

Great Sitkin (1987), *a 5,742-ft (1,740-m) volcano, is a vent inside the caldera of an older shield volcano on the well-glaciated Great Sitkin Island, which is covered in a layer of dark pumice 20 ft (6 m) thick.*

Mount Cleveland, *a symmetrical 5,675-ft (1,730-m) cone on Chuginadak Island, is one of the Aleutians' most active volcanoes. This dramatic peak is a prominent feature of the beautiful Islands of Four Mountains.*

Kiska *(1962)*
Little Sitkin
Cerberus
Tanaga *(1914)*
Kanaga *(1996)*
Garitoi *(1996)*
Adak
Andreanof Islands
Korovin *(2006)*
Atka
Seguam *(1993)*
Yunaska *(1937)*
Amukta *(1997)*
Kagamil *(1929)*
Carlisle (1987)
Okmok *(2008)*
Vsevidof *(1957)*
Nikolski
Bogoslof *(1992)*
Makushin *(1995)*
Akut *(1992*
Unala
Fox Island

Bering Sea

Rat Islands

The Aleutian Megathrust is a very active fault line that is responsible for the numerous earthquakes in southern Alaska.

Aleutian Trench

TECTONIC ACTIVITY

The distinctive chain of islands and peaks that make up the Aleutian Islands is the result of plate tectonics – the movement of the interlocking plates of the earth's crust that ride on the molten material (magma) in the mantle. At the subduction zone, the oceanic Pacific plate is being forced under the continental North American plate, creating the Aleutian Trench. North of this zone, fractures in the continental plate allow magma from below to migrate upward. When the pressure increases, the magma bursts through the crust in dramatic volcanic activity.

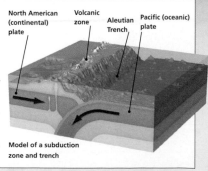

North American (continental) plate
Volcanic zone
Aleutian Trench
Pacific (oceanic) plate

Model of a subduction zone and trench

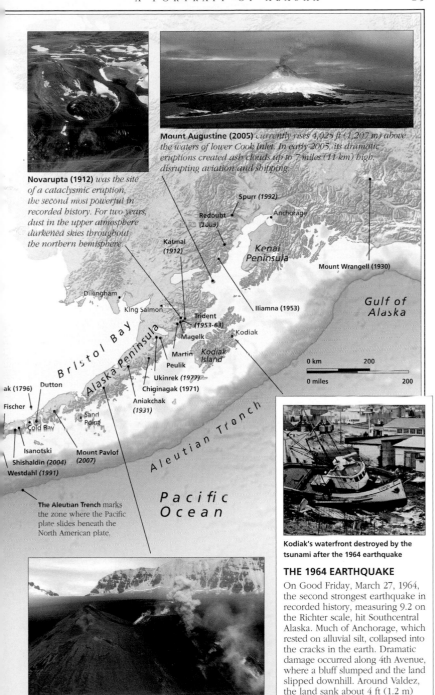

Novarupta (1912) *was the site of a cataclysmic eruption, the second most powerful in recorded history. For two years, dust in the upper atmosphere darkened skies throughout the northern hemisphere.*

Mount Augustine (2005) *currently rises 4,025 ft (1,207 m) above the waters of lower Cook Inlet. In early 2005, its dramatic eruptions created ash clouds up to 7 miles (11 km) high, disrupting aviation and shipping.*

Spurr (1992)

Redoubt (2009)

Anchorage

Katmai (1912)

Kenai Peninsula

Mount Wrangell (1930)

Dillingham

King Salmon

Gulf of Alaska

Trident (1953-63)

Iliamna (1953)

Magelk

Kodiak

Bristol Bay

Martin

Kodiak Island

0 km   200

0 miles   200

Peulik

Alaska Peninsula

Ukinrek (1977)

Chiginagak (1971)

ak (1796)   Dutton

Aniakchak (1931)

Fischer

Sand Point

Cold Bay

Aleutian Trench

Isanotski

Mount Pavlof (2007)

Shishaldin (2004)

Westdahl (1991)

The Aleutian Trench marks the zone where the Pacific plate slides beneath the North American plate.

Pacific Ocean

Mount Veniaminof (2008) *features a volcanic vent surrounded by a crater about 20 miles (32 km) in circumference that contains a glacier. This very active volcano has erupted several times in the early 21st century.*

Kodiak's waterfront destroyed by the tsunami after the 1964 earthquake

THE 1964 EARTHQUAKE

On Good Friday, March 27, 1964, the second strongest earthquake in recorded history, measuring 9.2 on the Richter scale, hit Southcentral Alaska. Much of Anchorage, which rested on alluvial silt, collapsed into the cracks in the earth. Dramatic damage occurred along 4th Avenue, where a bluff slumped and the land slipped downhill. Around Valdez, the land sank about 4 ft (1.2 m) and destroyed the town, while the resulting tsunami destroyed much of Valdez, Seward, and Kodiak.

Alaska's Glaciers

Much of Alaska's spectacular landscape has been shaped by 5,000 major and countless minor glaciers that scraped downhill from icefields in the coastal mountains, gouging out steep-sided valleys. As glaciers melted, valleys that were below sea level were filled by seawater to create long, narrow fjords. Although glaciers continue to reshape the landscape, most of these rivers of ice – the earth's largest reservoir of freshwater – are currently receding, and scientific research points to human-caused warming of the planet as the primary reason.

Crevasses *develop when stresses on the flowing ice cause large cracks in glaciers. The largest crevasses are found on steep sections of rapidly flowing ice.*

Outlet glaciers, *such as Mendenhall Glacier near Juneau, spill down steeply from icefields, creating ravines that serve as outlets for the icefield. They often flow into lakes created by the glacier's terminal moraine, a ridge of debris at the foot of the glacier.*

GLACIAL CHANGES

As glaciers flow downhill, friction against the rock melts the bottom ice, forming a "slide" so the glacier can surge ahead. Increasing air temperatures can cause melting at glacier faces, but can also cause surging, as higher temperatures mean more snowfall, and therefore, pressure, on parent icefields. Tidewater glaciers flowing into warming seas tend to recede due to higher water temperatures.

Lateral moraines are strips of ground rock on the edges of glaciers.

Bergy bits are large chunks of glacier ice or small icebergs, rising up to 13 ft (4 m) out of the water.

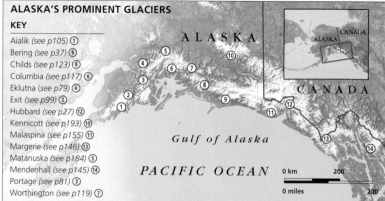

ALASKA'S PROMINENT GLACIERS

KEY

Aialik *(see p105)* ①
Bering *(see p37)* ⑨
Childs *(see p123)* ⑧
Columbia *(see p117)* ⑥
Eklutna *(see p79)* ④
Exit *(see p99)* ②
Hubbard *(see p27)* ⑫
Kennicott *(see p193)* ⑩
Malaspina *(see p155)* ⑪
Margerie *(see p146)* ⑬
Matanuska *(see p184)* ⑤
Mendenhall *(see p145)* ⑭
Portage *(see p81)* ③
Worthington *(see p119)* ⑦

ALASKA

CANADA

ALASKA

CANADA

Gulf of Alaska

PACIFIC OCEAN

0 km   200
0 miles   200

Valley glaciers are created when the weight of an icecap is great enough to make its edges flow downhill, creating rivers of ice that grind away underlying rock to form valleys. Valley glaciers are subdivided into outlet, tidewater, and piedmont glaciers.

Hanging glaciers in high mountain valleys may eventually become tributaries of a main valley glacier.

Medial moraines are wide, dark strips of debris and ground rock in the middle of valley or tidewater glaciers.

Icefields, *including the Juneau, Harding, and Bagley Icefields, are formed between high mountains when snow compresses into ice under the weight of additional snowfall. Liquid water beneath glaciers and shallow portions of icefields is revealed in deep wells called* moulins, *French for "mills." Peaks rising from icefields are called* nunataks.

Growler ice is a small chunk of floating ice that releases trapped air as it melts, making a growling noise.

HUBBARD GLACIER

Located near the town of Yukutat, Hubbard Glacier is North America's largest tidewater glacier, and one of the only advancing glaciers in Alaska. In 1986, it rammed across the mouth of Russell Fjord in just a few days, turning the fjord into a lake and trapping marine life on the wrong side of the ice wall. While the fjord has since reopened, the glacier still occasionally surges and may eventually seal off the fjord.

Fjords, *such as Prince William Sound's College Fjord, are narrow submarine valleys flanked by steep, glacier-carved walls that may erode into gentler slopes over time.*

Landscape and Wildlife

With its range of landforms and wild country, Alaska naturally supports a wealth of wildlife, not only in the mountains and forests, but also on the barren tundra, in the surrounding seas, and even in the cities and towns. In fact, Anchorage has a healthy moose population, and bears are occasionally sighted in city parks. Perhaps the most reliable wildlife viewing venue is Denali National Park. Visitors to the park's interior are typically treated to sightings of grizzlies, moose, caribou, Dall sheep, and a host of birds and smaller animals. A wealth of marine mammals – sea lions, sea otters, seals, and whales – abound in the Gulf of Alaska, Bering Sea, and the Arctic Ocean. Sightings are practically guaranteed on Inside Passage cruises, and on day cruises and ferry trips in Southeast Alaska, Prince William Sound, and the Kenai Fjords.

Orcas *are often seen in the Gulf of Alaska and its sheltered bays, where visitors can also spot other marine mammals such as seals and otters.*

TEMPERATE RAINFOREST
The islands of the eastern Gulf Coast and Southeast Alaska form the world's largest expanse of temperate rainforest *(see p131)*. Conifers such as Western hemlock and Sitka spruce dominate, but there is also muskeg or spongy bog, composed of sphagnum moss, peat, and ground cover.

TAIGA AND BOREAL FOREST
The boreal forest *(see p161)*, which covers most of the Alaskan mainland, ranges from mixed birch to black and white spruce woodland. Low-lying, poorly-drained areas are typified by taiga, characterized by bog dominated by spindly black spruce.

Lynx *are the only wild cats native to Alaska. They are distinguished by long tufts on the tip of each ear and have unusually large paws that act as snowshoes in very deep snow and aid in winter hunting.*

Black bears *are the most common and widely distributed of North America's three species of bears* (see p109). *At about 5 ft (2 m) in length, they are the smallest. They range in color from black to almost white.*

Sitka black-tailed deer *are native to the Southeast, whose old-growth forests provide optimal foraging and habitat.*

Moose, *the largest member of the deer family, can weigh up to 1,500 lb (675 kg). Besides pondweed, they feed on willow, birch, and aspen twigs.*

ROCKY COASTLINES

In many places along the coast of the Gulf of Alaska and the Bering Sea, the land rises from the sea in rocky beaches and high cliffs that are frequently pummeled by storms and pounding waves. The seas, rich in plankton and fish, support both nesting birds and marine mammals, such as sea otters, seals, sea lions, and walruses. Below the high tide line, seaweed beds and tide pools provide a habitat for mollusks and soft-bodied creatures such as octopuses and jellyfish.

Northern fur seals *haul out on the Pribilof Islands to breed and bear pups. About 700,000 – half of the world population of northern fur seals – gather here every summer. Over the last decade the population has declined sharply.*

Walruses, *with their distinctive coarse whiskers and ivory tusks, are seen mainly on rocky Bering Sea beaches, where males break their journey northward to their breeding grounds around the Arctic Ocean.*

HIGH MOUNTAINS AND ICEFIELDS

The alpine areas of Alaska are found in the high mountain ranges that arc along the southern coast of the state and in the peripheral ranges crossing the Interior and Arctic regions. The southern ranges are capped by extensive icefields that give rise to the valley glaciers that carve intermontane valleys and fjords.

ARCTIC TUNDRA

Most of Arctic and Western Alaska is covered with Arctic tundra *(see p225)*, which ranges from rolling expanses covered by low shrubs and miniature grasses to spongy tussocks and vast open plains. Despite the harsh climate, the shallow soils support a diversity of plant life including flowers, berries, and lichen.

Dall sheep *inhabit alpine meadows and steep slopes, fleeing to rocky crags to escape pursuers. These herbivores are rarely found below the timberline.*

Musk oxen, *hunted to extinction in Alaska, were reintroduced from Greenland in the 1930s. Qiviut, their soft, warm underhair, is spun into fiber.*

Hoary marmots *burrow on alpine slopes and use high-pitched whistles as alarm signals. These rodents hibernate for seven months.*

Caribou *in Alaska number about a million individuals. Herds of up to 400,000 migrate annually between summer and winter ranges that can be up to 250 miles (400 km) apart.*

Birds of Alaska

Common redpoll

From enormous trumpeter swans to tiny hummingbirds, Alaska's bird life is varied and prolific, with 437 identified species and over 60 incidental visitors. Bald eagles can be spotted in old-growth timber, while sandpipers and peeps scurry around at the water's edge. Countless migratory birds summer in Alaska, and loons, snow geese, and herons can be seen at lakes and ponds across the state. On the remote Pribilofs, red-legged kittiwakes, puffins, crested auklets, and many others nest on the storm-battered sea cliffs.

Bird-watching *is popular on coastal cruises, such as this tour at Glacier Bay.*

CLIFF-NESTERS

Many Alaskan seabirds nest on sea cliffs to protect their nests and hatchlings from predators. The best places to see nesting gannets, fulmars, petrels, cormorants, puffins, kittiwakes, and other cliff-nesting birds include Glacier Bay, Kenai Fjords National Park, and the Pribilof Islands.

Thick-billed murres inhabit large cliff colonies, but do not build nests, instead laying their eggs on bare rock.

Glaucous gulls, *among the world's largest gulls, live on the Pribilof Islands (see pp216–17) and on the western and northern coasts, from the Yukon-Kuskokwim Delta to Canada's northern regions. The similar, but smaller, Glaucous-winged gull breeds along Alaska's southern coasts.*

Black-billed magpies *have a lustrous green iridescence on their wings and tails. They can be seen in open country, but need birch, cotton-woods, or shrubs for nesting.*

WINTER BIRDS

Most nesting and migratory birds in Alaska go south in winter, but Steller's jays, magpies, ravens, and ptarmigan are year-round residents. The availability of food in towns has changed the migratory patterns of ducks and geese and it is often possible to see them in mid-winter in the Southeast. Chickadees, nuthatches, and other small birds that winter in Alaska can also be seen around bird-feeders in the south.

The raven *has long been revered by indigenous peoples as the creator of the world and bringer of daylight. These intelligent corvids especially like to raid urban dumpsters.*

The willow ptarmigan, *the official state bird, is seen all year round. Its plumage, brilliant white in winter, becomes a mottled brown in summer to blend in with the forest floor.*

FRESHWATER BIRDS

During the spring and summer mating season, Alaska's lakes and muskeg attract ducks, snow geese, trumpeter and tundra swans, blue herons, loons, and several species of grebes. Sandhill cranes, which perform an elaborate mating dance, can easily be seen in Creamer's Field in Fairbanks *(see p174).*

Red-legged kittiwakes, found in the Pribilof Islands, build cliff nests made of mud, grass, and kelp

Arctic terns, *frequently observed swooping over lakes throughout Alaska, migrate 25,000 miles (40,000 km) each year between their Arctic breeding grounds and their wintering grounds in Antarctica. Usually smaller than gulls, they will attack anything – even humans – that approaches their chicks.*

The red-throated loon, *much rarer than the iconic common loon, is one of Alaska's five loon species. Their haunting calls are signature sounds of the North American wilderness.*

Trumpeter swans, *with wingspans of up to 7 ft (2 m), are the world's largest waterbirds. Surprisingly efficient flyers, they migrate at altitudes up to 10,000 ft (3,000 m) at speeds up to 60 mph (100 kph). They are most readily seen in their nesting grounds on the Copper River Delta (see p123).*

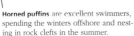

Horned puffins are excellent swimmers, spending the winters offshore and nesting in rock clefts in the summer.

Snowy owls *are perhaps the most spectacular summer birds on the Arctic coast. Diving from the sky with outstretched talons, these birds can drive away even an advancing caribou.*

RAPTORS

Alaska is home to a variety of raptors, not the least of which is the US national bird, the magnificent bald eagle. Denali National Park *(see pp166–9)* and other parts of the Interior also have a healthy population of golden eagles. Other common raptors include merlins, red-tailed hawks, harriers, ospreys, and numerous species of owls.

Bald eagles, *although established across the Lower 48, are found in their greatest numbers in Alaska. From October to December, thousands of eagles gather along the Chilkat River, but they can also be readily spotted almost anywhere in southern Alaska from late spring to early fall.*

Russian Culture in Alaska

While modern Alaska is tied ideologically to mainstream USA and traditionally to its own Native cultures, there are also remnants of 18th- and 19th-century Russian colonization. The distinctive crosses and onion-domed spires of Orthodox churches across Alaska attest to the fact that the colonizers were not just concerned with trade, but also brought with them their religious convictions, converting many Native Alaskans to their faith. Today, most Southwest Alaska villages still have a Russian Orthodox majority population.

Russian Big Diomede (right) and US Little Diomede (left) lie in the Bering Strait

Icons include All Saints of Alaska: Innocent, Herman, Jakov, Juvenali, and Peter the Aleut.

A Russian priest *and settlers gather with Native Tlingit people in traditional dress in this photograph taken in Sitka circa 1900.*

Deacon doors in this chapel have icons of St. Stephen (left) and St. Lawrence (right).

Alexander Baranov *(1747–1819) is honored with this statue in Sitka, where he once lived. Attracted to Alaska by the fur trade, he became the manager of the Russian-American Company in 1790 and the first Colonial Governor of Russian America in 1799.*

The analogian displays icons for worshipers, who may not approach the iconostasis.

OLD BELIEVERS

In 1652, Patriarch Nikon of Moscow ordered reforms to traditional Orthodoxy and excommunicated any dissidents. Many of the dispossessed, calling themselves Old Believers, fled to Siberia to escape persecution. In 1945, to escape the Soviet system, many migrated to Brazil and eventually to the USA. In the late 1960s, one group established several villages around Nikolaevsk, which are modern Alaska's only Russian settlements. Currently, about 2,000 Old Believers, who still speak Old Russian, live largely by hunting, fishing, trapping, and farming.

Old Believer women working in the fields near Nikolaevsk

The New Archangel Dancers, *Sitka, perform Russian folk songs and dances to promote Alaska's Russian heritage.*

The Holy Assumption of the Virgin Mary Russian Orthodox Church, *in Kenai, was completed in 1895. A distinctive crown-shaped cupola marks this National Historic Landmark*

The iconostasis separates the church from the altar and symbolizes separation between the human world and the Divine. Only men may pass this wall.

The Russian Bishop's House *is the oldest intact Russian building in Sitka. Built in 1843 by the Russian American Company as the Bishop's residence, it also functioned as an orphanage, school, and seminary.*

The altar, behind the iconostasis, is where the priest celebrates the Holy Liturgy.

St. Nicholas Russian Orthodox Church *(1893), was founded for Juneau's mostly Tlingit Orthodox community.*

ORTHODOX INTERIORS
The interiors of Russian Orthodox churches are simple in layout, but are lavishly decorated with rich colors and beautiful, vibrant icons, as seen here in the chapel at St. Herman's Theological Seminary in Kodiak. In most Orthodox churches there are no pews, as worshipers are expected to stand in deference to Christ's suffering.

St. Michael's Russian Orthodox Cathedral, *in Sitka, was begun in 1844 when the original cornerstone was laid by Bishop Veniaminov. Destroyed by fire in 1966, the church was rebuilt and reconsecrated by 1976.*

Spirit houses *grace the churchyard behind St. Nicholas Russian Orthodox Church in the tiny Athabaskan village of Eklutna. Each of these structures is a gravesite and is decorated according to individual family traditions.*

Cruising the Inside Passage

First time and repeat passengers fill cruise ships every year to sail the Inside Passage and experience some of the most breathtaking vistas this sliver of Alaska can offer. The Inside Passage is usually remote, remarkable, and ultimately rewarding in rain or shine. Majestic tidewater glaciers, gouged-out valleys, and impenetrable forests compete for views of whales, bears, and eagles. Along with bustling ports of call, cruising here makes perfect sense. Cruise ships call on quaint fishing outposts, hidden coves, and small cities that dot the coastline – many in places inaccessible except by boat or floatplane.

Tracy Arm *twists into the mainland from Stephens Passage and rewards with a blanket of icebergs, created by the calving Sawyer Glaciers.*

LOCATOR

—— Area of main map

Skagway, a slice of Gold Rush mining history, nestles at the end of narrow Taiya Inlet.

⑦ Skagway

⑥ Haines

Haines sits in a gorgeous location on the Chilkat Peninsula, below the Fairweather Range.

Juneau ⑤

Gustavus

To the Gulf Route
(see pp36–37)

Hoonah is a quietly fascinating Tlingit settlement along Icy Strait where humpback whales are frequently sighted.

④ S

Juneau, the nation's smallest state capital, boasts a vibrant tourist economy that caters to cruise ship passengers.

Glacier Bay (see pp146–7) *is almost entirely water access only. Cruise ships easily bring their passengers within camera range of some of the park's 12 spectacular tidewater glaciers.*

PORTS OF CALL

① **Ketchikan** see pp128–9
② **Wrangell** see pp134–5
③ **Petersburg** see p138
④ **Sitka** see pp140–41
⑤ **Juneau** see pp142–5
⑥ **Haines** see pp148–9
⑦ **Skagway** see pp150–51

Sitka's *mix of Russian and Tlingit culture makes it a fascinating port of call and its protected location within a verdant valley is stunning. Most sights are within walking distance of the docks.*

Petersburg *lies at the north end of the Wrangell Narrows, a barely navigable passage lined with dense forests, hunting and fishing lodges, and homes for rugged vacationers. The town retains its strong Norwegian influence and remains less explored than Ketchikan or Juneau.*

PLANNING A CRUISE

Cruises *either sail a round trip through the Inside Passage from a port to the south (often Seattle or Vancouver), or cruise one way adding on the Gulf Route and starting or ending at Anchorage.*
Consider splashing out *on a cabin with a balcony, or at least with a window, for great views.*
Take *memory cards, and batteries for your camera.*
For more information *on booking and planning see pp264–71.*

Misty Fiords National Monument (see p130) *is on the itinerary of many smaller ships, which conduct slow tours of its placid waters. This protected area is a wonderland of bottomless fjords and granite escarpments laced with waterfalls.*

Wrangell is a laid-back town at the mouth of the Stikine River. The totems at Chief Shakes Island are a highlight.

KEY

- - - Suggested route

Kake

③ Petersburg

② Wrangell

KUIU ISLAND

Ketchikan ①

PRINCE OF WALES ISLAND

Prince Rupert, Canada

0 km 50
0 miles 50

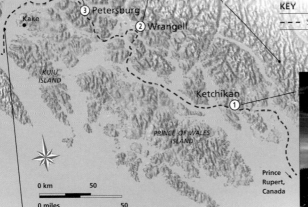

Frederick Sound *is the widest body of water in the Inside Passage and serves as a nutrient-rich feeding ground for Pacific Ocean humpback whales. They rise above the water with jaws gaping during feeding.*

Ketchikan *welcomes more than 800,000 cruise ship visitors every season. Many visitors head to Tlingit presentations at Saxman Village and Totem Park.*

Cruising the Gulf Route

Vast seascapes and endless mountain ranges are
the great attraction of a Gulf of Alaska cruise. The
shoreline has relatively few conventional or convenient cruise destinations; instead of ports, the
wildernesses of national parks and nature refuges
line up one after another. Mammoth calving glaciers,
such as the Hubbard, are top of the itinerary on all
cruise lines and many passengers tack on a multi-
day trip north from Seward to Denali *(see pp166–9)*.
Most ships transit the Gulf's wild expanse between
Whittier or Seward and Juneau during the night, so
stargazing might be the best prescription.

College Fjord (see p117) *snakes
towards the pinnacles of the Chugach
Range, dazzling at every turn. The
dense network of tidewater glaciers
were named for Ivy League schools.*

LOCATOR

— Area of main map

Whittier has become an
important port of call, as it is
so close to Anchorage and on
Passage Canal, an inlet just off
beautiful Prince William Sound.

Anchorage

③ Whittier

④ Seward

PRINCE WILLIAM SOUND

MONTAGUE ISLAND

Cook Inlet

0 km   50

0 miles   50

Seward *is the beginning or
end point for some cruises
sailing the Gulf of Alaska.
Nestled between mountains
and the sea, this attractive
city has plenty of charm.*

PORTS OF CALL

① **Cordova** see p122
② **Valdez** see pp118–19
③ **Whittier** see p116
④ **Seward** see pp98–101

Prince William Sound's *fragile environment has made a
partial recovery since 1989's disastrous Exxon Valdez oil spill
(see p119). Wildlife sightings are practically guaranteed.*

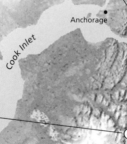

Valdez, *a coastal port between the two flanks of the vast Chugach National Forest, is notable for being at the end of the famed Trans-Alaska Pipeline. Large cruise ships do not stop here.*

PLANNING A CRUISE

Cruises through *the Gulf of Alaska are usually part of a one-way trip from either Vancouver or Seattle to Anchorage and also include the Inside Passage.*

Ships *dock in Seward or Whittier and passengers travel to or from Anchorage via plane or train.*

A tour to Denali *will take at least three nights; the train trip is spectacular (see pp294–5).*

For more information *on booking and planning see pp264–71.*

Hubbard Glacier (see p27), *Alaska's longest tidewater glacier, stretches across 6 miles (10 km) of Yakutat Bay's headwaters. Massive columns of ancient ice tumble from the glacier's face with the sound of thunder followed by a dull splash.*

2) Valdez

KEY
‒ ‒ ‒ Suggested route

Malaspina Glacier, at 1,500 square miles (3,890 square km), is the largest piedmont glacier in North America. It was named for the 18th-century Spanish explorer, Alejandro Malaspina.

① **Córdova**

● Alaganik

Cape Yakataga

KAYAK ISLAND

Icy Bay was formed within the last century when four tidewater glaciers retreated. Its icy waters provide spectacularly isolated sea kayaking.

Bering Glacier dramatically surges forward up to 328 ft (100 m) per day about every 20 years, sometimes filling the lake at its foot with calving icebergs.

Yakutat *(see p155),* a tiny Tlingit town on the route to Hubbard Glacier, boasts one of the most dramatic coastal locations on the continent.

To the Inside Passage *(see pp34–35)*

Cordova, *inaccessible by road and rail, is an occasional port of call for small ships. Originally the terminus of the Copper River and Northwestern Railway (see p187), which served the copper mines at Kennicott, today it is a pleasant fishing town.*

Dogsledding

Dogsled crossing sign

The Native peoples of Alaska's northern regions have long relied on dogsleds as essential survival tools in the winter, using them while hunting, trading, or moving camp. As other people moved to Alaska, dogsleds continued to play an important role, delivering medicine, food, and mail. While the practical use of dogsleds has now been replaced by snowmachines, dogsledding, locally called "mushing," is popular as a recreational activity and is the official state sport.

Historical image of Alaskan mail carriers delivering mail via dogsled

Dog sleds are built on wooden or aluminum runners, with an area in the front to carry freight, passengers, or tired or injured dogs.

Wheel dogs, at the very back, help in steering the sled.

Alaskans *traditionally made sleds of wood, bone, sinew, and rawhide, but modern sleds are made of wood, steel, plastics, Kevlar, and aluminum. Here, Inupiat elder Don Smith works on a sled in his workshop in Kiana, near Kotzebue.*

Mushers either stand on the runners of the sled or jog behind or alongside.

THE SLED TEAM

For mushers, dogsledding is as much an art form as a sport. In the harsh winter wilderness, the close interplay of human and dog is symbiotic: for the musher, the dog team is a faithful lifeline in an exposed environment, while for the dogs, the musher is a trusted companion who supplies sustenance. The dogs are directed not by reins, but by the musher's spoken commands to the lead dogs, who guide the others accordingly.

SLED DOGS

Malemutes, Siberians, Samoyeds, and other purebred huskies are popularly associated with dogsledding, but are rarely used as sled dogs. Most mushers prefer mixed-breed dogs that are bred for speed and endurance.

Wind-resistant kennels *provide shelter for sled dogs at home. On the trail, they sleep outdoors on hay, eating meat and fish for energy and warmth. Bred for Alaskan winters, they perform best at about -29° C (-20° F).*

Dog team transport, *when the dogs are not running, is in mobile kennels mounted on the back of pick-up trucks.*

Denali Park Rangers *use sleds to patrol the park in winter, but summer visitors can watch demonstrations of dogsleds adapted for use on trails.*

ALASKA'S DOGSLED RACES

Dogsled races feature in winter festivals all over Alaska, but the best-known mushing event is the famed Iditarod. Other popular races include the Yukon Quest, Glennallen's Copper Basin 300, which is a qualifier for the Iditarod, and the World Championship Sled Dog Races. Racers come from all over the world to serve apprenticeships with established mushers and to learn how to care for the dogs and cope with the elements.

Team dogs follow the swing dogs and provide a steady pulling action.

Lead dogs, in the front, follow the musher's commands.

Swing dogs back up the lead dogs and assist in steering.

The Yukon Quest *is one of Alaska's major dogsled races. The 1,000-mile (1,600 km) race follows a Gold Rush and historic mail delivery route between Whitehorse, Canada, and Fairbanks, Alaska.*

The World Championship Sled Dog Races *take place on a short track around Anchorage during the Anchorage Fur Rendezvous. This weekend event focuses more on speed and strategy than on endurance, which is the main factor in long-distance mushing.*

Dogsled team pulling out of the Iditarod starting line

THE LAST GREAT RACE ON EARTH

Historically, the Athabaskans called their hunting grounds Haiditarod, "the distant place." In 1910, the derivation Iditarod was given to the rough trail between Seward and Nome. In 1925, dog teams transported live-saving diphtheria serum to epidemic-stricken Nome along a portion of this trail. To commemorate this feat, a dogsled race between Anchorage and Nome was initiated in 1973 by legendary musher Joe Redington, affectionately known as the "Father of the Iditarod." Held in early March, this annual event begins with a ceremonial start in Anchorage and restarts the next day from Willow. Each year, the race follows one of two alternating courses. The leaders usually complete the 1,100-mile (1,760-km) run in about nine days.

Sportfishing in Alaska

Sportfishing is Alaska's most popular sport, and Alaskans fish regularly while outsiders often make it their main reason to visit the state. Some visit in the hopes of shipping home a crate of frozen fish, but for most the real attraction is the opportunity to spend some solitary time outdoors. However, anglers in the best fishing areas may find themselves up against hordes of competing fishermen. Remote sites and wilderness lodges offer more serene experiences. Those whose chief objective is to catch fish will find lakes and streams so prolific that success is practically guaranteed, even when several anglers are competing.

Fishing lure

Catch-and-release fishing *is a popular pastime that also maintains breeding stocks.*

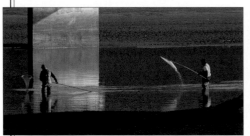

Dipnetting *is a favored way of catching Copper River red salmon and the small and greasy hooligan (eulachon) in Turnagain Arm (see pp80–81). Only Alaska residents are permitted to use dipnets.*

FLY FISHING

Fly fishing, which involves the use of a long, light rod, an artificial fly made of fur, feathers, or yarn, and a heavy line that helps to place the fly accurately, is used primarily to catch salmon and trout in smaller lakes, rivers, and streams. The most rewarding fly fishing is found in wilderness waterways accessed by bush plane.

SPECIAL FISHING TOURS

Anglers in Alaska can choose from a range of sportfishing packages, which typically include transportation, tackle, food, and accommodation. Tours range from deep-sea fishing charters to superb fishing adventures at remote lodges that are approachable only by floatplane.

Charter fishing tours *involve chartering a boat with a guide for half a day or a full day. Sportfishing vessels can travel far from shore to find the best sportfishing grounds for enthusiastic anglers looking for a good catch.*

Fly-in fishing, *a quintessential Alaskan experience, involves a floatplane flight to a remote lake for some quiet angling.*

Combat fishing *is common in Kenai Peninsula rivers when the salmon are running. Competing anglers stand elbow-to-elbow, trying to land one of the thousands of fish going upstream.*

Waterproof waders made of a synthetic rubber are essential gear for anglers in Alaska.

Deep-sea fishing *for the huge halibut known as "barn doors" is especially popular around Homer and Deep Creek on the Kenai Peninsula.*

ALASKAN SPORTFISH

Alaska offers keen anglers excellent fishing opportunities, and a wide variety of game fish are available in the state's waterways and along the coasts. Salmon is the most popular catch, but halibut, trout, and grayling are also highly prized.

King (chinook) salmon, *the largest of all Pacific salmon, are relatively common in Bristol Bay and the Kenai River.*

Arctic grayling, *a game fish, is found in clear, cold streams in the Interior between April and September.*

Halibut, *which occasionally weigh over 300 lb (135 kg), are found in the Gulf of Alaska, especially around Homer.*

Red (sockeye) salmon *run from May to mid-August in Southwest, Southcentral, and Western Alaska.*

Rainbow trout, *found in rivers from Southeast Alaska to the Kuskokwim Delta, are best fished in spring and fall.*

Arctic char *are found in clear, fresh waters in Interior and Southern Alaska between May and September.*

ALASKA THROUGH THE YEAR

Alaskans are festive types and nearly every town and village has evolved its own celebrations. Events that are not music or sports related typically focus on a local commodity, historic or ethnic event, some sort of novelty, or a natural phenomenon, such as events based around the midnight sun or sea ice. The atmosphere ranges from the elegant formality of the Sitka Summer Music Festival to uninhibited revelry at the Talkeetna Moose Dropping Festival. Summer festivals are often boisterous, round-the-clock affairs, while winter events give people the opportunity to get out of the house during the darkest days of the year. On Alaska Day and the Fourth of July, the entire state joins in the festivities, usually with displays of fireworks, but some communities often stage large celebrations that draw people from across the state.

Bird's-eye view of the rides at the Alaska State Fair

SPRING

In the spring, as the days grow longer, the ice is starting to break up, the birds are beginning to return, and Alaskans are gearing up for summer activity. Some communities try to get a jump on the excitement by staging early festivities, but the weather can be unpredictable, with snow possible in April and May.

APRIL

Alaska Folk Festival *(mid-Apr)*, Juneau. This weeklong festival features the hottest folk and bluegrass performers from around Alaska and the Northwest. Participants can also attend free dance workshops at the festival.
Alyeska Spring Carnival *(3rd week)*, Girdwood. This popular spring festival is the ski resort's finale for the season, with a freestyle competition, kids' games, and the Slush Cup, where skiers and snow boarders attempt to cross an icy pond at full speed. Most end up very wet and cold.

MAY

Copper River Delta Shorebird Festival *(1st week)*, Cordova. The return of shorebirds to the Copper River Delta is marked with three days of bird-related activities.
Kachemak Bay Shorebird Festival *(1st full weekend)*,

Musicians performing at the Sitka Summer Music Festival

Homer. A wooden boat festival, nature walks, and bird-oriented activities honoring 100,000 shore-birds on the beaches of Kachemak Bay.
Little Norway Festival *(weekend nearest May 17)*, Petersburg. A vibrant celebration of the town's Norwegian roots, including a traditional *bunad* dress competition, parade, and Norwegian delicacies.
Great Alaska Craftbeer and Homebrew Festival *(3rd weekend)*, Haines. This competition between home- and microbrewers is an excellent opportunity to taste some unusual beers.
Crab Festival *(Memorial Day weekend)*, Kodiak. The end of the crabbing season is marked with music, festivities, and races, including one in which teams wearing heavy survival suits swim out to boats in the harbor.

SUMMER

Summer is understandably the favorite season of most Alaskans, and communities organize an explosion of festivities designed for both locals and tourists. Attendees can plan on partying late into the midnight brightness.

JUNE

Sitka Summer Music Festival *(three weeks in Jun)*, Sitka. This popular event attracts international classical musicians every summer.

Book chamber music performances in advance.

Copper River Wild Salmon Festival *(2nd week)*, Cordova. This event commemorates the famous Copper River reds with a dance, salmon banquet, and a marathon race along the Copper River Highway.

Midnight Sun Festival *(Jun 21)*, Fairbanks. The festival features live music, a classic auto show, and the Alaska Goldpanners Midnight Sun Baseball Game, played by natural light at midnight.

Nalukataq *(late Jun)*, Barrow. A midsummer festival that celebrates the end, and hopefully the successes, of the spring whaling season with Inuit games, a feast, and a blanket toss.

Alaska Highland Games *(last weekend)*, Eagle River near Anchorage. Visitors can see the hammer toss, stone and caber throws, eat haggis, and listen to bagpipe music.

JULY

Independence Day *(Jul 4)*, across Alaska. While there are statewide celebrations, Seward has the biggest event with its Mount Marathon race. Seldovia and Skagway are also popular venues.

Talkeetna Moose Dropping Festival *(2nd weekend)*, Talkeetna. This very popular festival includes a parade, a 3-mile (5-km) run, and a

Participating in the World Eskimo-Indian Olympics in Fairbanks

moose-nugget toss contest. The highlight, however, is the Mountain Mother contest, in which women wearing hip waders and carrying a stuffed "baby" on their backs complete a course of river crossing, grocery carrying, wood chopping, archery, fly-casting, and diaper changing, and top it all off by making a cream pie.

World Eskimo-Indian Olympics *(mid-Jul)*, Fairbanks. This Native event includes an array of traditional games, including the kneel jump, toe kick, blanket toss, ear pull, and greased pole walk.

Alaska Bearpaw Festival *(mid-Jul)*, Eagle River near Anchorage. On offer are bear-oriented events, including a parade, a teddy bear

picnic, Miss Bear Paw Pageant, and a 300-yard (270-m) dash called the Tri-Bear-a-Thon.

Fairbanks Golden Days *(3rd week)*. An air show and a host of citywide activities are part of this event, which ends with a grand parade featuring a junk truck and a "hoosegow" (jail) wagon.

Deltana Fair *(last weekend)*, Delta Junction. A carnival, rodeo, and outhouse and mud bog races are on offer at this agricultural fair.

AUGUST

Talkeetna Bluegrass Festival *(1st weekend)*, Mile 102, Parks Highway. This festival is a Woodstock-style camp-out, with non-stop partying. Despite the name, bluegrass is conspicuously absent, while rock, folk, and blues predominate.

Blueberry Festival *(1st weekend)*, Ketchikan. The humble blueberry is honored with pie-eating contests, art exhibitions, folk music, food stalls, and even a slug race.

Seward Silver Salmon Derby *(mid-Aug)*, Seward. Alaska's most famous salmon derby offers a $10,000 grand prize and a total purse of $150,000.

Southeast Alaska State Fair *(3rd week)*, Haines. This fair features a farmers' market, a lumberjack show, pig races, a dog show, and live music.

Crowds at the Fourth of July parade in downtown Seward

Bald eagles crowding cottonwood trees in the fall, Haines

FALL

As tourists and seasonal workers leave, birch trees turn yellow, the air fills with the scent of woodsmoke, and over half the state's population ends up at the Alaska State Fair. With winter approaching, the frenetic activity of summer begins to wind down, with one last burst of excitement on Alaska Day.

SEPTEMBER

Alaska State Fair *(Aug–Sep)*, Palmer. This extremely popular 11-day event attracts visitors from all over the state with agricultural exhibits (including gargantuan vegetables), livestock auctions, art, food and retail booths, rides, music and theater performances, lumberjack shows, and other daily events.
Kodiak State Fair and Rodeo *(1st weekend)*, Kodiak. Stock car racing, a rodeo, and live music are the highlights of this small fair.
Labor Day *(1st Mon)*, across Alaska. Although this is celebrated statewide, Nome hosts the quirkiest events, including a Rubber Duck Race and a Bathtub Race.
Klondike Trail of '98 International Road Relay *(early Sep)*, Skagway to Whitehorse. This demanding relay attracts up to 150 teams of 10 runners each, who race along the 110-mile (176-km) Klondike Highway between Skagway and Whitehorse, Canada, following the 1890s Gold Rush trail.

OCTOBER

Alaska Day *(Oct 18)*, across Alaska. Celebrated statewide, this day marks Russia's handing over of Alaska to the US in 1867. Sitka has one of the largest festivals, featuring wonderful Russian costumes and dances, a parade, and a re-enactment of the flag-raising ceremony.

NOVEMBER

Alaska Bald Eagle Festival *(2nd week)*, Haines. Live music, photography workshops, and lectures fête the phenomenal return of the bald eagles to the Chilkat Valley in the fall.

Carrs/Safeway Great Alaska Shoot-Out *(Thanksgiving weekend)*, Anchorage. The University of Alaska Anchorage hosts top basketball teams in one of the largest pre-season tournaments in the US.

WINTER

In early winter, Christmas preparations dominate, and Alaska's snow and cold provide a quintessential holiday atmosphere. After New Year, those who haven't migrated to warmer climes participate in winter festivities, including ice-sculpture contests, indoor sports, dogsled races, and ski events.

DECEMBER

Wilderness Woman *(1st weekend)*, Talkeetna. Pitting women against each other in

Taking an icy dip in the Polar Bear Jump-Off, Seward

order to gain the favor of Talkeetna's single men, this competition includes snowmachine driving, wood chopping, and providing a sandwich and beer to a bachelor watching TV. It winds up with a Bachelor Auction.
Colony Christmas *(2nd weekend)*, Palmer. Old-fashioned Christmas festival echoing the Matanuska Valley Colony of the 1940s with reindeer sleigh rides, fireworks, caroling, and food.

World Ice Art Championship, Fairbanks

JANUARY

Russian Orthodox Christmas *(Jan 7)*, across Alaska. Russian Orthodox communities mark Christmas with both solemn commemorations and joyous celebration. Traditions include "starring," in which carolers carry a decorated star from house to house singing religious carols called *koyadki*.
Polar Bear Jump-Off *(3rd weekend)*, Seward. People jump into icy Resurrection Bay dressed up in costumes.

FEBRUARY

Iceworm Festival *(1st weekend)*, Cordova. Iceworms, small, thin worms that actually do inhabit glacial ice, are the inspiration for this wacky winter event. A 150-ft (45-m) long iceworm is paraded through the streets, and there is a carnival, dress-up competition, talent show, and the crowning of Miss Iceworm.
Yukon Quest International Sled Dog Race *(early Feb)*, Whitehorse to Fairbanks or vice versa. The race follows a route along the Yukon River and over the wild mountains between Fairbanks and Whitehorse.
Anchorage Fur Rendezvous *(Feb–Mar)*, Anchorage. Originally meant to bring fur trappers and buyers together, Fur Rondy features a snow sculpture

competition, the World Championship Sled Dog Races, and a run with the reindeer.
Nenana Ice Classic *(Feb–Apr)*, Nenana. Bets are laid on the exact minute that the ice breaks up on the Nenana River, with all correct entries splitting the purse.

MARCH

Iditarod Trail Sled Dog Race *(early Mar)*, Anchorage to Nome. This classic race is ceremonially flagged off from Anchorage and restarts in Willow the next day, arriving in Nome nine days later.
World Ice Art Championship *(early Mar)*, Fairbanks.

Huge blocks of ice are sculpted into exotic and artistic forms. Dozens of teams, including participants from China, Japan, and Russia, take part in this impressive competition.
Bering Sea Ice Golf Classic *(at the end of the Iditarod race)*, Nome. Golf on the frozen Bering Sea, with orange golf balls and painted greens.
Pillar Mountain Golf Classic *(late Mar)*, Kodiak. A one-hole, par 70 golf game played up the slopes of 1,400-ft (424-m) Pillar Mountain, with the aim of hitting the ball into a bucket at the summit.

Team starting off in the Iditarod Trail Sled Dog Race

The Climate of Alaska

Alaska's wide range of climates can be divided into six major zones. The Southeast experiences mild winters and cool, rainy summers. Shielded from the Gulf of Alaska by mountains, the region around Cook Inlet has longer, colder winters and shorter, warmer summers than elsewhere around the Gulf. The Aleutians have year-round stormy, blustery weather. The coldest winter temperatures are found in the Interior, where -40° C (-40° F) or lower is not uncommon, although the summer more than compensates with sunny days up to 32° C (90° F). Arctic winters are not as cold as those in the Interior, but snow can linger until July. The alpine climate is dictated by terrain and altitude.

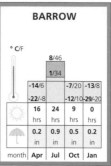

BARROW

°C/F		8/46		
		1/34		
	-14/6		-7/20	-13/8
	-22/-8		-12/10	-29/-20
	16 hrs	24 hrs	9 hrs	0 hrs
	0.2 in	0.9 in	0.5 in	0.2 in
month	Apr	Jul	Oct	Jan

CLIMATE ZONES

- Arctic (cold dry): Short, cool summer and long, cold winter.
- Interior (cold to hot): Extremely cold winters and warm summers.
- Southcentral (cold to warm): Variable winter, warm summer.
- Alpine (variable): Weather depends on terrain and altitude.
- Bering Sea (mild and stormy): Year-round blustery conditions.
- Southeast Maritime (cool wet): Cool rainy summer, mild winter.

ARCTIC OCEAN

Barrow

Chukchi Sea

A L A

Nome

St. Lawrence Island

Norton Sound

Bering Sea

Nunivak Island

DUTCH HARBOR

°C/F	13/55			
		8/46	7/44	
	3/38		2/35	1/34
	-2/28			-4/24
	14 hrs	16 hrs	11 hrs	8 hrs
	2.0 in	2.4 in	4.2 in	2.8 in
month	Apr	Jul	Oct	Jan

Average daily maximum temperature

Average daily minimum temperature

Daily hours of sunshine mid-month

Average monthly rainfall

Bristol Bay

Cold Bay

Dutch Harbor

Aleutian Islands

0 km	200
0 miles	200

FAIRBANKS

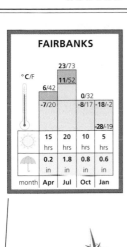

	23/73		
°C/F 11/52			
6/42			
		0/32	
-7/20		-8/17 -18/-2	
			-28/-19

☼	15 hrs	20 hrs	10 hrs	5 hrs
☂	0.2 in	1.8 in	0.8 in	0.6 in
month	Apr	Jul	Oct	Jan

Late summer sun shines on Nome's timber buildings

THE MIDNIGHT SUN

Due to Alaska's northerly location, and bisected as it is by the Arctic Circle, it never really gets dark here between late May and mid-July. At this time of the year, the long daylight hours spark a frenzy of late-night activities among the Alaskans, who play golf and baseball at midnight, and after work, set off on a day's worth of projects before going to bed. Even as far south as Ketchikan, the midnight twilight obscures the stars in late June, and in Barrow, Alaska's northernmost town, the sun does not set for two and a half months from May to July. On June 21, the summer solstice, the sun sets for just two hours in Fairbanks.

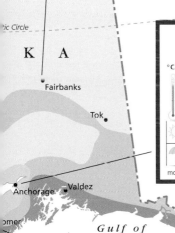

Arctic Circle

K | A

• Fairbanks

Tok •

• Anchorage • Valdez

Homer

Gulf of Alaska

Juneau

PACIFIC OCEAN

ANCHORAGE

	18/65		
°C/F 11/51			
7/44		4/40	
-2/29		-2/28 -6/21	
			-13/08

☼	15 hrs	18 hrs	10 hrs	6 hrs
☂	0.6 in	1.9 in	1.9 in	0.8 in
month	Apr	Jul	Oct	Jan

JUNEAU

	18/64		
°C/F 9/48 9/48		8/47	
0/32		3/37	
			-2/29
			-8/18

☼	14 hrs	18 hrs	10 hrs	7 hrs
☂	2.9 in	4.2 in	7.8 in	4.3 in
month	Apr	Jul	Oct	Jan

HOMER

	15/60		
°C/F 7/44 8/47 7/44			
		0/32	
-2/28			-2/28
			-8/17

☼	14 hrs	18 hrs	7 hrs	10 hrs
☂	1.2 in	1.6 in	2.9 in	2.5 in
month	Apr	Jul	Oct	Jan

THE HISTORY OF ALASKA

Known to the Aleut peoples as Alaxsxaq, "The Great Land," Alaska has been defined by cycles of prosperity and stagnation. Russian traders in the 18th century were followed by Gold Rush prospectors in the 1890s who struggled north with dreams of fantastic wealth. The discovery of North Slope oil in the 1960s led to a new boom that not only drew people to Alaska and rejuvenated its economy, but continues to affect the state and its fortunes today.

During the Pleistocene era between 1.8 million and 11,000 years ago, the growth of continental ice sheets caused sea levels to drop temporarily and expose shallow sea floors. The sea floor between Asia and North America formed a land bridge known as Beringia. This relatively dry and ice-free area provided access across open tundra to Alaska. As a result, the Alaskan Interior became a migration corridor from Central Asia to other parts of the North American continent. This led some anthropologists to believe that Alaska was the point of entry for some of the first people to set foot on the continent.

However, timelines differ between researchers. Some believe that the first groups of hunter-gatherers arrived from Siberia as recently as 12,000 years ago, but other evidence suggests that the first migration may have taken place as early as 30,000 to 25,000 years ago. Despite such discrepancies, it is generally thought that this early migration brought the ancestors of the modern Athabaskan, Tlingit, Haida, and Tsimshian peoples,

Inuit woman, circa 1904

who are still resident across Alaska. By about 15,000 years ago, most of the continental ice covering Alaska had melted, closing off the Bering land bridge but opening up migration routes deeper into the continent. Although opinions vary, modern scientific thought suggests that most contemporary Native groups across the Americas are descended from these Central Asian migrants.

It is estimated that the first Inuit peoples arrived in western Alaska by *umiaq* (skin boat) after the ice had melted. Some researchers date this to 8,000 years ago, while others claim it was as recent as 4,500 years ago. These hunters, familiar with Arctic coastal conditions, followed a maritime hunting culture along the Bering Sea and Arctic Ocean coasts. Over the next few thousand years, they spread farther southeast to the Cook Inlet region and east through northern Canada as far as Greenland. The Aleut settled in Southwest Alaska, as evidenced by the remains of their ancient *barabaras* or *ulax* (semi-subterranean sod dwellings).

TIMELINE

Inuit stone harpoon blade

30,000–12,000 BC First settlers cross the Bering land bridge to Alaska	**10,000 BC–AD 1000** At least 5,000 sites of human habitation across Alaska	**1000–1700** First Inuit settlers arrive in upper Cook Inlet region

30,000 BC	20,000 BC	10,000 BC	AD 1	AD 1000

23,000–7,500 BC Wisconsin Ice Age and migrations east and south	**8,000–4,500 BC** Inuit and Aleut migration to Alaska from Asia by *umiaq* (skin boat)	**2,500–1,500 BC** Inuit migrations into Canada and as far away as Greenland	**1700** Dena'ina Athabaskans begin settling around upper Cook Inlet

◁ **Painting depicting the signing of the Alaska Treaty of Cessation, March 30, 1867**

Color engraving dated between 1820 and 1840 depicting Alaska during Captain Cook's 1778 voyage

EUROPEAN EXPLORERS AND THE RUSSIAN ERA

It is possible that the first European to sight Alaska was the Spaniard Bartolomeo de Fonte, who is said to have sailed up the Inside Passage in 1640. Semyon Dezhnev, the first Russian in the region, saw the Bering Strait in 1648 and reported that a "great land" existed to the east. He was followed in 1728 by Vitus Bering, a Dane sailing for Tsar Peter the Great. Sailing through the Bering Strait, he claimed the land for the Russian Empire. In 1741, Bering set out on another voyage, with Alexei Chirikov as the commander of the second vessel. Chirikov landed on Prince of Wales Island in Southeast Alaska, paving the way for the eventual establishment of Russian America. Bering did not survive the journey, but his crew returned with sea otter pelts. Their success inspired many hunters and traders, known as *promyshleniki*, who headed for Alaska, exploiting not only the land's natural wealth, but also the labor of the Aleuts.

By 1772, a Russian settlement at Unalaska was harvesting the prized sea otter pelts throughout the Aleutians. Two years later, Spanish captain Juan Perez reported a Russian presence on Prince of Wales Island. In 1778, on his third and final voyage, British captain James Cook sailed the *Resolution* up the Southeast Alaskan coast and through Cook Inlet to the site of present-day Anchorage in his unsuccessful attempt to find the Northwest Passage to Europe.

To discourage British interest in the region, merchant and head of the Russian-American Company, Grigory Shelikov, established the first permanent Russian community at Three Saints Bay on Kodiak Island in 1784. Eight years later, he was granted a fur monopoly by Tsarina Catherine II. Over the next decade, both George Vancouver, who had been one of Cook's lieutenants, and Alejandro Malaspina of Spain, explored the Southeast and the Gulf of Alaska for their respective countries. Despite their efforts,

TIMELINE

1725 Bering explores the area east of the Russian mainland

Vitus Bering

1733 On Bering's second expedition, Georg Wilhelm Steller conducts nature studies in Alaska

1764 Clashes between Russians and Aleuts

1781 Grigory Shelikov establishes Russian-American fur trading company

1720	1740	1760	1780

1728 Bering sails through Bering Strait, but does not land in Alaska

1741 Alexei Chirikov reaches Prince of Wales Island; Bering dies on Bering Island in the Komandorski Islands

1772 Russian settlement established at Unalaska

1784 Shelikov sets up a town on Kodiak Island

Russian influence in the region continued to expand, and at one stage the colony extended as far south as Fort Bragg in northern California.

Under the directorship of former sales representative Alexander Baranov, the Russian-American Company was granted a trade monopoly by Tsar Paul I in 1799. He was also authorized to make Sitka the seat of colonial government. Just two years later, the Russian fort at Sitka was attacked and destroyed by Tlingit protesting their forced allegiance to the tsar. Despite the defeat, the Russians returned in 1804 and Sitka was rebuilt as a veritable stockade. In 1824, Russia, Britain, and the United States signed a treaty forming the boundaries of Russian America and British Canada roughly along Alaska's current boundaries.

William H. Seward, US Secretary of State

region. At the same time, overhunting of sea otters and fur seals caused a sharp decline in the profitability of the fur trade, which was replaced by fishing, shipbuilding, and lumbering. Realizing that American traders and Britain's Hudson Bay Company already had interests in Alaska, Russia began to lose enthusiasm for its distant and increasingly unproductive colony.

In 1859, Tsar Alexander II authorized his agent, Baron Edward de Stoeckl, to negotiate the sale of Alaska to the United States.

Initially, Congress was reluctant to consider the purchase, especially during the 1861–65 Civil War. In 1866, California fur companies expressed interest in the Russian-American Company but it wasn't until 1867 that Secretary of State, William H. Seward, championed the cause of purchasing Russian interests in North America. President Andrew Johnson and the US Congress agreed to buy Alaska for the paltry sum of $7.2 million or – as is frequently noted – about 2 cents an acre. At Sitka on October 18, 1867, ownership was officially transferred and the US flag was raised. Despite the low price, the American public generally thought Alaska was a waste of money, and dubbed the new acquisition "Seward's Folly," "Seward's Icebox," "Walrussia," and "Uncle Sam's Attic."

THE SALE OF ALASKA

By the 1830s, the Russian population of Sitka had grown to around 1,300, with Baranov emerging as the most powerful man in the North Pacific

Hand-colored woodcut depicting Sitka in 1869

1867 political cartoon on the purchase of Alaska

1799 Tsar Paul I grants trade monopoly to Russian-American Company; Baranov sets up Russian fort and political capital at Sitka		**1848** New England whalers begin commercial whaling in Alaskan waters	**1867** US Secretary of State William H. Seward purchases Alaska for $7.2 million
1800	**1820**	**1840**	**1860**
1791 George Vancouver of Britain and Alejandro Malaspina of Spain explore Southeast Alaska	**1840** Russian Orthodox diocese established for Alaska	**1859** Russian attaché Edward de Stoeckl is granted authority to negotiate the sale of Alaska to the US	**1861** American Civil War begins

The Gold Rush

In the decade after the US purchase of Alaska, there was very little interest in the new acquisition, but this changed in 1880 when gold was found at the site of present-day Juneau. Little had come of earlier strikes on the Kenai Peninsula and in the Stikine Valley, but the Juneau find sparked off a fresh wave of interest. With the discovery of gold in the Klondike and in the beach sands of Nome in the late 1890s, a frenzied Gold Rush began. By the time it ended around 1905, interest in Alaska had waned again, but a small number of adventurous homesteaders continued to venture north in search of opportunity.

KEY

☐   Gold Rush territory 1867–1905

---   Key routes to gold mining areas

Transport and communication routes *were set up as a result of the Klondike Gold Rush. Telegraph lines were laid and the White Pass and Yukon Route Railroad was built in 1898 to link Skagway with the Klondike, opening up the Interior to the outside world.*

Gold pans were used to separate river gravel and alluvial gold.

Streams carried the gravel that contained gold.

Steamships *were used by people who had the means to sail up the Yukon River to the gold-fields. Others took the All-American Route from Valdez across Valdez Glacier and up the Copper River system to the Yukon River.*

"Grubstakes" *were carried by all prospectors on the Chilkoot Trail, who hauled load after load of supplies over the steep pass. Fearing that unprepared miners would face starvation, Canadian officials required each man to carry a year's worth of supplies and food.*

Women travelers *such as Edith Van Buren* (left) *and Mary Hitchcock ushered in a new phase of Klondike history – while prospectors struggled to reach the goldfields, they sailed up the Yukon into Dawson as tourists in 1898.*

Capturing the popular imagination, *the Gold Rush was well represented in prose, poetry, and movies. Charlie Chaplin's* The Gold Rush *(1925), with the Tramp as a gold prospector in the Klondike, portrayed the harsh conditions faced by the prospectors.*

Tents served as home to prospectors in the northern wilderness, and tent cities sprang up around major discoveries.

Gold Rush literature *includes the works of Robert Service* (see pp200–1). *Known as the "Bard of the Yukon," Service immortalized this era with his poetry, which includes "The Spell of the Yukon," "The Cremation of Sam McGee," and "The Call of the Wild," which are popular even today.*

GOLD PANNING

In the river valleys of Interior Alaska and the Klondike, prospectors staked claims and set up operations to extract placer gold, particles of gold found in alluvial or glacial deposits concentrated in wilderness streams. Early prospectors used little more than shovels and gold pans, while others set up simple water-powered dredges.

Gold Rush mining tools *were usually basic, and included sluice boxes, gold pans, pickaxes, and shovels. Modern placer miners use gasoline dredges to process the gravel.*

After the Gold Rush, *most prospectors returned home penniless, having squandered their riches on frontier vices. By the 1920s, seams began to play out, and although the World War II ban on gold mining was lifted in 1946, postwar inflation made mining unprofitable. Operations such as Independence Mine* (see pp86–7) *began closing down, leaving derelict mines and dredges strewn across Alaska.*

Timber structures being built on Main Street in Anchorage in 1915

THE GOLD RUSH

After the purchase of Alaska, few Americans had any interest in the state. However, the discovery of gold near Juneau in 1880 and subsequently in the Canadian Klondike focused outside attention on Alaska and led to the Gold Rush that lasted for nearly two decades. By the time the Gold Rush era ended around 1905, most Americans had lost interest in Alaska, but a small, steady stream of hardy men continued to head north in search of land to homestead. In 1900, the capital was moved from Sitka to Juneau, and by 1906, Alaska had a non-voting member in Congress; it gained official Territorial status barely six years after that.

DEVELOPING THE NEW TERRITORY

In the years leading up to World War II, an increasing population and interest in timber resources and seafood transformed the new territory from a useless outpost to a viable part of the USA. In the 1920s, Alaskan Natives, along with other Native Americans, were granted voting rights and then US citizenship. The Alaska Railroad between Seward and Fairbanks was completed in 1923, rejuvenating the city of Anchorage, which had sprung up in 1914 as a railway construction camp and service center for miners from the Kenai Peninsula.

During the Great Depression of the mid-1930s, President Franklin D. Roosevelt's New Deal established the Matanuska Valley Colony at Palmer. Some 200 farming families, mostly from the Midwest states of Minnesota and Wisconsin, were resettled here to try their hand at farming and raising dairy cattle. Although the project enjoyed only limited success, the area remains Alaska's most productive farming region.

Workers marching back to camp during the construction of the Alaska Highway, 1942

TIMELINE

Gold panning in Nome

1884 US Congress passes Organic Act, providing education to all residents of Alaska

1891 First oil claims staked in Cook Inlet

1900 Alaska's capital moved from Sitka to Juneau

1914 Tent city of Anchorage founded as a construction camp for the Alaska Railroad

1880 — 1890 — 1900 — 1910

1872 Gold discovered around Sitka

1880 Joe Juneau and Richard Harris unearth gold near present-day Juneau

1896 Gold discovered in the Klondike in Canada

1902 Gold found near Fairbanks

1912 Novarupta erupts; Alaska becomes a US Territory

THE WAR YEARS

When Japan attacked Pearl Harbor on December 7, 1941, the American government realized the vulnerability of Alaska's position in the North Pacific, with Anchorage as close to Tokyo as it is to Washington, DC. Fears of invasion were well-founded and the Japanese launched an air attack on the Aleutians on June 3, 1942. Four days later, they captured Attu

US troops carrying a wounded soldier on Attu Island in 1943

Island, taking the locals prisoner. The US government was quick to retaliate. Hundreds of other islanders were evacuated to Southeast Alaska, troops and about 70 US Navy ships were dispatched to the Aleutians, and military bases were established at Akutan, Amchitka, and Adak. The islands were successfully recaptured by August 1943.

During this period, a large portion of the state's current highway system was developed. The greatest project was the 1,440-mile (2,304-km) Alaska Highway, which connected Alaska to the rest of the US by road *(see pp298–9)*. This phenomenal feat involved punching a route through trackless territory, felling trees, and bridging wild rivers. Despite incredible hardships, the project was completed in eight months and 12 days, and the road was opened on October 25, 1942.

STATEHOOD

In 1942, Anchorage had a population of just 7,724, but the development brought about by the war caused that number to increase to 43,314 by 1945. Several other towns grew almost as dramatically. At this point, it was clear that Alaska had matured and was on the road to eventual statehood. In 1955, Alaskans elected delegates to a constitutional convention, which would draft a constitution for the new state. The resulting document was adopted the following year, and in 1958 President Dwight D. Eisenhower signed the Statehood Bill that made Alaska the 49th state of the US on January 3, 1959.

Mile 0 marker of the Alaska Highway in the town of Dawson Creek, Canada

Alaska State flag and US flag

1923 Completion of the Alaska Railroad

1942 Japanese invade the Aleutian Islands; Alaska Highway completed

1955 Alaskans elect delegates to a constitutional convention

1956 Voters adopt the new Alaskan constitution

| 1920 | 1930 | 1940 | 1950 | 1960 |

1924 Congress extends citizenship to Native Americans

1922 Native voting rights established

1935 Matanuska Valley Project brings families from the US Midwest to farm in Alaska

1943 US forces finally repel the Japanese from the Aleutians

1959 Alaska becomes a state on January 3

Anchorage's 4th Avenue a day after the massive 1964 Good Friday earthquake

THE OIL BOOM

In 1957, oil was discovered in Cook Inlet and by the mid-1960s, platform installations were producing 200,000 barrels of oil per day. However, a major setback occurred on March 27, 1964, when one of the 20th century's strongest earthquakes – 9.2 on the Richter scale – rocked Southcentral Alaska, causing widespread destruction. Due to a low population density, the loss of life was minimal and property damage was limited to $500 million. Despite this tragedy, Alaska continued to grow. In 1968, the Atlantic-Richfield Company (ARCO) drilled an exploratory well at Prudhoe Bay on the Arctic coast and discovered an estimated 9.6 billion barrels of recoverable oil reserves on state-controlled land. Alaska sold oil leases worth $900 million, and six years later, the Alyeska Corporation began construction of the Trans-Alaska Pipeline and the black gold rush was on. Thousands of workers flooded into Alaska for well-paying pipeline jobs and 39 months and $8 billion later, the oil began to flow. The resulting oil revenues were used to establish the Alaska Permanent Fund in 1982, which now serves as a state savings account and pays an annual dividend to every resident of Alaska.

ANCSA AND ANILCA

In 1971, Congress passed the then controversial Alaska Native Claims Settlement Act (ANCSA), which attempted to compensate Alaska Natives for the loss of their lands. The

Endicott Oil Production Island at Prudhoe Bay on Alaska's North Slope

TIMELINE

1968 The first oil is pumped at Prudhoe Bay	**1971** ANCSA (Alaska Native Claims Settlement Act) passed		**1980** ANILCA (Alaska National Interest Lands Conservation Act) passed	**1985** Alaska purchases Alaska Railroad from federal government
1965	**1970**	**1975**	**1980**	**1985**
1964 Good Friday earthquake seriously damages Anchorage, Valdez, Seward, and Kodiak	**1969** North Slope oil leases sold for $900 million	**1976** Willow selected as the new capital site	**1977** Trans-Alaska Pipeline completed	**1989** *Exxon Valdez* hits Bligh Reef and spills oil into Prince William Sound

Workers cleaning oil-covered rocks after the *Exxon Valdez* spill

to the land for subsistence purposes. City and town dwellers, however, who are constitutionally entitled to the same access to fish, water, and wildlife, also want to be permitted to exercise their rights. After more than two decades, the dispute continues.

The 1989 *Exxon Valdez* oil spill *(see p119)* just off the coast of Valdez cost the company billions of dollars and damaged both the delicate ecology of Prince William Sound and the public opinion of Alaska's oil industry. However, fossil fuels continue to finance state government and fuel the enormous US market for petroleum products. Debates about opening the remote Arctic National Wildlife Refuge to oil drilling and developing a natural gas pipeline are ongoing, but in recent years, a diversifying economy has lessened Alaska's reliance on primary natural resources in favor of tourism and service industries.

Act transferred 68,750 sq miles (178,000 sq km) of land to 12 newly established and potentially profit-making Native Corporations, which roughly coincided with tribal and sub-tribal boundaries. Alaska Natives were made shareholders in their respective corporations and given substantial control over the assets. This arrangement effectively avoided the Reservation system used in the Lower 48 and nullified any claims to Native sovereignty.

In 1980, President Jimmy Carter signed the Alaska National Interest Lands Conservation Act (ANILCA), which set aside 162,500 sq miles (420,870 sq km) as protected wilderness. As a result, a host of national parks were created, including Wrangell-St. Elias, Kenai Fjords, Gates of the Arctic, and Katmai. Unfortunately, interpretation of other facets of ANILCA have since created rifts between urban residents and rural Alaska Natives, who do not consider their homeland to be "wilderness." Many of them feel that they should have priority access

Aialik Bay in Kenai Fjords National Park, which was created in 1980 under ANILCA

1994 Due to high cost projections, voters reverse capital move initiative; Juneau stays the capital	2004 10,000 sq miles (26,300 sq km) of Alaska burn in the worst wildfire season since statehood	2007 Climate scientists call global warming "unequivocal" and point to dramatic changes in the Arctic that threaten Alaska's wildest places	2009 Eruption of Mount Redoubt spreads ash over south central Alaska

1995	2000	2005	2010	2015

1997 Japanese freighter runs aground and spills fuel at Unalaska	2000 Alaska Airlines plane crashes off California coast	2006 Mount Augustine erupts, with pyroclastic flows and plumes of ash	

Eruption of Mount Augustine, 2006

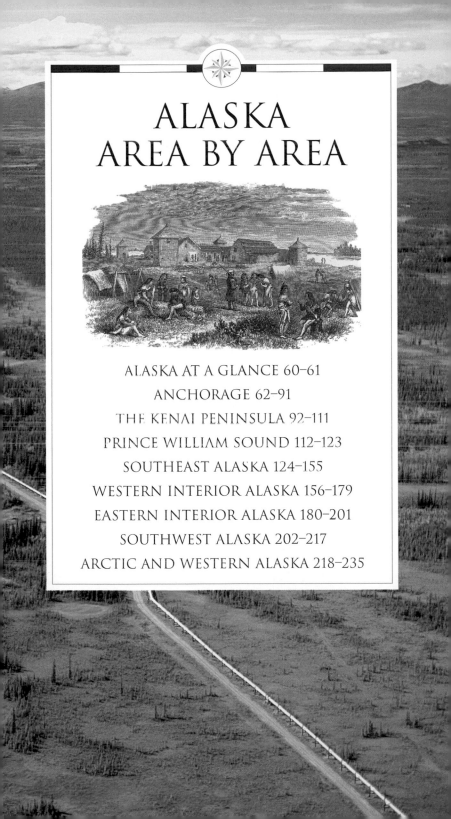

ALASKA
AREA BY AREA

ALASKA AT A GLANCE 60–61

ANCHORAGE 62–91

THE KENAI PENINSULA 92–111

PRINCE WILLIAM SOUND 112–123

SOUTHEAST ALASKA 124–155

WESTERN INTERIOR ALASKA 156–179

EASTERN INTERIOR ALASKA 180–201

SOUTHWEST ALASKA 202–217

ARCTIC AND WESTERN ALASKA 218–235

Alaska at a Glance

Thanks to its plate tectonics and glaciation, Alaska has a magnificent array of landforms. In Southeast, forested hills and ice-covered peaks rise above deep, winding fjords. Farther north, rugged mountains and rivers fringe the highways. Beyond the main routes, Alaska offers a wealth of variations on the wilderness theme, including temperate rainforests, Arctic tundra, volcanic islands, and boreal forests. Wildlife is plentiful and adventure activities abound, ranging from Nordic skiing to whitewater rafting. Anchorage, Fairbanks, and Juneau provide urban counterpoints to Alaska's wild expanses, offering excellent museums, restaurants, hotels, and shopping opportunities.

Barrow (see pp226–7), *well above the Arctic Circle, is the northernmost settlement in the US.*

Kenai Fjords National Park (see pp104–105), *near Seward, draws kayakers and day cruisers with its rugged coastlines, high peaks, icefields, and glaciers. The seas here, rich in crustaceans, fish, and plankton, host a wide variety of marine mammals.*

ARCTIC AND WESTERN ALASKA
(see pp218–35)

SOUTHWEST ALASKA
(see pp202–17)

THE KENA PENINSUL
(see pp92–1

The Aleutians *(see pp212–15)* are a long chain of stormy volcanic islands.

Katmai National Park (see pp210–11) *takes in a vast wilderness of icy lakes, volcanic landscapes, and a wild sea coast. The McNeil and Brooks Rivers have bountiful salmon runs that attract brown bears.*

◁ The Trans-Alaska Pipeline stretching across a vast taiga landscape near Gulkana

Denali National Park (see pp166–9) is Alaska's top visitor attraction. Its name comes from Mount McKinley, known to the Native peoples as Denali, which is an Athabaskan word meaning "The Great One." The park is home to moose, Dall sheep, caribou, and grizzlies.

Kennicott (see pp188–9) in Wrangell-St. Eltas National Park, was the processing site for the area's prolific copper mines. The remaining ghost town is now the park's most popular destination.

0 km   300

0 miles   300

EASTERN
INTERIOR
ALASKA
(see pp180–201)

WESTERN
INTERIOR
ALASKA
(see pp156–79)

ANCHORAGE
(see pp62–91)

PRINCE
WILLIAM
SOUND
(see pp112–23)

SOUTHEAST ALASKA
(see pp124–55)

Columbia Glacier (see p117), west of Valdez, spills down from the Chugach Mountains to calve icebergs into Prince William Sound, whose waters are a favorite of kayakers and anglers.

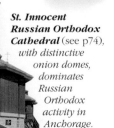

St. Innocent Russian Orthodox Cathedral (see p74), with distinctive onion domes, dominates Russian Orthodox activity in Anchorage.

The Beaver Clan House (see p129), in Saxman Totem Park near Ketchikan, provides a feel for Alaska's intriguing Native cultures.

ANCHORAGE

S pread across an alluvial plain between the lofty Chugach Range and the waters of Cook Inlet, Anchorage is Alaska's largest city. In less than a century since its founding in 1914, this former tent city has grown into the economic, commercial, and transport hub of the state. With excellent museums, theaters, parks, and shops, Anchorage is not only the perfect urban foil for Alaska's wilderness, but an ideal jumping-off point for adventures farther afield.

The original tent city on the shores of Ship Creek was a service camp for the Alaska Railroad. An early sale of lots led to the growth of downtown Anchorage on the nearby bluffs, while the banks of Ship Creek developed into the town's port, shipping, and industrial district.

The massive Good Friday earthquake of 1964 destroyed parts of Anchorage, but construction of the Trans-Alaska Pipeline in the 1970s completely changed the profile of the city. A large share of oil revenue came to Anchorage, leading to an explosion of growth. The downtown area was revitalized with new sports arenas, civic centers, and performing arts venues, and outlying suburbs were integrated into the urban area. Today, the municipality of Anchorage, with a population of over 280,000

people, includes not only the city proper, but also the Elmendorf Air Force Base and Fort Richardson Military Reservation, several villages along Turnagain Arm, and a string of suburbs, including Eagle River and Eklutna, along Knik Arm. It also takes in the vast swathe of Chugach State Park, which brings the "real Alaska" right to the city's back door. To the north, the growing Matanuska-Susitna Borough provides space and a more outdoorsy lifestyle than is possible in Anchorage proper.

All year round, travelers will find numerous good hotels and excellent restaurants. In the summer, however, downtown Anchorage comes into its own, bustling with visitors from across the world who stop off to see the sights and prepare for adventures in the more remote parts of the state.

Native Alaskans performing traditional dances at the Alaska Native Heritage Center

◁ *Crystal Lattice*, a contemporary sculpture by Robert Pfitzenmeier, Anchorage Museum

Exploring Anchorage

The historic downtown area and the older
neighborhoods of Smuggler's Cove and
Turnagain form the core of Anchorage. The
main sights of interest – including the
Alaska Public Lands Information Center,
Anchorage Museum, and Town Square –
are centered around this core, within
walking distance of one another. Avenues
in this central area run east-west and are
numbered, while streets run north-south
and are lettered from A Street west-west-
ward and named alphabetically for
Alaskan towns from Barrow Street eastward.

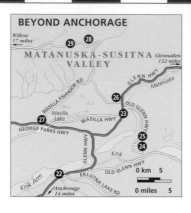

BEYOND ANCHORAGE

SIGHTS AT A GLANCE

Areas of Natural Beauty
Bodenburg Butte ㉕
Hatcher Pass ㉙
Hilltop Ski Area ⑱
Lake Hood and Lake Spenard ⑬
Ship Creek Salmon Viewing Platform ⑩
Tony Knowles Coastal Trail ⑪

Parks and Theme Parks
Alaska Botanical Garden ⑳
Alaska Zoo ⑰
Chugach State Park pp78–9 ⑲
Eklutna Historical Park ㉒
H2Oasis ⑯
*Independence Mine State Historical
    Park pp86–7* ㉘
Musk Ox Farm ㉖
Reindeer Farm ㉔
Resolution Park ⑥

Tour
Turnagain Arm Tour pp80–81 ㉑

Museums and Theaters
4th Avenue Theater ⑤
Alaska Aviation Heritage Museum ⑫
*Alaska Native Heritage
    Center pp72–3* ⑧
Alaska State Trooper Museum ②
Anchorage Museum pp68–9 ①

Buildings, Neighborhoods,
and Towns
Alaska Public Lands Information
    Center ④
Alaska Wild Berry Products ⑮
Log Cabin Visitor's Information
    Center ③
Oscar Anderson House ⑦
Palmer ㉓
Spenard ⑭
St. Innocent Russian Orthodox
    Cathedral ⑨
Wasilla ㉗

Signpost reflecting the city's self-
proclaimed status as an air crossroads

A   B   C

KEY

■	Place of interest
✈	International airport
🚂	Railroad station
🚌	Bus station
ℹ	Visitor information
✉	Post office
P	Parking
✝	Church
⊞	Cemetery

GETTING AROUND

The main sights, concentrated in downtown Anchorage, are best explored on foot. While People Mover buses connect the Dimond Center, Downtown, and Muldoon Transit Centers with most parts of town, the most convenient way to explore farther afield is by car. The Seward Highway is the main north-south corridor, while the main east-west route is the Glenn Highway. Anchorage International Airport, 4 miles (6 km) southwest of the city center, handles domestic and international flights and is served by taxis and buses. Alaska Railroad operates a year-round service between Anchorage and Fairbanks and summer trains to Seward and Whittier.

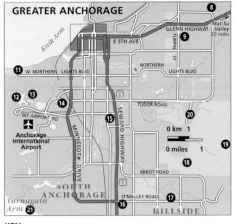

GREATER ANCHORAGE

KEY

■	Area of the main map

SEE ALSO

- *Where to Stay* pp242–3
- *Where to Eat* pp256–8

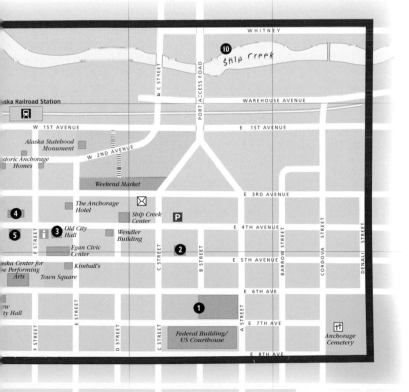

Street-by-Street: Downtown Anchorage

Although Anchorage began as a tented construction camp on the shores of Ship Creek, the 1915 sale of lots shifted its center to the site of present-day downtown Anchorage. After almost a century of growth and development, along with restoration work after the massive 1964 earthquake, downtown Anchorage today features a mix of historic buildings and modern high-rises interspersed with small private homes. Containing an open-air weekend market, a variety of shops, and most of the city's main sights, as well as a lovely town square and pleasant ornamentation including public artwork and flower baskets hanging from lampposts, this compact area is a joy to explore on foot.

Anchorage's busy 4th Avenue filled with visitors and locals

The Anchorage Market and Festival sells Alaskan arts and crafts, finger food, and fresh produce.

Alaska Public Lands Information Center
The Center has details on Alaska's millions of acres of wild places, including Denali and 14 other national parks ❹

4th Avenue Theater
The Art Deco-style 4th Avenue Theater, which was built in 1947, survived the Good Friday earthquake of 1964 ❺

★ **Log Cabin Visitor Information Center**
This picturesque downtown log building has an oft-photographed sign showing the distance to other cities around the globe ❸

STAR SIGHTS

- ★ Town Square
- ★ Log Cabin Visitor Information Center
- ★ Anchorage Museum

For hotels and restaurants in this region see pp242–3 and pp256–8

Balto's Statue
This champion sled dog's bronze statue stands outside the turreted Wendler Building.

WILD SALMON ON PARADE

In the tradition of the international Cow Parade, Anchorage has established the annual Wild Salmon on Parade competition. Local artists, sponsored by participating businesses, produce whimsical, light-hearted fibreglass interpretations of Alaskan salmon, such as *Unangax A Salmon*, wearing an Aleutian beaded hat, and *Salmon Pow*, a tribute to comic book art. Over the summer, they are on display across downtown Anchorage. At the end of the season, the fish are auctioned off at a Fish Fry & Buy dinner and the proceeds donated to local charitable organizations.

A Wild Salmon on Parade entry

Alaska State Trooper Museum
Founded in 1991, one of the most prominent exhibits in the museum is a sparkling fully restored 1952 Hudson Hornet patrol car ❷

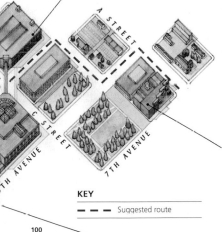

KEY

– – – Suggested route

0 meters   100
0 yards   100

★ Anchorage Museum
One of the state's premier museums, this houses excellent collections of historical artifacts, as well as traditional Native and modern Alaskan art ❶

★ Town Square
With over 9,000 plants, this is a popular lunch and concert spot. In the winter, it boasts an ice rink and hosts the New Year's fireworks display.

The Wyland Whale Mural
Created freehand by Robert Wyland in 1994, the mural depicting a family of whales is painted on a wall east of the Town Square.

Anchorage Museum ❶

Covering 170,000 square feet, including 2 acres (1 ha) of landscaped public space, Alaska's largest museum reopened in 2009 following a $106-million expansion. The museum houses exhibits on Alaskan history, science, and Native culture, along with some of the state's finest art. The Imaginarium Discovery Center is a high-light, as are the planetarium and artifacts from the Inupiat, Yup'ik, Athabaskan, and Southeast Alaskan Native cultures. Additionally, the museum hosts approximately 20 visiting exhibits annually from around the world.

Sculpture outside the museum

The slick, modern facade of the Anchorage Museum

GALLERY GUIDE

The Imaginarium Discovery Center covers much of the first floor, which also houses the Alaska Resource Center (open for public research) and the Art of the North gallery that features a broad scope of Alaskan and Circumpolar North art through the ages. The second level galleries exhibit native and contemporary art, and explore 10,000 years of Alaskan history. Changing exhibits are displayed on level three, which also gives access to the fourth floor gallery from where there are views of the Chugach Mountains.

The Arctic Studies Center houses a remarkable and large collection of Native art on loan from the Smithsonian.

Fourth floor

Third floor

★ **Mount McKinley** by Sydney Laurence
Considered one of Alaska's most popular painters, Sydney Laurence (1865–1940) is perhaps best known for his series of paintings of Mount McKinley, including this iconic depiction of the mountain in enigmatic Alaskan light. Several of Laurence's atmospheric landscapes are on display at the museum.

STAR EXHIBITS

★ Imaginarium Discovery Center

★ *Mount McKinley* by Sydney Laurence

Main entrance

First floor

KEY

- ☐ The Alaska Gallery
- ■ Imaginarium Discovery Center
- ☐ Special exhibits
- ☐ Art of the North
- ☐ Arctic Studies Center
- ☐ Conoco Phillips Gallery
- ☐ Alaska Resource Center
- ☐ Planetarium
- ■ Non-exhibition space

VISITORS' CHECKLIST

625 C Street. **Map** E5.
Tel 929-9200. 🚌 2, 14.
🕐 mid-May–mid-Sep:
9am–6pm daily, open until 9pm
on Thu; mid-Sep–mid-May.
www.anchoragemuseum.org

Vintage Hudson Hornet patrol car,
Alaska State Trooper Museum

Alaska State Trooper Museum ❷

245 W 5th Ave. **Map** E4.
Tel 279-5050, (800) 770-5050.
🚌 to Downtown Transit
Center. 🕐 10am–4pm Mon–Fri,
noon–4pm Sat. 🛗 🗐 www.
alaskatroopermuseum.com

Second floor

Prospector's Cabin
*A diorama in the Alaska Gallery
shows a log cabin with a
prospector weighing gold using a
small balance scale.*

Yup'ik Ceremonial Mask
*This traditional Yup'ik mask,
made of wood, feathers, and
pigment, was created in the
Kusko-kwim Delta circa 1900.
Masks represented characters
and experiences in performances
and stories.*

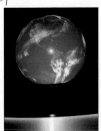

**★ Imaginarium
Discovery Center**
*This kid-friendly
science space has
many hands-on
attractions, such as
a floor that responds
to human movement.*

Founded with a handful of
officers in 1941 as the Alaska
State Highway Patrol, Alaska's
law enforcement agency also
served as the Territorial Police
and the State Police before
being named the Alaska State
Troopers in 1967. The museum
was established in 1991.

In the early days, the
Troopers protected half a
million square miles (1,295,000
sq km) of territory using the
fairly basic technology of the
time. One display exhibits a
typical 1940s law enforcement
office, where sealskin boots,
snowshoes, a clunky period
radio, typewriter, and telephone illustrate the wide
range of duties a trooper was
expected to fulfill.

The most popular exhibit is
the shiny 1952 Hudson Hornet
patrol car, one of the fastest
vehicles of its era, now lovingly
restored. Other displays
showcase memorabilia from
the days of the US Marshals,
including a poster offering a
$1,000 reward for Alaska's
first serial killer, Edward
Krause, who killed ten people
between 1912 and 1915.
Another intriguing device is
the Harger Drunkometer, a
confounding forerunner of
the modern breathalyzer.

The picturesque Log Cabin Visitor Information Center

Log Cabin Visitor Information Center ❸

546 W 4th Ave. **Map** D4. **Tel** 276-4118. 🚌 to Downtown Transit Center. ◯ Jun–Aug: 7:30am–7pm daily; May & Sep: 8am–6pm daily; Oct–Apr: 9am–4pm daily. ♿
www.anchorage.net

Operated by the Anchorage Convention and Visitors Bureau, this helpful center is located in the heart of downtown Anchorage. The flower-bedecked sod-roofed log cabin is a favorite spot for photos, and outside the center there are equally picturesque signposts showing the distance in miles to many international cities. The main visitor center fills a second building. Here you'll find an abundance of visitor brochures, free guides to nearby parks, and other publications, plus helpful staff to answer your travel questions. It is possible to plan your whole trip in advance by getting in touch through the website.

Alaska Public Lands Information Center ❹

605 W 4th Ave. **Map** D4. **Tel** 271-2737, (866) 869-6887. 🚌 to Downtown Transit Center. ◯ mid-May–early Sep: 9am–5pm daily; early Sep–mid-May: 10am–5pm Mon–Fri. **www**.alaskacenters.gov

The Federal government manages more than 60 percent

of Alaska lands, including 15 national parks, the nation's 2 largest national forests, 16 national wildlife refuges, and millions of acres of other public lands. This information center, which is housed within the old Federal Building, has displays on Alaska's wildlife and natural areas, a plethora of books and other publi-cations, and an auditorium for nature videos and talks. The center aims to encourage both visitors and residents to sustain the natural and cultural resources of Alaska.

If you're looking for information on anything from buses into Denali or bush flights into Arctic National Wildlife Refuge, this is a great place to ask experienced staff. Daily historical walks are also offered. It is located across the street from the Log Cabin Visitor Infor-mation Center. There are also branches in Fairbanks, Tok, and Ketchikan.

Classic neon sign of Anchorage's 4th Avenue Theater

4th Avenue Theater ❺

630 W 4th Ave. **Map** D4.
Tel 257-5635. 🚌 to Downtown Transit Center. ◯ May–Sep: 8am–10pm daily; Oct–Apr: 10am–6pm Mon–Fri. ♿ 🏛

Designed in 1941 in classic Art Deco style by B. Marcus Priteca, the old 4th Avenue Theater, also known as the Lathrop Building, is the quintessential Anchorage landmark. Construction began in 1947 at the cost of one million dollars US, and the building opened to the public with the film *The Al Jolson Story*. With 960 seats spread over its main floor and the balcony, the 4th Avenue Theater served as the city's only movie house for over four decades. The complex also included a restaurant, facilities for Lathrop's radio and television stations, and in 1959 a penthouse apartment was added.

Remarkably, the theater survived the destructive 1964 Good Friday earthquake *(see p25)*, which leveled other buildings along 4th Avenue. A restoration project in the mid-1980s revived its opulent Italian marble and walnut wood interiors which are adorned with bronze relief murals depicting scenes from Alaskan history. Looking up at the ceiling, visitors will see the eight twinkling stars of Ursa Major – better known as the Big Dipper – which is featured on the Alaska state flag. Capacity was also increased to 1,100 seats during the refurbishment.

In 2006, the theater nearly fell victim to demolition, but a catering firm bought the building and it was used for a time as a venue for special events. The building is now owned by the Rasmuson Foundation, and the Anchorage Convention and Visitors Bureau have converted it into a meeting space.

URBAN WILDLIFE IN ANCHORAGE

Urban moose climbing up the front steps of an Anchorage house

While Anchorage may not be representative of the Alaskan wilderness, it is home to an array of wild denizens. Along with a host of birds and squirrels, moose are resident across the city. All year round, lone bulls and mothers with calves may be seen raiding gardens, snarling traffic, and causing serious accidents that often do more damage to the car than to the moose. In addition, both brown and black bears inhabit city parks and have been known to harass joggers and cyclists on city trails, while red foxes may be observed prowling the sidewalks.

The Captain Cook Monument, a life-size bronze statue, in Resolution Park

Resolution Park ❻

300 L St. **Map** B4. 🚌 to Downtown Transit Center. ⏱ 24 hrs daily. ♿

Named after Captain Cook's flagship, Resolution Park offers visitors one of the best views in Anchorage, taking in Cook Inlet and both Mount Susitna (a magnificent low mountain to the northwest, also known as The Sleeping Lady) and spectacular Mount McKinley on a clear day. The active volcanoes south of Mount KcKinley, Mount Spur, and Redoubt are also visible.

The centerpiece of this small park is the **Captain Cook Monument**, commemorating the 200th anniversary of James Cook's exploration of Alaska. An 18th-century British naval officer and explorer with a natural talent for physics and mathematics,

Cook led several expeditions around the world. In 1776, on his third voyage in HMS *Resolution*, he sailed north along the continent's west coast in search of the Northwest Passage (a navigable link between the Atlantic and Pacific Oceans), and passed the present-day site of Anchorage, giving his name to Cook Inlet. Derek Freeborn's life-sized bronze statue, based on the one in Whitby, UK, from where Cook first set sail, was donated to Anchorage during the US Bicentennial celebrations in 1976.

Just one block east, in front of the Carr-Gottstein Building, is Josef Princiotta's fabulous 1973 bronze sculpture, **The Last Blue Whale**. Adding a wonderful sense of perspective is a small beleaguered boat on the ripples of water near the tail of the gigantic whale.

Oscar Anderson House ❼

420 M St. **Map** B4. **Tel** 274-2336. 🚌 to Downtown Transit Center. ⏱ Jun–mid-Sep: noon–5pm Mon–Sat; mid-Sep–May: by appt. 🚫 💳 ♿

This historic home was built in 1915 by Oscar Anderson, a Swede who is said to have been the 18th resident of the original tent city of Anchorage. While still living on the beach after his arrival in town, Anderson established the Ship Creek Meat Company and the Evan Jones Fuel Company. Due to a shortage of building materials, his house, the first permanent wood-frame structure in town, had only one and a half stories and measured just 800 sq ft (72 sq m). Anderson lived here until his death in 1974, and two years later, it was deeded to the City of Anchorage by his widow.

The building has since been meticulously restored to reflect the period in which it was built, and is listed on the National Register of Historic Places. Various exhibits reveal the history of the city, and many of Anderson's original belongings are on display, including a working 1909 player piano. A Swedish Christmas open house is held here in traditional style each December. Next to the house, **Elderberry Park** offers great views of Knik Arm and the chance to spot beluga whales.

Oscar Anderson House, Anchorage's oldest wood-frame building

Alaska Native Heritage Center ⓼

Situated in a lovely wooded corner of Anchorage, the Alaska Native Heritage Center uses exhibits, workshops, and outdoor displays to preserve and perpetuate Native Alaskan culture. One of Anchorage's most popular attractions, this educational and cultural institution gives visitors the opportunity to experience a range of diverse Native traditions at a single site. Among the center's highlights are five Native "villages," which are based on broad tribal groupings that draw upon cultural similarities or geographic proximity. Native Alaskans throughout the site interpret aspects of their cultures.

Raven the Creator, by John Hoover, at the Welcome House

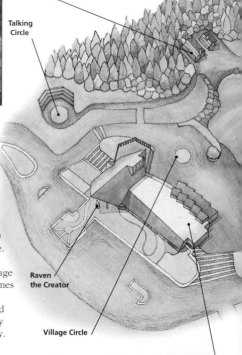
Talking Circle

Southeast Alaska Natives Village Site
Revealing the cultures of the Tsimshian, Eyak, Tlingit, and Haida peoples of Southeast Alaska, this site consists of a simple, undecorated clan house and a carving shed where Native artists work on totem poles.

EXPLORING THE CENTER
The center sprawls across 26 acres (10 ha) of land not far from downtown Anchorage. A trail winds around a large central lake, leading past five Native villages and a Village Circle and Talking Circle where Native games are often demonstrated. The center also presents workshops, films, storytelling, and numerous other cultural programs. To fully explore the site will take at least half a day.

Raven the Creator

Village Circle

★ **Welcome House**
The first stop for visitors, the Welcome House contains the Hall of Cultures, with craft displays and historical exhibits and the Gathering Place, where Native dancers, storytellers, and drummers perform.

STAR SIGHTS

★ Welcome House

★ Athabaskan Village Site

The Aleut and Alutiiq Village Site occupies a *ciqlluaq*, (also known as a *barabara* or *ulax*), a traditional semi-subterranean sod-covered home of Southwest Alaska.

The Inupiat and St. Lawrence Yup'ik Village Site is housed in a *qargi*, a community house usually made from sod blocks laid over whalebone frames.

VISITORS' CHECKLIST

Muldoon Rd North, exit from Glenn Hwy. **Map** F1. **Tel** 330-8000, (800) 315-6608. Free shuttle from Anchorage Museum mid-May–mid-Sep: 9am–5pm daily; open for special events in winter (late Sep–early May). discounted rates for seniors and children up to 16, free for kids under 6. www.alaskanative.net

The Yup'ik and Cup'ik Village Site features a circular *qasgiq*, or men's house. Here, visitors can watch Native Alaskans in traditional clothing interpret the Yup'ik way of life.

Lake Tiulana forms a natural centerpiece for the village tour.

★ **Athabaskan Village Site**
This site consists of a large earth-floored log cabin that served as a traditional Athabaskan home. Here, Athabaskan docents explain the use of the home's various rooms and demonstrate traditional tools and implements.

THE WELCOME HOUSE
Beyond the information desk and gift shop in the entrance area is the circular Gathering Place, an arena for traditional performances. Beyond the Crossroads foyer are the theater and the Hall of Cultures, with exhibits and stands where Native artisans create and sell their work. There is also a large research library.

The unique Welcome House entrance ushers visitors into the center

Exit to the village sites

Main entrance

Library exit

KEY

	Crossroads
	Theater
	Hall of Cultures
	Library
	Gathering Place
	Non-exhibition space

the nearby salmon hatchery releases up to 250,000 king salmon smolt, which swim downstream into Cook Inlet, spending seven years at sea before returning to spawn. To the north of the bridge across Ship Creek, a viewing platform gives visitors the opportunity to observe the salmon crowding their way upstream and jumping at the weir.

In the summer, anglers in hip-waders descend to the riverbanks in hopes of reeling in one of the 5,000 fish that are caught here each year. To fish here requires an Alaska fishing license, which is available in local shops. Fishing derbies may yield up to $10,000 for lucky anglers who catch specially tagged fish.

Tony Knowles Coastal Trail ⓫

Western end of 2nd Ave. **Map** E1.
🚌 7A. ♿

The most popular biking and jogging trail in Anchorage, the Tony Knowles Coastal Trail passes the attractive Elderberry Park on the downtown waterfront and follows the coastline south to Kincaid Park. One of the highlights along the 11-mile (17-km) trail is Westchester Lagoon, where walkers can observe waterfowl or cross over to the gravel beaches of Knik Arm. On clear days, there are great views across Cook Inlet to the volcano, Mount Spurr. Midway along the route, Earthquake Park has exhibits on the devastating 1964 Good Friday earthquake, which created the dramatic bluff visible here.

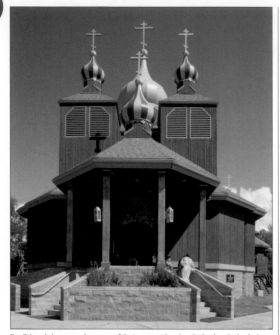

Traditional domes and crosses of St. Innocent Russian Orthodox Cathedral

St. Innocent Russian Orthodox Cathedral ❾

401 Turpin St. **Map** F1. **Tel** 333-9723. 🚌 8. ⬜ only for services.
♿ 🚫 ✝ 6pm Sat, 9am Sun.
www.sicanc.org

The heart of Russian Orthodox activity in the Anchorage area, this beautiful cathedral was named in honor of the erudite 18th-century bishop Ioan Veniaminov. After his arrival in Unalaska in the early 1820s, he built churches and schools, developed a written version of the Aleut language, and produced an Aleut Bible, for which he was canonized in 1977 as St. Innocent. Due largely to the efforts of such missionaries, Alaska is today the leading diocese of the Russian Orthodox Church in the Western Hemisphere.

The most striking features of St. Innocent are its 12 blue onion domes. As with most Orthodox places of worship, the cathedral is full of beautifully colored icons, paintings, and religious artifacts. Although the cathedral is usually closed to the public, its opulent interior can be seen during services, on feast days, or during other significant events of the Russian Orthodox calendar.

Ship Creek Salmon Viewing Platform ❿

North side of Ship Creek footbridge, off Whitney Ave. **Map** E3. ⬜ 24 hrs. **Derby tickets** available at the cabin next to Comfort Inn on the south bank of Ship Creek.

Flowing between downtown and the Port of Anchorage, Ship Creek is a mecca for urban fishermen. Each year,

Cyclists pedaling down Anchorage's scenic Tony Knowles Coastal Trail

1928 Stearman on display, Alaska Aviation Heritage Museum

At the southern end of the trail, the 2 sq miles (5.7 sq km) Kincaid Park, a forested glacial moraine area, offers excellent summer hiking and a network of Nordic ski trails in the winter. The park also has the city's largest population of moose.

Alaska Aviation Heritage Museum ⓬

4721 Aircraft Dr. **Map** E1. **Tel** 248-5325. ▦ 7A. ◯ mid-May–mid-Sep: 9am–5pm daily; mid-Sep–mid-May: 9am–5pm Wed–Sun. ▨ ♿ 🏠 www.alaskaairmuseum.org

Located on the shores of Lake Hood, the Alaska Aviation Heritage Museum is a must-see for anyone interested in the lives and achievements of traditional bush pilots and their planes. There is detailed coverage of the state's World War II history, including the Japanese invasion, along with collections of artifacts, photographs, aviators' clothing, and newspaper accounts of highlights in Alaskan aviation.

The museum also preserves an extensive collection of historic aircraft, including a 1928 Stearman bush plane that was among the first to land on Mount McKinley in 1932, one of only two remaining 1928 Hamilton Metalplanes, Merle "Mudhole" Smith's 1929 Cordova Airways TravelAir, and a 1929 Loening seaplane first flown to Alaska Territory in 1946 by former governor Jay Hammond. A 100-seat theater is available for viewing a library of film footage about Alaska's early pilots.

Lake Hood and Lake Spenard ⓭

Lakeshore Drive. **Map** E1. ▦ 7A. ◯ 24 hrs. ♿

Keeping Anchorage in touch with the Alaska that exists beyond its urban boundaries, this is the largest and busiest floatplane base in the US. It handles up to 800 takeoffs and landings per day and anyone chartering a bush flight into a remote area will probably depart from here. The best viewpoint to watch the flights is behind the Department of Transportation building. A lakeside park features a roped-off swimming area.

Anchorage's Lake Hood and Lake Spenard floatplane base

Spenard ⓮

Map E1. ▦ 7.

Anchorage's funky Spenard district was once a separate town, connected to downtown by the winding Spenard Road. Visitors to the neighborhood may come across a scattering of less-than-reputable businesses, throwbacks to Spenard's grittier days.

Despite its past and its somewhat unsavory reputation, Spenard is rapidly becoming a fashionable neighborhood. The derelict buildings and trailer parks are giving way to houses, health food eateries, second-hand shops, motels, and atmospheric bars and clubs. The corner of Spenard and Northern Lights has a REI store (see p89), along with a Kaladi Brothers coffee shop and one of Alaska's finest bookstores, Title Wave Books.

Floatplane taking off from the Lake Hood and Lake Spenard complex

BUSH FLYING IN ALASKA

Visitors who wish to fly into a remote lodge or enjoy a wilderness fishing trip are likely to employ an Alaskan bush pilot. These legendary aviators fly across untracked country, land on lakes and gravel bars, and defy natural conditions that most conventional pilots prefer to avoid. About 1 in 50 Alaskans has a pilot's license, and the state supports over 290 charter companies. Careful preparations are essential as drop-offs and pickups are prescheduled and can be disrupted by bad weather or unforeseen circumstances.

Village buildings at Anchorage's popular Alaska Wild Berry Products

Alaska Wild Berry Products ⑮

5225 Juneau St. **Map** F1. **Tel** 562-8858. 🚌 60. ⏱ late May–Oct: 10am–9pm Sun–Thu, 10am–10pm Fri & Sat; Nov–early May: shorter hours daily. ● Thanksgiving, Christmas, and New Year's Day. 🎦 🔥 🚻 🅿
www.alaskawildberryproducts.com

Located on the banks of the scenic Campbell Creek, Alaska Wild Berry Products is a popular tourist attraction. Perhaps the most interesting sight is the world's largest chocolate waterfall, a 20-ft (6-m) cascade of melted chocolate, which conjures up images of Roald Dahl's *Charlie and the Chocolate Factory*. Through observation windows, visitors can view the kitchens, which produce the company's signature jams and sweets.

A stroll around the Wild Berry Park and Village leads to a trail and reindeer enclosures. The attached Sourdough Mining Company serves traditional Alaskan fare and holds gold panning demonstrations. Visitors staying downtown can call to schedule a free pickup.

H2Oasis ⑯

1520 O'Malley Rd. **Map** F2. **Tel** 522-4420, (888) 426-2747. 🚌 2. ⏱ mid-May–mid-Sep: 10am–9pm daily; mid-Sep–mid-May: 3–9pm Mon, Wed, & Fri, 10am–9pm Sat–Sun, & school holidays. 🎦 🔥 🚻 **Riverwalk** ⏱ 7–10am Mon, Wed, & Fri.
www.h2oasiswaterpark.com

Alaska's only indoor water park, H2Oasis has activities for all age groups. The Lazy River encircling the park

offers tubing opportunities as well as a **Riverwalk**, a fitness walk in slow running water, thrice a week. A Wave Pool provides body surfing at a balmy 27° C (80° F) – even in winter. The Pirate Ship features water cannons and slides for children. Visitors can barrel down a 500-ft (150-m) water coaster on an inflatable raft, or body-slide down the tamer enclosed water tube. Swimmers can later relax in a whirlpool spa.

Alaska Zoo ㉒

4731 O'Malley Rd. **Map** F2. **Tel** 356-2133. 🚌 492. ⏱ mid-May–mid-Sep: 10am–5pm daily; mid-Sep–mid-May: 9am–9pm Tue & Fri. 🎦 🔥 🚻 🅿 **www**.alaskazoo.org

In 1966, the Crown Zellerbach Pulp Company staged a contest, offering either $3,000 or a baby elephant as the

Sign at Alaska Zoo, south of Anchorage

grand prize. To the company's surprise, the Anchorage grocer who won chose the baby elephant. Eventually, Annabelle the Asian elephant was donated to local horse rancher Mrs. Seawell, who decided that the community needed a public zoo. The Alaska Children's Zoo opened in 1969, developing slowly into what is today the sprawling Alaska Zoo.

Although Annabelle is no longer alive, visitors can see a host of Alaskan and exotic animals. There are enclosures for moose, reindeer, and Dall sheep. Waterfowl ponds provide a habitat for tundra and trumpeter swans. There are snow leopards and Siberian tigers, as well as a brown bear, polar bears, Bactrian camels, and even an African elephant. Children will enjoy the petting zoo.

Hilltop Ski Area ⑱

Upper Abbot Rd. **Map** F2. **Tel** 346-2167. ⏱ winter: 3–8pm Mon–Thu, 3–9pm Fri, 9am–9pm Sat & Sun. 🎿 🔥 disabled adaptive skiing programs available. 🅿 🚻 🅿
www.hilltopskiarea.org

New skiers and those without the time or money to head for the larger Alyeska Resort in Girdwood will appreciate the 30-acre (12-ha) Hilltop Ski Area, Anchorage proper's

Families enjoying the tropical environs of H2Oasis

For hotels and restaurants in this region see pp242–3 and pp256–8

Cemetery of the Eklutna Historical Park with its brightly painted "spirit house" graves

only ski resort. Here, the longest run (2,090 ft/637 m) offers a gradient that drops a gentle 295 ft (90 m). There are numerous other runs of varying difficulty. Access to the ski slopes is provided by a rope tow and a chairlift. In the adjacent Hillside Park, Nordic skiers will find 22 miles (32 km) of groomed cross-country trails.

Chugach State Park ⑲

See pp78–9.

Alaska Botanical Garden ⑳

4601 Campbell Airstrip Rd. **Map** F1. **Tel** 770 3692. 🚌 1, 75. ⬜ mid-May–mid-Sep: 9am–9pm daily; mid-Sep–mid-May: daylight hours. 🎫 🚶 Jun–Aug: 1pm daily. 🦽 limited access. 🅿 **www**.alaskabg.org

Amid the beautiful birch and spruce forests of Far North Bicentennial Park nestles the 110-acre (44-ha) Alaska Botanical Garden. Opened in 1993, the area features a formal herb garden, two perennial gardens, an alpine rock garden, and a wildflower path dotted with erratic boulders left behind by glaciers. Boreal flora is showcased with over 1,100 perennials and 150 native species of hardy flowering plants, shrubs, and other northern vegetation (see p161). The 1-mile (2-km)

long interpretive Lowenfels Family Nature Trail follows the north fork of Campbell Creek, which is home to a summer run of king salmon. The trail offers views of the Chugach Range and reveals the geological history of the Anchorage Bowl. In the summer, the area is ideal for photography and bird-watching, and in the winter, the various trails serve as Nordic ski routes. As moose and bears inhabit the area, dogs are not allowed.

Blue poppies, Alaska Botanical Garden

Turnagain Arm Tour ㉑

See pp80–81.

Eklutna Historical Park ㉒

Mile 26, Glenn Hwy. **Map** B2. **Tel** 688-6026. 🚌 Anchorage–Mat-Su. ⬜ mid-May–mid-Sep: 10am–4pm Mon–Fri; mid-Sep–mid-May: by appt. 🎫 🦽 ✝ 9–10:30am Sun. 🅿

Forming the centerpiece of the tiny village of Eklutna, the Eklutna Historical Park was established to preserve and portray the heritage of the Athabaskan people. Founded in 1650, it is the oldest continually inhabited village in the Anchorage area. With the coming of Russian missionaries in the early 19th century, most of the locals converted

to Russian Orthodoxy, as evidenced by the onion-domed St. Nicholas church. The adjacent cemetery has over 100 graves covered with colorful "spirit houses," decorated according to individual family traditions. Early 20th-century implements used here and Athabaskan beadwork and snowshoes can be seen at the Heritage House museum.

A 3-mile (5-km) return walk, over the Glenn Highway and through birch forests, leads to scenic **Thunderbird Falls**. During the winter, this 200-ft (60-m) high cascade becomes a spectacular icefall.

Hiking in the lush landscape below Thunderbird Falls near Eklutna

Chugach State Park ⑲

Encompassing almost 770 sq miles (2,000 sq km), Chugach State Park is America's third largest state park, and one of the most accessible from an urban area. This fabulously scenic glaciated region, situated right in Anchorage's backyard, includes icefields, glaciers, high peaks, forests, and mountain lakes, all within hiking distance of the city. While no roads cross the park, there are several hiking trails through spectacular scenery, as well as plenty of opportunities to view wildlife, including moose, black and brown bears, Dall sheep, mountain goats, marmots, and a host of smaller animals. Birdlife is profuse, especially along the park's many rivers, and close-up views of salmon are available from a platform near the Eagle River Nature Center.

Hikers passing through meadows on Crow Pass Crossing

KEY

🅰	Campground
ℹ	Visitor information
═══	Highway
══	Minor road
▬ ▬	Trail
▬▬▬	Alaska Railroad
▬ ▬	Park boundary
△	Peak

Symphony Lake
Cold, clear Symphony Lake, along the South Fork of the Eagle River, lies in a deep valley between the glaciated peaks of the Harmony Mountains.

★ Flattop Mountain
Alaska's most climbed mountain, the 3,510-ft (1,070-m) Flattop makes a popular outing for visitors who can manage the steep 1,310-ft (393-m), two-hour long ascent.

STAR SIGHTS

- ★ Flattop Mountain
- ★ Eklutna Lake
- ★ Eagle River Nature Center

Map labels:
GLENN HIGHWAY · Peters · Eagle · Fort Richardson · GLENN HWY · Anchorage · SEWARD HWY · Ship Creek · South Fork · Symphony Lake · Powerline Pass Trail · Flattop Mountain 3,510 ft · Indian Creek Trail · Alaska Railroad · Powerline Pass · Rabbit Lake · Bird Creek Trail · Bird Creek · Bird · Bird P...

0 km   5
0 miles   5

For hotels and restaurants in this region see pp242–3 and pp256–8

★ Eklutna Lake
The glacial blue waters of Eklutna Lake sparkle in the sun. The campground at the lake offers pleasant picnic and camping spots, while the lakeshore trail provides access to challenging alpine hikes up Twin Peaks and Bold Ridge.

The Mitre
Hikers on the trail to Eklutna Glacier are treated to close-up views of this spectacular 6,600-ft (2,000-m) high peak. The mountain is best viewed along the East Fork of the Eklutna River.

EXPLORING THE PARK
From the Eagle River Nature Center, the easy half-mile (1-km) Rodak Nature Trail and 3-mile (5-km) Albert Loop Trail lead to grand views of the Eagle River Valley. A popular day hike is the 6-mile (10-km) return hike to Echo Bend on the Old Iditarod Trail, which connects Eagle River with Girdwood.

Hikers on the Crow Pass Crossing can book the Forest Service public use cabin at the toe of Raven Glacier.

★ Eagle River Nature Center
The center has maps, books, and exhibits on the landscape and wildlife of the park. Viewing decks and spotting scopes offer visitors great views of the river valley and the surrounding peaks.

Turnagain Arm Tour ㉑

The curious name of the 50-mile (80-km) long fjord known as Turnagain Arm was bestowed by explorer Captain James Cook in 1778. He was forced to "turn again" after discovering that it was impossible to navigate a sea route between Cook Inlet and the fabled Northwest Passage. Today, a drive along the Arm's shore makes a rewarding day trip from Anchorage. A lovely stretch of the 120-mile (200-km) Seward Highway, which connects Anchorage and Seward *(see pp98–9),* follows the fjord's north shore through Chugach State Park, offering spectacular views of the Kenai Mountains and Chugach National Forest.

Driving along the scenic Seward Highway next to Turnagain Arm

Anchorage Coastal Wildlife Refuge ①
Just south of Anchorage at Mile 117, a series of boardwalks provide views across Potter Marsh, frequented in the summer by nesting ducks, geese, swans, and other waterfowl.

KEY

△	Campground
▬	Tour
══	Main road
══	Minor road
▬ ▬	Trail
▬	Alaska Railroad
⁞⁞⁞	Road-rail tunnel
△	Peak

Beluga Point ②
At Beluga Point (Mile 110) visitors can observe Turnagain Arm empty and refill twice daily in a wall of water known as the bore tide, which ranges from 2 to 6 ft (60 cm–2 m), occasionally topping a dramatic 8 ft (2.5 m).

Anchorage

SEWARD HIGHWAY

Alaska Railroad

Cook Inlet

Bird

Turnaga[in]

Chugach

Nationa[l]

Resurrection Creek

Sixmile Creek

Hope

BELUGA WHALES

The distinctive whale known as the beluga *(Delphinapterus leucas)* is one of several beaked whales that inhabit the Arctic, North Atlantic, and North Pacific Oceans. The name beluga, meaning "the white one," was given by Russian explorers, who probably first observed them in the Bering Sea. These mammals are 13 to 15 ft (4 to 4.5 m) in length and weigh about 2,500 to 3,500 lbs (1,100 to 1,600 kg). In the summer, pods migrate into Turnagain Arm to feed and may be observed from the shore, although the Cook Inlet population has been declining dramatically in recent years, alarming scientists.

Beluga whale breaking the surface

Girdwood and Alyeska Resort ③

The village of Girdwood, 40 miles (65 km) from Anchorage, revolves around Alyeska, Alaska's most popular ski resort. Summer visitors can ride the gondola to the top of Mount Alyeska for sweeping views over the fjord and surrounding mountains.

TIPS FOR DRIVERS

Starting point: 12 miles (19 km) S of downtown Anchorage.
Length: 40 miles (64 km).
Stopping-off points: Bird Ridge Café and Bakery at Mile 100 is a good place to stop for a quick bite. The McHugh Creek Wayside at Mile 112 offers pleasant picnic spots. Potter Section House at Mile 115 houses the Chugach State Park Headquarters.
Campgrounds: Bird Creek at Mile 101 offers good, basic sites.

Crow Creek Trail ④

From the end of Crow Creek Road, a 4-mile (6-km) trail climbs past Gold Rush relics to Crow Pass, which has fine views of Raven Glacier.

The "Drowned Forest" ⑤

At the head of the fjord, the highway passes through a ghostly "drowned forest" of bleached dead trees, created after the 1964 earthquake *(see p25)* caused the land to slump 4 ft (1.2 m) and the sea rushed in.

Begich-Boggs Visitors' Center ⑥

Built on a terminal moraine left by the receding Portage Glacier beside Portage Lake, the center has exhibits on Alaskan glaciers. The film *Voices from the Ice* is screened hourly and describes the dynamics of valley glaciers.

Portage Glacier ⑦

One of Alaska's most visited glaciers, Portage Glacier extends into Portage Lake and is best viewed on cruises from the visitors' center. A level 2-mile (3-km) loop track leads to the foot of nearby Byron Glacier.

Brilliant foliage along the Matanuska River ▷

Hay bales on a Mat-Su Valley farm near Palmer

Palmer ㉓

42 miles (70 km) NE of Anchorage.
Map C1. 🏛 *8,000.* 🚌 *from
Anchorage.* 🚩 *723 S Valley Way,
745-2880.* 🚂 *Fri.* 🎪 *Alaska State
Fair (Aug–Sep), Colony Christmas
(Dec).* **www**.palmerchamber.org

Best known as a farming
community, the compact
town of Palmer nestles below
the peaks of the Talkeetna
Range in the narrow valley
of the glacial Matanuska
River. Founded as a social
experiment in 1935 as part
of President Franklin Delano
Roosevelt's New Deal, it was
settled by 200 Midwestern
families *(see p54)*. Each family
in the newly established
Matanuska Colony was given
40 acres (16 ha) of land for
vegetable farming, growing
hay, and raising dairy cattle.
Today, while farming is still
important, Palmer's outskirts
are rapidly turning into bed-
room suburbs for Anchorage,

due mainly to the city's
dwindling land and high
costs. The surrounding
Matanuska and Susitna
Valleys, popularly abbreviated
to Mat-Su, are now
among the fastest-
growing regions
of Alaska.
Well worth visiting
is the **Colony House
Museum**, which reflects
one of the five basic
farmhouse styles
available to the
Colony farmers. Inside, their
story is told with old newspaper articles, period furnishings, and artifacts.
For 12 days in August and
September, Palmer hosts the
Alaska State Fair *(see p44)*,
the state's biggest annual
event, drawing nearly half of
Alaska's population. The fair
features the valley's famous
giant vegetables, as well as
other agricultural displays,
crafts, livestock, food and
retail booths, live music, a

**Reindeer at the
farm near Palmer**

rodeo, Native dancing and
blanket tossing, and a range
of competitions.

🏛 **Colony House Museum**
316 E Elmwood Ave, Palmer.
Tel 745-1935. ◻ *Jun–Aug:
10am–4pm Tue–Sat.* 📷

Reindeer Farm ㉔

7 miles (11 km) S of Palmer at Mile
11.5, Old Glenn Hwy. **Map** C1.
Tel 745-4000. 🚗 ◻ *May–mid-Sep:
10am–6pm daily.* 📷 ♿ 👶

Located in one of the original
Colony farmhouses on the flat
farmlands off the Old Glenn
Highway, the Reindeer Farm
offers visitors the
opportunity to see
reindeer close-up.
Children are invited
to hand-feed and
pet the animals, and
can also meet an
elk, a moose, and a
black-tailed deer.
Those inclined to
outdoor activities can
join a horseback trail ride.

Bodenburg Butte ㉕

Adjacent to the Reindeer Farm
at Mile 11.5, Old Glenn Hwy.
Map C1. 🚗

Rising out of the farmlands on
the Knik River flats south of
Palmer, the 900-ft (270-m)
high Bodenburg Butte is one
of the Matanuska Valley's
most prominent landmarks. It
was created when Knik
Glacier rode over a small
knob of resistant bedrock,
leaving a glacier-scraped
dome known as a *roche
moutonnée*. Once used for
military training, it is now a
popular picnic and hiking
spot with a windy summit
from where parasailers can
launch out over the flats. The
steep trail leading to the summit starts opposite Reindeer
Farm and soon passes from
the stands of birch at the base
into open grassy ridges and
rocky bluffs near the top. The
two-hour long round trek is
worth it for the views from
the summit, which take in the
Palmer area and Knik Glacier.

GREEN GIANTS

**Gargantuan cabbage
from the Mat-Su**

Alaskans are rightfully proud of the
produce grown in the Matanuska
Valley. The growing season may be
short, but thanks to the long summer
days, vegetables continue to grow
around the clock, resulting in enormous
carrots, turnips, zucchini, and other
produce. At the annual Alaska State Fair,
awards are given for the largest vegetable of each variety. The record-winning
rutabaga (swede) was 75 lb (34 kg),
while the largest pumpkin weighed in at
a whopping 942 lb (428 kg). The most
popular annual competition is for the cabbage – the world-
record holder, grown in Wasilla in 2009, tipped the scales
at 127 lb (38 kg), winning the $2,000 grand prize. Local
farmers and gardeners are still trying to break that record.

Abandoned snow-covered Mat-Su Valley barn near Bodenburg Butte

Musk Ox Farm ㉖

8 miles (13 km) N of Palmer at Archie Rd, Mile 50, Glenn Hwy. **Map** C1 **Tel** 745-4151. 🚌 🚻 *May–Sep: 10am–6pm daily, Oct–Apr: by appt.* ♿ 🅿 🚻 www.muskoxfarm.org

The Musk Ox Farm is home to the only domestic herd of musk oxen in the world. Hunted to extinction in Alaska in the 19th century, they were reintroduced from Greenland in the 1930s. Musk oxen now inhabit Nunivak Island, the Seward Peninsula, and the North Slope of Alaska.

Anthropologist John Teal started the farm in Fairbanks in 1964. Now located in Palmer, the farm gathers *qiviut*, the fine underwool of the musk ox, and distributes it to Native women. They spin and knit the *qiviut* into soft, warm garments using patterns and motifs unique to their villages. The farm is open to the public and runs short tours.

Wasilla ㉗

45 miles (72 km) N of Anchorage. **Map** C1. 🏘 *5,500.* 🚏 🚌 *from Anchorage.* 🛈 *Mat-Su Convention and Visitors Bureau, Tel 746-5000.* www.alaskavisit.com

Essentially a long strip of unfocused development along the Parks Highway, Wasilla was founded in 1917 as a railroad halt. It began to grow when the Parks Highway was completed in the 1970s, eventually becoming the commercial center of the Mat-Su Borough. Although not the prettiest Alaskan town, Wasilla does have several worthwhile attractions. Most of these sights are clustered north of the railroad station, off the highway at the Old Wasilla Townsite Park. The park includes historic homes, the original Wasilla School, an old barn

Iditarod Trail insignia

and blacksmith shop, a reconstructed bathhouse, and the Dorothy Page Museum, named for the woman who founded the Iditarod Trail Sled Dog Race *(see p39)* with musher Joe Redington.

The **Museum of Alaska Transportation and Industry**, formerly the Air Progress Museum of Anchorage, was renamed and shifted to Palmer after a fire. When it outgrew that site in 1992, it moved to its present home west of Wasilla. In addition to a large gallery and exhibit hall, the museum has an outdoor collection that includes *umiaqs* (skin boats), railway memorabilia, and vintage steam engines, aircraft, and vehicles.

Situated on the Iditarod Trail, the **Knik Museum and Musher's Hall of Fame** is located in an old roadhouse. Visitors can see objects from the now-defunct town of Knik, as well as Iditarod exhibits, such as race trophies, charcoal drawings of past winners, and a presentation on famous Alaskan mushers.

🏛 **Museum of Alaska Transport and Industry**
5 miles (8 km) W of Wasilla at Mile 47, Parks Hwy. **Tel** 376-1211. 🕐 *May–Sep: 10am–5pm daily.* ♿ www.museumofalaska.org

🏛 **Knik Museum and Musher's Hall of Fame**
Mile 13.9, Knik Rd. **Tel** 376-7755. 🕐 *Jun–Aug: 1–6pm daily.* ♿

Bull musk oxen facing off on a snowy plain

Independence Mine State Historical Park ㉘

Most people associate gold mining in Alaska with the placer gold *(see p53)* diggings in the Klondike. However, starting in 1906, a gold-bearing quartz lode was being tapped in the Talkeetna Mountains. Two mines were established in the scenic mountain valley of the Little Susitna River, the Alaska Free Gold Mine on Skyscraper Mountain and the Independence Mine on Granite Mountain. In 1938, the two were merged into the Alaska-Pacific Consolidated Mining Company. Although the mines were producing large amounts of gold, the activity was deemed non-essential during World War II, and after the war, government restrictions on private ownership of gold spelled the end of the mine. The site was designated a State Historical Park in the late 1970s.

Mine buildings scattered across Fishhook Valley

The New Mess Hall, constructed in 1941, had a well-equipped kitchen, bakery, butchery, scullery, and a dining hall that seated 160 persons.

The Administrative Building was used as an office, storeroom, and bunk house during an attempt to reopen the mine in 1946.

Mechanical and repair shops housed plumbing, carpentry, and electrical operations.

The New Bunk House was built in 1940 to house 50 people. It also contained rooms used for classes and for screening films.

★ **Bunk Houses**
Three of the larger buildings at Independence Mine served as bunk houses. One was built in 1939 and functioned as a supply warehouse, engineering office, and school. A small, well-appointed building nearby had self-contained housing units for top mine officials.

The Manager's House was constructed in 1939 to house the mine manager's family and guests. Today, the distinctive building serves as the park's Visitor Center and administrative headquarters.

EXPLORING THE MINE

To fully explore the park's historic buildings and ruins will take two to three hours. The Main Trail is an easy, level route that begins at the Manager's House and loops past the Mess Hall, Administrative Building, and Bunk Houses, with a short detour to the Museum (Assay Office). The more challenging 20-minute Hard Rock Trail climbs the tundra-covered hillside to an overlook near the Water Tunnel Portal and Mine Shops. Guided tours of the mine last between 60 and 90 minutes.

STAR SIGHTS

★ Bunk Houses

★ Mill Complex

An ore conveyor brought ore into the mill where it was sorted and crushed to extract the gold.

The Hard Rock Trail leads to a park overlook near the Water Tunnel Portal.

The Assay Office now houses the site museum.

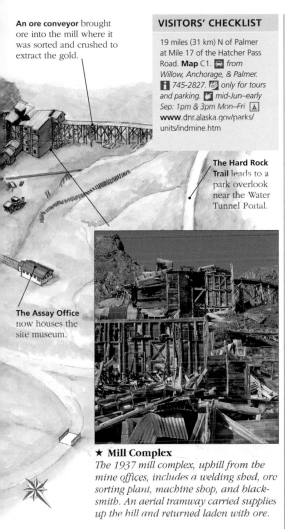

★ **Mill Complex**

The 1937 mill complex, uphill from the mine offices, includes a welding shed, ore sorting plant, machine shop, and blacksmith. An aerial tramway carried supplies up the hill and returned laden with ore.

Hatcher Pass Road winding through the Independence Mine area

Hatcher Pass ②⑨

21 miles (34 km) N of Palmer at Mile 19 of the Hatcher Pass Road. **Map** C1. 🚌 *from Anchorage, Willow, & Palmer. The pass may be closed from September to May; check in advance.*

Beyond Independence Mine, the Hatcher Pass Road climbs up onto the "tail" of the Talkeetna Range that reaches westward toward Willow and makes a wonderful driving or biking route. The road is paved only as far as the Independence Mine turn-off and Hatcher Pass Lodge at Mile 17. Shortly after, at Mile 19, it crosses 3,886-ft (1,166-m) Hatcher Pass, one of Alaska's highest road passes, before twisting for another 31 miles (50 km) to Willow.

Just beyond the pass, the road passes through the Summit Lake State Recreation Site. The lake itself is a small alpine tarn in a glacial cirque, or steep-walled basin, and is accessed by a trail around its perimeter and along the bluff overlooking it. The inspiring views take in the Susitna Valley, Willow Creek, and the Alaska Range in the distance.

In the summer, Hatcher Pass is an excellent paragliding venue, and a number of hiking trails, including the popular Gold Mint Trail, take off into the peaks and valleys. In the winter, the attraction is the network of Nordic skiing and snowmachining trails that lead into the wilds of the Talkeetna Mountains.

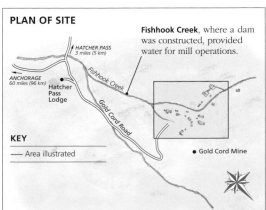

PLAN OF SITE

Fishhook Creek, where a dam was constructed, provided water for mill operations.

HATCHER PASS 3 miles (5 km)

ANCHORAGE 60 miles (96 km)

Hatcher Pass Lodge

Gold Cord Road

KEY

— Area illustrated

● Gold Cord Mine

SHOPPING IN ANCHORAGE

Anchorage is arguably the best place in Alaska to pick up gifts and souvenirs that are unique to the state. Throughout downtown, numerous small shops sell inexpensive gifts and mementos, while a range of higher quality shops and art galleries offer Alaskan art and photography, furs, local foods, Native arts and crafts, and antiques. Mainstream shopping ranges from

Sign, Anchorage Weekend Market

warehouse-like box stores, such as Fred Meyer outlets, to large shopping malls and the more upmarket Nordstrom store. Due to its position as a jumping-off point for adventure activities, the city is also an excellent place to pick up outdoor supplies, and several local outlets sell camping, hiking, cycling, boating, hunting, and fishing gear to help prepare for outdoor adventures.

Soapstone carvings on display at Anchorage's Weekend Market

MARKETS AND FAIRS

Every Saturday and Sunday, between mid-May and mid-September, from 10am to 6pm, the **Anchorage Market and Festival** fills the parking lot downtown at 3rd Avenue and E Street, selling Alaskan crafts, souvenirs, freshly cooked food, and clothing. From June to August, at the Northway Mall grounds in East Anchorage, the **Wednesday Market** sells similar items from 11am to 5pm. The ultimate informal shopping experience is undoubtedly the annual **Alaska State Fair** *(see p44)* in Palmer.

ALASKAN ARTS AND ANTIQUES

The best way to find unusual Alaskan photography, art, and original creations is to attend the First Friday

openings of art galleries. The **Iditarod Trail Store** sells official Last Great Race patches, dog booties, posters, and other memorabilia. A legacy of the Gold Rush, Alaskan gold makes excellent jewelry, souvenirs, and investment items. The **Alaska Mint** sells Alaskan gold and silver coins and medallions. The gift shop at the **Anchorage Museum** has a fine selection of works by Alaskan artists, including traditional pieces. In the summer, local artists have their wares on display in the atrium. In addition, a number of fine art galleries dot downtown Anchorage.

NATIVE ARTS AND CRAFTS

Alaska's most unique product is clothing made of *qiviut*, the fine underwool of the musk ox, sold at the **Oomingmak Musk Ox Producers' Co-operative**. *Ulus*, rounded knives used by Native women, are also popular.

Most gift shops sell them but the **Ulu Factory** has the largest selection of authentic knives. Other gifts include baskets made of grass, bark, and baleen (also called whalebone), beaded purses and belts, and fine scrimshaw art on ivory and bone. The **Alaska Native Medical Center Craft Shop** sells high quality Native objects from all over Alaska. At the **Alaska Native Heritage Center** *(see pp72–3)*, visitors can watch artists at work and purchase gifts from the on-site shop. **One People** is a cooperative shop selling authentic Native arts and crafts.

While shopping for Native art, especially soapstone carvings, it is best to be careful, as items mass-produced abroad are occasionally sold as Native art. The state-run Silver Hand program guarantees that products tagged with the Silver Hand label were made by Native Alaskans using Alaskan materials. However, the program is not universal, and plenty of legitimate crafts do not carry the label.

Pottery and wood-crafted ducks for sale in an Anchorage shop

ALASKAN FOODS

10th and M Seafoods sells smoked fish and freshly caught salmon, and will also smoke, freeze, and package visitors' own catch of fish or game for the trip home. **Alaska Sausage and Seafood** will turn hunters' moose, caribou, or deer into sausage products, and sells smoked salmon and reindeer sausage. **Alaska Wild Berry Products** (see p76) is the best place for Alaskan berries made into jam and sweets. Exotic seafood is available at the two **New Sagaya's Markets**, the city's prominent Oriental groceries.

DEPARTMENT STORES

The main shopping malls in Anchorage are occupied by department stores of varying price and quality. The most down-to-earth choice is the **Dimond Center**, which features The Gap and Old Navy for clothing and Best Buy for electronics. The midtown **Sears Mall** has a large Sears Department Store, which sells clothing and appliances, while the downtown **5th Avenue Mall** is best known for its Nordstrom store. There are also a large number of box stores, massive outlets that sell just about everything at discounted prices. The most pleasant of these are the **Fred Meyer** stores, which also have a grocer, bakery, and deli. The cheapest places are the membership warehouses **Costco** and **Sam's Club**. **Wal-Mart** stores sell a variety of functional items at low prices.

SPORTING GOODS

Due to its outdoor orientation, Anchorage is an excellent place to stock up on gear before heading out into the wilderness on a camping, hiking, backpacking, fishing, hunting, whitewater rafting, or kayaking trip. One of the most popular stores in town is **REI** (Recreational Equipment Incorporated), a membership retailer that mainly stocks equipment, clothing, and lightweight gear for non-motorized sports. **Alaska Mountaineering and Hiking**, a similar outlet nearby, sells gear from a range of manufacturers and is aimed primarily at rock climbers and mountaineers. For keen hunters, anglers, and campers, there is no better outfitter than the mind-boggling **Sportsman's Warehouse**, which offers everything from camouflage clothing, winter gear, footwear, and salmon smokers to hunting hides, rifles, pontoon boats, and skinning knives.

Visitors who are in town in the cold season and want to try out some winter sports can drop by **Play It Again Sports** and pick up warm clothing, as well as used and new skiing, skating, snowshoeing, and hockey equipment at discounted prices.

DIRECTORY

MARKETS AND FAIRS

Wednesday Market
Northway Mall. Map F1. *Tel 272-5634.* www.anchoragemarkets.com

Anchorage Market and Festival
3rd Ave & E St. Map D4. *Tel 272-5634.* www.anchoragemarkets.com

ALASKAN ARTS AND ANTIQUES

Alaska Mint
429 W 4th Ave. Map D4. *Tel 278-8414.* www.alaskamint.com

Iditarod Trail Store
5th Avenue Mall, 320 W 5th Ave. Map E4. *Tel 276-2350.* www.iditarod.com

NATIVE ARTS AND CRAFTS

Alaska Native Medical Center Craft Shop
4315 Diplomacy Dr. Map F1. *Tel 729-1122.*

One People
425 D St. Map D4. *Tel 274-4063.*

Oomingmak Musk Ox Producers' Co-operative
604 H St. Map C5. *Tel 272-9225.* www.qiviut.com

Ulu Factory
211 W Ship Creek Ave. Map E3. *Tel 276-3119.* www.theulufactory.com

ALASKAN FOODS

10th and M Seafoods
1020 M St. Map E1. *Tel 272-3474.* www.10thandmseafoods.com

Alaska Sausage and Seafood
2914 Arctic Blvd. Map E1. *Tel 562-3636.* www.alaskasausage.com

New Sagaya's Markets
3700 Old Seward Hwy. Map F1. *Tel 561-5173.*

900 W 13th Ave. Map E1. *Tel 274-6173.* www.newsagaya.com

DEPARTMENT STORES

5th Avenue Mall
320 W 5th Ave. Map E4.

Costco
330 W Dimond Blvd. Map E2. *Tel 344-6436.* www.costco.com

Dimond Center
Dimond Blvd & Old Seward. Map F2. *Tel 344-2581.* www.dimondcenter.com

Fred Meyer
7701 Debarr Rd. Map F1. *Tel 269-1700.* www.fredmeyer.com

Sam's Club
8801 Old Seward Hwy. Map F2. *Tel 522-2333.* www.samsclub.com

Sears Mall
Benson & Seward Hwy. Map E1. *Tel 264-6695.* www.mallatsears.com

Wal-Mart
8900 Old Seward Hwy. Map F2. *Tel 344-9900.* www.walmart.com

SPORTING GOODS

Alaska Mountaineering and Hiking
2633 Spenard Rd. Map E1. *Tel 272-1811.* www.alaskamountaineering.com

Play It Again Sports
2636 Spenard Rd. Map E1. *Tel 278-7529.* www.playitagainsports.com

REI
1200 W Northern Lights Blvd. Map E1. *Tel 272-4565.* www.rei.com

Sportsman's Warehouse
8681 Old Seward Hwy. Map E2. *Tel 644-1400.* www.sportsmanswarehouse.com

ENTERTAINMENT IN ANCHORAGE

While Anchorage may be better known as a launching pad to the wilderness, it nonetheless offers a range of entertainment that is more vibrant than most other Alaskan cities. The seemingly endless daylight hours of summer are ideal for outdoor activities, while in autumn and winter, indoor pursuits such as concerts, theater, opera, and ballet are available. The Alaska Center for the Performing Arts, in downtown Anchorage, is renowned for its cultural events, while the Sullivan Arena hosts rock concerts and sporting events. The city also has numerous cinemas, bars, and nightclubs, many of which offer live entertainment and excellent locally produced brews.

INFORMATION AND TICKETS

Published every Thursday, the *Anchorage Press* is the best source of information on art exhibitions, concerts, festivals, and sports. This free weekly paper is distributed to businesses across the city. The **Anchorage Convention and Visitors' Bureau** also keeps abreast of upcoming events. Tickets for most programs can be easily bought at the Alaska Center for the Performing Arts or obtained directly from the various venues. Alternatively, **Ticketmaster** outlets can be found at Fred Meyer stores around the city.

THEATER AND CONCERTS

Major theater and musical productions are staged at the Atwood Concert Hall, the Discovery Theater, and the Sydney Laurence Theater, all located in the **Alaska Center**

The log cabin theme at Chilkoot Charlie's in Anchorage

for the Performing Arts. The **Anchorage Opera**, the **Alaska Dance Theatre**, the **Anchorage Symphony Orchestra**, and the **Anchorage Concert Association** perform at the center. The **Sullivan Arena** hosts pop and rock concerts, while plays and small classical music shows are held at the Wendy Williamson Auditorium, the Arts Theater, and the Arts Recital Hall at the **University of Alaska Anchorage**.

CINEMA

While there are no art film venues in Anchorage, a number of multiplex cinemas such as **Dimond Center 9 Cinemas** and **Century 16 Cinemas** screen popular first-run films. Showing inexpensive second-run movies, the **Bear Tooth Theatre Pub** also offers some excellent microbrewery beer and good food in a bar-and-restaurant environment. For extensive film critiques, there is the *Anchorage Press*, while cinema listings are outlined in the city's main newspaper, the *Anchorage Daily News*.

CULTURAL PRESENTATIONS

The large open theater at the **Alaska Native Heritage Center** *(see pp72–3)* plays host to a range of Native arts, theater, dance, and sports demonstrations. The **Anchorage Museum** often features visiting art exhibitions *(see pp68–9)*. On the first Friday of every month, galleries across Anchorage hold art openings, usually attended by showcased artists. During the winter, the downtown **Dena'ina Civic and Convention Center** hosts a variety of cultural events as well.

CLUBS AND BARS

Anchorage enjoys a vibrant nightlife, with a good variety of clubbing and drinking venues on offer. For rock, pop, and sheer mayhem, the hotspot is **Chilkoot Charlie's**, popularly nicknamed "Koot's." Downtown, head to **Humpy's Great Alaskan Alehouse** for live music, a packed dance floor, microbrews on draught, and tasty pub grub.

Traditional dance performance at the Alaska Native Heritage Center

Anchorage Glacier Pilots playing the Bucs at Mulcahy Stadium

Blues Central at the Chef's Inn is well-known for live blues and soul. **Cyrano's Off Center Playhouse** and the **Organic Oasis** (see p256) often showcase live jazz evenings.

For fans of the amber fluid, microbreweries at the **Glacier Brewhouse** and the **Snow Goose** (see p257) conjure up a fantastic selection of beers.

SPORTS

Although Anchorage has no major league baseball or NHL hockey team, it takes pride in sport. During the summer, the Alaska Minor Baseball League's **Anchorage Glacier Pilots** and **Anchorage Bucs** play in town. The **University of Alaska Anchorage (UAA)**

Seawolves basketball team hosts the **Great Alaska Shootout** in late November, and the **Alaska Aces** hockey team play at the Sullivan Arena in winter. The **World Championship Sled Dog Races** are held in February, while the **Iditarod Trail Sled Dog Race** is flagged off in early March.

CHILDREN

With an array of children's activities on offer, Anchorage promises to be a fun experience for the family. The Children's Gallery at the **Anchorage Museum** (see pp68–9) caters specifically to youngsters with its extraordinary **Imaginarium Discovery Center**, home to a host of fun activities. The **Alaska Zoo** (see p76) offers a wonderful day out for kids.

DIRECTORY

INFORMATION AND TICKETS

Anchorage Convention and Visitors' Bureau
546 W 4th Ave. **Map** D4
Tel 274-3531.
www.anchorage.net

Anchorage Press
540 E 5th Ave. **Map** F1.
Tel 561-7737. www.
anchoragepress.com

Ticketmaster
Tel 562-4800.
www.ticketmaster.com

THEATER AND CONCERTS

Alaska Center for the Performing Arts
621 W 6th Ave. **Map** D5.
Tel 263-2900. www.
myalaskacenter.com

Alaska Dance Theatre
2602 Gambell St. **Map** F1.
Tel 277-9591. www.
alaskadancetheatre.org

Anchorage Concert Association
430 W 7th Ave,
No. 200. **Map** D5.
Tel 272-1471. www.
anchorageconcerts.org

Anchorage Opera
1507 Spar Ave. **Map** E4.
Tel 279-2557. www.
anchorageopera.org

Anchorage Symphony Orchestra
400 D St No. 230. **Map** D4. **Tel** 274-8668. www.
anchoragesymphony.org

Sullivan Arena
1600 Gambell St. **Map** F1.
Tel 279-0618 (Box Office).
www.sullivanarena.com

University of Alaska Anchorage
Department of Theatre and Dance, 3211 Providence Dr. **Map** F1. **Tel** 263-2787 (Box Office). http://
theatre.uaa.alaska.edu

CINEMA

Bear Tooth Theatre Pub
1230 W 27th Ave. **Map** E1. **Tel** 276-4200. www.
beartooththeatre.net

Century 16 Cinemas
301 E 36th Ave. **Map** F1.
Tel 929-3456.

Dimond Center 9 Cinemas
800 E Dimond Blvd. **Map** F2. **Tel** 566-3327.

CULTURAL PRESENTATIONS

Dena'ina Civic and Convention Center
600 W 7th Ave. **Map** D5.
Tel 263-2850.
www.anchorage
conventioncenters.com

CLUBS AND BARS

Blues Central
825 W Northern Lights
Blvd. **Map** E1.
Tel 272-1341.

Chilkoot Charlie's
1071 W 25th Ave,
Map E1. **Tel** 279-1692.
www.koots.com

Cyrano's Off Center Playhouse
4th Ave & D St. **Map** D4.
Tel 274-2599.
www.cyranos.org

Humpy's Great Alaskan Alehouse
610 W 6th Ave. **Map** D5.
Tel 276-2337.
www.humpys.com

SPORTS

Alaska Aces
804 E 15th Ave, Suite C.
Map E1. **Tel** 258-2237.
www.alaskaaces.com

Anchorage Bucs
1317 W Northern Lights
Blvd No. 2. **Map** E1.
Tel 561-2827. www.
anchoragebucs.com

Anchorage Glacier Pilots
207 E Northern Lights
Blvd No. 105. **Map** E1.
Tel 274-3627.
www.glacierpilots.com

Great Alaska Shootout
3211 Providence Dr.
Map F1. **Tel** 786-1250.
www.shootout.net

Iditarod Trail Sled Dog Race
Box 870800, Wasilla.
Map B1. **Tel** 376-5155.
www.iditarod.com

University of Alaska Anchorage (UAA) Seawolves
3211 Providence Dr.
Map F1. **Tel** 786-1250.

World Championship Sled Dog Races
400 D St No. 200.
Map D4. **Tel** 274-1177.
www.furrondy.net

THE KENAI PENINSULA

*requently referred to as Alaska's Playground for the range of
outdoor activities it offers, the Kenai Peninsula is a microcosm
of the state. Its eastern half has forested slopes and icefields, and
a coast cut by deep fjords and dramatic valleys that usher glacier ice
into the sea. The west is gentler, with muskeg bog, rolling, lake-studded
lowlands full of wildlife, and seas that brim with marine life.*

Situated on the western edge of
the Gulf of Alaska, the peninsula derives its name from
the Kenaitze people of the
Dena'ina Athabaskans, who
moved here from the interior
regions of Alaska. With
the coming of the Russians in the
late 18th century and the establishment of the towns of Ninilchik and
Kenai, Native culture began to
gradually fade away and the peninsula became one of the main centers
of Russian influence in Alaska.

After the US purchased Alaska in
1867, the area remained a backwater
until the discovery of gold near Hope
in the 1890s. Since then, Seward has
gained importance as a center for
transportation and shipping, Homer
thrives on its fisheries, and the
production of oil and natural gas in
Cook Inlet drives the economy
around Kenai and Soldotna. The
entire peninsula has also benefitted
from tourism. Its proximity to
Anchorage and its diverse landscape
has helped make the region
one of the most populated,
best connected, and most
visited in the state. With its
relatively dense road
network, the Alaska
Railroad, the Marine Highway, and
the cruise ship port at Seward, the
peninsula is an easily accessible
destination for most independent
travelers and those on package tours.

The area offers stunning drives that
wind through the spruce forests of
the Kenai Range. Kenai Fjords
National Park and many state parks
offer campsites, beaches, and miles
of hiking trails. In the summer,
outdoors enthusiasts bound for
activity-packed weekends crowd
onto the scenic Seward Highway,
while anglers gravitate toward the
Kenai River, or opt for deep-sea
fishing in Kachemak Bay. For those
interested in soaking up Russian
ambience and history, the towns of
Ninilchik, Nikolaevsk, and Seldovia
make good stopping-off points.

Rolling fields and verdant mountains of the Kenai Peninsula

◁ Fresh catch of halibut and other fish displayed on the dock at Seward

Exploring the Kenai Peninsula

The varied landscape of the Kenai Peninsula takes in everything from fjords and glaciers to forests and muskeg. Kenai Fjords National Park contains the Harding Icefield, one of the largest in the US. The peninsula also features three very distinctive urban areas – practical Seward, the bustling, commercial Kenai-Soldotna region, and free-spirited Homer. These towns boast some excellent attractions, including Seward's Alaska SeaLife Center and Homer's Oceans and Islands Visitors' Center, as well as good places to stock up on supplies for outdoor activities. For the adventurous, the Kenai River is ideal for rafting and combat fishing, while the Resurrection Pass Trail is Alaska's most popular multi-day hiking route.

Resurrection Creek along Resurrection Pass Trail, near Hope

SIGHTS AT A GLANCE

Towns and Cities
Anchor Point ⑮
Clam Gulch ⑬
Cooper Landing ③
Homer ⑰
Hope ①
Kenai ⑩
Moose Pass ②
Nikolaevsk ⑯
Ninilchik ⑭
Seward ⑥
Soldotna ⑨
Sterling ⑧

National and State Parks
Captain Cook State
    Recreation Area ⑪
Kenai Fjords National
    Park pp104–105 ⑦
Kenai National Wildlife
    Refuge ⑫

Area of Natural Beauty
Kenai River ④

Tour
Resurrection Pass Trail p97 ⑤

GETTING AROUND
It is easiest to explore the region with an organized tour or by car. The Seward Highway links the Kenai Peninsula to Anchorage, while the Sterling Highway runs along the peninsula's west coast. In the summer, daily Homer Stage Lines buses connect the main sights and Park Connection buses run directly to Denali National Park. Also in the summer, there is a daily Alaska Railroad service from Seward, and the Marine Highway ferry *Tustumena* calls at Seward, Homer, and Seldovia. Homer, Kenai, and Soldotna are served by year-round scheduled flights from Anchorage.

Cook Inlet

CAPTAIN COOK ST.
RECREATION ARE

Nikishka Bay

Nikiski

Beaver Lake

STEP

KENAI ⑩

SOLDOTNA ⑨

Kalifonsky

Cohoe

⑬ **CLAM GULCH**

Tustur Lak

Crooked

NINILCHIK ⑭

*Deep Creek State
Recreation Area*

①

Deep Creek

*Stariski State
Recreation Area*

**ANCHOR
POINT** ⑮

⑯ **NIKOLAEVSK**

*Kachema
Selo*

*Kachemak
City*

HOMER ⑰

*Grewingk
Glacier*

*Halibut
Cove*

*Kachemak
Bay*

*Yalik
Glacier*

Seldovia

*Kachemak Bay State
Wilderness Park*

Port Graham

English Bay

*Elizabeth
Island*

*East Chugach
Island*

*Perl
Island*

0 km   20

0 miles   20

For additional map symbols *see back flap*

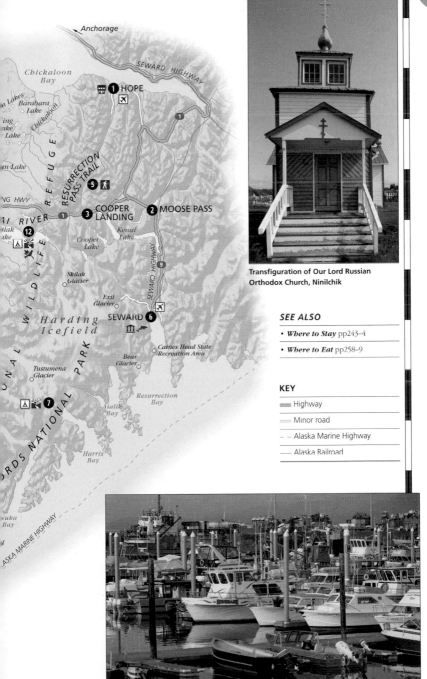

Transfiguration of Our Lord Russian
Orthodox Church, Ninilchik

SEE ALSO

- **Where to Stay** pp243–4

- **Where to Eat** pp258–9

KEY

━━━ Highway

─── Minor road

‒ ‒ Alaska Marine Highway

──── Alaska Railroad

Charter vessels and fishing boats at the Small Boat Harbor on the Homer Spit

Seaview Café and Bar on the main street of Hope

Hope ❶

88 miles (141 km) W of Anchorage.
Road Map B3. 🚶 *130*. ✈ 🚗
🎪 *Wagon Trail Run (3rd weekend in Jul)*. **www**.advenalaska.com/hope

The historic gold-mining town of Hope nestles in a deep valley next to the south shore of Turnagain Arm *(see pp80–81)*. Named after Percy Hope, a 17-year-old prospector, Hope's heyday was in the late 1890s, when it was a rollicking Gold Rush town. By the end of the decade, however, many of the town's inhabitants had pulled up stakes and headed for the Klondike goldfields.

Today, despite its proximity to Anchorage and the Seward Highway, Hope remains a quiet place. Most visitors stroll around town and visit the 1902 log social hall and the old 1896 general store, now home to the Seaview Café and Bar *(see p258)*. Recreational opportunities here include camping at the Porcupine Campground, rafting on Six-Mile Creek, and hiking on the Gull Rock Trail. More energetic hikers can try the **Resurrection Pass Trail**, which passes both historic and modern-day gold diggings.

Moose Pass ❷

98 miles (158 km) S of Anchorage.
Road Map B3. 🚶 *220*.
🚌 *Anchorage–Seward*. **Tel** 288-3101. 🎪 *Moose Pass Summer Festival (weekend nearest 21 June)*.
www.moosepass.net

Moose Pass village began life in 1912 as a construction camp on the Alaska Railroad. The area was named in 1903, after, it is said, a moose blocked the

passage of a mail-carrying dog team. To the west of the Seward Highway stands a landmark waterwheel, constructed in 1976 by the Estes Brothers who still run a grocery located in the adjacent 1928 building. Moose Pass sits on the south side of Trial Lake, and a local air taxi provides flightseeing trips.

North of Moose Pass, a salmon hatchery next to North Trail Lake is the starting point of the **Johnson Pass Trail**. Following the lakeshore, the trail climbs over its namesake before descending to Granite Creek at Mile 62.9 of the Seward Highway.

Cooper Landing ❸

98 miles (158 km) S of Anchorage.
Road Map B3. 🚶 *360*.
🚌 *Anchorage–Homer*. **Tel** 595-8888. ℹ *Mile 48, Sterling Hwy*.
www.cooperlandingchamber.com

Named after Joseph Cooper, who was the first to discover gold in the area in 1894,

Cooper Landing was one of the few places in Alaska that continued producing gold into the 20th century. The town sprawls along the Sterling Highway in a string of eateries, lodges, gift shops, and fishing fitters. At the **K'Beq Kenaitze Footprints Heritage Site**, Dena'ina Natives share their traditions through interpretive walks featuring archeological sites. Local artists make and sell Dena'ina arts and crafts.

Kenai River ❹

Road Map A3. 🚌 *Anchorage–Homer*. 🔲

Originating between high peaks above the glacier-blue Kenai Lake, the Kenai River rushes westward from Cooper Landing, where whitewater rafting, kayaking, and canoeing are on offer. The Kenai then passes the mouth of the Russian River before flowing out of the mountains and onto the flats around Skilak Lake.

Among the world's most productive salmon streams, the lower Kenai is the original combat fishing river, with fierce competition among anglers for fishing space. People flock to the river on summer weekends, temporarily making the Sterling Highway one of Alaska's busiest roads. Continuing west from its Skilak Lake outlet, the river flows past innumerable public campsites and private cabins to its mouth at Kenai.

The Kenai River flowing swiftly past Cooper Landing

Resurrection Pass Trail ❺

The 38-mile (61-km) Resurrection Pass Trail on the Kenai Peninsula is Alaska's most popular multi-day hiking route. Beginning at the Kenai River along the Sterling Highway, it climbs through spruce forest and past Juneau Creek Falls into the subalpine zone. The trail crosses the 2,600-ft (780-m) Resurrection Pass before descending along Resurrection Creek to the trailhead near the gold mining village of Hope. An alternative is to hike the 10-mile (16-km) Devil's Pass Trail from Mile 39.5 on the Seward Highway, and then take the Resurrection Pass Trail to either Hope or the Sterling Highway.

TIPS FOR WALKERS

Starting point: Kenai River at the Sterling Highway. Due to the net altitude loss, it is best to hike the trail from south to north.
Length: the 38-mile (61-km) trail can take between two and six days to cover.
Accommodation: there are several forest service public use cabins along the trail. It is essential to pre-book (see p241).

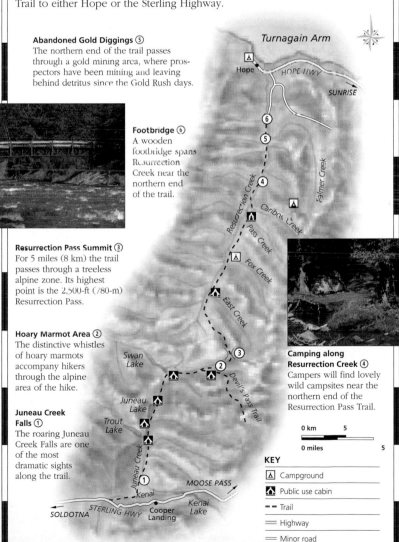

Abandoned Gold Diggings ❺
The northern end of the trail passes through a gold mining area, where prospectors have been mining and leaving behind detritus since the Gold Rush days.

Footbridge ❻
A wooden footbridge spans Resurrection Creek near the northern end of the trail.

Resurrection Pass Summit ❸
For 5 miles (8 km) the trail passes through a treeless alpine zone. Its highest point is the 2,500-ft (780-m) Resurrection Pass.

Hoary Marmot Area ❷
The distinctive whistles of hoary marmots accompany hikers through the alpine area of the hike.

Juneau Creek Falls ❶
The roaring Juneau Creek Falls are one of the most dramatic sights along the trail.

Camping along Resurrection Creek ❹
Campers will find lovely wild campsites near the northern end of the Resurrection Pass Trail.

Turnagain Arm

Hope · HOPE HWY · SUNRISE

Resurrection Creek · Caribou Creek · Palmer Creek · Pass Creek · Fox Creek · East Creek

Swan Lake · Juneau Lake · Trout Lake · Juneau Creek · Devil's Pass Trail

Kenai · MOOSE PASS · Kenai Lake

SOLDOTNA · STERLING HWY · Cooper Landing

0 km 5
0 miles 5

KEY

△ Campground
🏠 Public use cabin
- - Trail
═ Highway
═ Minor road

Seward ⑥

Considered to have one of Alaska's most scenic locations, Seward is also known for its saltwater salmon fishing, its rollicking Independence Day celebrations, and its access to Kenai Fjords National Park (see pp104–105). Although the Russians set up a shipyard here in 1793, the town was founded in 1903 by John Ballaine, who decided that its deepwater port would be an ideal location for a railhead. The railway came to fruition in 1923 and Seward thrived, but the 1964 earthquake destroyed most of the town. However, Seward was rebuilt, and to mark its revitalisation, its newspaper was named the Phoenix Log.

Ship's anchor on display at Seward's waterfront

🐝 Benny Benson Memorial

&

Located next to the lagoon just west of the Seward Highway stands a memorial honoring Benny Benson and his contribution to Alaska. Carved on Alaska stone by artist Damon Capurro, the memorial is engraved with the words of the Alaska flag song by Marie Drake and Elinor Dusenbury.

In 1926, George Parks, the governor of Alaska, asked schoolchildren to submit ideas for a state flag with essays explaining their design. Of the 142 entries submitted, the judges' unanimous choice was that of Benny Benson, a 13-year-old Alutiiq boy who lived at Seward's Jesse Lee Orphanage. Benson's essay explained that the flag's blue field represented the Alaska sky as well as the forget-me-not, the state flower. The North Star stood for the future State of Alaska, the most northerly in the Union, while the Great Bear constellation symbolized strength. Alaska's flag is now generally regarded as the most beautiful of all the US state flags (see p55).

🎿 Seward Waterfront

& 🍴 🖼 🚻

Situated a short distance away from the small boat harbor and downtown Seward, the waterfront lies within easy reach of the port, rail depot, and airport. For most of the year, row upon row of yachts, pleasure craft, and fishing boats peacefully bob in the waters beneath the snow-covered peaks across the bay.

In the summer, however, the waterfront transforms into a bustling tourist complex. Here, the town's thousands of visitors and cruise ship passengers can organize tours and fishing trips, join Kenai Fjords cruises, plan outdoor activities, and shop for gifts in a growing number of souvenir shops. At the southern end, the shops give way to an often packed tent and RV campground that stretches along the shore for almost 2 miles (3 km).

🏛 Kenai Fjords National Park Information Center

1212 4th Ave. **Tel** 224-7500.
☐ late May–early Sep: 8:30am–7pm daily; winter: 8am–5pm Mon–Fri.
& 🚻 **www**.nps.gov/kefj

The handsome building that houses the Kenai Fjords National Park Information Center sits on the Seward waterfront. It features several exhibits detailing aspects of the glaciation that created the park's spectacular landscapes, as well as the wildlife and prolific birdlife that inhabit it (see pp104–105). A free video runs intermittently, outlining natural history and park landscapes, including remote sites that few visitors are able to reach.

🏛 Seward Museum

Jefferson & 3rd. **Tel** 224-3902.
☐ mid-May–mid-Sep: 10am–5pm; winter: by appointment. 🎥 & 🚻

The Seward Museum offers visitors a glimpse of the town's history, from the first Russian entrepreneurs to its reconstruction after the 1964 earthquake. One exhibit features the residence of illustrator and political activist Rockwell Kent, who spent a winter on Fox Island in

Kenai Fjords National Park Information Center on the Seward Waterfront

Visitors exploring the magnificent Exit Glacier

Resurrection Bay. Perhaps the most enigmatic exhibit is a clock that stopped at the moment the earthquake struck, and has read 5:36 ever since.

➤ Alaska SeaLife Center
See pp100–1

🌲 Caines Head State Recreation Area
🚢 water taxi from Seward. 🗺
🏠 🅰 www.dnr.alaska.gov/parks/units/caineshd.htm

During World War II, the US Army built Fort McGilvray on the rocky headland known as Caines Head, as well as a

dock at North Beach and a garrison at South Beach. The area still has ammunition storage bunkers and gun emplacements used to guard the port and Resurrection Bay when Alaska's Aleutian Islands were attacked by Japanese forces.

The shale covered beaches are ideal for anglers, and sea kayakers will enjoy paddling here. Hiking is also possible, but the 3-mile (5-km) walk from Tonsina Point is possible only at low tide, so hikers on the return trip will probably need to camp overnight. Note that the remains of the South Beach garrison are unstable.

VISITORS' CHECKLIST

127 miles (204 km) S of Anchorage. **Road Map** B4.
🚶 3,000. ☒ 🚌 🚆 🛥 🚻
Mile 2, Seward Hwy; 224-8051.
🎣 Seward Silver Salmon Derby (mid-Aug). **www**.seward.com

🌲 Exit Glacier
8 miles (13 km) W of Seward on Exit Glacier/Herman Leirer Rd.
🚻 224-7500. 🗺 🎣 🅰 limited.
🏠 🅰 www.nps.gov/kefj

The impressive Exit Glacier, 2,500 ft (762 m) high and 3 miles (5 km) long, is the only part of Kenai Fjords National Park that is accessible by road. Pouring down from Harding Icefield, it is the most readily accessible walk-up glacier in Alaska. From the seasonal visitors' center at the end of the road, a short wheelchair-accessible trail leads to a hiking route across the rocky terminal moraines to the glacier face. The energetic can hike the steep 4-mile (6-km) Harding Icefield Trail up the western flank of Exit Glacier to the vast Harding Icefield. Camping is not permitted on the trail, but there is a public use cabin and free campground nearby.

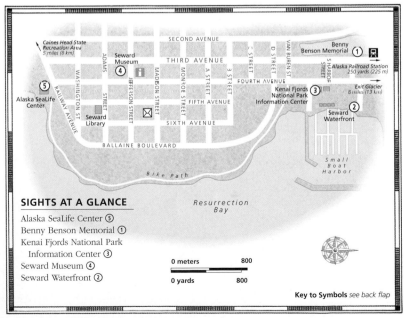

SIGHTS AT A GLANCE
Alaska SeaLife Center ⑤
Benny Benson Memorial ①
Kenai Fjords National Park
    Information Center ③
Seward Museum ④
Seward Waterfront ②

0 meters	800
0 yards	800

Key to Symbols see back flap

Seward: Alaska SeaLife Center

On the lovely Resurrection Bay waterfront in Seward, the Alaska SeaLife Center integrates museum exhibits, aquarium displays, and hands-on experiences to provide an educational introduction to the maritime world of Alaska's southern coasts. Initially conceived as a coldwater marine research and rehabilitation facility to study and protect sealife and provide public education – especially in the aftermath of the 1989 *Exxon Valdez* oil spill *(see p119)* – the center was opened in May 1998 and has since grown into one of Alaska's best-loved attractions. Highlights include several innovative tours and a series of spectacular tanks with underwater viewing windows that allow visitors to look at a variety of creatures in naturalistic habitats.

Façade of the extensive Alaska SeaLife Center in Seward

The Resurrection Bay Overlook provides an opportunity to view harbor seals, sea otters, whales, and birds in their natural habitat.

The Harbor Seal Habitat resembles a rocky coastline where seals can be seen in great numbers.

★ **Windows to the Sea**
Visitors enjoy close-up views of fish, harbor seals, octopuses, and Woody, an affable Steller sea lion.

★ **Encounter Tours**
Among several hands-on Encounter Tours is the Octopus Encounter, where participants meet a giant Pacific octopus, and can feel octopus suckers grab onto their hands.

STAR SIGHTS

★ Windows to the Sea

★ Encounter Tours

★ Discovery Touch Pool

★ Seabird Habitat

GALLERY GUIDE
Windows to the Sea on the first floor provides underwater views of Alaskan sealife. The second floor has a host of exhibits, including the Discovery Pool and the Seabird Habitat, showcasing various aspects of the marine world.

Entrance

★ Discovery Touch Pool

The pool offers a hands-on experience of Alaska's underwater world. Children enjoy touching such creatures as sea cucumbers, starfish, anemones, and sea urchins, as well as underwater plant life.

The Research Deck Overlook provides a view of the animals involved in rehabilitation or research projects.

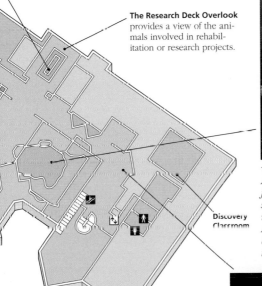

★ Seabird Habitat

A large aviary on the second floor encloses cliffs housing a selection of the bird species that inhabit the islets in the Gulf of Alaska. Diving seabirds are visible in the tank in the Windows to the Sea exhibit below.

Discovery Classroom

Second floor

The research and rehabilitation facilities are designed to combine scientific study, wildlife rehabilitation, and public education.

First floor

KEY

▦	Windows to the Sea
▦	Aquariums
▦	Rugged Coast Gallery
▦	Salmon Stream
▦	The Resurrection Bay Overlook
▦	Research Facilities
▦	A Closer Look
▦	Non-exhibition space

Bering Sea Gallery

This gallery contains a series of images and illustrative displays about Alaska's marine ecosystem. Attractive cutouts and interactive kiosks explain various facets of the state's sealife and address rehabilitation concerns.

Seward's harbor flanked by the peaks of the Kenai Mountains ▷

Kenai Fjords National Park ❼

Covering 950 sq miles (2,460 sq km), Kenai Fjords
National Park takes in some of Alaska's finest and most
accessible coastal scenery, glacial landscapes, and
diverse marine wildlife. The crown of the park is the
Harding Icefield. This vast expanse of ice, interrupted
only by an occasional *nunatak (see p27)*, feeds the
glaciers that flow down from the heights to form the
park's deep valleys and fjords. The seas, rich in fish,
crustaceans, shellfish, and plankton, also provide a
habitat for a range of readily observed birds and marine
mammals, including sea otters, Dall porpoises, Steller
sea lions, and several whale species.

KEY

☐ Kenai Fjords National Park

Calving Glaciers
*Tidewater glaciers such as
Holgate Glacier regularly calve
icebergs into the fjords in the
park. Kayakers must watch out
for large waves generated by
falling house-sized chunks.*

KEY

ℹ	Visitor information
===	Highway
===	Minor road
---	Park boundary

0 km   5

0 miles   5

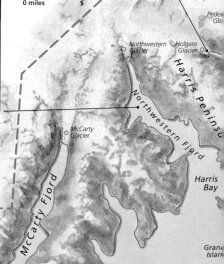

Whale-Watching
*Summer visitors often spot sounding or
breaching whales in these waters, which
serve as summer feeding grounds for humpbacks and migratory routes each spring and
fall for gray whales. Minke whales and pods
of porpoises are also seen in the summer.*

STAR SIGHTS

★ Harding Icefield

★ Fjord Cruises in
  Aialik Bay

★ Steller Sea Lion Rookery

★ Harding Icefield

The 70-mile (113-km) long and 30-mile (48-km) wide Harding Icefield stretches across the Kenai Mountains and creates all of Kenai Fjord's glaciers. Hikers can access it via a steep trail from Exit Glacier. The icefield also draws skiers keen to explore its farthest reaches.

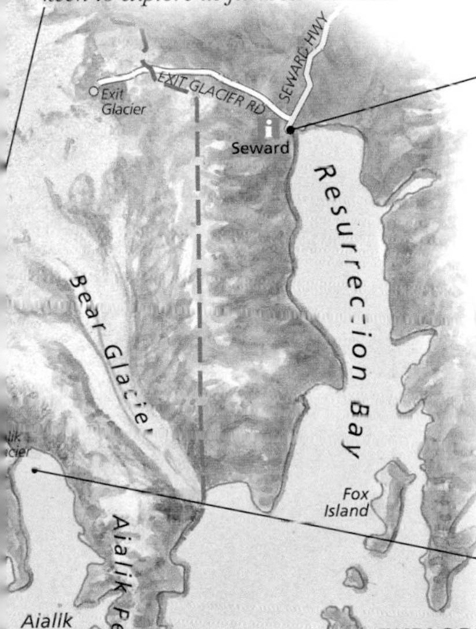

The Kenai Fjords National Park Information Center *(see p98)* in Seward issues backcountry permits and provides information.

★ Fjord Cruises in Aialik Bay

This 20-mile (32-km) long fjord is the most popular destination for day cruises. Visitors are usually guaranteed a dynamic show as huge chunks of ice calve off the towering face of Aialik Glacier.

EXPLORING THE PARK

Kenai Fjords' only road ends at the Exit Glacier car park where an easy half-mile (1-km) trail leads to good views of the glacier face. A challenging 6-mile (10-km) return trail goes up to Harding Icefield, which can also be visited on a helicopter tour. To see the park's wildlife and calving glaciers, visitors can hire kayaks for multi-day trips or join a half- or full-day fjords cruise with Seward-based operators *(see p275)*.

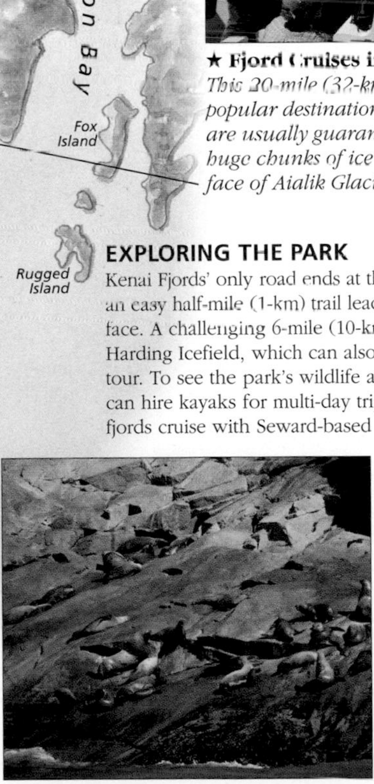

★ Steller Sea Lion Rookery

On the lonely, rocky outcrops of Chiswell Islands, passengers on day cruises can approach one of Alaska's most prominent Steller sea lion rookeries. The islands also have impressive bird cliffs with nesting puffins and kittiwakes.

[Map labels: Exit Glacier, SEWARD HWY, EXIT GLACIER RD, Seward, Resurrection Bay, Bear Glacier, Aialik Peninsula, Aialik Bay, Fox Island, Rugged Island, Chiswell Islands, laska]

Sterling ❽

134 miles (215 km) SW of
Anchorage. **Road Map** A3.
🏃 5,000. 🚌 Anchorage–Homer.

The name of the game in the
5-mile (8-km) strip known as
Sterling is fish. Nearly all the
businesses along the Sterling
Highway cater to the anglers
who flock to the town when
the salmon are running. This
community is also home to
numerous private recreational
cabins on the banks of the
Kenai River.

Anyone who has ever
wanted to try their hand at
landing a monster salmon will
find plenty of equipment and
advice in Sterling, as well as
along the highway between
here, Soldotna, Kenai, and
Homer. The area's most worthwhile site is **Skilak Lake**,
featuring lovely wild lakeside
campsites and hiking trails.
In the winter, the area's many
frozen lakes, including Seven
Lakes and Hidden Lake, make
a pretty sight, but in the summer, the congestion around
this area can be frustrating.

Soldotna ❾

148 miles (238 km) SW of
Anchorage. **Road Map** A3.
🏃 4,000. ✈ 🚌 Anchorage–
Homer. ℹ 44790 Sterling Hwy;
262-9814. 🛒 Farmer's Market,
Saturdays in summer. **www**.
soldotnachamber.com

As the primary commercial
and service center of the
Kenai Peninsula, Soldotna

**Log cabin at the Soldotna Historical
Society Museum**

Holy Assumption of the Virgin Mary Russian Orthodox Church, Kenai

features fast food franchises,
stores, and visitor accommodation options. Founded in
the 1940s as a retail hub at
the junction of the Sterling
and Kenai Spur Highways,
it was incorporated only in
1967. While the area experienced steady growth, unbridled sprawl, and congestion
in the late 20th century, much
of the surrounding land
remains protected under
federal management.

Five sites around town,
Soldotna Visitors' Center,
Rotary Park, Soldotna Creek
Park, and the Centennial and
Swiftwater Campgrounds,
have set up "Fishwalks" along
the Kenai River. These boardwalks, designed to protect the
fragile riverbank, allow public
access to the river for fishing
and salmon-viewing.

On Centennial Park Road,
the **Soldotna Historical Society
Museum** features a collection
of homesteaders' cabins
from the 1940s. It also has a
Territorial log school, Native
artifacts, and a collection of
stuffed wildlife.

Kenai ❿

11 miles (18 km) NW of Soldotna.
Road Map A3. 🏃 7,000. ✈
🚌 Anchorage–Homer. ℹ 11471
Kenai Spur Hwy; 283-1991.
🎫 Kenai River Festival (2nd week-
end in Jun). **www**.visitkenai.com

The Kenai Peninsula's largest
city, Kenai is also one of
Alaska's best-preserved
historic communities. In 1791,
Russian fur traders came in
contact with the region's
Dena'ina Athabaskan people
and established St. Nicholas
Redoubt, the second permanent Russian settlement in
Alaska. In 1869, two years
after the purchase of Alaska,
the US Army built Fort Kenay
to provide a military presence
in the Cook Inlet region.
Extensive oil exploration
began in the 1950s, and the
Tesoro Alaska refinery at
Nikiski is now a major
economic player.

Visitors can stroll around
the historic Old Town near
the beach, which has the
1881 Parish Rectory House,

the 1906 St. Nicholas Chapel, a replica of Fort Kenay, and the onion-domed **Holy Assumption of the Virgin Mary Russian Orthodox Church**. Founded in 1846, the church's present building was constructed between 1894 and 1895. The interior is decorated with Russian artifacts, some from the early 19th century.

In spring, the salt marsh at **Kenai Flats State Recreation Site**, across the Warren Ames Bridge over the Kenai River, attracts large flocks of Siberian snow geese. With interpretive panels, picnic tables, a boardwalk and viewing scope, it will delight birders. A bit farther west, on Cannery Road, a salmon cannery compound dating from 1922 has been converted into Kenai Landing, an atmospheric complex consisting of shops, a restaurant, bar, theater, and museum.

The old salmon cannery complex at Kenai Landing, Kenai

Captain Cook State Recreation Area ⓫

25 miles (40 km) N of Kenai at Mile 36, Kenai Spur Hwy. **Road Map** A3. 262-5581. www.dnr.alaska.gov/parks/units/captcook.htm

Located on the shores of Cook Inlet, the Captain Cook State Recreation Area is named after British explorer Captain James Cook, who explored the area in 1778. One of Alaska's quieter parks, its forests, lakes, streams, and beaches offer picnic sites, hiking routes, and camping at the large Discovery Campground, as well as swimming, canoeing, and fishing in Stormy Lake. Wildlife, including moose, bears, loons, and sandhill cranes, can be spotted in the park. The beach is popular with agate hunters, but visitors should avoid the dangerous mud flats just offshore.

Along the dead-end road to the recreation area, visitors can pick up supplies and look around the oil town of **Nikiski**, 9 miles (14 km) to the south. Formerly called North Kenai, this town began as a homesteading area in the 1940s and grew with the discovery of oil in Cook Inlet. At the end of Nikiski Beach Road, fine views open up across Nikishka Bay and the Cook Inlet oil drilling platforms, and beyond to the active volcano Mount Spurr. The large domed Nikiski pool, funded by the oil companies, boasts a hot tub and a winding 136-ft (41-m) water slide that is very popular with residents and visitors.

Kenai National Wildlife Refuge ⓬

Road Map A4. Anchorage–Homer. Ski Hill Rd, 43655 Kalifornsky Beach Rd, Soldotna; 262-7021. http://kenai.fws.gov

The Alaska National Interest Lands Conservation Act of 1980 (see p57) changed the name of the Kenai National Moose Range to the Kenai National Wildlife Refuge, and expanded it to its current area of almost 3,125 sq miles (8,094 sq km). The refuge covers high peaks, glaciers, muskeg, and lake-studded bog. This landscape provides habitat for a range of wildlife, from mountain goats, Dall sheep, and bears to moose, caribou, and wolves. The refuge is also home to lynx, coyotes, and waterfowl such as trumpeter swans and migratory birds.

Kenai National Wildlife Refuge sign

Access to the refuge's wild southern part can be challenging, but the northern areas feature several public campgrounds, 200 miles (322 km) of hiking trails, and two world-class canoe routes. The 80-mile (128-km) **Swanson River Canoe Route** links over 40 lakes with the Swanson River, ending in the Captain Cook State Recreation Area. The 60-mile (96-km) **Swan Lakes Loop** is a system of 32 lakes, accessible from the Swanson River and Swan Lake Roads. Equipment can be hired and tours organised in nearby towns.

Lakes and forests at the Kenai National Wildlife Refuge

Clam Gulch **⑬**

23 miles (37 km) S of Soldotna.
Road Map A3. 🚶 *180.*
🚌 *Anchorage–Homer.*

As its name might suggest, the highlight at Clam Gulch is clamming. The village itself is small, consisting of a few houses and some services, but beneath the sands of the beautiful Cook Inlet coast lie some of the world's most productive razor clam beds. At low tide, this is the best place in Alaska to dig for these delicious treats.

Diggers will need rubber boots, a clam shovel, bucket, and an Alaska fishing license *(see p41)*. The daily limit per person is 60 clams. The clams are usually about 6 inches (15 cm) beneath the surface. A small dimple in the sand indicates the presence of a clam, but it is best to dig to the side to avoid breaking its shell. Clams will attempt to flee by burrowing into the sand, so diggers may well have to give chase. It is best to carry the clams in a bucket of saltwater, adding a bit of corn meal to let them clean themselves before they are cooked.

Ninilchik **⑭**

40 miles (65 km) S of Soldotna.
Road Map A4. 🚶 *780.*
🚌 *Anchorage–Homer.* ℹ️ *567-3571.* 🎣 *King Salmon Weekends.*
www.ninilchikchamber.com

This traditional Russian-era Native village, whose name means "peaceful riverside place," is centered around the 1901 **Transfiguration of Our Lord Church**. The photogenic onion-domed church sits beside a rambling Russian Orthodox cemetery and offers fine views across the inlet. While the church is open for Sunday services, it is closed to the public on other days.

The Ninilchik River, a short walk to the north of the Visitors' Center, and Deep Creek, to the south, are world-class salmon fishing streams. Deep-sea charters provide access to offshore halibut and salmon. On the King Salmon

Weekends before the start of the season on June 30, the Deep Creek State Recreation Area Campground and the Ninilchik River Campground fill up and spill over into surrounding private sites and RV parks. Anglers will probably enjoy the scene, while others may prefer quieter areas.

Anchor Point sign highlighting its location on the highway system

Anchor Point **⑮**

61 miles (98 km) S of Soldotna.
Road Map A4. 🚶 *2,000.* 🚌
Anchorage–Homer. ℹ️ *Sterling Hwy, opposite Anchor River Inn; 235-2600.*
www.anchorpointchamber.org

Named after an anchor that the British explorer Captain James Cook lost on his voyage up Cook Inlet, the Anchor Point community was established by homesteaders in 1949. The major attraction at this westernmost point on the contiguous US Highway system is the Anchor River, with its abundant supply of king and silver salmon, and

rainbow, Dolly Varden, and steelhead trout. The seas around the area are rich in saltwater salmon and halibut.

Anglers usually stay at the Anchor River State Recreation Area at Anchor Point. Those who prefer a quieter campsite can opt for the beautiful (and angler-free) Stariski State Recreation Area north of Anchor Point. The park is perched on a bluff with views across Cook Inlet to the volcanoes beyond.

Nikolaevsk **⑯**

64 miles (103 km) S of Soldotna.
Road Map A4. 🚶 *400.* 🚗

Settled in 1960, Nikolaevsk village is home to the Old Believers, a sect of Russian Orthodoxy that broke away from the mother church and settled in Siberia after the 17th-century religious reforms *(see pp32–3)*. Those who wound up in Alaska established Nikolaevsk and several surrounding villages.

Visitors arriving along the 9-mile (14-km) drive from Anchor Point might feel as if they have passed through a time warp. With distinctive architecture and demeanor, the villagers' lifestyle has only been lightly touched by the 21st century. One exception is an enterprising local woman who runs the Samovar Café *(see p258)* and a gallery of costumes and artwork.

There is a lovely Russian Orthodox Church which is worth a look, but its interior is closed to the public.

The traditional Transfiguration of Our Lord Church, Ninilchik

The Bears of Alaska

Most visitors to Alaska want to see bears, and nearly everyone does. One often hears, "When you're in Alaska, you're never far from a bear," and while that does not hold true for the Aleutian Islands, the rest of the state is prime bear habitat. Alaska is home to three species of bears – black, brown, and polar. Alaskan brown bears are further divided into two kinds, the smaller grizzlies of the Interior and the enormous brown bears of Southwest Alaska. They are not a true subspecies, however, and the size variations are due only to differences in their diet. Active in summer, many bears become dormant in winter, retreating to dens and living on fat reserves. Cubs are often born during dormancy. Bears can be aggressive, particularly when protecting cubs or competing with each other during the breeding season.

Brown bears, *numbering about 40,000 in Alaska, are resident from the Southeast to the Arctic. The smaller grizzlies eat more vegetation, whereas Kodiaks (see p207), which can measure up to 12 ft (4 m) tall when standing on their hind legs, eat a high protein fish diet.*

Black bears, *which measure an average of 5 ft (1.5 m) in length, are the smallest Alaskan bears. These predominantly vegetarian bears are found everywhere in Alaska except the Arctic tundra and the Aleutian Islands.*

BEAR SAFETY

YOU ARE IN BEAR TERRITORY
Do Not Leave Food Unattended
Unattended items subject to
Impound and $50 Fine
11 AAC 12.230

Bear safety sign

- Store food in a bear-proof container, and cook away from tents. Never eat or keep snacks in your tent.
- In a bear encounter, do not run, as that may elicit a chase response.
- In a defensive attack, curl up in a ball with knees tucked into the stomach, arms wrapped around the face, and hands laced behind the back of the neck.
- In an aggressive attack, fight back with as much strength as possible. Poke at the bear's eyes and nose, punch it in the face, and try to hit it with a hiking pole or stick.
- Polar bears are the only species that stalk humans, and in an aggressive attack, a firearm will provide the only reasonable protection.

Polar bears, *which inhabit the Arctic Ocean coastline, subsist mainly on marine mammals. Swimming across open water, they spend most of their lives roaming the ice floes in search of seals, but come ashore in the fall to breed (see p227).*

BEAR	IDENTIFICATION	BEST TIMES TO SEE	BEST PLACES TO SEE
Black (*Ursus americanus*)	Black or cinnamon coat; pointed muzzle	Spring, summer, and fall	Anan Creek Wildlife Observatory
Brown (*Ursus arctos*)	Dark brown to blond coat; prominent shoulder hump	Summer to fall	Denali National Park and Katmai National Park
Polar (*Ursus maritimus*)	Creamy coat; longer neck than other bears	Spring and fall	Barrow and Kaktovik

Ramp to the small boat harbor on Homer Spit

Homer ⑰

84 miles (135 km) S of Soldotna.
Road Map A4. 🏠 5,200. ✈ 🚐
🚢 ℹ *201 Sterling Highway, 235-7740.* 🐦 *Kachemak Bay Shorebird Festival (1st weekend in May).*
www.homeralaska.org

Founded in 1895 and named for Homer Pennock, a New York con man who spent a few months in the area, Homer sells itself as the "end of the road." It is a refuge for visitors, artists, and anglers, as well as some modern-day Pennocks. In 1886, Homer got its first post office, and in the late 1890s, a coal-shipping settlement occupied the tip of Homer Spit that runs into Kachemak Bay. However, the village was abandoned in 1902 when the coal seams became unviable. The handful of residents who remained in town turned to farming and fishing. From 1910 onwards, Homer expanded from a fishing village into a pleasant small town.

Homer continues to attract outsiders, causing rapid development of its bluffs and foothills. For visitors, the town means bird-watching, halibut fishing, shopping for local arts, and visits to the nearby Kachemak Bay State Park. Homer also boasts the world-class Alaska Islands and Oceans Visitors' Center and several interesting museums.

Pratt Museum insignia

🏛 Pratt Museum

3779 Bartlett St. **Tel** 235-8635.
⭕ *Mid-May–mid-Sep: 10am–6pm daily; mid-Sep–mid-May: noon–5pm Tue–Sun.* 📷 🎫 ♿ *botanical garden only.* 🖥 **www**.prattmuseum.org
Homer's natural history museum covers the geology, flora, fauna, and oceanography of the peninsula, as well as homesteader and Native cultures. The Kachemak Bay exhibit uses photographs, videos, and interactive computer programs to provide a sense of the place. Detailed coverage of the 1964 earthquake and the 1989 *Exxon Valdez* oil spill *(see p119)* is displayed downstairs. Trails through the botanical gardens outside the main building lead past 150 identified species of local plants. The Harrington cabin displays artifacts from Homer's 1940s homesteading era.

Exhibits inside Homer's Pratt Museum

🏛 Bunnell Street Arts Center

106 W Bunnell St. **Tel** 235-2662.
♿ 🚫 🖥 **www**.bunnellstreet gallery.org
Drawn by its scenic location, several artists made Homer their home, and as a result, sundry street fairs, workshops, and galleries sprang up. One of the most renowned is the Bunnell Street Arts Center, which was founded by an artists' group in 1989. Housed in the 1937 Old Inlet Trading Post building, which was once a commercial hub for homesteaders, the gallery now showcases contemporary fine art.

🏛 Alaska Islands and Oceans Visitors' Center

95 Sterling Hwy. **Tel** 235-6961.
⭕ *late May–early Sep: 9am–6pm daily; winter: noon–5pm Tue–Sat.* ♿
🖥 **www**.islandsandocean.org
This highly worthwhile stop is probably the finest center of its kind in Alaska. A wealth of original exhibits, including a replica of a Bering Sea seabird rookery and a recording of conservationist and researcher Olaus Murie dictating his journal, detail the natural history of the Alaska Maritime National Wildlife Refuge and the Kachemak Bay Research Reserve. Visitors can also hike along a boardwalk to Beluga Slough's tidal marshes or watch an award-winning film on the Aleutian Islands.

🦅 Carl E. Wynn Nature Center

E Skyline Dr. *Tel 235-6667.* 🚌
⏰ *mid-Jun–early Sep: 10am–6pm
daily.* 📷 📹 ♿ *limited.* 🏠 www.
akcoastalstudies.org/wynn.htm

This center is set amid spruce forests and meadows on the bluffs overlooking Homer. Formerly the homestead of naturalist Carl E. Wynn, it was donated to the Center for Alaskan Coastal Studies in 1990. Visitors can enjoy bird-watching, stroll amid wild-flowers, or explore the variety of vegetation from upland coastal forests to boreal forests. The center also offers guided walks highlighting local wildlife and shrubs.

Wildflowers at the Carl E. Wynn Nature Center outside Homer

🦅 Homer Spit

🍴 🏨 🚻 🏕️

Thought to be a remnant of an ancient glacial moraine, Homer Spit has been spared from the ravages of the sea by reclamation and rock walls. This is Homer's main tourist district, taking in the small boat harbor, the ferry terminal, a hotel, myriad eateries, and a host of fishing charter companies. The **Salty Dawg Saloon**, with its distinctive lighthouse tower, is listed as a maritime landmark. Around 1900, it served as the headquarters for the Cook Inlet Coal Fields Company. Today, this atmospheric drinking den is unmissable.

The Spit is also a camping venue with communities of RVs and tents strung along the northern shore.

Rocky Island off Kachemak Bay State Park

Seldovia

20 nautical miles (32 km) S of Homer. 👥 *280.* ✈ *charter float-plane from Homer.* ⛴ *from Homer.*
🎵 *Summer Solstice Music Festival (3rd weekend in Jun).*
www.seldoviachamber.org

Seldovia was inhabited by Dena'ina people as early as the 16th century. Russians settled here around 1800, naming the place Zaliv Seldevoe (Herring Bay). In the early 20th century, the area's flourishing herring trade increased the town's population to about 2,000, but the boom was shortlived.

Today, Seldovia is a small fishing village with an active Native association. Visitors can stroll along the waterfront boardwalk, explore the Village Tribe Museum and Visitors' Center, and visit the 1891 St. Nicholas Russian Orthodox Church, which crowns a hill overlooking the harbor.

Salty Dawg Saloon lighthouse, Homer Spit

🦅 Kachemak Bay State Park

8 nautical miles (12 km) across the bay from Homer. *Tel 235-7024.* ⛴
from Homer. 🏕️ 🎣
www.alaskastateparks.org

Alaska's first state park and one of the largest coastal state parks in the US, the Kachemak Bay State Park and the adjoining Kachemak Bay State Wilderness Park take in 625 sq miles (1,619 sq km) of islands, forests, glaciers, beaches, and rocky coastlines. This critical habitat area supports several species of marine life, including whales and sea otters, land mammals such as coyotes and black bears, and birds that include eagles and puffins. About 90 miles (145 km) of hiking trails lace the waterfront area of the park, across the bay from Homer. Trails from primitive beach campsites lead to ridges and remote coastlines.

Halibut Cove

12 miles (19 km) SE of Homer.
👥 *35.* ⛴ *from Homer.*
www.halibutcove.com

Halibut Cove happily receives short-term visitors, but is keen to avoid the unbridled growth of Homer. This scenic little cove makes an excellent launch point for hikes into the adjacent Kachemak Bay State Park. There is also a restaurant and several lodges, as well as a number of artists' galleries. The most renowned of these is the Cove Gallery of Diana Tillion, who uses octopus ink for her works. A local charter boat company provides twice-daily summertime tours from Homer to Halibut Cove.

PRINCE WILLIAM SOUND

T*he northernmost extent of the Gulf of Alaska, Prince William Sound is a large bay studded with forested islands. Lying to the east of the Kenai Range and south of the heavily glaciated Chugach Range, the massive sound is roughly twice the size of Massachusetts, with convoluted coasts lined with large tidewater glaciers and sheltered waters that harbor a rich variety of wildlife.*

Home to the Eyak, Dena'ina, and other Native peoples, the Prince William Sound area was first explored in 1778 by the British captain James Cook and by the Spanish explorer Don Salvador Fidalgo in 1790, both of whom were searching for the elusive Northwest Passage. The first serious scientific study of the area was conducted in June 1899 by the Harriman Expedition, which included eminent scientists and artists. Much of their vast collection of specimens, illustrations, and photographs is now at the Smithsonian Institution in Washington, DC.

In the early decades of the 20th century, the area's economy received a boost when Cordova became the railhead for the Copper River and Northwestern Railway. In the 1970s, Valdez, by virtue of being the northernmost ice-free port in North America, was chosen as the site of the marine terminal for the Trans-Alaska Pipeline. Since then, oil tankers have shared the shipping lanes with Marine Highway ferries, fishing boats, kayakers, and, more recently, cruise ships calling into the port of Whittier.

Despite the environmental damage suffered in the 1989 *Exxon Valdez* oil spill, most of the sound has come back, at least on the surface, although herring fisheries have never recovered. Marine life is recovering and wildlife watching cruises can be very rewarding. Bird-watchers will enjoy the kittiwake colonies near Whittier and the migratory birds of the Copper River Delta. Kayaking among the ice floes in the bay is another popular activity, as is hiking on the glaciers.

Fisherman's Memorial overlooking Cordova's boat harbor

◁ Russian Orthodox church in Tatitlek Native village, eastern Prince William Sound

Exploring Prince William Sound

Alaska's greatest concentration of tidewater glaciers form the highlight of Prince William Sound. Three main towns, prosperous Valdez, cozy Cordova, and tiny Whittier, flank the sound. They serve as bases for popular cruises that visit Blackstone Bay, College Fjord, and the massive Columbia Glacier, and offer opportunities to view seals, whales, and sea otters. East of Cordova, the arresting beauty of the Copper River Road makes for a wonderful drive through the bird-watching area of Alaganik Slough and the Copper River Delta to the Childs Glacier and famed Million Dollar Bridge.

Sign for Childs Glacier next to Million Dollar Bridge, Cordova

Private yachts and boats crowding Whittier's Small Boat Harbor

SIGHTS AT A GLANCE

Towns and Cities
Cordova ❻
Valdez ❺
Whittier ❶

Areas of Natural Beauty
Blackstone Bay ❷
College Fjord ❸
Columbia Glacier ❹
Copper River Highway ❼

GETTING AROUND

Scheduled flights operate between Anchorage, Valdez, and Cordova. In the summer, Alaska Marine Highway ferries do daily runs between Whittier, Valdez, and Cordova. Private vehicles can get to Valdez on the Richardson Highway, and flights connect Valdez and Cordova with Anchorage. A toll tunnel from the Seward Highway provides access to Whittier. While there's no outside road access to Cordova, it's worth taking a vehicle on the ferry in order to drive the Copper River Highway. Perhaps the best way to see the sound, however, is on an organized cruise from Whittier or Valdez.

KEY

▬▬	Highway
▭▭	Minor road
——	Alaska Railroad
– –	Alaska Marine Highway
△	Peak

Marshland at Alaganik Slough near Cordova, Prince William Sound

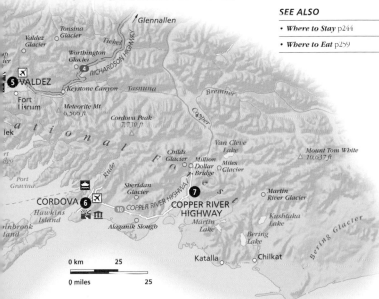

SEE ALSO

- *Where to Stay* p244

- *Where to Eat* p259

Ice floes in the bay near Columbia Glacier, Prince William Sound

Pleasure boats docked at Whittier, at the western edge of Prince William Sound

Whittier ❶

59 miles (95 km) SE of Anchorage.
Road Map E4. 🏔 *300.* 🚗 *from Anchorage via Portage.* ⛴ *from Valdez and Cordova.* **www.** whittieralaskachamber.org **Anton Anderson Memorial Tunnel** 🕐 *15 mins hourly in each direction.* **www.**tunnel.alaska.gov

Whittier's name came from the adjacent Whittier Glacier, named after the American poet John Greenleaf Whittier. Founded in 1943, when the US Army used this ice-free port to build an Alaska base, the town was made accessible by the 3-mile (5-km) Anton Anderson road-rail toll tunnel, which connects Turnagain Arm with Passage Canal, an arm of Prince William Sound.

Despite its spectacular setting, surrounded as it is by glaciers and thundering water-falls, Whittier is probably one of Alaska's oddest towns. The army, not especially concerned with aesthetics, housed their personnel in Soviet-style high-rise apartment buildings. After

the army left in 1960, the few hundred residents who stayed behind continued to live in two towers, one of which, the 14-story Begich Towers, has now been converted into con-dominiums. The town's other occupied building is the less obtrusive Whittier Manor. Most residents are accustomed to unflattering remarks about these buildings, and even seem proud of the undeniably quirky architecture.

One of Whittier's main attractions is a large colony of black-legged kittiwakes in the cliffs across Passage Arm, which can be viewed on sea kayaking trips. Lovers of the outdoors will also enjoy the 26 Glacier Cruise run by **Phillips Cruises and Tours**. The cruise boats travel deep into Barry Arm and College Fjord, offering visitors close-up views of wildlife and glaciers.

Phillips Cruises and Tours
519 W 4th Ave, Anchorage.
Tel 276-8023, (800) 544-0529.
🕐 *May–Sep: 1pm daily.*
www.26glaciers.com

Blackstone Bay ❷

Road Map E4. ⛴ *from Whittier.*

One of Alaska's most dramatic sights, the 18-mile (29-km) long Blackstone Bay lies at the foot of three calving tide-water glaciers – Blackstone, Beloit, and Northland. These choke the upper portion of this spectacular fjord with growler ice, bergy bits, and small icebergs *(see pp26–7)*.

From the campground at the southern end of Willard Island, campers have a front-row view of nature's intrigu-ing displays, as well as a minor lesson in physics. As chunks calve off the glaciers, three types of waves appear. First, light waves make the calving visible to observers. Several seconds later, a sound wave arrives, carrying the thunder-like crack of the breaking ice. Finally, after a minute or so, the waves created by the big splash roll onto the shore.

Even though it is possible to visit Blackstone Bay on a day cruise from Whittier, it is popular as a venue for sea kayakers, who typically take two days to reach Willard Island in the middle of the fjord. Although it can be an enjoyable experience to paddle around between the bergs, visitors should be careful not to approach the glacier faces or be caught on an incoming tide. Pieces of ice, pushed by the forceful current, can crush a kayak.

Sea kayakers gliding past Blackstone Glacier, Blackstone Bay

For hotels and restaurants in this region see p244 and p259

College Fjord ❸

Road Map E4. 🚢 *tour from Whittier.* 🎥

The College Fjord arm of Prince William Sound and the neighboring Harriman Fjord include an impressive concentration of easily accessible tidewater glaciers, as well as myriad valley glaciers and hanging glaciers *(see pp26–7)*.

In 1899, New York railroad magnate Edward Harriman launched a scientific expedition along the Alaskan coast, including College Fjord, where he named the glaciers after the Ivy League colleges attended by the scientists on board his ship, the *George W. Elder*. As one travels into the fjord, the glaciers on the left are named for women's colleges and those on the right for men's schools. Chunks as large as a house often calve from the massive 300-ft (90-m) high glacier faces.

Columbia Glacier ❹

Road Map E3. 🚢 *tour boats from Valdez.* 🎥

During the 1980s, 40-mile (64-km) long, 2,000-ft (600-m) thick Columbia Glacier was a highlight on the Alaska Marine Highway route

Black-legged kittiwakes perching on a small ice floe

KITTIWAKES

The towering cliffs across Passage Arm from Whittier are home to a colony of thousands of black-legged kittiwakes *(Rissa tridactyla)*. During the summer nesting season they can be seen wheeling around the precarious cliff faces where they nest, breed, and hatch their chicks. With a relatively rapid wingbeat, kittiwakes are highly maneuverable and able to land on narrow cliff ledges even in strong winds. In the winter, these pelagic gulls spend most of their time on the open ocean, feeding on small fish and plankton.

between Whittier and Valdez. Ferries would typically stop amid the groups or rafts of sea otters and icebergs laden with harbor seals, and blast their horns with the hope that the vibrations would cause the glacier to calve.

However, in the early 1980s, Columbia Glacier began to surge at a pace as great as 115 ft (35 m) per day, calving icebergs into Prince William Sound much faster than snow compression on the ice field could replace it. It is thought that the melting ice created a cushion of water beneath the main ice sheet, allowing the glacier to progress without being impeded by the friction of ice against rock. As a result of the calving, however, the glacier has receded about 6 miles (10 km) in the past decade and can no longer be readily accessed by ferry. It calved so much ice that it choked the waters between its 3-mile (5-km) wide face and its terminal moraine with large icebergs that froze together. Currently, this active glacier is most readily accessed on day cruises and private tour boats from Valdez.

Cruisers aboard a tour boat approaching Columbia Glacier, Prince William Sound

Display of a trapper's cabin, Valdez Museum

Valdez ❺

304 miles (487 km) E of Anchorage.
Road Map E4. 🏘 *4,000.* ✈
🚌 *irregular service from Fairbanks.*
🚢 *from Whittier, Cordova.* ℹ *200
Fairbanks Dr, 835-4636.*
www.valdezalaska.org

The most important town of
the Prince William Sound
region, Valdez was named
after the bay Port Valdez,
which in turn, was named
by Spanish explorer Don
Salvador Fidalgo after Spanish
naval officer Antonio Valdes y
Basan in 1790. The town was
founded in 1897 about 4
miles (6 km) east of its current location as a jumping-off
point for prospectors heading
to the Klondike goldfields.

With the discovery of
copper in the Wrangell
Mountains, Cordova became
the terminus of the Copper
River and Northwestern
Railway *(see p187)* and Valdez
slid into decline. In the early
20th century, however, Valdez

became the terminus for a
wagon road to connect the
nearby Fort Liscum with Fort
Egbert on the Yukon River.
After the 1964 earthquake
utterly destroyed Old Valdez,
the town was rebuilt at its
present location.

As the northernmost ice-free
port in North America, it was
chosen to be the terminus
of the Trans-Alaska Pipeline
(see p186), which brought
prosperity to the town during
its construction.

Modern Valdez
enjoys a lovely
setting between
the mountains and
the sea. Day trips
and organized cruises
to northeastern Prince
William Sound pro-
vide good wildlife
viewing, including
sightings of whales,
seals, sea otters,
and birds around
Columbia Glacier.

**Pipeline Workers'
Monument**

🏛 Valdez Museum
217 Egan Dr. *Tel* 835-
2764. 🕐 *summer: 9am–5pm daily;
winter: 1–5pm Mon–Sat.* 🎟 ♿ ⬛
Remembering Old Valdez 436 S
Hazelet Dr. *Tel* 835-5407. 🎟 ♿ ⬛
www.valdezmuseum.org
This excellent museum, which
takes at least two hours to
explore fully, reveals the
history of Valdez and Prince
William Sound, as well as the
Alaskan oil industry. The
museum's most well-known
display is probably the 1886
hand-pumped Ahrens steam
fire engine, lovingly polished
and tended. A replica of the
Pipeline Workers' Monument,
dedicated to the men who

built the pipeline, is among
the displays. There are photographs depicting the 1964
earthquake and Valdez's
rebirth as an oil town, as well
as Native artifacts and
mockups of an old miner's
cabin, a period photography
studio, and a historic 1880s
bar. The *Exxon Valdez* spill
gets rather minimal coverage.

The **Remembering Old
Valdez** exhibit, housed in
an old warehouse nearby,
contains a 1:20 scale model
of Old Valdez as it appeared
before the 1964 earthquake.
It also has a number of
historic vehicles and a high-
tech exhibit on earthquakes.
A visit to the actual site of
Old Valdez, east of town,
will give visitors an idea
of the devastation that
occured there.

🏛 Whitney Museum
303 Lowe St. *Tel* 834-1690. 🚗 ◯
May–mid-Sep: 9am–7pm daily. 🎟 ♿
www.pwscc.edu/museum.shtml
For more than half a century,
philanthropists Maxine and
Jesse Whitney traveled around
the villages of Alaska, buying
art and other items
directly from artists and
craftsmen. In the 1980s,
they donated their
collection to the Prince
William Sound
Community College.
This museum is
thought to have the
world's largest
private collection
of Native Alaskan
art, artifacts, and
stuffed wildlife.
It houses some of the
finest examples of
Inuit scrimshaw, as well as a
ship and an aircraft carved
entirely of ivory. One room
is filled with nothing but
baskets, another is dedicated
to historic Gold Rush exhibits,
and yet another to fascinating
rocks and minerals.

There is also an extensive
collection of Native dolls,
garments, weapons, masks,
and household implements.
In addition, the museum
contains larger exhibits such
as an old Inuit kayak with
whale baleen stays, a lovely
Russian prayer rug, and a sofa
made of moose horn.

**Ahrens steam fire engine occupying
pride of place in Valdez Museum**

For hotels and restaurants in this region see p244 and p259

Hiking the challenging trail up to the face of Worthington Glacier

Keystone Canyon

Mile 12.8 Mile 15.9 on the Richardson Highway.

This canyon was named after the Keystone State (Pennsylvania) by Captain William Ralph Abercrombie, following a failed 1884 expedition to sail up the Copper River to the Yukon. Keystone Canyon contains both the Richardson Highway, one of Alaska's most scenic highways and buried stretches of the Alaska Pipeline.

East of Valdez, at Mile 13, two great waterfalls spill down the slopes into the slate-gray Lowe River. A paved turnout provides access to **Horsetail Falls**, north of the highway. A bit farther along, the lovely **Bridal Veil Falls** tumble down into a deep, rainbow-flanked pool. Farther east, the highway climbs out

of the canyon into an alpine landscape beneath the ice-sculpted spires of the eastern reaches of the Chugach Range.

Worthington Glacier

Mile 28. / on the Richardson Highway.

www.alaskageographic.org

The Worthington Glacier, protected in the Worthington Glacier State Recreation Site, flows steeply down the icy peak of the 6,130-ft (1,840-m) high Girls Mountain in a series of fingers that extend to within 430 yards (400 m) of the road. Visitors can admire the scene from below or follow the challenging Ridge Trail up the glacier's lateral moraine and right to its face. There is an information desk and a small shop, which also provides shelter.

The Blueberry Lake State Recreation Site, 4 miles (7 km) south of the glacier, makes a great stop. North of the campground is **Thompson Pass**, Alaska's snowiest spot.

Spectacular cascade of Horsetail Falls, Keystone Canyon

EXXON VALDEZ OIL SPILL

On March 23, 1989, the tanker *Exxon Valdez*, under the command of Captain Joseph Hazelwood, was forced to change course to avoid an iceberg near the mouth of Columbia Bay. The ship struck Bligh Reef and started leaking oil. As much as 11 million gallons (42 million liters) of oil spilled into the sound. Clean-up crews were slow to respond, and although dispersants were eventually applied, the weather was too calm for them to be effective. Even a week later, only a few skimmer vessels had been deployed. The oil contaminated 1,500 miles (2,400 km) of

Cleaning an oil-covered bird after the oil spill

coastline, killing fish, whales, seals, sea otters, and birds. Nearly 10,000 workers were employed to count dead wildlife and clean up the sound and surrounding areas, often wiping the black sludge off rocks by hand. The effort cost Exxon $1.25 billion. In 1991, the State of Alaska and the federal government reached an out-of-court settlement, requiring Exxon to pay $1 billion in restitution. In 1994, a class-action suit awarded $5.2 billion in damages but Exxon appealed and a much smaller settlement of $507m was granted in 2009.

Columbia Glacier flanking island-studded Prince William Sound ▷

Cordova ❻

50 miles (80 km) SE of Valdez. **Road
Map** E4. 🚶 2,200. ✈ 🚢 Valdez,
Whittier. 🛈 401 1st St, 424-7260.
🎭 Iceworm Festival (1st weekend in
Feb), Copper River Delta Shorebird
Festival (1st week of May), Copper
River Wild Salmon Festival (2nd week
of Jun). **www**.cordovachamber.com

Smaller than nearby Valdez,
rainy little Cordova offers a
slice of the independent, self-
sufficent character of "old
Alaska" that has faded in
more accessible places along
the road system. There is a
quiet charm in wandering its
steets or strolling past the fish
canneries. This scenic town is
linked to the outside world
only by plane or the ferries of
the Marine Highway.

Initially a Gold Rush town,
Cordova became the Copper
River and Northwestern
Railway railhead, linking the
copper mines at Kennicott
(see pp188–9)
with the coast.
The railroad
functioned
until the mines
closed down in
1938. Although
Cordova was
badly damaged
by the 1964
earthquake, it
bounced back
as a fishing
town and is
known for its
Copper River reds, prized
salmon that are shipped fresh
to restaurants both inside and
outside Alaska.

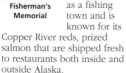

**Fisherman's
Memorial**

Snow-capped mountains overlooking the boat harbor, Cordova

🏛 Cordova Historical Museum

622 1st St. **Tel** 424-6665. ⬤ late
May–early Sep: 10am–5pm Thu & Fri;
winter: 1–5pm Tue–Sat. 🎦 🛥 🖰
This small museum, housed
in the Centennial Building,
features several interesting
exhibits. In addition to works
by Alaskan artists, including
painter Sydney Laurence (who
spent some time in Cordova
around 1900), the museum
houses an old skin-covered
canoe and a collection of
antique photographs. One
exhibit explains the effects
of the 1964 earthquake and
another showcases Cordova's
Iceworm Festival (see p45),

held in February to relieve the
stress of wintertime cabin
fever. There is a thoughtful
display on the Copper River
and Northwestern Railway,
along with examples of
copper jewelry and
implements. A video show-
cases high points in the
town's history.

🏛 Prince William Sound Science Center

Seafood Lane, Cordova Harbor.
Tel 424-5800. ⬤ 9am–5pm Mon–
Fri. 🛥 **www**.pwssc.org
Founded immediately after
the 1989 oil spill, this scientific base at Cordova harbor's
entrance is home to teams of
research scientists studying
the Prince William Sound ecosystem. The center offers a
fine view from
the deck over-
looking the water.
The researchers
here can answer
questions and
provide insights
into the long-term
effects of the
Exxon Valdez oil
spill on the sound
and its ecology.
The center also
offers numerous educational
programs. These include
holding field trips and science

**Logo, Prince William
Sound Science Center**

projects for families and
adults, informative scientific
seminars in isolated communities around Prince William
Sound, and summer camps
for local schoolchildren.

🏛 Ilanka Cultural Center

110 Nicholoff Way. **Tel** 424-7903.
⬤ summer: 10am–5pm Mon–Fri,
other times by appointment.
🎦 donations accepted. 🛥 🖰
Situated opposite the
Fisherman's Memorial on
Nicholoff Way, the Ilanka
Cultural Center was founded
to preserve the culture of the
Eyak tribe, and in fact the
last Native speaker of the
Eyak language died in 2008.
The Eyak people's stories are
told in an interesting collection of artifacts and photographs. Other
exhibits include a
complete orca
skeleton and a
contemporary
subsistence totem
pole. The work of
carver Mike
Webber, the pole is
intended to reflect
the foods, clothing,
and dance regalia
of the tribe. The
center also provides studio
space for Eyak artisans to
produce their work.

Copper River Highway ❼

Road Map E4. 🚗 🅰 *Childs Glacier.*
Forest Service *612 2nd St, Cordova;*
424-7661. **www**.fs.fed.us/r10/
chugach

There is little to prepare visitors for the arresting beauty of the 48-mile (77-km) drive along the Copper River Highway between Cordova and the end of the road at the **Million Dollar Bridge**. Along the way, a number of short hiking trails and roadside views, as well as abundant wildlife and a few obligatory sights, will easily fill up a full day.

The gravel road, which is always open for visitors, and usually free of snow by late April, follows the roadbed of the historic Copper River and Northwestern Railway. At Mile 4, a marker provides information on its construction and history. At Mile 5.7, the road passes the Forest Service's **Eyak River Trail**, a 2-mile (3-km) hike, which includes a long boardwalk over muskeg. The variety of birdlife found here makes it a favorite walking trail of birders.

About 7 miles (11 km) north along a side road from Mile 13.7, a short walk leads onto the terminal moraine of **Sheridan Glacier**, with fine views of its blue ice. The steep 3-mile (5-km) Sheridan Ridge Trail climbs to a good view. After another 4 miles (6 km) along the highway, a rugged side route leads south to **Alaganik Slough**, which

Million Dollar Bridge across the Copper River near Cordova

has a picnic site and a 990-ft (300-m) elevated boardwalk over a wetland. Vast watery views are on offer, replete with colorful wildflowers such as irises. Every summer, thousands of waterfowl, including 7 percent of the world's trumpeter swans, descend on this spot to nest, and countless shorebirds screech overhead.

Beginning around Mile 25 for 10 miles (16 km), the view from the road takes in more water than land as the route crosses the **Copper River Delta** over a series of bridges and causeways. Once across the river, the road passes through birch and cottonwood forests to its end at the Million Dollar Bridge. This impressive structure, a part of the Copper River and Northwestern Railway, actually cost a million dollars to build in 1910. It had to be constructed in the winter to avoid the summer advance of

Wild iris at Alaganik Slough

the adjacent **Childs** and **Miles Glaciers**. The northernmost span collapsed in the 1964 earthquake and it took nearly 40 years of makeshift repairs to reopen it to traffic. The road, however, ends barely a mile or so farther on. Views from the bridge take in both Childs Glacier and the expansive Miles Glaciers, which has receded over a mile (2 km) since the bridge was built. There is a small five-site campground at Childs Glacier, offering excellent views of the glacier face across the roiling gray Copper River. Campers here are treated to an all-night symphony of thunder-like booms and cracks as the glacier calves. Signs dotted around the area warn visitors that about once a year, the calving of large chunks into the water generates waves of up to 40 ft (12 m) that have been known to wash across the campground.

Childs Glacier near Million Dollar Bridge along the Copper River Highway

SOUTHEAST ALASKA

*N**ature prevails throughout the Panhandle, a narrow 400-mile (640-km) strip of islands and coastline that reaches southeastward from the Alaskan mainland. The spectacular scenery of Southeast Alaska, from the threaded passageways of the Alexander Archipelago to the rugged Coast Mountains, combines with its easy accessibility to make it one of Alaska's most visited regions.*

For the Tlingit, Haida, and Tsimshian peoples who have inhabited this area for thousands of years, Southeast Alaska has provided not only beauty, but also bounty – seas full of fish, wildlife to hunt, and a wealth of enormous trees to provide wood for homes and boats. When the first Russians arrived, the Native peoples fought to defend their homeland, but were ultimately forced to accept the inevitable political, economic, and lifestyle changes that were introduced by the newcomers.

Fortunately, many of the traditional ways of the Native peoples have been preserved, not only in museums, but in villages with significant indigenous populations. Several towns, especially Wrangell and Sitka, have grown around Russian forts, while the discovery of gold was the impetus for the creation of Juneau and Skagway. In 1900, the discovery of gold near Juneau along with its strategic location along the Klondike route led to its becoming the capital of Alaska, taking over from Sitka. Other towns, such as Ketchikan and Petersburg, grew around fisheries, canneries, and timber mills.

Today, Southeast Alaska is the favored venue for most Alaska cruises *(see pp.34–5)*, and the region sees large numbers of visitors each summer. With local economies increasingly dependent upon tourism, ports such as Ketchikan, Skagway, and Sitka cater to cruise ship passengers with a variety of day tours and shopping opportunities. A limited number of ships are also permitted to enter Glacier Bay National Park, a UNESCO World Heritage Site, with its renowned whale-watching and glacier viewing opportunities.

Tour boat passengers admiring a glacier in Glacier Bay National Park

◁ Detail of an unrestored 19th-century totem pole, Ketchikan

Exploring Southeast Alaska

The Southeast, often the first part of the state seen by visitors traveling north, is archetypal Alaska. The main towns – bustling Ketchikan, beautiful Sitka, friendly little Wrangell, and Juneau, the capital – enjoy spectacular settings along narrow ocean channels next to rainforested slopes and glaciated peaks. The Tongass National Forest covers almost the entire region, including lush Prince of Wales Island and Misty Fiords National Monument. Anan Creek Wildlife Observatory and Admiralty Island National Monument offer excellent bear viewing, while Glacier Bay National Park and Juneau Icefield offer awe-inspiring vistas.

Eagle-topped totem pole at Saxman Totem Park near Ketchikan

SIGHTS AT A GLANCE

Towns, Cities, and Islands
Haines ⑮
Hyder ④
Juneau ⑬
Ketchikan ①
Metlakatla ②
Petersburg ⑧
Prince of Wales Island ⑤
Sitka ⑩
Skagway ⑯
Tenakee Springs ⑪
Wrangell ⑥
Yakutat ⑳

National and State Parks
Admiralty Island National
   Monument ⑫
Anan Creek Wildlife
   Observatory ⑦
*Glacier Bay National Park
   pp146–7* ⑭
Misty Fiords National
   Monument ③

Areas of Natural Beauty
Mitkof Highway ⑨
Tatshenshini-Alsek Rivers ⑲

Tours
Gold Rush Routes pp152–3 ⑰
Haines Cut-Off Tour p154 ⑱

SEE ALSO

• **Where to Stay** pp244–7

• **Where to Eat** pp259–61

Creek Street above Ketchikan Creek, Ketchikan

GETTING AROUND

The best way to get around Southeast Alaska is by plane, both on the scheduled flights that connect Skagway, Juneau, Sitka, Wrangell, Petersburg, and Ketchikan, and the floatplanes that fly to remote homesteads and lodges. The Alaska Marine Highway is a lifeline, with ferries connecting most towns. Other companies provide access to Prince of Wales Island and Glacier Bay National Park. Although Haines, Skagway, and Hyder are linked to the Canadian highway system, the lack of continuous roads within the region means that cars are not very helpful in getting around, except along the limited highways around individual towns.

The cloud-obscured eastern cliffs of Glacier Bay National Park

KEY

- ▬ Highway
- ▬ Minor road
- -- Alaska Marine Highway
- ▬ International border
- △ Peak

0 km   50

0 miles   50

Cruise ship anchored at Ketchikan, a popular stop on cruise routes

Ketchikan ❶

235 miles (378 km) S of Juneau.
Road Map F5. 🏠 8,000. ✈ ⛴
Bellingham–Skagway. 🛈 131 Front
St, 225-6166, (800) 770-3300. 🐾
Blueberry Festival (1st weekend in
Aug). **www**.visit-ketchikan.com

Situated on the southwestern
end of Revillagigedo Island,
Ketchikan likes to call itself
Alaska's First City, because it
is the first Alaskan city that
visitors see when arriving on
a cruise ship or ferry.

Originally a Tlingit fish
camp called Kitschk-Hin
(meaning "thundering eagle
wings creek"), the town's
growth started in 1885 when
Irishman Mike Martin staked
a claim near Ketchikan Creek
and set up a fish cannery.
By the 1930s, the town's
dozen canneries had earned
it the title Salmon Capital
of the World. Its other big
economic resource, the
Ketchikan Pulp Company's
paper mill at Ward Cove,
operated for over 40 years
until it shut down in 1997.

Despite that major loss,
Ketchikan bounced back.
Today, Alaska's fourth largest
city thrives as a major stop for
cruise ships and as a regional
service center. Built on pilings,
the city center lies along the
waterfront, while older neighborhoods climb the slopes of
nearby hills accessible by steep
streets and wooden staircases.

🏛 Great Alaskan Lumberjack Show

Spruce Mill Way. **Tel** 225-9050.
🚌 Ketchikan city bus.
◯ May–Sep: four shows daily when
cruise ships are in port. 🌐 ♿ 🅿
www.lumberjacksports.com
Held in an amphitheater on
the site of the old Ketchikan
Spruce Mill, this lively show
displays hand-sawing, tree-
climbing, and log-rolling. It
is all done in a spirit of fun,
and the actors and lumberjack
competitors are so engaging
that much of the audience
seems happy to participate.
The original 1898 mill was the
world's largest spruce mill
and provided work for lum-
berjacks who prepared timber
for the Gold Rush, for building aircraft during World War
II, and for local canneries.
The mill finally closed in 1993,
with the pulp mill at Wards
Cove closing four years later.

🏛 Southeast Alaska Discovery Center

50 Main St. **Tel** 228-6220. 🚌
Ketchikan city bus. ◯ May–Sep:
8am–5pm Mon–Sat, 8am–4pm Sun;
Oct–Apr: 10am–4:30pm Tue–Sat. 🌐
♿ 🅿 **www**.fs.fed.us/r10/tongass/
districts/discoverycenter
Both a museum and a visitors'
center for the 26,000-sq mile
(68,000-sq km) Tongass
National Forest, the lush temperate rainforest which covers
the region, the Southeast
Alaska Discovery Center is a
mine of information. Totem
poles from the region's three
main Native cultures, Tlingit,
Haida, and Tsimshian are
displayed, and the historical,
cultural, natural, and economic
story of Southeast Alaska is
told through exhibits. Other
displays feature traditional
Tlingit salmon-drying, forest
ecosystems, and local fishing
techniques such as purse sein-
ing, gillnetting, and trawling.

Silver salmon sculptures at the
Southeast Alaska Discovery Center

🚻 Creek Street

🚌 Ketchikan city bus.
🍴 🖼 🅿 Dolly's House ◯ May–
Sep: 8am–5pm daily when cruise
ships are in port. 🌐
A pedestrian boardwalk built
on pilings over Ketchikan
Creek, Creek Street was the
town's red-light district for
half a century. In the early
1900s, well-heeled newcomers

Dolly's House built on the pilings of Creek Street

to the north side of town decided to clean up the neighborhood by banishing the "working girls" to the south side. Creek Street was soon notorious for its bars and bordellos, and it was here that Frenchie, Black Mary, and Dolly Arthur plied their trade.

Most of their houses have been turned into shops and eateries, but **Dolly's House** is now a museum. Visitors learn interesting facts about those bawdy days, such as how Creek Street's construction lent itself to surreptitious trap-door deliveries of alcohol after it was banned by the 1917 Bone Dry Law.

The street is a perfect spot to watch spawning salmon swim upstream. Visitors can also take the funicular from the end of the street up to the Cape Fox Lodge or follow the Married Man's Trail, once used by men hoping for a clandestine Creek Street encounter.

⌂ Saxman Totem Park

2 miles (4 km) S of Ketchikan at Mile 2.5, S Tongass Hwy. **Tel** 225-4846. 🚌 Ketchikan city bus. ☐ daily in summer. ☑ ☐ ☐ www.capefoxtours.com
Founded in 1894, the Native village of Saxman today has the finest display of totem poles in Southeast Alaska. The village was settled by Tlingit from the villages of Tongass and Cape Fox at the southern tip of Alaska, who were persuaded to move here by Presbyterian missionaries. Begun in the late 1930s as a Civilian Conservation Corps (CCC) project, Saxman Totem

Totems along a forest walkway, Totem Bight State Historical Park

Park has grown into a popular attraction. In addition to the renovated poles brought from surrounding villages, there is the colorful Beaver Clan House and the Frog Wall, which features dozens of frog faces. A large carving shed houses the workshops of Alaska's best totem carvers.

⌂ Totem Bight State Historical Park

10 miles (16 km) N of Ketchikan. 🚗 ☐ 9883 North Tongass Hwy, 247-8574. 🚌 Ketchikan city bus. ☑ ☐ www.dnr.alaska.gov/parks/units/totembgh.htm
As Europeans established permanent settlements in

Southeast Alaska, many Natives joined them, and their traditional villages fell into ruins. In 1938, the CCC launched a project to restore old totem poles that lay rotting in abandoned villages. Native carvers were hired to re-create the damaged poles, which were placed in a forested site near the Tongass Narrows, and by 1942, 15 poles and a clan house had been completed. In 1970, Totem Bight was designated a State Historical Park. Today, a walkway between the totems leads to the water and a replica clan house that once would have held 30 to 50 people.

Detail of a totem pole at Saxman Totem Park near Ketchikan

TOTEM POLES

Alaska's Tlingit, Haida, and Tsimshian peoples carve at least six types of totem poles to support buildings, tell stories, and honor people or special events. Never meant to be objects of veneration, poles were cultural symbols, carved of western red cedar with designs that included stylized clan totems, such as Raven, Beaver, Frog, Bear, Wolf, and Killer Whale, and painted in symbolic colors. Due to the iron tools gained by trade with Europeans, the mid-19th century saw an especially prolific carving period. This ended with the arrival of missionaries in the late 19th century, who discouraged pole raisings and potlatches, the gifting feasts that accompanied them. Pole carving was revived in the 1930s by the CCC, which launched a project to restore old poles and commission locals to carve new ones. Today, master carvers still create poles and pass on the craft to apprentices.

Metlakatla's boat harbor on Annette Island

Metlakatla ❷

18 miles (29 km) SW of Ketchikan.
Road Map F5. ⚐ *1,400.*
✈ *Ketchikan.* ⛴ *from Ketchikan.*
ℹ *886-8687.* **www**.
metlakatlatours.net

Located on Annette Island
southwest of Ketchikan,
Metlakatla was founded in
1887 by Scottish clergyman
Father Duncan. After falling
out with the
church in Old
Metlakatla,
Canada, he
fled to Annette
Island with
over 800 of his

Sign, Annette
Island Reserve

Tsimshian fol-
lowers *(see p23).*
In 1891, the US
Congress gave them possession of the island. Because the
Tsimshian rejected ANCSA in
the early 1970s *(see p56),* they
retained their sovereignty, and
Annette Island is now Alaska's
only Indian reservation, with
an economy dependent on
fishing and the timber industry.
Metlakatla's main appeal
lies in its quiet, small-town

atmosphere. The **Duncan
Cottage Museum** contains
Father Duncan's educational
and medical materials, musical instruments, and a phono-
graph built by Thomas Edison
himself. The **Le Sha'as
Tsimshian** clan house is worth
a visit to watch dance performances and totem carvers at
work. There's also a pleasant,
short hike up Yellow Hill for
great Inside Passage views.

Misty Fiords National Monument ❸

22 miles (35 km) E of Ketchikan.
Road Map F5. ✈ *charter floatplane
from Ketchikan.*

Misty Fiords is a hidden gem,
not only because it's little-
known outside the Southeast,
but also because it's often hidden in pouring rain behind a
bank of clouds. Characterized
by wild fjords, alpine lakes,
roaring waterfalls, rainforests,
snowy peaks, and soaring
3,000-ft (915-m) granite cliffs,

the site was first identified in
the 1793 journals of Captain
George Vancouver, one of
Captain Cook's lieutenants.
The profuse wildlife includes
bears, deer, mountain goats,
bald eagles, and whales.
With time, sufficient gear,
and lots of effort, it's possible
to kayak from Ketchikan to
Misty Fiords, but most people
prefer to fly or take a boat
tour. Charters can provide
drop-off and pick-up flights for
kayakers. Several cruise lines
also visit the area *(see pp34–5).*

Hyder ❹

2 miles (4 km) W of Stewart
(Canada), 75 miles (120 km) E of
Ketchikan. **Road Map** F5. ⚐ *100.*
✈ *Stewart.* ⛴ *Stewart–Terrace.*
ℹ *5th Ave, Stewart, (250) 636-9224.*
🎪 *International Rodeo (2nd week in
Jun), International Days (1st weekend
in Jul).* **www**.stewart-hyder.com

Isolated from the rest of Alaska
by a roadless range of mountains, Hyder sits on the US
border at the end of Canada
Route 37A. Despite the fact
that it works on Canadian
time, has a Canadian phone
code, and sends its children
to Canadian schools, it enjoys
a very Alaskan atmosphere.
For visitors, the town is an
attraction in itself, with its historic buildings and more bars
per capita than any town in
Alaska. The scenic but rough
25-mile (40-km) long **Granduc
Road** heads north from Hyder,
following the Salmon River
past old gold mines to a grand
view of Salmon Glacier. The
area also has a large number
of brown bears, and salmon
crowd the streams in summer.

New Eddystone Rock rising from Behm Canal in the atmospheric Misty Fiords National Monument

For hotels and restaurants in this region see pp244–7 and pp259–61

Alaska's Temperate Rainforests

Characterized by lush, rain-soaked mosses, lichens, shrubs, and ferns sheltering beneath enormous coniferous trees, the forests of Southeast Alaska make up the northern extent of the world's largest temperate rainforest. Much cooler than their tropical counterparts, temperate rainforests have climatic conditions that are marked by average summer temperatures of less than 16° C (61° F), a cool dormant season, and at least 55 inches (140 cm) of precipitation per year. At the southern end of the Panhandle, the rainfall can exceed 200 inches (508 cm) per year, but moving north, it decreases to around 60 inches (152 cm) near Juneau. The most prominent trees in Alaska's rainforest are the Sitka spruce and western hemlock, followed by mountain hemlock, yellow cedar, and western red cedar. Rarer conifers include mountain juniper, subalpine and silver fir, and Pacific yew.

Rainforest trees typically live from 200 to 1,000 years. When they fall, they decompose into a rich organic material that nourishes vegetation.

Ferns prefer moist conditions with low levels of light and thrive under the temperate rainforest cover.

FLORA AND FAUNA

Alaska's temperate rainforest includes a canopy composed of tall coniferous trees, while smaller shade-loving trees and shrubs make up the understory. On the damp, shady forest floor grow ferns and large-leafed plants. Fauna species include river otters, pine martens, and boreal toads.

Devil's Club, a spiny plant, dominates the floor of the rainforest where little sunlight filters through.

The Tongass National Forest, *the world's largest temperate rainforest, covers the Southeast Alaskan mainland and over 1,000 islands, and includes Wrangell Narrows, a narrow waterway between Mitkof and Kupreanof Islands.*

Sitka black-tailed deer, *endemic to the region, feed on the native hemlock, berries, and lichens.*

Epiphytic mosses and lichens *draw nutrients and moisture directly from the air, using the host trees just for support.*

Porcupines, *second in size to beavers among Alaskan rodents, are nocturnal animals.*

Prince of Wales Island ⑤

Named for the son of King George III by
Captain George Vancouver in 1793, Prince of
Wales Island lies mostly within the Tongass
National Forest. The third largest island in the
US after Hawaii and Kodiak, it is home to
both the Haida and Tlingit peoples, as well
as a number of outsiders attracted by its
beauty and solitude. It is laced with 1,400
miles (2,240 km) of small old logging roads,
half of which are passable by cars. One of the
most interesting activities here is simply to drive
through the forests and muskeg of the interior.
Access to the island is either by ferry from
Ketchikan or Wrangell, or by floatplane.

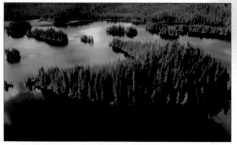

Densely forested islets off Prince of Wales Island

Craig

90 miles (145 km) W of Ketchikan.
🚶 1,200. ✈ charter floatplane.
⛴ to Hollis. ℹ 300 A, Easy St, 755-
2626. www.craigalaska.com
The largest town on the island,
Craig is also its only community without a Native majority.
It was named for Craig Millar
who, with the help of local
Haida, set up the first saltery
on Fish Egg Island in 1907,
followed by a sawmill and a
salmon cannery. Due to poor
salmon runs, fishing declined
in the 1950s, but in 1972, the
large Head Sawmill, north of
Craig, boosted the town's fal-
tering economy. Today, Craig
is the island's service center,
with a bank, hotel, gas station, and several restaurants.

Klawock

5 miles (8 km) N of Craig. 🚶 850.
✈ ⛴ to Hollis. ℹ Mile 23.4,
Hollis–Craig Hwy, 755-2626.
Named for the first Tlingit
settler, Kloo-wah, the village
of Klawock was originally a
summer fishing camp. A
trading post and saltery were
set up here in 1868, and a
decade later, it became the

site of Alaska's first salmon
cannery. Today, the town
boasts a hatchery on the
shores of Klawock Lake, a
sawmill, a log-sorting yard,
and a dock for loading timber.
In keeping with the timber
theme, electricity is provided
by a wood-fired generator.
   Klawock Totem Park, next to
the town library, has about 20
restored poles from Tuxekan,
a Tlingit winter village to the
north. Across the Hollis-Craig
highway from
the Chamber
of Commerce is
the Gaan Ax Adi
Clan House, with
a carving shed
where visitors
may sometimes
see new totems
being carved.
The airport, the
only one on the
island, has an
unattended 6,000-
ft (1,800-m)
paved runway
with pilot-
controlled light-
ing, remarkable
given its location.

KEY

✈	Airport
✈	Floatplane base
⛴	Ferry port
ℹ	Visitor information
═	Minor road

```
0 km          30
|———————————|
0 miles        30
```

Tlingit totem poles in the village of Klawock

Students paddling a traditional Haida canoe carved by them

Hydaburg

45 miles (72 km) SE of Craig.
🏔 380. ✈ charter floatplane.
As rural Alaskan towns go,
the little Haida village of
Hydaburg is as picturesque
as it gets. Although the town
was not founded until 1912,
when the three villages of
Sukkwan, Howkan and
Klinkwan combined, Haida
peoples have occupied the
area since the 18th century,
when they migrated from
British Columbia. Today, the
town has the largest Haida
population in Alaska.

Hydaburg's totem park is
well worth a visit. Its collection of restored totems, with
their unique emphasis on
pastel colors, stands apart
from others in the region.

Thorne Bay

39 miles (63 km) NE of Craig. 🏔 480.
✈ floatplane from Ketchikan. ⛺
Nestled between rolling hills
and the sea, Thorne Bay was
named in honor of Frank
Manley Thorn, superintendent
of the US Coast and Geodetic
Survey in the 1880s. During its
heyday in the mid-20th century, Thorne Bay was North
America's largest logging
camp, but the mill closed in
the 1990s and the economy
now depends on fishing.

A popular visitor attraction
here is the **Honker River
Canoe Route**, which begins at
Coffman Cove Road and winds
through a chain of lakes down
to Thorne Bay. The area also
has several campsites, forest
service cabins, hiking trails,
and picnic areas.

Kasaan

49 miles E of Craig. 🏔 55.
✈ charter floatplane.
Deriving its name from the
Tlingit word for "pretty town,"
Kasaan does indeed have a
lovely setting between
forested mountains and the
sea. It was founded in 1892
when mining and fishing jobs
attracted the Haida here from
the now-abandoned Old
Kasaan. Today, most Kasaan

residents depend on their
harvests of deer, fish, shrimp,
and crab.

In the 1930s, the Haida Chief
Sonihat built the Whale clan
house, and the various totems
around the village were transferred to the same site, forming the **Kasaan Totem Park**. A
15-minute trail through beach-
side woods leads to the park,
where the decaying poles and
clan house, almost swallowed
by the undergrowth and
unspoilt by commercial trap-
pings, lend an authentic air to
the picturesque scene.

El Capitan Cave

Mile 50, N Prince of Wales Rd.
Tel 828-3304. ✈ ⭘ late May–
early Sep: Thu–Sun. 🚫 🅿
mandatory: 9am, noon, & 2pm
daily.
Sited northwest of Whale Pass,
El Capitan Cave is the largest
and longest of the limestone
caves dotted around the karst
region of northern Prince of
Wales Island. In these caves,
paleontologists have uncovered human remains dating
back about 9,500 years, the
oldest found in the region.
A 12,300-year old brown bear
skeleton was discovered in
El Capitan Cave, while a more
remote cave yielded a 45,000-
year old bear skeleton.

Over 2 miles (3 km) of
passageways in El Capitan
Cave have been surveyed.
Guided tours using helmets
and headlamps are offered.
Reservations must be made
two days in advance, but rare
walk-ins are allowed. Young
children under 7 years are not
allowed in the cave. The tour
begins with a steep climb up
367 steps, and a fair degree of
physical fitness is required.

FORESTRY IN SOUTHEAST ALASKA

Since the late 19th century, forestry and forest
products have been an economic factor in the
Tongass National Forest, and from the 1940s to
1990s, they were the mainstay of Alaska's economy. The prime western hemlock and Sitka spruce
of Southeast Alaska were exported, while lower
quality timber was reduced to pulp for the paper
industry. In the 1990s, economic and environmental pressures combined with decreasing harvest
limits caused the closure of the Sitka and Ketchikan
mills. Today the industry plays only a minor role
in Alaska's economy.

Worker adjusting truckload of logs for delivery

Wrangell's harbor against the backdrop of the Coast Mountains

Wrangell ❻

80 miles (128 km) N of Ketchikan.
Road Map F5. 🏔 *1,700.* ✈ *from
Ketchikan.* ⛴ *from Ketchikan, Peters-
burg, or Coffman Cove.* ℹ *296 Outer
Dr, 874-2381.* ♿ 🐦 *Stikine River
Birding Festival (early May).*
www.wrangell.com

Founded as Redoubt St.
Dionysius in 1833 by the
Russians, the original fort on
this site was intended to protect Russian fur trading interests from the British and
Spanish. The local Tlingit,
under Chief Shakes V, recognized the economic benefits
of cooperation with the
Russians and joined them at
the redoubt in 1834. In the
same year, combined Tlingit
and Russian forces managed
to repel the British forces led
by Peter Skeen Odgen, who
had attempted to establish a
fur trading post. In 1868, after
Alaska's transfer to the US,
the Americans established a
military fort that they named
after the head of the Russian-
American Company *(see p50)*,
Baron Ferdinand von Wrangel.

Today, Wrangell is a friendly
little town, attracting a few
adventurous visitors and a
handful of small cruise ships in
the summer. The real draw is
the Stikine River, just outside
town, as well as Anan Creek
and outlying parts of Wrangell
Island, both popular for wildlife viewing. From the town,
forest roads lead to free camp-

grounds, the loveliest of which
are at Nemo Point, 14 miles
(22 km) south of town, offering
wonderful high altitude views
over Zimovia Strait.

🏛 Wrangell Museum
296 Outer Dr. **Tel** 874-3770.
🚗 ⬜ *May–Sep: 10am–
5pm Mon–Sat; Oct–Apr:
1–5pm Tue–Sat.* 💳
♿ 🛍
Housed in the
modern James and
Elsie Nolan Visitors'
Center, the Wrangell
Museum contains a
wonderful collection
of artifacts. The large
entryway features
the original 17th-
century houseposts of the
Frog Clan from the Tlingit
Tribal House on Chief Shakes
Island. Electronic lighting on

Tlingit housepost,
Wrangell Museum

the ceiling of the lobby
simulates the undulations of
the aurora borealis. Museum
displays begin with the natural history of the region and
proceed chronologically
through exhibits on Native
culture, the fur trade, military
history, the Stikine
Gold Rush, fishing,
and forestry. The
museum is also a
repository for thou-
sands of historic
images and numer-
ous audio and video
records, which are
available for viewing.
The town's visitor
information office
and convention cen-
ter are located in the center.

🚩 Chief Shakes Island
Shakes St.
Accessible by a wooden
walkway across an arm of the
harbor, Chief Shakes Island is
a park and a repository for
Tlingit totems dating from
1840 to 1940. Opened in
1940, the large replica **Tlingit
Tribal House**, a National
Historic Site, was named Ck!
Udatc Hit ("House of Many
Faces") in reference to the
human visages in its design.
Inside are replica houseposts
of the Frog Clan, and dotted
around the park are several
distinctive totems. The peaceful park overlooks the picturesque harbor, and on sunny
days, its green lawns make a
perfect spot to relax.

Totem pole and Tlingit Tribal House
on Chief Shakes Island

🏛 Petroglyph Beach State Historic Site

Half a mile (1 km) N of Wrangell at Grave St. 🚐 ◯ *24 hrs* ♿ *limited.*
Archeologists believe that an ancient culture already occupied the Wrangell area before the modern-day Tlingit arrived. Evidence suggests that these early groups were here around 10,000 years ago, at the end of the last Ice Age, and that they established subsequent settlements 5,000 and 3,000 years ago. It is thought that these early people made some of the 40 petroglyphs that adorn the rocks of the beach. However, the artwork reveals little information about their culture, except that the simplest spiral and sun designs match petroglyphs found as far away as South America. The petroglyphs of wolves, bears, and orcas found on the same beach were probably carved by the Tlingit. Most of the petroglyphs, carved on boulders scattered along several hundred feet of beach, have been eroded over time by the sea. A visitors' platform provides access to the beach, where the state has reproduced the most interesting petroglyphs to allow visitors to make rubbings of the carvings without damaging the originals.

Kayaking in the blue waters of the Stikine River

Petroglyph of a fish on a boulder

🐾 Stikine River

🚢 *tour boats.* 🎣 ⛺ 🅰
The glacier-fed Stikine River is the biggest draw for visitors to Wrangell. Originating in the mountains of British Columbia, the 360-mile (576-km) river flows through 30 miles (48 km) of the Stikine-LeConte Wilderness on the Alaskan mainland to its mouth across the narrows near Wrangell.

Several companies organize jetboat tours, which head upstream through spectacular mountain scenery and past waterfalls and the iceberg choked face of Shakes Glacier. There is a delightful lunch spot here, overlooking the glacier. There are also good opportunities to see harbor seals, black bears, spawning salmon, and the world's largest summer concentration of bald eagles. A popular destination is **Chief Shakes Hot Springs**, where open-air hot tubs offer soaking in a wild setting.

⚑ Muskeg Meadows Golf Course

Mile 0.5, Ishiyama Dr. **Tel** *874-4653.* 🚐 *or phone for pickup from town.* ◯ *Apr–Nov: 9am–6pm.* 📶 🖥 📷 www.wrangellalaskagolf.com
The non-profit Wrangell Golf Club was established in 1993 to carve a nine-hole, par 36 course from the muskeg bog for which it was named. From 1995 to 1998, volunteers cleared trees, laid wood pulp to create the fairways, planted grass, and installed the greens, resulting in a beautiful course set amid spruce and cedar rainforest. This is the world's only golf course with a rule that states that if a raven steals a golf ball, it can be replaced without penalty, provided the golfer has a witness.

Anan Creek Wildlife Observatory ❼

31 miles (50 km) S of Wrangell. **Road Map** F5. **Tel** *874-2323.* ✈ *by floatplane.* 🚢 *tour boat.* ◯ *year-round.* 📶 ⛺ *book in advance.* **Permits** *required Jul 5–Aug 25, book at 525 Bennett St, Wrangell.*

Located on the Cleveland Peninsula, Anan Creek is the site of one of Alaska's greatest pink salmon runs. The fish are slowed by a waterfall half a mile (1 km) inland, which attracts large numbers of hungry brown and black bears. Adjacent to the falls, a wildlife observatory, which is actually a large viewing platform, allows visitors close up views of the feeding bears. During the salmon run, sea otters, harbor seals, and bald eagles can also be spotted along the shore near the mouth of Anan Creek.

While wildlife is usually visible all summer, permits are needed to visit the observatory in July and August. Only 60 permits are issued for each day. Four permits are also available for those staying at the nearby Anan Bay public use cabin – the only accommodation available in the area. However, local tour operators pre-book permits and make them available to visitors on their tours.

Black bear feeding with cub at the rapidly flowing Anan Creek

Spectacular blue face of Hubbard Glacier, Yakutat Bay ▷

Houses built on pilings above Hammer Slough in Petersburg

Petersburg ❽

32 miles (51 km) N of Ketchikan.
Road Map F5. ⚑ *3,000.*
✈ *from Ketchikan, Wrangell, &
Juneau.* ⛴ *from Ketchikan, Sitka,
Wrangell, & Juneau.* ⓘ *1st & Fram
St, 772-4636.* ⚐ *Little Norway
Festival (weekend nearest May 17).*
www.petersburg.org

Named for Norwegian settler
Peter Buschmann, Petersburg
nestles on sheltered Mitkof
Island beside a calm sea.
Buschmann, who arrived to
homestead in the area in 1890,
initiated the development of
the town. By 1900, realizing
that glacier ice could be used
to preserve fish, he set up the
Icy Strait Packing Company
cannery. By the 1920s, jobs
created by the town's businesses had attracted over 600
people. Petersburg now has
crab, shrimp, salmon, and
herring fisheries, as well as
Alaska's largest halibut fleet.

Petersburg enjoys spectacular
mountain views that include
the precipitous Devil's
Thumb, towering at 9,077 ft
(2,767 m) and straddling the
Canadian border about 40
miles (64 km) away. The
major attractions for visitors
are the beautiful hinterlands
of Mitkof Island and neighboring Kupreanof Island,
which offer superb hik-
ing, camping, fishing,
boating, and kayaking.

⚏ Sing Lee Alley
Built on pilings above
Hammer Slough, this
picturesque board-
walk is one of
Petersburg's oldest
historic streets. At
No. 23, the distinc-
tive Sons of Norway Hall,
built by Norwegian immi-
grants in 1912, has graceful
decorative scroll paintings
called *rosemaling* on its
façade. The adjacent Bojer

Wikan Fishermen's Memorial
Park features a statue of Bojer
Wikan, a local fisherman lost
at sea. The replica Viking ship
Valhalla, used in the Little
Norway Festival, is kept here.
The street also boasts pleasant
cafés and a bookshop.

⛫ Clausen Memorial
Museum
203 Fram St. **Tel** 772-3598.
⬜ *May–early Sep: 10am–5pm
Mon–Sat.* ⬤ *public holidays.*
⛿ ⓘ **www**.clausen
museum.net

Bojer Wikan statue,
Sing Lee Alley

The compact Clausen
Memorial Museum
showcases the history
and culture of the
Petersburg and
Kupreanof Island
area. Besides a
replica of a 1970s-era fish
packer's office, it features
a fish trap, a collection of
old nautical and fishing gear,
and a Tlingit dugout canoe.
The most popular exhibit,
however, representing every
angler's dream, is the 125-lb
(56-kg) stuffed king salmon.

Mitkof Highway ❾

Road Map F5. ⛊ ⓘ *12 N Nordic
Dr, 772-3871.* ⓐ **www**.fs.fed.us/
r10/tongass/districts/petersburg

The scenic Mitkof Highway
follows the coastline from
Petersburg to the southern
end of Mitkof Island. At Mile
14.5, a lovely boardwalk trail

Sons of Norway Hall with the Viking ship *Valhalla*, Sing Lee Alley

For hotels and restaurants in this region see pp244–7 and pp259–61

crosses the muskeg to access some picnic spots and the salmon run at **Blind River Rapids**. Wintering trumpeter swans can be seen from mid-October to December at the Swan Observatory at Mile 16. Not far ahead, at Mile 18, the Crystal Lake Hatchery and Blind Slough Recreation Area offer scenic picnic sites.

The beautiful **Man Made Hole** at Mile 20 was once a quarry that has filled with water to form a lake. A gentle trail winds around its perimeter on boardwalks and gravel. At Mile 22, the pretty Ohmer Creek Campground offers visitors free camping at the island's only public campsite.

Sitka

See pp140–41.

Brightly painted houses at Tenakee Springs flanking the calm inlet

Tenakee Springs ⑪

48 miles (78 km) N of Sitka. **Road Map** F5. 🏚 100. ⛴ Sitka–Juneau. 🛈 736-2207. **Bathhouse** at the end of the ferry dock. ◻ men: 2–6pm & 10pm–9am daily; women: 9am–2pm & 6–10pm daily.

Situated on the eastern shores of Chichagof Island, the village of Tenakee Springs takes its name from the Tlingit Tinaghu, meaning "Copper Shield Bay," after three prized copper shields that were lost in a storm in Tenakee Inlet.

Historically, the town's main attraction was the 42° C (108° F) hot spring, which made the area bearable in all seasons. In 1895, a **Bathhouse** was built to enclose the spring,

Mud flats and forests on Admiralty Island

and 1899 saw the launch of Snyder's Mercantile, which is still run as a general store.

Modern Tenakee Springs is a community of retirees, residents, and weekend visitors from Juneau, stretching along a single picturesque street. Vehicles are not allowed and most people walk in town.

Admiralty Island National Monument ⑫

43 miles (70 km) NE of Sitka. **Road Map** F5. ✈ charter floatplane from Juneau. ⛴ Sitka–Angoon; tour boat Juneau–Pack Creek. 🛈 586-8800 🖼 📷 ⚠ 🅰 **Permits** required for Pack Creek Jun–mid-Sep, book online. **www**.fs.fed.us/r10/tongass/districts/admiralty

Called Kootznoowoo (meaning "Fortress of Bears") by the Tlingit people, Admiralty Island National Monument

sprawls across 1,492 sq miles (3,865 sq km). Lying within the Tongass National Forest, almost 98 percent of this lush rainforest is a designated wilderness area. The main site of interest for wildlife enthusiasts is **Pack Creek** in the Stan Price State Wildlife Sanctuary at the island's northeast corner. This area is home to the world's densest population of brown bears. Sitka black-tailed deer can be seen along the shore, and Mitchell, Hood, Chaik, and Whitewater Bays contain porpoises, seals, and sea lions. Summer access to the tidal estuary and bear-viewing tower is by permit only.

The sole settlement on the island is **Angoon**, a small Native village accessible via the Marine Highway. Kayakers and canoeists will enjoy the **Cross-Island Canoe Route**, which connects Angoon with Mole Harbor, on the island's eastern shore, by a series of lakes, streams, and portages.

LITTLE NORWAY

Peter Buschmann's success in Petersburg inspired many of his countrymen to follow him to Alaska in search of fjords, fishing, and opportunity. Nicknamed Little Norway, the town reflects its Norwegian heritage in the decorative details on buildings and the souvenirs on offer. On the weekend nearest Norwegian Independence Day on May 17, the town celebrates the Little Norway Festival (see p42) with a Norwegian feast and *bunad* (traditional dress) fashion show. The *Valhalla* leads a parade of revelers

The replica Viking ship *Valhalla*, Sing Lee Alley

clad in Norwegian flags and Viking attire. Even if it rains – and it usually does – a good time is had by all.

Sitka ⑩

One of Alaska's most beautiful towns, Sitka sits beside an island-studded sea on the west coast of Baranof Island. The lure of hunting sea otters for their pelts led the Russians to set up Redoubt St. Michael in the year 1799. After local Tlingit destroyed the fort in 1804, the Russians established the fortified town of Novo Archangelsk. By 1808, this was the capital of Russian America and was flourishing economically and culturally. When the US bought Alaska in 1867, the town's name was changed to Sitka, a contraction of Shee Atiká, the Tlingit name for the settlement. Today, Sitka's economy is based on tourism and a large fishing and cold-storage industry.

Tlingit totem poles on display at the Sheldon Jackson Museum

Detail of ceremonial Native canoe, Isabel Miller Museum

🏛 Isabel Miller Museum

330 Harbor Dr. *Tel* 747-6455, 747-5516 *(performance information).* ◻ mid-May–late Sep: 8am–5pm daily; late Sep–mid-May: 9am–5pm Sun–Fri, 11am–3pm Sat. 📷 donations accepted. ♿ ◻
www.sitkahistory.org

Housed in the Harrigan Centennial Hall, the Isabel Miller Museum, named for the local benefactor who established it, outlines Sitka's history from the Russian era to the present. In addition to a model of Sitka at the time of its transfer to the US, museum highlights include Tlingit art, tools, and spruce baskets. There are also trade beads, Russian weapons, historic photographs, and a unique "tea brick." These bricks of compacted Cantonese tea were acquired by the Russians from the Chinese in exchange for the sea otter pelts that formed the basis of Russian Alaska's economy.

Outside, a large Haida ceremonial canoe is on display beneath a canopy. In the summer, the New Archangel Dancers perform in traditional Russian costume for tourists.

🔼 St. Michael's Russian Orthodox Cathedral

Lincoln St. *Tel* 747-8120. ◻ May–Sep: 9am–4pm Mon–Fri, or when cruise ships are in port; winter: by appt. 📷 ♿ limited. 🚫 🔼 6:30pm Sat, 10am Sun.

This onion-domed cathedral is the quintessential Sitka landmark. The cornerstone was laid by Bishop Veniaminov *(see p74)* in 1844, and construction was completed in 1848. The present church is a replica of the original, which burned down in a fire in 1966. Although locals managed to rescue the paintings, icons, chandelier, and the partially melted bronze bells, the large library of works in Russian, Tlingit, and Aleut languages was lost. One of the surviving artifacts, the Madonna of Sitka, has been credited with miraculous healings. The reconstruction, in fire-resistant materials, was begun in 1967 and finished in 1972, and the new cathedral was consecrated in 1976. Visitors can attend services.

Dome and spire of St. Michael's Russian Orthodox Cathedral

🏛 Sheldon Jackson Museum

104 College Dr. *Tel* 747-8981. ◻ mid-May–mid-Sep: 9am–5pm daily; mid-Sep–mid-May: 10am–4pm Tue–Sat. 📷 ♿ ◻
www.museums.state.ak.us

From 1888 to 1898, the Presbyterian Reverend Sheldon Jackson traveled around Alaska

representing the US educational system. In the course of his travels, he collected the indigenous artifacts that are displayed here, including hunting tools, masks, kayaks, and reindeer sleighs. Each summer, Native artisans come to the museum to demonstrate their crafts. The museum shop offers a variety of Native hand-crafted goods and artwork.

✈ Alaska Raptor Center

1000 Raptor Way. **Tel** 747-8662.
🚌 Community Ride. ◯ late May–
early Sep: 8am–4pm daily. 🅿 🎫
♿ 🏠 www.alaskaraptor.org

One of the state's best
raptor hospital and
rehabilitation centers, the
non-profit Alaska Raptor
Center treats injured ravens
and raptors such as eagles,
falcons, owls, and hawks,
and tries to re-adapt them to
life in the wild. Seriously
wounded birds become
Raptors in-Residence and are
used in educational programs
for visitors.

♛ Russian Bishop's House

Lincoln & Monastery Sts. **Tel** 747-
6281. 🚌 Community Ride. ◯
May–Sep: 9am–3pm daily; winter:
by appt. 🅿 🎫 ♿
www.nps.gov/sitk

The oldest building in Sitka,
this 1843 structure is one of
the few surviving examples of
secular Russian architecture.
The original building was
made from spruce by Finnish
woodworkers, who

**Bald eagle in the compound of
the Alaska Raptor Center**

introduced Baltic-style
opulence to Russian America.
Despite the building's flam-
boyance, its first occupant,
Bishop Veniaminov, lived a
simple monastic life.

Over the years, the building
has served as an orphanage,
seminary, and school. The last
Russian bishop moved out in
1969 and the building was
purchased in 1972 by the US
National Park Service for restoration. On the main floor is
a model of Novo Archangelsk
as it looked in 1845 and a col
lection of icons and relics. To
see the library, chapel, and
Bishop's quarters, it is necessary to join a guided tour.

VISITORS' CHECKLIST

96 miles (155 km) NW of
Petersburg. **Road Map** F5.
🚶 9,000. ✈ 🚢 🛈 303
Lincoln St (upstairs), 747-5940.
🎭 Sitka Summer Music Festival
(three weeks in Jun); Sitka
Whalefest (early Nov)
www.sitka.org

redoubt from the Tlingit.
Just behind the Blockhouse
lies the overgrown Russian
cemetery, where hundreds
of graves recall 18th- and
19th-century Russian Sitka.

♛ Sitka National Historical Park

106 Metlakatla St. 🚗 🛈 747-6281.
◯ public hols. 🎫 ♿ 🏠
www.nps.gov/sitk

Alaska's oldest federal park
was established in 1910 to
commemorate the 1804 Battle
of Sitka. In 1802, Tlingit
warriors of the Kiks.adi tribe
attacked the Russian redoubt,
killing most of the Russian
and Aleut personnel. Seeking
revenge, the Russians
returned with four ships and
beseiged the Tlingit fort. After
much bloodshed, Russians
entered the fort to find that it
had been abandoned by the
Tlingit. Today, the site is part
of the park. From the visitors'
center and museum, trails
lead through rainforest past
totem poles brought here in
1905 from Prince of Wales
Island. To the east is the site of
the Tlingit fort and the actual
battleground, while to the
north, across the creek, trails
lead to the Russian Memorial.

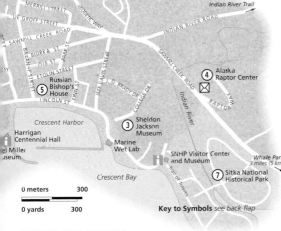

**Prince of Wales Island totem pole,
Sitka National Historical Park**

SIGHTS AT A GLANCE

Alaska Raptor Center ④
Blockhouse and Russian
   Cemetery ⑥
Isabel Miller Museum ①
Russian Bishop's House ⑤
Sheldon Jackson Museum ③
Sitka National Historical Park ⑦
St. Michael's Russian Orthodox
   Cathedral ②

♛ Blockhouse and Russian Cemetery

Kogwanton & Marine Sts.
Blockhouse ◯ late May–early
Sep: noon–4pm Sun.
Cemetery ◯ 24 hrs.

North of St. Michael's sits a
reconstruction of an octagonal
two-story blockhouse used by
the Russians to shield their

Juneau ⑬

Often described as a little San Francisco due to its hilly setting, Alaska's capital is located between Mount Juneau and Mount Roberts along Gastineau Channel. Joe Juneau and Dick Harris' 1880 discovery of gold in Gold Creek and Juneau's strategic location on the route to the Klondike goldfields established its importance and led to it taking over the role of Alaska's capital from Sitka in 1900. In the mid-1970s, Alaskans voted to move the state capital to Willow, but due to projected costs, they reversed the decision in 1982.

Gold Rush-era mining display at the Alaska State Museum

Pleasure craft and fishing boats anchored in Juneau

🏛 Alaska State Capitol Building

4th & Main. 🚌 3 & 4. ◷ 9am–4:30pm Mon–Fri, 10am–4pm Sat. 🎫
Designed to serve as the seat of Territorial Government, this gracious marble Art Deco building was completed in 1931. It now houses the Alaska State Legislature and the offices of the Governor and Lieutenant Governor. A state map made from a slice of the Alaska Pipeline is on display near the staircase, and decorative details throughout the building showcase aspects of the state's culture, lifestyle, and economy. Free tours are available Monday to Saturday in summer. The Legislature is in session January to March.

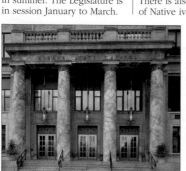

Façade of the Alaska State Capitol Building

🏛 Alaska State Museum

395 Whittier St. Tel 465-2901.
🚌 3 & 4. ◷ mid-May–mid-Sep: 8:30am– 5:30pm daily; mid-Sep–mid-May: 10am–4pm Tue–Sat. 🎫
🚹 🛈 www.museums.state.ak.us
The Alaska State Museum has an impressive collection reflecting many facets of Alaskan history, ranging from prehistoric times to modern days. On the ramp to the second floor is a mock rainforest, complete with recorded bird-song and a replica bald eagle nest. Displayed along the walls of the ramp are a range of Native artifacts, including dolls, masks, baskets, and models of traditional canoes. There is also a collection of Native ivory "billikens" upstairs. These chubby elf-like figurines have now become mainstays of the Alaskan tourist trade. Russian America is represented by a collection of icons and samovars, while numerous mining tools bring the Gold Rush to life. Other highlights include a

mineral collection, the pen used by President Dwight Eisenhower to sign the bill that gave Alaska its statehood, and a children's area with hands-on activities.

0 meters   200
0 yards   200

Key to Symbols see back flap

SIGHTS AT A GLANCE

Alaska State Capitol Building ①
Alaska State Museum ②
Mount Roberts Tramway ⑤
Red Dog Saloon ④
Wickersham State Historical Site ③

🏛 Wickersham State Historical Site

213 7th St. **Tel** 586-9001. ☐ mid-May–mid-Sep: 10am–4pm Tue–Sat; winter: by appt. 🗺 donations accepted.

The historic Wickersham house, built in 1898, was once the home of Judge James Wickersham, who served as the voice of the law in over half of Territorial Alaska. As a delegate to the US Congress, the judge introduced an Alaska Statehood Bill in 1916, planting the seeds of an idea that would come to fruition in the 1950s. After his death in 1939, his niece Ruth Allman opened the house to the public. In 1984, the house and its relics were purchased by the state and turned into a museum.

🍺 Red Dog Saloon

278 S Franklin St. **Tel** 463-3658. 🚍 3 & 4. ☐ May–Sep: 9am to late, daily. ♿ 🍴 🖥 📷 **www**.reddogsaloon.com

During Juneau's mining heyday in the late 19th century, the Saloon offered alcohol, entertainment, and dancing to travelers and local miners. The Harris family bought the place in 1973 and turned it into a bar. While popular with cruise passengers and other visitors, it offers a good range of meals and drinks in a retro setting that includes a collection of interesting memorabilia.

🚠 Mount Roberts Tramway

490 S Franklin St. **Tel** 463-3412. 🚍 3 & 4. ☐ May–Sep: 8am–9pm daily 🗺 ♿ 🍴 🖥 📷 **www**.goldbelttours.com

The tramway up the slopes of Mount Roberts offers panoramic views along Gastineau Channel and across to Douglas Island. At the summit, the Mountain House has a gift shop, restaurant, and the Chilkat Theater, which screens a film on Tlingit culture. The short Alpine Loop trail winds through meadow and forest, past several Tlingit carvings, with a short side trip to Father Brown's Cross. The energetic can forgo the tramway and hike up the mountain from the end of Sixth Street.

Mount Roberts Tramway cable car moving past forested slopes

🏛 Last Chance Mining Museum

1001 Basin Rd. **Tel** 586-5338. 🚌 ☐ mid-May–late Sep: 9:30am–12:30pm & 3:30–6:30pm daily. 🗺

The only remnants of the Juneau goldfields are the historic buildings and relics of the Last Chance Mining Museum. It is located in the mine's old service center, which once housed dormitories, assay offices, and machine repair shops. The museum displays what was once the world's largest air compressor, mining tools, and a three-dimensional representation of the mine tunnels that wind through the adjacent mountain.

View of downtown Juneau from the upper Mount Roberts Tramway station

Exploring Beyond Juneau

Downtown Juneau lies between the Coast Range and Gastineau Channel, so most of the city's residential areas are found on the coast of precipitous Douglas Island, as well as in the scenic side valleys and along the coastal, forest-studded Glacier Highway to the northwest. The city bus system extends only as far as the Mendenhall Valley loop, but with a rental car, it is possible to explore the spectacular hinterlands. More adventurous visitors can join helicopter tours of the Juneau Icefield.

SIGHTS AT A GLANCE

Alaska Brewing Company ②
Glacier Gardens ③
Juneau Icefield ④
Macauley Salmon Hatchery ①
Mendenhall Glacier ⑤
Shrine of St. Therese
   de Lisieux ⑥

KEY

☐ Juneau

✈ International airport

⛴ Ferry terminal

▬ Highway

═ Minor road

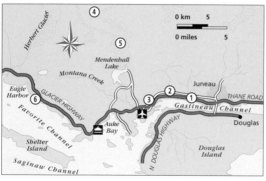

🏛 Macauley Salmon Hatchery

2697 Channel Dr, 3 miles (5 km) N of downtown Juneau. *Tel* 463-4810. ▦ 3 & 4. ⬤ *May–Sep: 10am–6pm Mon–Fri, 10am–5pm Sat & Sun.* 🎟 ☑ ⛄
☐ www.dipac.net

A working hatchery that provides fry to stock streams in many areas of Southeast Alaska, the Macauley Salmon Hatchery is an interesting place to visit. Inside, over 100 species of local sealife are on view in a number of large saltwater aquariums. Outside the building, walkways lead past several tanks where fry of various ages are fed and reared until they are ready for release into the surrounding waterways. Small salmon are also released into nearby Twin Lakes for recreational anglers. Between June and October, a 450-ft (135-m) fish ladder provides easy access for pink and chum salmon returning to the hatchery to spawn and produce their fry. Visitors can purchase a range of salmon products in the hatchery shop.

🏛 Alaska Brewing Company

5429 Shaune Dr. *Tel* 780-5866. ▦ 3 & 4. ⬤ *May–Sep: 11am–6pm daily; Oct–Apr: 11am–5pm Thu–Sun.* ☑ ⛄ ☐
www.alaskanbeer.com

Home-brewers Geoff and Marcy Larsen started the Alaskan Brewing Company in 1986 when they uncovered an ingredient list for a popular beer brewed during the 19th-century Gold Rush. This recipe became the base for their winning formula for Alaskan Amber. The popularity of their beers grew, and today their company is the state's only fully-fledged brewery. In 1987, they produced 1,600 barrels of Amber and currently, the company annually distributes about 125,000 barrels of award-winning amber, pale ale, stout, and smoked porter throughout the western states.

A free hour-long tour explains the brewing process and includes displays of brewing equipment. Beer samples are available, and it is also possible to buy discounted cases of beer.

🌿 Glacier Gardens

7600 Glacier Hwy. *Tel* 790-3377. ▦ 3 & 4. ⬤ *May–Sep: 9am–6pm daily.* 🎟 ☑ ⛄ ☐
www.glaciergardens.com

Nearly surrounded by the Tongass National Forest, the 52-acre (21-ha) Glacier Gardens is a pleasant blend of groomed gardens and natural rainforest, including a series of artificial streams and ponds flanked by lovely plantings. A collection of upended tree stumps, salvaged from a devastating 1984 mudslide, form planters for colorful hanging gardens of petunias, begonias, and fuschias.

From the greenhouse, a succession of rainforest trails leads to boardwalks and a platform offering dramatic views of Gastineau Channel. For those who do not want to climb the steep hillside, the admission price includes transport by an electric golf cart through the woods, as well as a running commentary on the rainforest environment.

Unusual tree-stump planters, Glacier Gardens

Mendenhall Glacier on the shores of Mendenhall Lake near Juneau

Juneau Icefield

accessible by flightseeing or helicopter tour only. www.fs.fed. us/r10/tongass/districts/mendenhall
Juneau Icefield sprawls across 1,500 sq miles (3,885 sq km) of the Coast Range, with its highest peak, the 8,584-ft (2,616-m) Devil's Paw, straddling the US-Canada border.

The icefield feeds about 40 large and 100 small glaciers. Of all Juneau Icefield's glaciers, only Taku Glacier continues to advance and calve into Taku Inlet.

The most readily accessible portion of the icefield is the retreating Mendenhall Glacier. A hike to the rest of the vast white wilderness of the ice field can be quite challenging, and most visitors opt for helicopter or flightseeing tours, some of which additionally offer adventurous summer dogsled rides across the ice. Also available are ice climbing classes, with instruction and gear provided.

Mendenhall Glacier

Glacier Spur Hwy. *Tel* 789-0097. 3 & 4. 789-6640. May–mid-Sep: 8am–7:30pm daily; Oct–Apr: 10am–4pm Thu–Sun. summer only; free in winter. www.fs.fed.us/r10/tongass/districts/mendenhall
Spilling into the Mendenhall Valley from Juneau Icefield, the large Mendenhall Glacier was first called Auke Glacier after the nearby Tlingit village, Aak'w Kwaan. In 1892, it was renamed in honor of physicist Thomas Mendenhall, who surveyed the international border between Canada and Southeast Alaska.

Several trails access the glacier. The East Glacier Loop follows the glacial trimline, while the West Glacier Trail goes up to the glacier's west face. The Moraine Ecology Trail has information panels explaining the regeneration of vegetation on deglaciated areas. The Photo Point Trail is lined with benches and interpretive panels, and provides the best vantage points to capture panoramic shots of the glacier.

At **Mendenhall Lake**, which is often choked with icebergs calved from the glacier, the huge curving glass wall of the visitor center offers fabulous views of the glacier across the lake. An exhibit hall has information on glaciers, and a theater shows films on icefield geology. A salmon-viewing platform and a fish-cam provide views of spawning salmon moving up Steep Creek.

Shrine of St. Therese of Lisieux

Mile 23, Glacier Hwy. *Tel* 780-6112. Apr–Sep: 8:30am–10pm; Oct–Mar: 8:30am–8pm. limited. late May–early Sep: 1:30pm Sun. www.shrineofsainttherese.org
This peaceful Catholic pilgrimage site lies on Shrine Island at the end of a 400-ft (120-m) pedestrian causeway from the mainland. The serene chapel, built of beach stone, occupies a lovely forested spot with views across the sea to the distant peaks of the Chilkat Range. It is dedicated to the 19th-century French saint, Therese de Lisieux, who was chosen by the first Bishop of Alaska, Joseph Raphael Crimont, as the patron saint of the state. The shrine also contains the 14 Stations of the Cross, a prayer labyrinth, and the Marian Gardens.

The Shrine of St. Therese on a forested islet west of Juneau

Glacier Bay National Park ⑭

The 5,000-sq mile (13,000-sq km) area surrounding Glacier Bay was designated a National Park in 1980 and declared a UNESCO World Heritage Site in 1992. Historically, the park has served as an open-air laboratory for studies on the recolonization of formerly glaciated lands by plants and wildlife. For visitors, Glacier Bay is best known for its tidewater glaciers and deep fjords, and is also a popular destination for wildlife enthusiasts. Its forests and alpine areas are home to bears and mountain goats, while in the summer, its waters are alive with migrating humpback whales. Although most visitors take an organized cruise, kayaking is also an enjoyable option.

LOCATOR MAP

☐ Glacier Bay National Park

— - International border

0 km   10

0 miles   10

★ **Margerie Glacier**
Of the dozen tidewater glaciers that calve into the bay, Margerie Glacier is the most visited. It was once a tributary of the Grand Pacific Glacier, which has retreated 70 miles (112 km) in the past 200 years.

★ **Fairweather Range**
The forbidding Fairweather Range, which culminates at the 15,300-ft (4,590-m) high Mount Fairweather, was the source of the ice that created the park's deeply indented fjords. The range continues to feed the glaciers on the western peninsula of the park.

STAR SIGHTS

★ Margerie Glacier

★ Fairweather Range

★ Bartlett Cove

For hotels and restaurants in this region see pp244–7 and pp259–61

Whale-Watching at Glacier Bay

Black and white killer whales (orcas), humpback whales, and fast-swimming minke whales can frequently be spotted. As boats are not allowed within 500 yards (450 m) of the whales, it is worth carrying binoculars.

★ Bartlett Cove

Several easy hikes are available around Bartlett Cove, the only developed area within the park. It has a visitor center, park headquarters, a lodge, and a campground.

EXPLORING THE PARK

While short, easy hikes loop through the forests around Bartlett Cove, the best views of Glacier Bay are from the water, and most visitors see the park either on cruises or organized boat tours that typically go up to the face of Margerie and Grand Pacific Glaciers. Smaller boats provide drop-off services for people wishing to explore on their own.

Gustavus

The village of Gustavus, just outside the southeast corner of the park, prospered in the 1920s as a fishing port. It offers accommodation and other visitor services, and operators here run tours and rent kayaks for private trips.

Former officers' quarters at Fort Seward, Haines

Haines ⑮

75 miles (120 km) N of Juneau. **Road Map** E4. 🏚 1,400. ✈ to Juneau & Skagway. 🚢 ⓘ 122 2nd Ave, 766-2234. 🎪 Great Alaska Craft Beer & Home Brew Festival (3rd week of Apr), Southeast Alaska State Fair (3rd week of Aug), Alaska Bald Eagle Festival (2nd week of Nov). www.haines.ak.us

Founded by Presbyterian missionaries in 1881, Haines sits on a site known to the indigenous peoples as Dei-Shu, or "end of the trail."

Early residents were quick to take advantage of the plentiful fish in adjacent Lynn Canal, the country's deepest and longest fjord. By 1900, commercial fishing and canning had grown into major enterprises. The building of Fort Seward brought further economic benefits. In 1939, a sawmill was developed to support a nascent timber industry.

was the state's first permanent army post and the mainstay of Haines' economy. Locally refered to as Chilkoot Barracks to avoid confusion with the town of Seward *(see pp98–9)*, the fort was used as a training base during the two World Wars. Decommissioned in 1947, it was bought by five World War II veterans who set up a series of small businesses. Today, it houses art galleries, restaurants, a replica Tlingit clan house, and a center for Native arts.

Haines boasts a mild climate and spectacular setting and over the years has attracted many artists and entrepreneurs. In addition to several galleries and a renowned microbrewery, it has a winery that makes unusual wines from fireweed, birch sap, and onions. There are excellent hiking trails around town, including the Mount Ripinsky and Mount Riley Trails and the easy 2-mile (4-km) Battery Point Trail.

🏛 Fort Seward

⏰ 24 hrs. 🔢 ⌾
Named for William H. Seward, President Andrew Johnson's Secretary of State who instigated the purchase of Alaska, Fort Seward was built in 1903. Complete with barracks, officers' quarters, carpentry shops, and smithies, the fort

Indigenous copper shield

🏛 Sheldon Museum

11 Main St. **Tel** 766-2366. ⭘ mid-May–Sep: 10am–5pm Mon–Fri; Oct–mid–May: 8am–5pm Mon–Fri. 🧇 ⎆ www.sheldonmuseum.org
Established in 1924, the museum grew around a private collection of artifacts from the early days of European settlement in the upper Chilkat Inlet area. The original collection has been augmented by relics from the Gold Rush era and the fishing and timber industries, as well as by Chilkat blankets, basketry, and a single-log dugout canoe. The area's Russian history is reflected in colorfully painted Russian trunks. There are also shipping artifacts, including an old lens from Lynn Canal's Eldred Rock Lighthouse.

Eldred Rock Lighthouse sitting in the middle of spectacular Lynn Canal

Model woodcarver at the Hammer Museum

🏛 Hammer Museum

108 Main St. **Tel** 766-2374. ☐ *mid May–early Nov: 10am–5pm Mon–Fri; all other times: by appt.* ● *public hols.* 🖼 🍴 **www.** hammermuseum.org

The Hammer Museum is Alaska's contribution to the world's most unique museums. Over 1,500 hammers of varying sizes are on display, painstakingly collected by owner Dave Pahl. They served a variety of purposes, from blacksmithing and mining to cracking nuts and stunning cattle. Highlights include Colonial-era and Industrial Revolution hammers, an 800-year-old Tlingit slave-killing hammer found on a Southeast Alaska beach, all put in historical context. There are also some model woodcarvers salvaged from the Smithsonian Institution in Washington, DC. Visitors are invited to identify hammers whose purpose is not yet known.

🏔 Mount Ripinsky

Rising above Haines, the 3,610-ft (1,083-m) Mount Ripinsky affords the best view over the town and its stunning hinterlands, extending as far as Skagway and almost to Juneau. North of the town center, from the trailhead at Young Road, a trail winds up the peak. Climbing gently for about 3 miles (5 km), it then ascends steeply through alpine meadows to the summit. Hikers should carry plenty of water, and allow at least seven hours for the strenuous round trip. Overnight camping is also possible beyond the North Summit. The less energetic can opt for an easier hike up 1,760-ft (528-m) Mount Riley, which is accessed by a trail from Mud Bay Road near Fort Seward, or along a spur trail from the Battery Point Trail that starts at the end of Beach Road, south of the town center.

🦅 Chilkat Bald Eagle Preserve

Mile 9.4 to Mile 25, Haines Cut-Off. 🚌 ♿ *limited.* **American Bald Eagle Foundation Center** 113 Haines Rd at 2nd Ave. **Tel** 766-3094. ☐ *late May–Aug: 9am–6pm Mon–Fri; 1–5pm Sat & Sun.* 🖼 ♿ 🎫 **www.**baldeagles.org

In the summer, Haines hosts a modest number of bald eagles that can be seen at the waterfront or along streams. In October and November, however, cottonwood trees along the Chilkat and Klehini River valleys in the 75-sq mile (195-sq km) Chilkat Bald Eagle Preserve fill with up to 3,500 eagles, who arrive to feed on Alaska's last salmon run after most other waterways have frozen solid. Within the preserve, several pull-offs along the Haines Cut-Off afford excellent viewing of this phenomenon, known as the Gathering of the Eagles, which has inspired Haines' annual Alaska Bald Eagle Festival.

Summer visitors who will miss this November event can stop by the **American Bald Eagle Foundation Center** in town, only 20 miles (32 km) away from the preserve. This non-profit foundation is dedicated to the protection and preservation of bald eagles. Using a diorama of the Chilkat Preserve, the center gives visitors a better understanding of how the eagles live in a delicate balance with their environment. The center also has a screening room where visitors can watch videos of the Gathering of the Eagles.

BALD EAGLES

The national bird of the US, the bald eagle (*Haliaeetus lucocephalus*) is the only eagle unique to North America. In this case, the word "bald" means not hairless, but white, a reference to its distinctive head color. In 1963, the bald eagle population in the Lower 48 states included just 417 breeding pairs, but by 2004 stringent conservation measures had raised that number to about 10,000 pairs. Currently, North America is home to 100,000 bald eagles – about half of which live in Alaska – leading the US Fish and Wildlife Service to suggest that they can be removed

Bald eagle taking flight from a tree

from the official threatened species list. While the Bald Eagle Protection Act makes it illegal to transport, trade, or possess any part of an eagle without a permit, indigenous peoples are allowed to use eagle feathers in their traditional dresses and ceremonies.

Skagway ⑯

After pioneers George Washington Carmack, Skookum Jim Mason, and Dawson Charlie discovered gold in the Klondike in the late 1890s, steamboat captain William Moore founded Skagway as a gateway to the goldfields. Over 30,000 prospectors passed through in the first year, seeking supplies and entertainment, and helping the town to boom. The 1900 completion of the White Pass and Yukon Route Railroad (WP&YR) made the trip easier, but the Gold Rush was already subsiding. Skagway was revived in the 1940s as an Alaska Highway construction staging camp, and today, the town's economy is driven mainly by tourism.

LOCATOR MAP

— Area illustrated

★ Arctic Brotherhood Hall
The front of this building, housing the Skagway Visitor Information Center, is decorated with thousands of pieces of driftwood.

★ Red Onion Saloon
The 1898 Red Onion still retains the bar from the days when it served as a saloon and brothel. It offers the Brothel Tour, conducted by appropriately clad young ladies.

Soapy Smith's Saloon

Chilkoot Trail Center

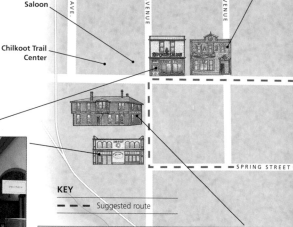

STATE STREET

1ST AVE.

2ND AVENUE

3RD AVENUE

SPRING STREET

KEY

— — — Suggested route

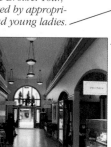

White Pass and Yukon Route Railroad Depot
In the summer, daily trains set off from here, offering journeys through stunning scenery.

STAR SIGHTS

★ Arctic Brotherhood Hall

★ Red Onion Saloon

★ Skagway Museum

Klondike Gold Rush NHP Visitors' Center
Now the Klondike Gold Rush National Historical Park Visitors' Center, the original WP&YR depot, built using packing crates and salvaged lumber, was hurriedly constructed in 1898 to handle the flood of prospectors.

Corrington Museum
Built in 1975, the Corrington Building houses an ivory gift shop and displays Native basketry, a mammoth tusk, and a collection of walrus ivory scrimshaw.

VISITORS' CHECKLIST

15 miles (24 km) NE of Haines.
Road Map E4. 🏠 *850*. ✈ *from Juneau and Haines.* 🚢 *from Fraser and Bennett Lake, BC (Canada).* 🚌 *from Fraser, BC (Canada).* 🚐 *from Haines and Juneau.* 🛈 *Broadway, between 2nd & 3rd Aves., 983-2854* 🎊 *Soapy Smith's Wake (Jul 8).* **www.**skagway.org **White Pass and Yukon Route Railroad** 2nd Ave. **Tel** *983-7217, (800) 343-7373.* **www.**wpyr.com

Eagle's Hall, built in 1898, hosts the Days of '98 show, re-creating the Frank Reid-Soapy Smith shootout.

Nome Saloon, a Gold Rush drinking hall, now houses a jewelry shop.

Library

STATE STREET

7TH AVENUE

8TH AVENUE

BROADWAY

5TH AVENUE

6TH AVENUE

Mollie Walsh Park

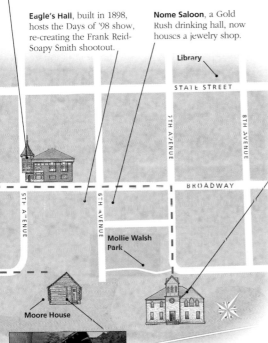

Moore House

★ Skagway Museum
The 1899 faux-Gothic McCabe College first functioned as a private school, then the Federal Courthouse, jail, and Town Hall. It now houses the town museum, with displays on the Gold Rush, local Tlingit culture, and the infamous Soapy Smith.

0 meters	100
0 yards	100

Moore Cabin
Built in 1888 by Captain Moore, the town's founder, this is Skagway's oldest building. Its walls are papered with newspapers from the late 1800s.

SOAPY SMITH

Born Jefferson Randolph Smith in Georgia in 1860, Soapy earned his nickname after a swindle involving soap. In 1896, he arrived in Skagway, opened a saloon, and set himself up as an underworld boss and local philanthropist. His most notorious scams included a phony freight company and a fake telegraph office that would "wire" money across non-existent wires. In 1898, this uncrowned "king" of Skagway was killed after a shootout with city surveyor Frank Reid.

Historic image of Soapy Smith at the bar of his saloon

Gold Rush Routes ⑰

Along the old Gold Rush trail from Skagway, three separate routes link the port with the interior. The most famous is the Chilkoot Trail, starting at the site of Dyea and crossing Chilkoot Pass to Bennett Lake in Canada's British Columbia. Hikers can return by the narrow-gauge 1898 White Pass and Yukon Route Railroad, which runs from Skagway past vertical cliffs, over old bridges, and through tunnels from sea level to the 2,865-ft (860-m) high White Pass in just 20 miles (32 km). The third route, the picturesque Klondike Highway, is a good driving route that passes spectacular scenery on the opposite side of the Skagway River from the railway and continues to the Yukon Territory.

Rafting on the Chilkoot River at Dyea near Skagway

Lindeman ④

Now a campsite, Lindeman was a bustling lakeside tent town of 4,000 during the Gold Rush. While stampeders and their gear were carried by a steamer and barges across the lake in the summer, they had to walk across the frozen lake in the winter.

Chilkoot Pass ③

After struggling up the 3,525-ft (1,058-m) Chilkoot Pass on the US-Canada border, hikers can look forward to a down-hill run all the way to Bennett Lake. During the Gold Rush, stampeders crossing the border had to stop here to pay customs duties to the Royal Canadian Mounted Police.

Canyon City ②

In 1898, Canyon City had 1,500 residents and 24 businesses, but the town had disappeared within two years. All that is left today is the remains of a boiler once owned by a transportation company.

Dyea ①

Although it rivaled Skagway as Alaska's largest town during the Gold Rush (see pp52–3), nothing remains of Dyea but a few harbor pilings, a cemetery, and the wooden frontage of a land office. Thousands of prospectors, also called stampeders, set off from Dyea for the Klondike. Today, it is the trailhead for the Chilkoot Trail.

Mount Hoffman
6,080 ft

②

US
(ALA

Irene
Glacier

Mount Yeatman
5,670 ft

Mount Carmack
6,229 ft

①

Goat
Lake

⑧

Skagway

0 km   2

0 miles   2

Bennett Lake, British Columbia ⑤
In the winter of 1897, a town of over 20,000 people sprang up at Bennett Lake, as stampeders waited for the ice to break up. In May 1898, in the week after the thaw, about 7,000 boats set off for the goldfields. For modern hikers, the lake is the end of the Chilkoot Trail.

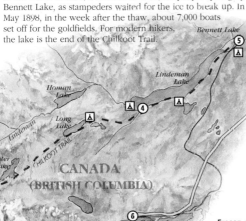

TIPS FOR WALKERS

Starting point: Dyea. Hikers returning on the WP&YR Railroad must pre-book at 983-2217.
Length: the Chilkoot Trail is 35 miles (56 km) and takes three to five days to hike.
Getting there: 9 miles (14 km) N of Skagway on Dyea Rd. There is a private bus service to Dyea.
Permits: needed for back-country travel; available at the Chilkoot Trail Center, Broadway & 1st Ave, Skagway.
Immigration: hikers must carry passports and clear Customs at the Chilkoot Trail Center, Skagway. Tel 983-9234.
www.nps.gov/klgo

KEY

🅰	Campground
🏠	Public use cabin
===	Klondike Highway
--	Chilkoot Trail
—	White Pass and Yukon Route Railroad
⬛⬛	International border
△	Peak

Fraser, near Bernard Lake ⑥
Beside beautiful Bernard Lake in an alpine valley, Fraser is a stop on the modern White Pass and Yukon Route Railroad. It also serves as Canada's Customs and Immigration post for travelers on both the railway and the Klondike Highway.

Denver ⑧
At Denver, the railway line crosses the east fork of the Skagway River. Here, the US Forest Service rents out a public use cabin sited in a historic railway caboose.

White Pass ⑦
About 7 miles (11 km) from Fraser, the railway crosses White Pass where, during the Gold Rush, Canadian police checked the grubstakes of stampeders on the White Pass Route. The modern trains, made up of 1890s rolling stock, are pulled by either steam or diesel locomotives.

Haines Cut-Off Tour ⑱

The scenic 146-mile (234-km) Haines Cut-Off, or Haines Highway, links Haines with the Alaska Highway. From Haines, the route follows the Chilkat and Klehini Rivers northward. Near the Canadian border, the road climbs steeply, gaining 3,000 ft (900 m) over 18 miles (29 km). For the next 50 miles (80 km), the road passes through the high alpine country of northern British Columbia before dropping into lake-studded forests to join the Alaska Highway at Haines Junction.

TIPS FOR DRIVERS

Starting point: Haines.
Length: 146 miles (234 km).
Stopping-off points: there is excellent whitewater rafting at Tatshenshini-Alsek Park at Dalton Post off the Haines Cut-Off. An overlook at Mile 78 offers photo opportunities. Dezadeash Lake at Mile 114 has primitive campsites.

KEY

▬▬ Alaska Highway
▬▬ Tour
═══ Major road
▪▬▪ International border
▬ ▬ Provincial border
△ Peak

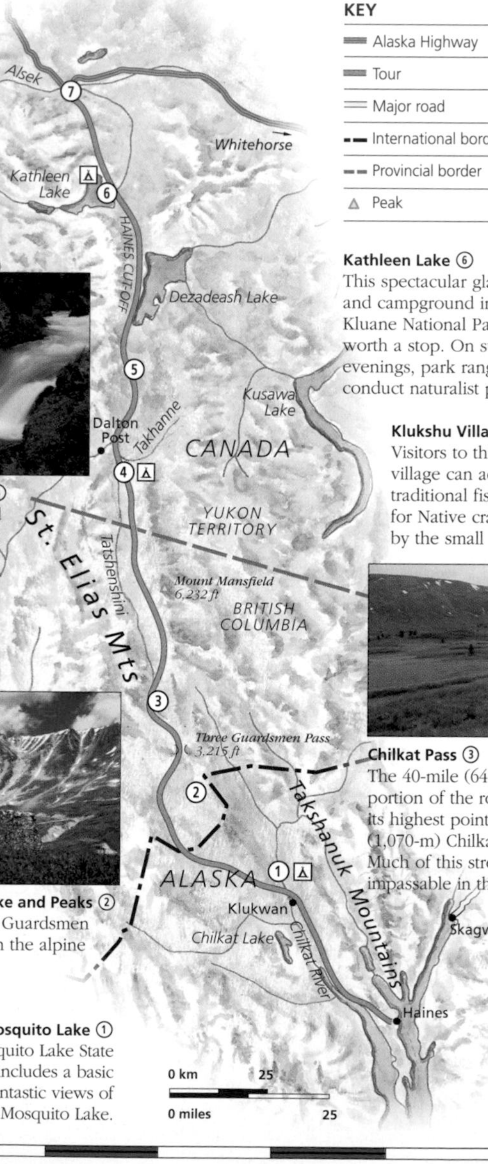

Haines Junction ⑦
This service center appeared in 1942 with the construction of the Alaska Highway, and is a staging point for trips into Kluane National Park.

Kathleen Lake ⑥
This spectacular glacier-fed lake and campground in Canada's Kluane National Park are well worth a stop. On summer evenings, park rangers often conduct naturalist programs.

Klukshu Village ⑤
Visitors to this indigenous village can admire the traditional fish traps, shop for Native crafts, and stop by the small museum.

Million Dollar Falls ④
Boardwalk trails and viewing platforms at the Million Dollar Falls campground provide great views of the tumbling Takhanne River.

Chilkat Pass ③
The 40-mile (64-km) alpine portion of the route reaches its highest point at 3,510-ft (1,070-m) Chilkat Pass. Much of this stretch may be impassable in the winter.

Three Guardsmen Lake and Peaks ②
The imposing Three Guardsmen Lake and Peaks lie in the alpine portion of the route.

Mosquito Lake ①
The small Mosquito Lake State Recreation Site includes a basic campground with fantastic views of high peaks across Mosquito Lake.

0 km   25
0 miles   25

Map labels: Alsek, Whitehorse, Kathleen Lake, HAINES CUT-OFF, Dezadeash Lake, Kusawa Lake, Dalton Post, Takhanne, CANADA, Tatshenshini, YUKON TERRITORY, St. Elias Mts, Mount Mansfield 6,232 ft, BRITISH COLUMBIA, Three Guardsmen Pass 3,215 ft, Takshanuk Mountains, ALASKA, Klukwan, Chilkat Lake, Chilkat River, Skagway, Haines

For hotels and restaurants in this region see pp244–7 and pp259–61

Tatshenshini-Alsek Rivers ⑲

Road Map E4.
Permits *mandatory, contact the Visitor Reception Center, Haines Junction, YT.* **www**.nps.gov/glba/planyourvisit/rafting.htm

The Tatshenshini River and its tributary, the Alsek, which are considered two of the world's best whitewater rafting and kayaking rivers, rise in the St. Elias Range of British Columbia and the Yukon Territory, respectively. From there, they flow 160 miles (256 km) through canyons and rapids and past numerous glaciers to the coast at the northern end of Glacier Bay National Park *(see pp146–7)*. A relatively clear stream, the Tatshenshini supports productive salmon runs, and visitors to Klukshu can see how the First Nations once caught salmon with fish traps and dried them for use in the winter.

The usual put-in site for the glacial Alsek is near Haines Junction, while Tatshenshini rafters put in at Dalton Post, near the Yukon Territory-British Columbia border. Most rafters run the rivers with commercial operators and experienced guides. For private trips on the Alsek, rafters need a wilderness permit from Canada's Kluane National Park. Rafters on both rivers must also obtain a permit for Glacier Bay National Park, citing a pre-specified take-out

Floating houses in Yakutat's harbor with Mount Augusta in the distance

time from Dry Bay at the mouth of the Tatshenshini, which will require a bush flight to Haines or Yakutat.

Rafters on the Alsek should be aware that the 10-mile (16-km) stretch through Turnback Canyon in British Columbia presents serious whitewater, and must be bypassed using a pre-organized helicopter portage. A highlight is the paddle past the icebergs of Alsek Glacier. There are no services along the way, so river runners need to be fully self-sufficient.

Yakutat ⑳

225 miles (362 km) NE of Juneau.
Road Map E4. 690.
 Yakutat Chamber of Commerce 784-3933. *Fairweather Days (Aug).* **www**.yakutatalaska.com

Located on the Gulf of Alaska at the southern edge of Wrangell-St. Elias National Park *(see pp192–3)*, Yakutat is

just 70 miles (110 km) from the 18,008-ft (5,490 m) Mount St. Elias, the second highest peak in the US.

The Russians were among the first outsiders in Yakutat, whose name means "where the canoes rest" in the Tlingit language. In 1805, the Russian-American Company built a fur trading post here, but it was destroyed by the Tlingit, who had been denied access to their traditional hunting and fishing lands. In 1886, minor gold deposits were discovered in the beach sands, but the area's economy took off only in 1903, when a cannery, sawmill, and railroad were established. Yakutat also served as a garrison and airstrip during World War II.

Due to its remote location, modern Yakutat sees few casual visitors. However, it has been discovered by fly-fishermen who come for steelhead and surfers who head to **Cannon Beach**, a popular place to surf the waves. The town also enjoys good views of a host of peaks and glaciers, including the galloping **Hubbard Glacier** *(see p27)* and the vast **Malaspina Glacier**, which is one of the largest in North America. Yakutat is a good base for exploring the southeast corner of Wrangell-St. Elias National Park, while the Russell Fjord Wilderness, which includes Harlequin Lake and Yakutat Glacier, is a 26-mile (42-km) drive away.

Rafters passing through a calm section of the Tatshenshini River

WESTERN INTERIOR ALASKA

The landscape of the sparsely populated Western Interior is covered with boreal forests, muskeg, taiga, and lakes. Dominated by a continental climate that creates the state's greatest climatic extremes, the region enjoys long summer days with almost round-the-clock sunlight and dramatic storms, and long, cold winter nights illuminated by the undulating colors of the aurora borealis.

This territory was first settled by Native Athabaskan peoples who, despite its exceedingly harsh environment, found it a region rich in wildlife and capable of providing meat for food, and skins for clothing and shelter during the bitterly cold winters. While much of the land is deemed unproductive by modern definitions, the first Europeans in the area, like the Athabaskans before them, managed to eke out a living in these bleak and difficult conditions. These pioneers, including early 20th-century prospectors near Fairbanks, built up a semblance of civilization in what was then considered the country's last frontier.

By the 1920s, engineers were using dredges to exploit deep seams of gold after placer gold *(see p53)* started to play out. World War II boosted the region's fluctuating fortunes and population, with huge military bases being set up to counter the Japanese threat *(see p55)*. There was another growth spurt in the 1970s when Fairbanks was chosen as the logistical headquarters of the Trans-Alaska Pipeline.

Across the heart of the region stretches the massive Alaska Range, crowned by Mount McKinley. Located within the popular Denali National Park, the peak is now the area's main draw. Denali and various state parks provide excellent hiking and wildlife viewing. Winter activities range from Nordic skiing to soaking in hot springs and viewing the aurora. Attractive towns, including Fairbanks, Alaska's second-largest city, historic gold dredges, and whitewater rafting all combine to draw steadily increasing numbers of visitors.

Brilliant aurora borealis undulating across the sky

◁ A Riverboat Discovery cruise on the Chena River near Fairbanks

Exploring Western Interior Alaska

Dominating the landscape of the Western Interior is Mount McKinley, North America's highest mountain. Popular Denali National Park, home of the massive peak, is on the itinerary of nearly every visitor to the state. Beyond Denali, summer visitors also enjoy Denali State Park, the rustic little town of Talkeetna, and the excellent museums of Fairbanks. The region also contains such little-known gems as Nancy Lake State Recreation Area to the south and Chena Hot Springs to the north. The uncrowded and mostly untarred Elliott, Steese, and Denali Highways, which lead into the heart of the northern wilderness, make not-to-be-missed drives.

Rafting the Nenana on the border of Denali National Park

KEY

▬▬	Alaska Highway
▬▬	Highway
▬▬	Minor road
───	Alaska Railroad
△	Peak

SIGHTS AT A GLANCE

Towns and Cities
Big Lake ❶
Cantwell ❼
Denali Park ❿
Ester ⓮
Fairbanks ⓯
Healy ⓬
Houston ❷
Nenana ⓭
Talkeetna ❺
Willow ❹

National and State Parks
Denali National Park pp166–9 ❾
Denali State Park ❻
Nancy Lake State Recreation
  Area ❸

Area of Natural Beauty
Nenana River ⓫

Tours
Denali Highway Tour p165 ❽
Steese Highway Tour p179 ⓰

Prudhoe Bay
Stever Village
DALTON HIGHWAY
△ Mount Tozi 5,500 ft
Rampart
Livengoo
⓫
Tanana
ELLIOT HIGHWAY
Minto
Yukon
Manley Hot Springs
Chatan
Tanana
Tolovana
NENANA ⓭
Anderson
Nenana
HEALY
DENALI ✕ 🏔 🚶 ⛺ ❾
Kantishna
NATIONAL
Toklat
Wonder Lake
DENAL PAR
CANTWEL ✕
PARK
Mount McKinley (Denali) 20,320 ft △
Mount Foraker 17,344 ft △
✕ 🏔 🚶 ❻
DENALI STATE
❸
PARK
Petersville
🏛
TALKEETNA ❺
Yentna
Trapper Creek
Mont Creek
Skwentna
WILLOW
🏕 ❹
NANCY LAKE STATE ❸ ❷
RECREATION AREA
❶ W
HOUSTON **BIG LAKE**

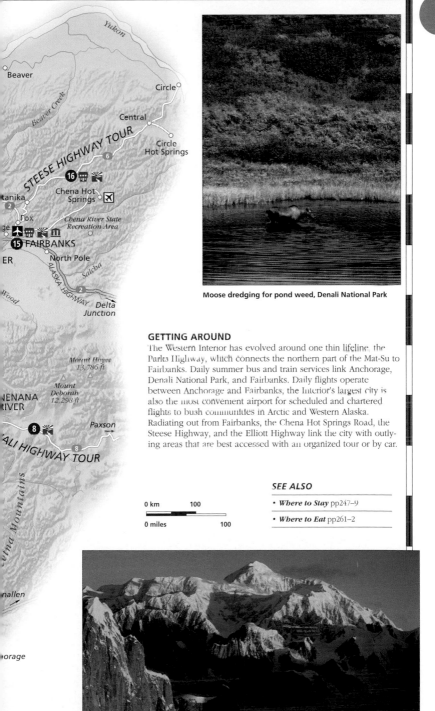

Moose dredging for pond weed, Denali National Park

GETTING AROUND
The Western Interior has evolved around one thin lifeline, the Parks Highway, which connects the northern part of the Mat-Su to Fairbanks. Daily summer bus and train services link Anchorage, Denali National Park, and Fairbanks. Daily flights operate between Anchorage and Fairbanks, the Interior's largest city is also the most convenient airport for scheduled and chartered flights to bush communities in Arctic and Western Alaska. Radiating out from Fairbanks, the Chena Hot Springs Road, the Steese Highway, and the Elliott Highway link the city with outlying areas that are best accessed with an organized tour or by car.

0 km   100
0 miles   100

SEE ALSO
• *Where to Stay* pp247–9
• *Where to Eat* pp261–2

A floatplane flying across Mount McKinley and the Alaska Range

Cottages lining the shoreline along Big Lake

Big Lake ❶

60 miles (96 km) N of Anchorage.
Road Map E3. 🏃 *2,200.* 🚗
🛈 *892-6109.* 🎊 *Fall Festival
Chili Cook-Off (mid-Sep).*
www.biglakechamber.org

Dubbed Alaska's Year Round
Playground, Big Lake lives up
to the moniker. In the summer,
the lake echoes with the roars
of motorboats, floatplanes, jet
skis, and fireworks, while in
the winter, it buzzes as snowmachiners take to the trails.
  While the community itself
is small, most of the surrounding lakes are lined with
the vacation cabins of city
dwellers trying to get away
to the outdoors. However, in
contrast to Big Lake's constant
hum of activity, many of these
lakes, including the Papoose
Twins, Big Beaver Lake, and
Horseshoe Lake, are quieter.
Nearly all have public boat
launches that offer access to
quiet sailing, kayaking, and
canoeing, as well as the
chance to view otters, muskrats, and nesting waterfowl.
  Devastating forest fires in
1996 burned much of the
area, which now provides a
first-hand look at the regeneration of the boreal forest.

Houston ❷

60 miles (96 km) N of Anchorage.
Road Map E3. 🏃 *1,300.*
🚌 *Anchorage–Fairbanks.*

Stretched out along the Parks
Highway, this small service
center is the only place in the
Matanuska-Susitna Valley

where fireworks can be
purchased legally. They are
banned in some parts of the
state, including Anchorage
and much of the Mat-Su, due
to the possibility of setting
wildfires. Fireworks stands are
permitted in only one area
near the southern end of the
town, and it is worth visiting
for their advertising alone. The
most imaginative is Gorilla
Fireworks, featuring enormous inflatable gorillas and a
range of psychedelic vehicles.

Nancy Lake State Recreation Area ❸

Nancy Lake Parkway, Mile 67.3 Parks
Hwy. **Road Map** E3. 🚗 🛈 *Nancy
Lake Ranger Station, 495-6273.* 📷
🏕 🏕 **www**.alaskastateparks.org

The Susitna Valley landscape
is dominated by the winding
ridges and small hills – eskers
and drumlins – left behind by
retreating glaciers. Here, the
low-lying bogs, forested
slopes, and lakes of Nancy

Lake State Recreation Area
provide a serene environment
for canoeing, fishing, and
wildlife watching. The highlight is the two-day **Lynx Lake
Loop** canoe trail, which winds
through 14 lakes and ponds.
Canoes can be rented at South
Rolly Lake in the summer.
Many lakes in this area have
beaver lodges and dams, and
every lake has at least one pair
of loons, whose haunting calls
punctuate summer evenings.
During the winter, the park's
trails and canoe route become
excellent Nordic ski trails and
snowmachine routes.

Willow ❹

70 miles (113 km) N of Anchorage.
Road Map E3. 🏃 *500.*
🚌 *Anchorage–Fairbanks.*

Founded in 1897 after the
discovery of gold in the
Talkeetna Mountains, Willow
flourished until the 1940s,
when mining stopped and the
town lapsed into obscurity.
It gained national visibility in
1976, when voters selected it
as their new state capital.
Investment poured in, land
prices skyrocketed, and
myriad plans surfaced for
the new "capital in the
wilderness." The hype
evaporated after a 1982
referendum in which
Alaskans declined to fund
the predicted costs of the
move from Juneau. The
town now serves as a
Parks Highway snack
stop, and, more importantly,
as the restart location for
the Iditarod *(see p45).*

Small roadside museum on the Parks Highway at Willow

The Boreal Forest

Most of Interior Alaska is cloaked in the vast circumpolar boreal forest that also covers much of subarctic Canada, northwestern Russia, Scandinavia, and Siberia. In hilly or well-drained regions, the term "boreal forest" includes dry lands, such as the rolling country around Fairbanks, which are typically covered in white or black spruce and birch. This region also includes

Alaskan blueberries

taiga, "little sticks" in Russian, which refers to the stick-like black spruce forest that dominates the typically boggy and low-lying muskeg that prevails in much of the Alaska's Interior. These rich, lake dotted lands produce a wealth of berries and are home to most of Alaska's lynx, bears, and forest-dwelling rodents such as beavers, porcupines, martens, and ermines.

Shrubs, mosses, and lichens form the ground cover beneath the trees.

Spruce, birch, and aspen are well-adapted to the typically thin topsoil.

BOREAL FAUNA

At different stages in its regrowth after a wildfire, the boreal forest supports a changing succession of wildlife. Northern hawk owls are among the first to inhabit the forest, followed by red foxes, martens, and spruce hens as the forest matures.

Black-capped chickadees, *tiny song birds, do not migrate in the winter and are evident all year round.*

Red squirrels *spend summer cutting and storing green spruce cones. They nest in trees, using ground burrows mostly as caches.*

Spruce hens, *marked by mottled feathers, usually nest at the base of a spruce tree.*

Northern hawk owls *are atypical of most owls because they hunt during the day, preying on voles, mice, and occasionally small birds.*

Martens, *who feed mainly on voles, have non-retractable claws, used for climbing as well as holding prey.*

Red foxes *are recognized by their white-tipped tails and black "stockings." These omnivores are found across the Alaskan Interior in hilly, forested country.*

Talkeetna 🟠

114 miles (183 km) N of Anchorage.
Road Map E3. 🎿 350. ✈
🚉 Anchorage–Fairbanks. 🚌
Anchorage–Fairbanks. 🛈 Parks Hwy
& Talkeetna Spur Rd, 733-2688.
🎭 Talkeetna Moose Dropping
Festival (2nd weekend in Jul),
Talkeetna Bluegrass Festival (1st
weekend in Aug), Wilderness
Woman (1st weekend in Dec).
www.talkeetnadenali.com

Climbers planning a trip at the Talkeetna Ranger Station

Talkeetna, meaning "meeting of the rivers" in the local Athabaskan language, began in 1896 as a trading post and eventually grew into a riverboat port supplying the 1910 Susitna Valley Gold Rush. There was a second wave of development when the Alaska Engineering Commission set up its headquarters here during the construction of the Alaska Railroad. Modern growth has been fueled by its favorable location near the spectacular Mount McKinley.

Any illusions of Talkeetna being the prototype of a small, quiet, pioneer town, will be quickly dispelled by the summer crowds. Although the town was bypassed by the Parks Highway when it was

AIRCRAFT CROSSING

Road sign, Talkeetna

built in the early 1970s, it still attracts a lot of traveler traffic: busloads of tourists admire its old-fashioned air, young backpackers wonder how to settle in permanently, and prospective climbers hope to scale Mount McKinley. Among the most popular activities in town are flight-seeing trips over Mount McKinley and touring the junction of the Susitna, Talkeetna, and Chulitna Rivers with **Mahay's Riverboat Service**. Mahay's also runs Denali wilderness tours and fishing tours on the Talkeetna River.

Mahay's Riverboat Service
Main St, Talkeetna. **Tel** (800) 736-2210. www.mahaysriverboat.com

Talkeetna Ranger Station
1st & B Sts. **Tel** 733-2231. 🕐 mid-Apr–early Sep: 8am–6pm daily; winter: 8am–4:30pm Mon–Fri. ♿ www.nps.gov/dena/planyourvisit/mountaineering.html
Maintained by the National Park Service, this ranger station provides year-round information for prospective climbers of Mount McKinley and other peaks of the Alaska Range. The staff also mails out free information on mountaineering regulations and fees. Inside, there is a reference library of books and maps on mountaineering and Mount McKinley. Rangers conduct free orientation programs for climbing expeditions, as well as general interest programs at the Talkeetna Historical Society Museum and the Talkeetna Alaskan Lodge.

🏛 **Talkeetna Historical Society Museum**
Off 1st St. **Tel** 733-2487. 🕐 summer: 10am–6pm daily; winter: by appointment. 🎫 www.talkeetnahistoricalsociety.org
Located next to the old airstrip, the Talkeetna Historical Society Museum consists of a complex of seven buildings. The main displays are housed in the red 1937 **Schoolhouse**, which had rooms for teachers on the floor above. Used as a school until 1971, it became the museum headquarters three years later. Today, it is packed with pioneer artifacts, photographs, and articles on old Talkeetna, including relics of bush pilot Don Sheldon and mountaineer Ray Genet.

The museum also includes the 1933 **Railroad Depot**, complete with a historic ticket

Climbers and bush plane on Kahiltna Glacier

MOUNTAINEERS AND GLACIER PILOTS

Mount McKinley, looming on the horizon, is Talkeetna's main draw. In 1947, Bradford and Barbara Washburn pioneered the West Buttress Route, which is the standard route in use today. Starting with a flight to the 7,200-ft (2,160-m) level of Kahiltna Glacier, it eliminates a long walk on Muldrow Glacier from McKinley's northern slope. Talkeetna legend Ray Genet became the first McKinley guide, and his friend Don Sheldon ferried climbers to and from Kahiltna Glacier. Today, dozens of Talkeetna pilots fly climbers, skiers, and sightseers to McKinley's slopes.

office, which replaced the original 1920s structure that burned to the ground. It was moved from the railway yard to its present location in 1990. The 1923 **Railroad Section House** was originally the home of the railway foreman and his family and crew. It now houses a mountaineering exhibit, including a 12-sq ft (3.5-sq m) scale model of Mount McKinley that is based on aerial photographs taken by renowned photographer, Bradford Washburn.

The town's oldest building, the 1916 **Ole Dahl Cabin**, the home of miner and barber Ole Dahl, was also salvaged by the museum, as were the 1924 **Harry Robb Cabin** and the 1920s **stables** operated by Belle McDonald.

🚩 Fairview Inn
Main & D Sts. *Tel 733-2423*.
www.denali-fairview.com
Built by Ben Nauman in 1923 as the overnight stop on the Alaska Railroad between Seward and Fairbanks, the Fairview Inn holds the laudable distinction of having possessed Talkeetna's first bathtub. Decorated with antlers, pelts, and local memorabilia, it was a community hall and drinking den for both locals and visitors. In 2003, it was decreed that no building

in downtown Talkeetna could be higher than the inn. After closing briefly, the Fairview reopened in 2006 and is now smoke-free. It is a great spot to meet locals and climbers, and to enjoy the occasional live band.

🚩 Nagley's Store
D & Main Sts. *Tel 733 3663.*
www.nagleysstore.com
Across the street from the Fairview Inn, Nagley's Store is one of Talkeetna's most charming buildings. Horace Nagley ran a shop at Susitna Station on the Big Su (the Susitna River), but dismantled it and reconstructed it on the Talkeetna riverfront between 1917 and 1921. In 1945, it was moved again on log rollers to its current site. Amazingly, it stayed open during the move. The store houses the town's only grocery and general store. Farther down Main Street is

Fairview Inn sign, downtown Talkeetna

the 1930s **Ole Dahl Cabin No. 2**, the home of miner Ole Dahl, the 1930s Norwegian-style **Helmer Ronning House**, and the 1917 **Frank Lee Cabin and Barn**, now housing the popular Talkeetna Roadhouse.

🚩 Talkeetna Cemetery
2nd & F Sts.
Talkeetna's quiet cemetery would be of little interest to visitors if it were not for the memorial commemorating climbers who have died on Mount McKinley over the years. It is a sobering reminder to those setting out that the mountain and its weather can be harsh opponents and are not to be taken lightly. Among the headstones is that of Talkeetna glacier pilot Don Sheldon, whose exploits are immortalized in the book, *Wager with the Wind*. He died in 1975 at the age of 56. Talkeetna's other hero, Ray Genet, is missing here as he was lost on Mount Everest in 1979 at the age of 48 and his body was never found.

McKinley Climbers Memorial in Talkeetna's wooded cemetery

Historic Nagley's Store in downtown Talkeetna

The enormous concrete Igloo at Mile 188.5 of the Parks Highway serving as a local landmark

Denali State Park ❻

135 miles (215 km) N of Anchorage.
Road Map E3. 🚌 *Anchorage–Fairbanks*. 🛈 *Alaska State Parks Office (Wasilla), 745-3975.* ♿ *limited.* 🅰 www.alaskastateparks.org

The majority of travelers drive past Denali State Park en route to the better-known Denali National Park *(see pp166–9)*, effectively creating this park's quieter charm. Established in 1970, Denali State Park sprawls over 507 sq miles (1,313 sq km), which is about half the size of Rhode Island.

The park offers uncrowded campgrounds, fabulous hiking trails, and views that equal those of its more renowned neighbor. **Denali Viewpoint South**, at Mile 134.7 of the Parks Highway, which bisects the park, offers the best panorama of Mount McKinley along the road system. The park's **Kesugi Ridge Trail**, a challenging 13- to 35-mile (21- to 56-km) long hike, follows an alpine ridge east of the Parks Highway, with superb mountain and glacier views from beginning to end. It is accessed from Little Coal Creek Trailhead at Mile 163.9 of the Parks Highway, with exits back to the highway via the Troublesome Creek, Ermine Hill, or Cascade Trails.

The flora of the park is dominated by white spruce and paper birch, as well as moss campion and mountain

avens. The park's varied landscape, with valley glaciers and great alpine ridges, as well as meandering lowland streams and Arctic tundra, make it the favored habitat of a wide range of wildlife, including caribou, moose, bears, wolves, and lynx. Beavers and muskrats inhabit the park's wet areas, while both marmots and pikas (small rabbit-like mammals) can be seen on treeless hillsides and rocky outcrops.

A few sights along the Parks Highway beyond the Denali State Park boundary at Mile 168.6 also demand attention. These include the dramatic **Hurricane Gulch** at Mile 174 and the **Igloo** at Mile 188.5. Built in the 1970s, this enormous structure (now abandoned) roughly marks the midway point between Anchorage and Fairbanks.

Cantwell ❼

210 miles (340 km) N of Anchorage.
Road Map E3. 🚶 *220.* 🚌 *Anchorage–Fairbanks*.

This small village takes its name from the Cantwell River, the former name of the Nenana River. This scenic area was originally inhabited by itinerant Athabaskan hunters, but the first person to settle there was trapper Oley Nicklie in the early 20th century. As more people settled there, Cantwell was designated a federally recognized tribal community. Today, a quarter of its residents are of Native descent. Cantwell, with a food shop and a motel, is a convenient refueling stop. It is also the western terminus of the Denali Highway.

NO-SEE-UMS

The biting midges known as no-see-ums are the smallest of the biting flies. Their peskiness quotient often surpasses that of mosquitoes, as they appear in swarms so thick that they are impossible to ignore. Alaska has 50 midge species, of which only a few actually bite. The variety found in the boreal forests of Interior Alaska, *Culicoides sanguisuga* (the

Tiny midges appear in swarms in the summer

Latin name appropriately means bloodsucker), raises large itchy welts, and can make life intolerable from late June through July. A DEET-based repellant will be effective, although some people swear by the Avon Skin-So-Soft repellant that is widely available.

Denali Highway Tour ❽

A trip across the fabulously scenic Denali Highway is an unforgettable experience. Built in 1957, it was the only link between Anchorage and Denali National Park until the completion of the Parks Highway in 1972. The Alaska Range runs along its length, offering spectacular views, and tundra and taiga forests on the route are home to moose, caribou, and grizzlies. Except for the first 21 miles (34 km) westward from Paxson and the last couple of miles, the route is gravel that ranges from smooth to rough and rutted.

TIPS FOR DRIVERS

Starting point: *Paxson.*
Length: *134 miles (214 km).*
Accommodation: *Tangle River Inn, Mile 20 (Tangle Lakes)* **www**.tangleriverinn.com. *Gracious House, Mile 82 (Susitna River)* **www**.alaskaone.com/gracious.
Stopping-off points: *waysides and parking areas along the route offer great photo opportunities.*
Note: *the highway is closed to traffic from October to mid-May.*

KEY

- 🅰 Campground
- ▬ Tour route
- ▬ Main road

Brushkana River ⑥
The highway crosses the Brushkana River at Mile 104.3. The campsite near the bridge is ideal for fishing.

Susitna River ⑤
The 260-mile (416-km) Susitna River, popularly called the Big Su, has its headwaters in the Susitna Glacier in the Alaska Range. The river has Class III to Class V rapids between here and Talkeetna.

Clearwater Creek Controlled Use Area ④
Gold was mined in the Clearwater Creek area in the early 20th century. Today, there is good hunting and fishing available here.

0 km 100
0 miles 100

McLaren Summit ③
At 4,086 ft (1,226 m), this is Alaska's second highest pass. The view north takes in several glaciers, including Susitna Glacier.

Tangle Lakes ②
Tangle Lakes, the headwaters of the Delta River, are popular for kayaking and fishing. The surrounding 350-sq mile (900-sq km) area includes several ancient Native hunting sites.

Summit Lake ①
Around Mile 4, several highway turnouts afford great views north to Summit Lake and Gakona Glacier.

Cantwell
Nenana
Brushkana
DENALI HIGHWAY
Susitna
Clearwater Mountains
DENALI HIGHWAY
McLaren
Delta Junction
Fielding Lake
Summit Lake
Paxson
Paxson Lake
RICHARDSON HIGHWAY
Gakona

Denali National Park 9

Alaska's top attraction, the expansive Denali National Park, sprawls across 9,420 sq miles (24,395 sq km) and is larger than the entire state of New Hampshire. Its highlight is, of course, the 20,320-ft (6,195-m) Mount McKinley, which dominates the surrounding landscape and is North America's highest peak. The park is world-renowned for its wildlife viewing, and visitors can expect to see a wide variety of animals. In the summer, Denali's tundra regions explode with wildflowers, while in September, they blaze with autumnal yellows, reds, and oranges. Just one road penetrates the backcountry; this single route, accessible only by the park's shuttle buses, crosses open tundra, boggy lowlands, and mountain passes to wind up at beautiful Wonder Lake.

Alaska Railroad
The train is a convenient way to get to the park from Anchorage or Fairbanks.

★ Wonder Lake
Wonder Lake, at the end of the park's shuttle route, affords one of the finest views of Mount McKinley. Visitors will find excellent summer blueberry picking around the lake campground.

Kantishna

McKinley

Won
Lak

EXPLORING THE PARK

With a full day, it is possible to take an early morning shuttle bus to Wonder Lake and still have an hour or two to explore on foot before catching the last bus back. As long as no wildlife is visible in the area, day hikers can get off the bus wherever they like and flag down a later bus back on a space-available basis. Some of the finest day hiking is found around the site of the Eielson Visitors' Center. Backcountry hiking and camping can be strenuous and requires a permit from the Backcountry Information Center.

Mount McKinley
20,320 ft

Mount Foraker
17,400 ft

Mount Hun
14,573 f

A l a s k a   R a n g e

Dall Glacier
Yentna Glacier
Lacuna Glacier
Kahiltna Glacier
Kahiltna Glacier

★ Mount McKinley
The snow-clad Mount McKinley is visible from many points on the Denali National Park Road. Athabaskans called the peak Denali, "The Great One," and most Alaskans continue to refer to Mount McKinley by its old name.

0 km   20

0 miles   20

★ **Polychrome Pass**
The Park Road crosses four high passes between Riley Creek and Wonder Lake. The overlook on Polychrome Pass offers a fabulous view across a wildly multicolored landscape.

VISITORS' CHECKLIST

125 miles (200 km) S of Fairbanks.
Road Map D3. **Tel** 683-2294
(Park HQ), 272-7275 (shuttle bus
& campground reservations).
Fairbanks or Anchorage, then bus
or train. from Anchorage or
Fairbanks. mid-May–mid-
Sep (weather permitting).
Denali Visitors' Center Mile 1.2,
Park Rd. mid-May–mid-Sep:
8am–6pm. **Wilderness Access
Center** Mile 0.6, Park Road. **Tel**
683 9274. mid-May–mid-Sep:
5am–8pm. **Backcountry
Information Center** Mile 0.6,
ParkRoad. mid-May–mid-Sep:
9am– 6pm. www.nps.gov/dena

Whitewater Rafting
The Nenana River (see p172), on the park's eastern boundary, offers exciting whitewater rafting.

KEY

Campground	
Airstrip	
Visitor information	
Highway	
Minor road	
Alaska Railroad	
Park boundary	
△ Peak	
Viewpoint	

WILDLIFE VIEWING AT DENALI

Wildlife viewing is one of Alaska's major attractions, and Denali National Park offers excellent opportunities to see Alaska's "Big Four" – grizzlies, moose, caribou, and Dall sheep. A variety of other animals and birds are routinely sighted, including the well-known wolf packs of Denali.

Grizzly bear roaming the park

Moose dredging for pond weed

Caribou browsing on the tundra

STAR SIGHTS

★ Wonder Lake

★ Mount McKinley

★ Polychrome Pass

Exploring Denali National Park

Most summer visitors to Alaska have Denali National Park on their itineraries, so a smooth visit requires pre-booking and advance planning. In the June to August peak season, it is not uncommon to have to wait several days for shuttle tickets or campsite bookings. For hikers, the park is divided into 43 backcountry units, each of which accommodates one group per night. Backcountry permits cannot be reserved, so access to high-demand units can require long waits. To get to the most appealing parts of the park, those without bookings should stop off at the Wilderness Access Center to organize their visit. Note that no private vehicles are allowed on the Denali National Park Road beyond Savage River.

Horseshoe Lake, a popular and easy hike from Park Headquarters

Denali National Park Headquarters Area

PO Box 9, Denali National Park.
Tel 683-2294. 🔗 🍴 🅿 🔺
The Park Headquarters area, near the main entrance at the eastern end of the park, is a necessary stop for all visitors. Around the Denali Visitors' Center, which has an information desk, there is a general store, a restaurant, a bookshop, a gas station, showers, and lockers. A mile (1.6 km) away, the Wilderness Access Center handles shuttle bus tickets and campsite reservations, while next door, the Backcountry Information Center issues free backcountry permits. Also worth a visit are the **Sled Dog Kennels**, accessible by free shuttle bus from the Denali Visitors' Center. Since the 1920s, rangers have used dogsleds to patrol the park. The dogs are so popular that rangers now offer mushing demonstrations in the summer.

The entrance area also has some smooth, well-managed trails. The Rock Creek and Mount Healy Overlook Trails both take half a day, while the Horseshoe Lake and Taiga Trails take an hour or two. As the park proper has no managed trails, hikers must be prepared for rough terrain and unbridged river crossings. They need to carry their camping gear and food, and must be adept at route-finding with a map and a compass or GPS.

Park shuttles go to all six of the park's campgrounds. All the sites have toilets, and four have potable tap water. It is advisable to reserve a place as far in advance as possible.

🚌 Denali National Park Road

Tel 272-7275 (bus reservations). 🚌 late May–mid-Sep: 6am–3pm at half-hour intervals from Park HQ; reserve in advance. 🎫 🔗 on some buses.
www.reservedenali.com
The Denali National Park Road leads 85 miles (136 km) into the heart of the park through a picturesque and wildlife-rich forest and tundra landscape. The area between Park Headquarters and **Savage River**, 15 miles (24 km) west of the entrance, is moose habitat. In the spring, visitors should look out for cow moose with calves. Beyond the river, the road grows increasingly scenic as it climbs onto alpine tundra, with herds of Dall sheep often visible on Primrose Ridge to the north.

Winding past braided rivers and colorful peaks, the road continues above the treeline to **Sable Pass**. **Polychrome Pass** at Mile 45 is another highlight. The stunning, vividly colored rocks of Polychrome Mountain were formed by volcanic action about 50 million years ago.

Park shuttle buses at the Stony Hill Overlook on the Denali National Park Road

For hotels and restaurants in this region see pp247–9 and pp261–2

Wolves sometimes hunt migrating caribou in this area, and visitors might spot a lone wolf on the road in the summer. Shortly after the road's highest point at the 3,980-ft (1,213-m) **Highway Pass**, visitors get their first good view of Mount McKinley at the **Stony Hill Overlook**. The road continues west to the **Eielson Visitor Center**. West of here, the road passes the foot of **Muldrow Glacier** and follows the wildly braided McKinley River to Wonder Lake. The one-way trip from Park Headquarters to the lake takes about six hours.

In an effort to control traffic pollution, only park shuttle buses are allowed on the Park Road beyond Savage River. The only exceptions are RV drivers who have a minimum three-night stay at the Teklanika campground.

🦌 Wonder Lake

Mile 84, Denali National Park Road. 🚌 from Park Headquarters. 🛖

Lovely Wonder Lake, at an altitude of just 2,090 ft (627 m), enjoys an unobstructed view of Mount McKinley, which rises a dramatic 18,230 ft (5,560 m) above the level of the lake. By comparison, the 29,035-ft (8,710-m) high Mount Everest rises only about 10,000 ft (3,000 m) from its base. On rare clear days, visitors are treated to the remarkable sight of the mountain reflected in

The original log-built 1919 Kantishna Roadhouse

the still waters of Wonder Lake. The region around the lake, characterized by expanses of tundra and blueberry bushes, is favored grizzly habitat, and campers at the Wonder Lake Campground frequently see bears and caribou. In nearby ponds, beavers can often be seen cutting willows, and moose can be spotted dredging for pond weed. For most visitors, the lake is the end of the usual route through the park, although the road and shuttle bus services continue on to Kantishna.

Kantishna

93 miles (150 km) W of Denali (McKinley) Village. 🏘 130. ✈ air taxi from Denali (McKinley) Village. 🚌 from Park Headquarters.

Located 7 miles (11 km) beyond Wonder Lake, tiny

Kantishna is one of many Alaskan settlements that started as mining camps. In 1905, the initial rush brought in at least 2,000 stampeders, who arrived to profit from the area's deposits of gold, silver, lead, zinc, and antimony. After ANILCA was passed in 1980 *(see p57)*, Denali National Park was expanded and Kantishna found itself surrounded by the park. In 1985, all mining, including that on private claims, was banned.

Today, Kantishna is little more than an airstrip and a collection of lodges. The 1906 recorder's and assayer's office and the original 1919 **Kantishna Roadhouse** can still be seen near the current roadhouse. Anglers who hold a state fishing license can also fish around Kantishna.

THE WOLVES OF DENALI

While most people come to Denali to see the "Big Four" – grizzly bears, moose, caribou, and Dall sheep – a very lucky few also have the chance to see timber wolves in the wild, or hear their haunting choruses. These canines number only 7,000 to 10,000 in Alaska, and only 100 or so individuals, in about a dozen packs, inhabit Denali National Park. Each pack, which includes an alpha male, a female, and their pups, requires between 200 and 800 sq miles (518 to

Timber wolf wandering through the scrub, Denali National Park

2,072 sq km). Adults usually weigh around 100 lb (45 kg), and have a brain twice as large as that of a domestic dog. Currently, Alaska's wolf population is healthy, but many sport and subsistence hunters maintain that wolves kill too many moose and caribou, and in response, the state government has instituted predator control programs. Denali's wolves are safe from officially sanctioned hunts, but once a pack roams beyond the boundaries of the park, there are no guarantees. Modern wolf researchers in Denali employ aircraft, radio collaring, and genetic studies to track and study the packs.

McKinley River flowing through vibrant autumn tundra against the backdrop of Mount McKinley ▷

Denali Village, the main service center for Denali National Park

Denali (McKinley) Village ⑩

124 miles (200 km) S of Fairbanks.
Road Map E3. 🕍 *170.* 🚂
Anchorage–Fairbanks. 🚌 *Anchorage–Fairbanks, park shuttle buses.*

This cluster of enormous hotels, RV parks, lodges, restaurants, and outdoor activity operators is the main service center for the Denali National Park area *(see pp166–9)*. Normally referred to as either Denali Village or Denali Park, this place was formerly just a roadside stretch of development, but a burgeoning number of hotels, shops, and tourist-driven businesses have earned it the moniker "Glitter Gulch." By any name, however, it would still be one of the busiest villages in the summer. Since the demolition of the Denali National Park Hotel, which provided well-heeled accommodations inside the park, visitors who want to appreciate Denali in comfort usually take hotel rooms here.

Visitors can also opt for less expensive options in Healy to the north, or Carlo Creek, 13 miles (21 km) south on the Parks Highway.

Nenana River ⑪

S of Nenana Bridge in Denali (McKinley) Village. **Road Map** E3.

Rising on Nenana Mountain in the Alaska Range, the 150-mile (240-km) long Nenana River tumbles down to join the Parks Highway at Mile 215. From this point on, the river and highway flow side by side. Spruce occasionally topple off the eroding banks, forming "sweepers," logs that float in the water and are a real navigation hazard for rafts and canoes.

Beyond Healy, the Nenana enters the flats north of the Alaska Range and flows more lethargically until it merges with the Tanana River at the village of Nenana. From the south side of the Nenana Bridge in Denali Park, thrilling whitewater rafting through the steep-sided Nenana Canyon is provided by three main outfitters: **Nenana Raft Adventures**, the **Denali Outdoor Center**, and **Denali Raft Adventures**. Difficulty levels range from easy Class I rapids to more challenging Class IV white-water. In the price of a half-day trip are included raingear, boots, personal flotation devices, and transfers to and from hotels in the area.

Denali Outdoor Center
Mile 238.5, Parks Hwy.
Tel 683-1925, (888) 303-1925.
www.denalioutdoorcenter.com

Denali Raft Adventures
Mile 238, Parks Hwy. **Tel** 683-2234, (888) 683-2234.
www.denaliraft.com

Nenana Raft Adventures
Mile 238, Parks Hwy. **Tel** 683-7238, (800) 789-7238.
www.raftdenali.com

Healy ⑫

113 miles (182 km) S of Fairbanks.
Road Map E3. 🕍 *650.*
🚌 *Anchorage–Fairbanks.*
ℹ️ *Mile 0.4, Healy Spur Rd; 683-4636.* **www**.denalichamber.com

North of Denali, the village of Healy has long been the service center for the Usibelli coal fields 3 miles (5 km) to the east. Discovered by Emil Usibelli in 1943, these fields contain the state's largest deposits of sub-bituminous coal. The mine now provides energy for Alaska's military bases, fuels Fairbanks' power plant, and exports coal.

Thrilling whitewater rafting on the Nenana River

For hotels and restaurants in this region see pp247–9 and pp261–2

Healy is best known as an inexpensive place to stay and plan a visit to Denali National Park. It is also well-known for the rough winter route from here to Kantishna *(see p169)*. Known as the **Stampede Trail**, the route is accessible by snowmachine in winter, but river crossings make it practically impassable in the summer. About 4 miles (6 km) north of Healy, the trail passes an old Fairbanks city bus. It was here that 24-year-old Chris McCandless expired of injury and starvation in 1992. He intended to live off the land, away from civilization, and to experience the raw Alaskan wilderness. His story is documented in Jon Krakauer's book *Into the Wild* and film of the same name.

Nenana ⓫

58 miles (93 km) S of Fairbanks.
Road Map E3. 450.
Anchorage–Fairbanks.
A St & Parks Hwy, 832-5435.
Nenana Ice Classic (Feb–Apr).

The little service center of Nenana lies at the confluence of the Nenana and Tanana Rivers. At the turn of the 20th century, it was known as Tortella or Tortilli, apparently

Old river tug, the *Taku Chief*, outside the Nenana Visitor Center

derivations of a long forgotten Athabaskan word. The town began as a trading post for river travelers, and eventually came to be called Nenana, which means "a good camp-site between the rivers." In the 1920s, it served as a railroad construction camp, and gained fame on July 15, 1923, when President Warren G. Harding drove in the golden spike that marked the completion of the Alaska Railroad between Seward and Fairbanks.

The old railroad depot at the end of Main Street houses the **Alaska Railroad Museum**. A block away, the log-built **St. Mark's Mission Church** is worth a visit, as is the *Taku Chief*, a river tug that once pushed barges down the Tanana. Today, it stands outside the Nenana Visitor Center. The **Alfred Starr Cultural Center** has displays on Native culture, plus a small gift shop.

Nenana is the site of the **Nenana Ice Classic** competition. Each year, people from all

across the state place bets on when the ice will go out on the Tanana. Any surge in the river ice shifts a four-legged "tripod" on shore, which pulls a cord, which in turn trips the clock on the adjacent tower. All correct entries split half the take and the organizers get the other half.

Four-legged "tripod" for determining ice breakup

Ester ⓬

6 miles (10 km) W of Fairbanks
Road Map E3. 240.
Anchorage–Fairbanks.

Northeast of Nenana on the Parks Highway is the old mining and Gold Rush town of Ester. In 1906, in its heyday, Ester had a population of 5,000. The Fairbanks Exploration Company built the Ester Gold Camp in the mid-1930s to service the area's dredging operations. The camp closed in the 1950s, but it was reopened as a tourist site in 1958. It closed in 2008, and if it does not reopen, it is expected that there will be an impact on summer tourism. Regardless, the town retains a pleasant, small mining village feel. Most residents are employed in Fairbanks or at the University of Alaska Fairbanks, although there are some small local businesses in the town. Today, Ester has a saloon, a library, fire station, post office, silversmith, numerous art studios, and three active gold mines.

Now closed, the Healy Clean Coal Plant generated energy using Usibelli coal

Fairbanks ⑮

Known as Alaska's Golden Heart, Fairbanks sprawls across the broad Tanana Valley. Italian immigrant Felix Pedro, who discovered gold near Chatanika, met miner E.T. Barnette, who was forced ashore here when his boat ran aground, and together, they founded Fairbanks in 1901. The two men convinced Dawson prospectors to come to Fairbanks, swelling its population to 18,000. Most boomers left when the seam played out in the 1920s, but the town's economy was bolstered by World War II and the construction of the Trans-Alaska Pipeline in the mid-1970s. Today, Alaska's second largest city enjoys a sense of stability that has outlasted both its rapid urbanization and its economic fluctuations.

Sandhill crane at Creamer's Field Migratory Waterfowl Refuge

The broad Chena River curving through the city of Fairbanks

movements, through much of the summer. Visitors can watch birds being banded at the Alaska Bird Observatory near the edge of the refuge.

🏛 Golden Heart Plaza

Next to the Chena River in the heart of Fairbanks, the Golden Heart Plaza attracts summer pedestrians with its green lawns and benches. Its centerpiece fountain contains Malcolm Alexander's 1984 sculpture, *The Unknown First Family*, depicting an Inuit family and dedicated to the spirit of all Alaskans. A block away is the Morris Thompson Cultural and Visitor Center, which provides a wealth of information and hosts Native cultural programs. The Doyon Building, across the foot-bridge, also displays a wealth of Native art.

🏛 Fairbanks Ice Museum

500 2nd Ave. **Tel** 451-8222.
○ May–Sep: 10am–8pm daily.
www.icemuseum.com
Housed in the historic Lacey Street Theater, the Fairbanks Ice Museum displays beautifully carved ice sculptures at a chilly -7° C (20° F). Some pieces are entries from the previous winter's World Ice Art Championships. This competition draws top ice sculptors from around the world, who turn massive 7,800-lb (3,500-kg) blocks of ice into works of art.

🦅 Creamer's Field Migratory Waterfowl Refuge

1300 College Rd. **Tel** 459-7307.
Red Line. ○ 24 hrs. ◐ Jun–Aug: 10am Mon–Thu, 7pm Wed.
Bird banding May: 6:30am–noon daily; Jun–mid-Jul & mid-Aug–Sep: 6am–noon daily.
www.creamersfield.org
The refuge was originally a dairy farm but was sold to the state in 1975, and as it had always attracted migratory birds, the Alaska Conservation Society expanded the acreage to turn it into Creamer's Field Migratory Waterfowl Refuge.

Today, the site offers good opportunities to view harriers, falcons, and swans. Sandhill cranes can be seen performing their unique dance, consisting of a series of bowing and hopping

University of Alaska Fairbanks Museum of the North
1 mile (1.6 km)

Riverboat Discovery
1 mile (1.6 km)

④ Pioneer Park

0 meters	700
0 yards	700

Key to Symbols *see back flap*

SIGHTS AT A GLANCE

Creamer's Field Migratory Waterfowl Refuge ③
Fairbanks Ice Museum ②
Golden Heart Plaza ①
Pioneer Park ④

🏛 Pioneer Park

2300 Airport Way. **Tel** 459-1087.
🚌 Blue & Red Lines. ◯ year-round.
📷 for some attractions. ♿ 🖥 📷
Museums ◯ late May–early Sep:
noon–8pm; winter: closed.
www.co.fairbanks.ak.us
A historical theme park in the
heart of Fairbanks, Pioneer
Park features gold panning, a
reconstructed Gold Rush
town, the railway car that
President Warren G. Harding
used while visiting Nenana
in 1923, and the SS *Nenana*,
a sternwheeler which operated on the Chena River from
1933 to 1956. The Native
Village Museum highlights
Athabascan culture, while
the Alaska Pioneer Museum
outlines the lives of early
settlers. Also worth a visit is

Vintage mining equipment in
Pioneer Park

the **Pioneer Park Air Museum**,
with its collection of vintage
aircraft and exhibits on
Alaska's aviation history.

🏛 University of Alaska Museum of the North

907 Yukon Dr, University of Alaska
Fairbanks. **Tel** 474-7505. 🚌 Blue,
Yellow, & Red Lines. ◯ mid-May–
mid-Sep: 9am–9pm daily; mid-Sep–
mid-May: 9am–5pm Mon–Sat. 📷
♿ 📷 **www**.uaf.edu/museum
Georgeson Botanical Garden 117
W Tanana Dr, UAF.
◯ May–Sep: 8am–8pm daily. 📷 📷
LARS Yankovich Dr, UAF. **Tel** 474-
7207. 📷 📷 May–Sep: 7 tours daily.
Packed with natural history,
cultural, and geographical
displays, the old wing of
the University of Alaska
Fairbanks Museum of the
North is well worth a visit.
Exhibits include the famous
Blue Babe, a mummified
Ice Age bison, a large collection of Inuit carvings,
and Native costumes.
The architecturally inspiring
new wing is designed to
represent mountain ridges,
ice, the aurora, and the tail
flukes of a sounding whale.
Inside, the two-story glass
view of the Alaska Range

complements the Rose Berry
Gallery of Alaska Art, which
exhibits works by renowned
Alaskan artists.
The university's **Large
Animal Research Station
(LARS)**, which studies musk
oxen and caribou, and the
Georgeson Botanical Garden
with its specialty gardens are
open to visitors as well.

🏛 Riverboat Discovery

Discovery Dr. **Tel** 479-6673. 🚌
Yellow Line. ◯ mid-May–mid-Sep:
8:45am & 2pm daily. 📷 ♿ 📷 📷
www.riverboatdiscovery.com
Perhaps the town's most
popular attraction, Riverboat
Discovery offers three-hour
long sternwheeler riverboat
cruises down the Chena
River on the *Discovery I*,
Discovery II, or *Discovery III*.
En route, a bush pilot displays field take-offs and landings from a grass runway on
the bank. There are visits
to the kennels of the late
Iditarod champion Susan
Butcher and to a recon-
structed Athabaskan village,
where guides explain Native
traditions. The cruise also
sails past the confluence of
the clear black waters of the
Chena River and the silty,
glacial Tanana River.

Riverboat Discovery sternwheeler cruising on the Chena River

The Aurora Borealis

The Fairbanks area is one of the best places in the world to see the aurora borealis or northern lights. The effect is visible as faint green, light yellow, or rose curtains, pillars, pinwheels, wisps, and haloes of undulating, vibrating light. During the greatest auroral storms, it appears as bright yellow, crimson, or violet streaks of light across the sky. While summer visitors will miss out due to the 24-hour daylight, there is a good chance of catching the celestial show on clear nights between late September and early April. Indigenous peoples had various explanations for these dancing lights. One legend said that they were the spirits of their ancestors, while another held that they were past and future events playing out across the sky.

Auroral undulations *are due to the eddies, fluctuations, and directional changes in the earth's magnetic field. During a single storm, the aurora can produce up to a trillion watts of electricity with a million-amp current. Some people claim that they can hear the aurora crackling and whirring, or feel its charged particles, although scientists doubt this.*

THE NORTHERN LIGHTS PHENOMENON

The aurora is caused by the interaction of the earth's magnetic field with charged particles from the sun. As the sun fuses hydrogen into helium, it emits particles of radiation – protons and electrons – that are shot into space. When this plasma stream of particles, known as the solar wind, blows past the earth, the earth's lines of magnetism draw them toward the points where these lines converge at the north and south magnetic poles. As the particles arrive in the ionosphere, they collide with gas atoms, causing them to emit light. The type of gas determines the color of the aurora.

Rare crimson aurora borealis over spruce and birch trees, Fairbanks

Vivid green aurora borealis shining above Bear Lake on Eielson Air Force Base

Exploring Beyond Fairbanks

Moving away from Fairbanks into the Fairbanks North Star Borough, the population thins and the vistas open up. This landscape of seemingly endless forested hills, broad river flats, and distant views of snow-capped peaks is the essence of Interior Alaska. Typically blue summer skies oversee it all, and in the winter, the aurora borealis is clearer and brighter than in Fairbanks, where it is obscured by the city lights.

SIGHTS AT A GLANCE

Chena Hot Springs ③
Chena River State Recreation
　Area ②
El Dorado Gold Mine ⑤
Elliott Highway ⑥
Gold Dredge No. 8 ④
North Pole ①

KEY

✈ International airport

▬ Main road

▭ Minor road

-- Trail

— Alaska Railroad

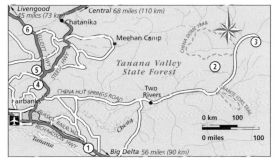

North Pole

15 miles (24 km) SE of Fairbanks. 🚗 *2,000.* 🚌 *Fairbanks' Green Line.* ℹ️ *125 Snowman Lane, 488-2281.* www.northpolealaska.com **Santa Claus House** 101 St. Nicholas Dr. *Tel 488-2200.* www.santaclaushouse.com
This town is nowhere near the North Pole, or even within the Arctic Circle, but here, the name is everything. Homesteaded in 1944, it was eventually sold to a developer who hoped to attract toy manufacturers by naming the new town North Pole. While manufacturers never materialized, the name inspired a Christmas spirit, as evidenced by such street names as Kris Kringle Drive, Mistletoe Lane, and Reindeer Alley. The **Santa Claus House**, next to the Richardson Highway, has a charming history and attracts youngsters with its enormous Christmas store, live reindeer, and the chance to speak with Santa. The community ushers in the Christmas season with a tree-lighting ceremony.

🎿 Chena River State Recreation Area

Mile 26, Chena Hot Spring Rd. 🚗 🏕️ www.dnr.alaska.gov/parks/units/chena
A wonderful park in Fairbanks' backyard, the Chena River State Recreation Area follows the clear Chena River as it winds between low, forested hills topped by rocky tors sprouting from alpine tundra. The river is ideal for fishing for Arctic grayling and easy kayaking. The surrounding hills have hiking trails, from short walks to multi-day routes. One popular walk goes uphill through birch and spruce to Angel Rocks, large outcrops with superb views. The excellent two-day **Granite Tors Trail** leads up into the hills to a free shelter overlooking the Plain of Monuments, a wide expanse dotted with towering volcanic rocks. It loops back down through forest and over boardwalks across a berry-studded muskeg bog. The three-day 29-mile (46-km) **Chena Dome Trail** climbs above the timberline onto alpine tundra, with views across the wilderness. In the winter, there is plenty of scope for Nordic skiing and aurora viewing.

🎿 Chena Hot Springs

Chena Hot Springs Rd, 57 miles (91 km) E of Fairbanks. *Tel 451-8104.* ✈️ *Chena Hot Springs.* ◯ *year-round.* 🛏️🚗♿🅿️📷🍴🛒🏕️ www.chenahotsprings.com
The most developed thermal spa in the state, Chena Hot Springs has functioned since 1905. It offers a complete resort experience with hot springs, pools (adults only), an indoor pool, spa therapies, and a range of other activities, such as canoeing and fishing.
Nordic skiing, sleigh rides, snowmachining, dogsledding, and, of course, aurora viewing make the spa more popular in the winter. A recent addition is the unique **Aurora Ice Museum**, which is open all year. It boasts an ice bar, ice decor, and average room temperatures of -2° C (28° F).

Visitors enjoying a soak in a rock pool at Chena Hot Springs

For hotels and restaurants in this region see pp247–9 and pp261–2

⛏ Gold Dredge No. 8

1755 Old Steese Hwy N.
📞 457-6058. ⏱ mid-May–mid-Sep:
9:30am–3:30pm daily.
🎫 hourly. & 🍴 🛍
www.golddredgeno8.com

Of all the old dredges in the state, Gold Dredge No. 8 is one of just two that are open to the public. Between 1928 and 1959, this behemoth extracted over 7.5 million ounces (210,000 kg) of gold. Guided tours explain the history and use of dredges, and also take in a display of Ice Age fossils and a reconstructed bunkhouse. A video depicts dredges in operation in the 1940s. Visitors are supplied with shovels and gold pans to try their hand at panning, and are allowed to keep anything they find.

Gold Dredge No. 8 moored along the Old Steese Highway

🏛 El Dorado Gold Mine

10 miles (16 km) N of Fairbanks at Mile 1.3 of the Elliott Hwy.
Tel 479-6673, (866) 479-6673.
El Dorado Shuttle from Fairbanks.
⏱ late May–early Sep daily.
🎫 🎟 mandatory. & 🛍
www.eldoradogoldmine.com

Opened during Fairbanks' 1902 Gold Rush, the El Dorado Gold Mine today gives visitors a brief taste of the prospecting experience in a two-hour long tour that faithfully explains gold mining methods used in the early days. The tour begins with a ride on a replica of the Tanana Valley Railroad. The train passes through a permafrost tunnel, where miners explain hard rock mining and point out fossils embedded in

Historic Manley Roadhouse in the village of Manley Hot Springs

the frozen earth. Prospectors then demonstrate panning and washing gravel to extract the gold, and the guides encourage visitors to try it themselves using "pay dirt." Any gold found is weighed to determine its current value. The gold can then be kept or turned into a quick necklace or locket by the mine's own jewelers.

🎣 Elliott Highway

Starts 11 miles (18 km) NW of Fairbanks, off the Dalton Highway.
Tolovana Hot Springs 100 miles (160 km) W of Fairbanks. **Tel** 455-6706. 🌐 www.mosquitonet.com/~tolovana **Manley Hot Springs** 152 miles (245 km) W of Fox.
Tel 672-3171.

Connecting Fairbanks with **Manley Hot Springs**, the winding, undulating Elliott Highway is a 152-mile (245-km) wilderness route through some of Interior Alaska's finest scenery. The landscape it passes through is especially lovely in early September, with the

bright autumnal colors of the birch and aspen forests.

At the tiny village of Livengood, the Dalton Highway (see pp222–3) turns north toward Prudhoe Bay while the Elliott Highway continues westward. At Mile 87, the road begins to climb to the trailhead for **Tolovana Hot Springs**, 11 miles (18 km) off the highway to the southeast. Pre-booking is essential for the springs. At Mile 98, the view opens up to take in the lake-studded Minto Flats, and a few miles later, a long side road turns south to the Athabaskan village of Minto.

The Elliott Highway ends at the pretty village of Manley Hot Springs, which boasts the Gold Rush-era Manley Roadhouse. The village's growth dates from 1902, when the site became a supply center for the nearby Tofty and Eureka Mining Districts. Today, the hot springs consist of three tubs in a spring-fed greenhouse filled with tropical plants.

Steel bucket used in gold dredging

DREDGING FOR GOLD

After early prospectors had taken most of Alaska's easily available gold, large mining companies employed mechanical dredges, which resembled massive houseboats beset with machinery. To get at the gold-bearing quartz, water cannons blasted away soil and gravel permafrost layers. Upon reaching the bedrock, a dredge was brought in, usually to a streambed, to gouge out the rock using steel buckets on a conveyor belt. The rock was then sifted by screens of diminishing size until it reached a riffle board, where mercury was introduced to bind with the bits of gold. Dredges crawled slowly upstream, creating dredge ponds in front of them and leaving artificial moraines behind.

Steese Highway Tour ⑯

From its start in Fox, the Steese Highway winds through the Alaskan Interior to Circle on the Yukon River *(see pp198–9)*. Built in 1927, the highway follows an early mail route. After passing rolling hills and low-lying muskeg, it travels through several river valleys, which are choked with mining residue, and then crosses a scenic alpine stretch. After Twelvemile Summit, it starts descending into the flatlands around the Yukon River. While the first 44 miles (71 km) are tarred, the rest of the route is gravel of variable quality.

TIPS FOR DRIVERS

Starting point: *Fox, 11 miles (18 km) N of Fairbanks.*
Length: *161 miles (259 km).*
Accommodation: *Chatanika Gold Camp Lodge (see p247) at Mile 28.6 has rooms and a good restaurant. At Mile 39, the Upper Chatanika River State Recreation Site has wooded riverside campsites, as does Cripple Creek Campground at Mile 60.*

KEY

▬▬ Tour route

— Minor road

– – Trail

△ Peak

0 km　　20

0 miles　　20

Circle ⑥
The highway ends at Circle, the largest town in the region until the rise of Dawson in the late 1890s. Early settlers chose its name believing that it lay astride the Arctic Circle – it is, in fact, about 55 miles (88 km) south of it.

Central ⑤
Unique exhibits at the town museum detail the history of Central, which was the heart of the Circle Mining District during the Gold Rush.

Birch Creek Access ④
River runners can launch at a facility at Mile 94, and put-in for a float to Mile 147.

Pinnell Mountain Trail ③
This 27-mile (43-km) trail follows an alpine ridge from Eagle Summit to Twelvemile Summit. Two free public shelters provide a roof for hikers along the route.

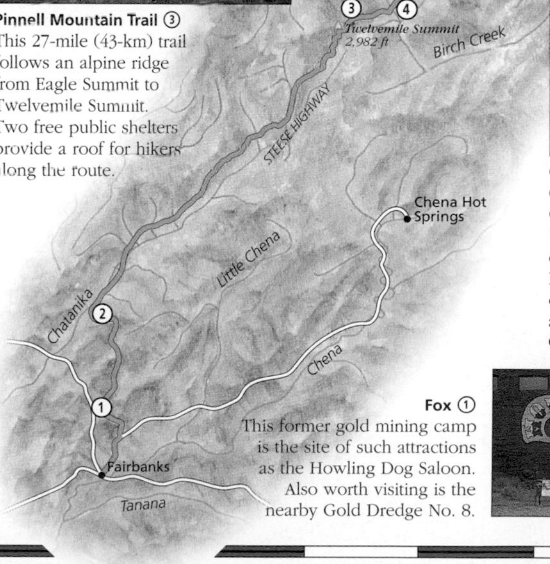

Porcupine Dome 4,915 ft

Twelvemile Summit 2,982 ft

Twelvemile House

Circle Hot Springs

Chatanika and Gold Dredge No. 3 ②
Chatanika was built in 1925 to supply local dredging operations. Dredge No. 3, which closed in 1962, stands a short hike away from Chatanika Lodge.

Chena Hot Springs

Fox ①
This former gold mining camp is the site of such attractions as the Howling Dog Saloon. Also worth visiting is the nearby Gold Dredge No. 8.

EASTERN INTERIOR ALASKA

The heart of the Klondike Gold Rush of 1898, the wild Eastern Interior reflects the popular image of Alaska for most outsiders. This "great, big, broad land 'way up yonder," so evocatively extolled in the poetry of Robert Service, is typified by hills laced with the gold-bearing streams that were the destinations of hopeful prospectors, and the icy peaks and glacial valleys that barred their way.

During the Gold Rush, towns sprang up in remote areas along the Yukon River and its tributaries. Dawson City, lying at the confluence of the Yukon and Klondike Rivers in Canada's Yukon Territory, became the commercial heart of the region. After most of the claims had been staked and the readily accessible gold had been extracted, many penniless prospectors opted to stay to homestead and pursue frontier lifestyles.

Shortly after the Gold Rush ended, copper was discovered at the turn of the century near Kennicott in the Wrangell Mountains, and the Copper River and Northwestern Railway was built from Cordova to export ore to the outside world. World War II necessitated the construction of the Alaska Highway in 1942, and the road not only opened up an access route through the Interior, but also boosted the economy of the region. In the 1970s, the area experienced a new boom – a black gold rush – as the Richardson Highway became the corridor for the Trans-Alaska Pipeline that connected the Prudhoe Bay oilfields with the Valdez terminal.

With the creation of Wrangell-St. Elias National Park in 1980, a thriving tourist industry took shape in the region. The park, a UNESCO World Heritage Site, is now on the itinerary of an increasing number of visitors. Visitors are also drawn by the numerous wildlife refuges and the mighty Yukon River, which flows across the northern part of the region, as well as by adventure activities, scenic drives, and historic towns.

The broad Yukon River winding across the Alaskan Interior near Circle

◁ Abandoned buildings at Kennicott within Wrangell-St. Elias National Park

Exploring Eastern Interior Alaska

Eastern Interior Alaska takes in not only vast swathes of
landscape crossed by gold-bearing streams, but also the peaks
of the Wrangell-St. Elias Mountains and the eastern Alaska
Range. Cutting through Wrangell-St. Elias National Park is one
of North America's most scenic drives, the Edgerton Highway/
McCarthy Road leading to Kennicott, an abandoned mining
town that is one of the state's most unusual attractions. Paxson
is famous for hosting the Arctic Man, a demanding snowmachining challenge, while farther north lie the appealing
communities of Eagle and Chicken. The mighty Yukon River
offers canoeing and whitewater rafting.

Hiking across the ridges of Matanuska Glacier

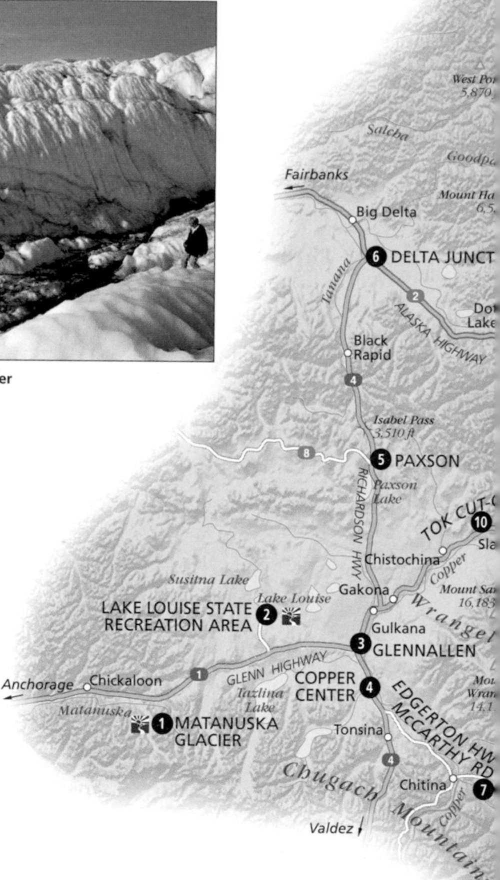

SIGHTS AT A GLANCE

Towns and Cities
Chicken ⑮
Copper Center ④
Dawson City ⑳
Delta Junction ⑥
Eagle ⑱
Glennallen ③
Kennicott pp188–9 ⑧
Northway ⑬
Paxson ⑤
Tok ⑪

National and State Parks
Jack Wade Dredge No. 1 ⑯
Lake Louise State Recreation Area ②
Tetlin National Wildlife Refuge ⑭
Tok River State Recreation Site ⑫
*Wrangell-St. Elias National
    Park pp192–3* ⑨
Yukon-Charley Rivers National
    Preserve ⑰

Areas of Natural Beauty
Edgerton Highway/McCarthy
    Road ⑦
Matanuska Glacier ①
Tok Cut-Off ⑩
The Yukon River pp198–9 ⑲

Birch Creek

Twenty-
Mile Vill.

Fairbanks

West Por
5,870

Saleba

Goodpa

Fairbanks

Mount Ha
6,5.

Big Delta

⑥ DELTA JUNCT

Do
Lake

Black
Rapid

④

Isabel Pass
3,510 ft

⑤ PAXSON

Paxson
Lake

TOK CUT-C

⑩

Sla

Chistochina

Susitna Lake

Lake Louise

LAKE LOUISE STATE ②
RECREATION AREA

Gakona

Mount Sa
16,185

Gulkana

③ GLENNALLEN

Wrangel

Anchorage   Chickaloon

GLENN HIGHWAY

COPPER ④
CENTER

Mou
Wran
14,1

Taxlina
Lake

EDGERTON HW
McCARTHY RD

① MATANUSKA
GLACIER

Tonsina

Chitina

④

⑦

Chugach

Valdez

Mountains

KEY

▬▬	Alaska Highway
▬▬	Highway
▬▬	Minor road
▬▬	International border
△	Peak

0 km   50

0 miles   50

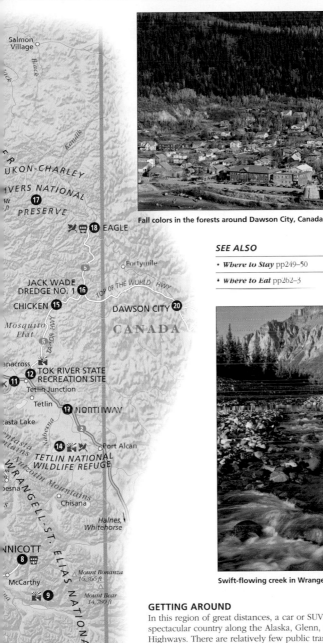

Fall colors in the forests around Dawson City, Canada

SEE ALSO

- *Where to Stay* pp249–50
- *Where to Eat* pp262–3

Swift-flowing creek in Wrangell-St. Elias National Park

GETTING AROUND

In this region of great distances, a car or SUV will open up the spectacular country along the Alaska, Glenn, and Richardson Highways. There are relatively few public transport links. One bus line connects Whitehorse, in Canada, with Anchorage and Fairbanks via the Glenn and Alaska Highways, respectively. In the summer, there is a daily bus between Glennallen and McCarthy. Popular guided tours serve as de facto bus links between Fairbanks, Tok, Chicken, Dawson City, and Eagle. In the summer, a riverboat operates daily along the Yukon River between Eagle and Dawson City. Bush planes provide scheduled flights to most regional tours.

The wide face of the Matanuska Glacier visible from the Glenn Highway

Matanuska Glacier ❶

Mile 101 on the Glenn Highway.
Road Map E3. **Tel** 745-2534, (888)
253-4480. 🚌 ⬜ May–mid-Oct.
🏔 ☑ 🖥 📷 www.matanuska
glacier.com

Drivers on the Glenn Highway cannot fail to notice the Matanuska Glacier, a broad, blue river of ice, descending 12,000 ft (3,600 m) to its 2-mile (3-km) wide face. It is thought that about 18,000 years ago, the glacier filled the entire Matanuska Valley and probably even flowed into Knik Arm near Palmer. Presently, it is advancing a foot (30 cm) a day.
Access to the glacier is via the privately owned Glacier Park, where hiking to the glacier face is permitted and hikes onto the ice with equipment and instruction can be organized. Drivers can stop at the free Matanuska Glacier State Recreation Site Wayside, which provides a lofty vantage point and interpretive panels. The Edge Nature Trail loops from here to another point with fine views.

Lake Louise State Recreation Area ❷

Mile 160 on the Glenn Highway.
Road Map E3. 🚗 ⬛ 441-7575.
⬜ May–Sep.

Not often visited by outsiders, the 26-sq mile (67-sq km) Lake Louise lies 19 miles (30 km) north of the Glenn

Highway. It was named in 1889 by Major Edwin F. Glenn of the US Geological Survey who reported its existence.
Much of the lakeshore lies within the Lake Louise State Recreation Area, which offers camping, swimming, berry picking, boating, and fishing for trout and grayling in the summer, and snowmachining and ice fishing in the winter.

Glennallen ❸

Mile 187 on the Glenn Highway.
Road Map E3. 🚶 1,000.
🚌 Anchorage–Whitehorse.
🛈 junction of Glenn & Richardson
Highways, 822-5555.
www.traveltoalaska.com

Deriving its name from two early explorers in the Copper River Valley, Major Edwin F. Glenn and Lieutenant Henry T. Allen, Glennallen is mainly a food and fuel service center at the junction of the Glenn and Richardson Highways, with a supermarket, restaurants, and a hotel. However, the town is beautifully

situated. Approaching on the Glenn Highway from Palmer, the mountains Sanford, Drum, and Wrangell, which seem impossibly lofty, rise above the flats beyond the town. In the summer, the haze of humidity and wildfire smoke make them appear even more dreamlike.

Copper Center ❹

100 miles (161 km) N of Valdez.
Road Map E3. 🚶 360. 🚌 from
Fairbanks to Valdez.

Dotted with historic buildings, the small town of Copper Center makes a worthwhile side trip off the Richardson Highway. In operation since 1896, the Copper Center Roadhouse still offers rooms and meals (see p249). In an old bunkhouse next to it, the **Copper Center Museum** is filled with artifacts such as birch baskets, an enormous mouse trap, and a kerosene tin cradle. It also has information on the Copper River and Northwestern Railway

Abandoned cabins around the small town of Copper Center

(see p187). The annex next door displays old tools and an antique snowmachine. A block away, in the Copper Center Bar, a scale replica of the railway winds across the ceiling, and a collection of historic railway photos decorates the walls. The town also boasts the region's first church, the 1942 log Chapel on the Hill; occasionally, the church screens historic videos about Copper Center.

Outside town, the beautiful **Wrangell-St. Elias National Park Visitors' Center** (see pp192–3) features a shop, information office, interpretive displays, and a nature trail.

🏛 Copper Center Museum

Copper Center Loop Road.
🕐 mid-May –mid-Sep: 11am–5pm.
🎫 donations accepted.

Rivers winding by the Denali Highway near Paxson

Paxson ❺

176 miles (283 km) SE of Fairbanks.
Road Map E3. 🏚 40 🚌 from Fairbanks to Valdez. 🎿 Arctic Man Ski and Snow-Go Classic (early Apr).
www.arcticman.com

The eastern anchor of the Denali Highway, the tiny village of Paxson consists of little more than a roadhouse, a café, and a gas station. However, for five days in early April, attendance at the Tesoro Arctic Man Ski and Snow-Go Classic makes it the fourth largest city in the state.

The area is dotted with vacation cabins along the shores of Paxson and Summit Lakes, and Paxson Lake has one of the best-maintained campgrounds in Alaska. The lake itself serves as a launching

THE ARCTIC MAN

The Arctic Man Ski and Snow-Go Classic is unsurpassed for sheer craziness. The contest attracts as many as 15,000 spectators to the tiny hamlet of Paxson. Each team has a snowmachine driver and a skier. After schussing down 1,700 ft (518 m) in less than 2 miles (3 km), the skier grabs a tow rope attached to the snowmachine. Pulled uphill at 80 miles (128 km) an hour, he lets go of the rope, slides over another mountain, and descends 1,200 ft (360 m) to the finish line.

Team participating in the Arctic Man Classic, Paxson

point for four-day rafting and kayaking trips on the Gulkana River, with Class II to Class III rapids (see p274).

North of Paxson, the area around Summit Lake provides long views across open tundra and beyond to glaciers on the southern slopes of the mighty Alaska Range.

Delta Junction ❻

98 miles (158 km) SE of Fairbanks.
Road Map E3. 🏚 1,000. 🚌 from Fairbanks to Valdez. 🛈 Richardson Hwy, 895-5068, (877) 895-5068.
🎪 Deltana Fair (last weekend in Jul).
www.deltachamber.org

In 1910, Delta Junction was little more than a roadhouse on the wagon road from Valdez to Fairbanks, but in the early 1920s, it grew as a construction camp for the Richardson Highway. After the Alaska Highway connected with the Richardson Highway here in the early 1940s, the town developed into a major

service center. Several private and governmental projects were set up here, including an Alaska Pipeline pump station and reindeer, yak, and elk farms. There were also bison farms, following the relocation of a herd from the Lower 48 states in the 1920s.

Delta Junction remains a small, rural outpost. The 1905 **Sullivan Roadhouse Museum** reveals pioneer life in Interior Alaska. Once located in the wilderness 14 miles (22 km) west of the modern town, it was moved here in 1996. Just outside town, the **Big Delta State Historical Park** includes the historic Rika's Roadhouse, with sweeping views along the Tanana River.

🏛 Sullivan Roadhouse Museum

Mile 267, Richardson Hwy. **Tel** 895-5068. 🕐 9am–4.30pm daily.
🎫 donations accepted.

⛩ Big Delta State Historical Park

Mile 275, Richardson Hwy. 🕐 May–Sep: 8am–8pm daily. ♿ 🏛 🎫

Log façade of Rika's Roadhouse in Big Delta State Historical Park

The Trans-Alaska Pipeline

When oil was discovered at Prudhoe Bay in 1968, no one knew how to transport it to market. It was eventually decided to lay an 800-mile (1,280-km) pipeline from the North Slope oil fields to the ice-free port of Valdez, where a pipeline terminal and shipping facility were to be built to handle the crude. Through the early 1970s, the Alyeska Pipeline Service Company worked on the pipeline design. Construction began on April 29, 1974, and was completed three years later at a cost of $8 billion. The first tanker, the *ARCO Juneau*, left Valdez filled with crude on August 1, 1977. Now run by a consortium, the pipeline transports 700,000 barrels of oil per day.

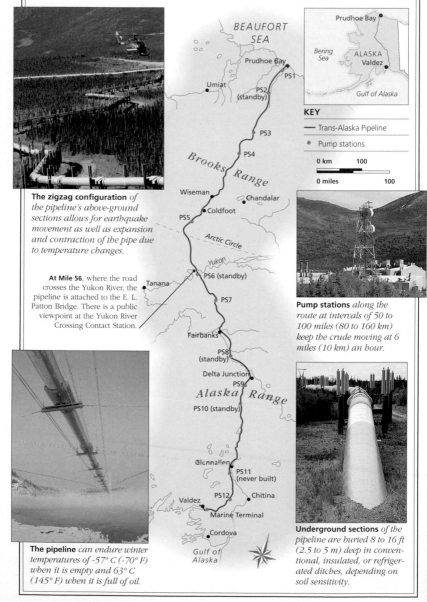

The zigzag configuration *of the pipeline's above-ground sections allows for earthquake movement as well as expansion and contraction of the pipe due to temperature changes.*

At Mile 56, *where the road crosses the Yukon River, the pipeline is attached to the E. L. Patton Bridge. There is a public viewpoint at the Yukon River Crossing Contact Station.*

The pipeline *can endure winter temperatures of -57° C (-70° F) when it is empty and 63° C (145° F) when it is full of oil.*

BEAUFORT SEA

Prudhoe Bay
PS1
Umiat
PS2 (standby)
PS3
PS4
Brooks Range
Wiseman
Chandalar
PS5 Coldfoot
Arctic Circle
Yukon
PS6 (standby)
Tanana
PS7
Fairbanks
PS8 (standby)
Delta Junction
PS9
Alaska Range
PS10 (standby)
Glennallen
PS11 (never built)
Valdez PS12 Chitina
Marine Terminal
Cordova
Gulf of Alaska

KEY

— Trans-Alaska Pipeline
• Pump stations

0 km   100
0 miles   100

Prudhoe Bay
Bering Sea
ALASKA
Valdez
Gulf of Alaska

Pump stations *along the route at intervals of 50 to 100 miles (80 to 160 km) keep the crude moving at 6 miles (10 km) an hour.*

Underground sections *of the pipeline are buried 8 to 16 ft (2.5 to 5 m) deep in conventional, insulated, or refrigerated ditches, depending on soil sensitivity.*

Camping at the Liberty Falls State Recreation Site

Edgerton Highway/ McCarthy Road **❼**

Off the Richardson Hwy at Mile 82.6. **Road Map** E3. 🚌
Backcountry Connection shuttle bus.

The Edgerton Highway/ McCarthy Road is among the most picturesque drives in North America. It begins calmly, gradually descending from the Richardson Highway into the Copper River Valley, with long views of the river's characteristic eroded bluffs. Entering Wrangell-St. Elias National Park *(see pp192–3)* at Chitina, the road follows the graveled railbed of the Copper River and Northwestern Railway (CR&NW) as it twists along above the Chitina River. Dramatically crossing the Kuskulana River, the road parallels the glaciated Wrangell Mountains to McCarthy, deep inside the park.

Chitina
66 miles (106 km) SE of Glennallen. 🏠 *130.* ✈ *scheduled flights.* 🚌 *Glennallen–McCarthy.* 🛈 *Chitina Ranger Station, 823-2205.*
Huddling in a narrow valley, Chitina was founded in 1908 as a halt on the CR&NW railway and a supply center for the copper mines at Kennicott. Of the few remaining original buildings, the former tinsmith's shop is the best restored and now houses an art gallery.

About 10 miles (16 miles) short of Chitina, the road passes camping and picnic spots at the **Liberty Falls State Recreation Site**. Entering a narrow canyon, it passes three lovely blackwater lakes before it reaches Chitina. Heading east from town, the road crosses the 1,378-ft (413-m) long Copper River Bridge, where subsistence fish wheels are visible. The river current turns the wheels, trapping salmon in the rotating baskets.

🚌 Kuskulana Bridge and Gilahina Trestle
🚌 *Glennallen–McCarthy.*
Perhaps the most dramatic reminders of the days when ore trains clattered along the CR&NW route are the two large railway trestles between Chitina and McCarthy. The incredible Kuskulana Bridge at Mile 17, built in 1910, is a three-span former trestle above the roiling Kuskulana River. At Mile 29, the road crosses the Gilahina River just downstream from the towering wooden Gilahina Trestle.

McCarthy
60 miles (96 km) W of Chitina. 🏠 *50.* 🚌 *Glennallen–Kennicott River bridge, then on foot or by shuttle bus.*
Homesteaded in 1906, McCarthy was a lively rest and supply town for workers at the Kennicott Mine in the early 20th century. During World War I, the rise in copper prices boosted McCarthy's economy. The town declined in 1938 when the mines and railway closed down, but its fortunes revived in the 1980s with the creation of Wrangell-St. Elias National Park.

Scenic little McCarthy retains much of its original flavor due to the well-preserved and restored buildings, some of which are still in use. The free **McCarthy-Kennicott Museum**, housed in the old Railway Depot, features historic photographs and artifacts from the two towns. Kennicott can be accessed by a shuttle bus or on foot along the Old Wagon Road out of McCarthy.

🏛 McCarthy-Kennicott Museum
Kennicott Road. 🕐 *late May–early Sep: 10am–6pm daily.*

The narrow Kuskulana Bridge 283 ft (85 m) above the Kuskulana River

COPPER RIVER AND NORTHWESTERN RAILWAY
With the discovery of copper in the Wrangell Mountains in 1900, railway builder Michael J. Heney began surveying the route and laying the track for the Copper River and Northwestern Railway from Cordova to the copper veins in the mountains. Given the difficult terrain, pessimists dubbed it the "Can't Run and Never Will." The Kennecott Corporation started a rival operation, but when a storm destroyed their railhead, they bought Heney's project and with an investment of $23 million, completed the railway in 1911.

Kennicott ⓼

Overlooking the spectacular Kennicott Glacier, Kennicott is a fascinating historical attraction. In 1900, while exploring the mountain east of the glacier, prospectors Clarence Warner and "Tarantula Jack" Smith discovered some of the richest deposits of copper ever found. Mining engineer Stephen Birch convinced wealthy East Coast families to finance the completion of the Copper River and Northwestern Railway to transport ore to Cordova. Over the years, nearly $200 million in copper was mined, but declining copper deposits and the high cost of railway maintenance led to the closure of the mine in 1938.

Kennicott Glacier Lodge, housed in a replica of a historic mine building

Mine buildings against the Wrangell Mountains

The machine shop, one of the most prominent buildings at Kennicott, held the metal-working and maintenance operations of the mine.

Workers' cottages dotted around the site and perched on the hillsides are now used as private homes.

Electrical shop

Storage shed

★ **Power House**

Power at Kennicott was generated by the large power plant which overlooks Kennicott Glacier. In this now partially restored building, four coal-fired steam boilers and two diesel generators provided enough steam and electricity for the entire mining operation.

STAR SIGHTS

★ Power House

★ Concentration/ Crusher Mill

★ Ammonia Leaching Plant

★ **Concentration/Crusher Mill**
In Kennicott's heyday, low grade ore was processed in the mill, which is the most striking building in the town. Remnants of the tramways that brought ore from the Bonanza and Jumbo Mines to the mill are still visible.

★ **Ammonia Leaching Plant**
Here, copper carbonates were extracted from treated ore that had passed through the crusher mill.

The historic railway depot now houses the Visitors' Center.

The General Manager's Office, Kennicott's oldest standing structure, had a large drafting room and was the heart of the mine's operations.

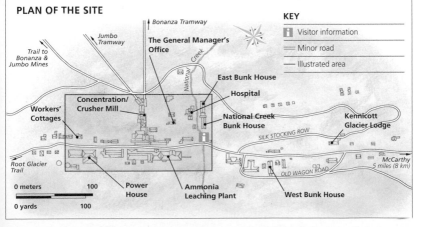

PLAN OF THE SITE

Bonanza Tramway

Jumbo Tramway

The General Manager's Office

Trail to Bonanza & Jumbo Mines

National Creek

Concentration/ Crusher Mill

East Bunk House

Hospital

Workers' Cottages

National Creek Bunk House

Kennicott Glacier Lodge

SILK STOCKING ROW

Root Glacier Trail

OLD WAGON ROAD

McCarthy 5 miles (8 km)

0 meters 100

0 yards 100

Power House

Ammonia Leaching Plant

West Bunk House

KEY

ℹ Visitor information

═ Minor road

─ Illustrated area

Erie Mine bunkhouse perched high on the mountains above Kennicott ▷

Wrangell-St. Elias National Park ❾

Wrangell-St. Elias National Park, the largest national park in the US – six times the size of Yellowstone – is a 20,000-sq mile (52,500-sq km) wilderness sprawling across the southeast corner of the Alaskan mainland. Dominated by the volcanic Wrangell Mountains and the glaciated St. Elias Range, the park has nine of the 16 highest mountains in the US. Designated a UNESCO World Heritage Site in 1992, the park contains remnants of historic mining sites and harbors a wealth of wildlife. Major activities include hiking, whitewater rafting, and taking flightseeing tours over the park's vast expanses.

KEY

☐ Wrangell-St. Elias National Park

Mount Wrangell
This 14,160-ft (4,300-m) volcano, which last erupted in 1900, was known to the Ahtna Athabaskans as K'elt'aeni, "The One That Controls." Its ice-filled summit caldera contains active fumaroles.

The Wrangell-St. Elias National Park Visitors' Center provides information and has a short nature trail leading to spectacular mountain views.

Copper River at Chitina
East of Chitina, the McCarthy Road (see p187) crosses the Copper River. The river crossing is surrounded by hills that are sometimes obscured by clouds of billowing dust.

STAR SIGHTS

★ Nabesna Road

★ Kennicott

★ McCarthy

★ Nabesna Road
Built in 1933 to access Nabesna Mine, this 42-mile (67-km) gravel road leads through muskeg and hills to the eponymous village. At Mile 36, a tough 5-mile (8-km) loop hike explores the area around the inactive Skookum Volcano.

VISITORS' CHECKLIST

Off the Richardson Highway.
Road Map E3. ⊠ *McCarthy.*
🚍 *to McCarthy.* ℹ *Wrangell-St.Elias National Park Visitors' Center, Mile 106.5 Richardson Highway; 822-7440. Ranger stations at Chitina and Slana.* ♿ *Visitors' Center & ranger stations only.* 🍴 📷 🏕 ☕ 🅰 *public campgrounds only on Nabesna Road.* www.nps.gov/wrst

KEY

ℹ	Visitor information
⊠	Airstrip
🅰	Campground
═	Highway
═	Minor road
▬ ▬	Trail
▬ ▬	Park boundary
△	Peak

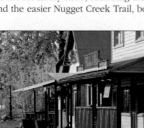

★ Kennicott
In the early 20th century, Kennicott (see pp188–9) was the site of rich copper mines. In the summer, rangers conduct tours of the abandoned buildings.

EXPLORING THE PARK

Given the distances, flights are needed to get to the heart of the park. Only the Nabesna and McCarthy Roads *(see p187)* penetrate the park, which offers hikes of varying lengths and difficulty levels. Two short trails at Kennicott, the easy 3-mile (5-km) return hike to Root Glacier and the straightforward but strenuous 9-mile (14-km) return hike to Bonanza Mine, offer magnificent views. Longer routes are accessible off the McCarthy Road, including the challenging Dixie Pass Trail and the easier Nugget Creek Trail, both two- to four-day hikes.

★ McCarthy
The old mining town of McCarthy (see p187) was a supply and support center for the workers at Kennicott. It is now accessed via a short walk or shuttle ride from the Kennicott River footbridge.

Swans paddling in a lake, just off Tok Cut-Off

Tok Cut-Off ⑩

Gakona Junction to Tok. **Road Map**
E3. 🚌 *Anchorage–Whitehorse.* 🅰

For drivers heading from
Anchorage to the Alaska
Highway, the scenic 125-mile
(200-km) Tok Cut-Off links
Glennallen with the village
of Tok. The southern half of
the route looks eastward on
to broad vistas of Mount
Drum, Mount Sanford, Mount
Jarvis, and Mount Blackburn
in the Wrangell Mountains. At
Mile 60 is the junction with
the Nabesna Road, which
leads east, past the town of
Slana and several hiking
trailheads into the northern
reaches of Wrangell-St. Elias
National Park *(see pp192–3)*.
  The Native village of
Mentasta Lake, the northernmost outpost of the Ahtna
Athabaskans, lies in the heart
of the Mentasta Mountains,
which form the easternmost
extent of the Alaska Range.
About 16 miles (26 km) short
of Tok, the Eagle Trail State
Recreation Site includes a
large campground and a steep
2-mile (3-km) trail to spectacular views over the surrounding hills and valleys.

Tok ⑪

206 miles (331 km) SE of Fairbanks.
Road Map F3. 🏠 *1,200.* 🚌 *from
Fairbanks and Anchorage to
Whitehorse.* ℹ️ *Tok Main St Visitors'
Center, Mile 1314, Alaska Hwy; 883-
5775.* **www**.tokalaskainfo.com

Situated in the upper Tanana
River Valley, at the junction
of the Tok Cut-Off and the
Alaska Highway, Tok is the
first major Alaskan town west
of the Canadian border. While
there have been Athabaskan
settlements in the region for
centuries, the modern town
came up as a housing site for
workers during the construction of the Alaska and Glenn
Highways in the 1940s. Tok's
economy was later enhanced
by a fuel line from Haines to
Fairbanks in 1954 and the
opening of a Loran station,
built in 1976 as an aid to
long-range navigation.
  Tok is now a service center
with a range of accommodation, RV parks, eateries, and
gas stations. It also has three
information centers: the Tok
Main Street Visitors' Center,
the Alaska Public Lands
Information Center next door,
and a Tetlin National Wildlife
Refuge ranger station about 5
miles (8 km) southwest of
town. The Fortymile Country,
a gold mining region with
historic and active claims,
stretches north over undulating landscape along the Taylor
Highway to the Yukon River.

Tok River State Recreation Site ⑫

5 miles (8 km) E of Tok at Mile 1309,
Alaska Hwy. **Road Map** F3. 🚌
Anchorage–Whitehorse. ⭕ *mid-
May–mid-Sep: daily.* 💯 🅰 **www**.
alaskastateparks.org

Located beside a sandy beach
on the eastern bank of the
Tok River, the Tok River State
Recreation Site is a popular
venue with both locals and
highway travelers. Families
spend sunny afternoons fishing and picnicking at this
lovely site, which also offers

Arctic poppies produce a burst of color in the village of Tok

good boating opportunities. Although the area was burned in the Tok wildfire in 1990 and in the devastating fires of 2004, the campground itself was spared and remains a pleasantly green place to stop and take a break.

In addition to 43 campsites, 10 of which have room for RVs up to 60 ft (18 m) long, there is a picnic shelter with drinking water and facilities, a boat launch, a short nature loop, and interpretive sign boards that describe the human and natural history of this part of Interior Alaska. A campfire area is provided on the beach.

Northway ⑬

59 miles (95 km) E of Tok. **Road Map** F3. 🏠 80. ✈ charter plane only. 🚌 Anchorage–Fairbanks.

This small village was named in 1942 to honor the local Athabaskan chief, Walter Northway, who passed away in 1993 at the age of 117. During the 1940s, the village served as an airstrip on the Northwest Staging Route, a chain of air bases and radio ranging stations that were built every 100 miles (160 km) from Edmonton, Alberta in Canada to Fairbanks, Alaska, to provide defense during World War II.

Visitors' Center at the Tetlin National Wildlife Refuge

Today, Northway remains the main US port of entry for private aviators arriving from the Lower 48 states. It is also the first US town for travelers arriving via the Alaska Highway. The modern settlement consists of three separate villages. Northway Junction lies right on the Alaska Highway, with a café, lodge, and gas station. The airstrip is on the Northway Road, 6 miles (10 km) south of the Alaska Highway, and another 2 miles (3 km) to the south is the Athabaskan Native village of Northway, where visitors can purchase basketry, Native moosehide and fur clothing, hats, gloves, and shoes decorated with fine beadwork.

Sandhill crane, a migratory visitor

Tetlin National Wildlife Refuge ⑭

E of Tok on the Alaska Highway. **Road Map** F3. 🚌 Anchorage - Whitehorse. 🏠 Mile 1229, Alaska Highway, 774-2245. 🅿 ♿ visitors' center only. 📷 ♿
http://tetlin.fws.gov

Snow-capped peaks, glacial rivers, open tundra, lakes, and endless forests and muskeg flats mark the 1,140-sq mile (2,955-sq km) Tetlin National Wildlife Refuge. Along with the Kenai National Wildlife Refuge (see p107), it is one of the two Alaskan refuges that are accessible by road. Situated under a bird migration corridor, the refuge attracts over 185 species of waterfowl, songbirds, and raptors. At least 115 of these, including the once threatened trumpeter swan, breed and nest in the refuge, and the annual migrations of sandhill cranes through the Tetlin corridor are spectacular events. In addition, some 25 hardy bird species remain in the refuge through the frigid winters of the Alaskan Interior.

The northern boundary of the refuge runs along the Alaska Highway, with seven interpretive turnouts and two free campsites. At Mile 1229 of the Alaska Highway, just west of the Canadian border, the visitors' center presents a wealth of natural history, wildlife, and cultural exhibits, as well as a spectacular view from its elevated deck.

Wildfire raging through forests in Interior Alaska

WILDFIRES IN ALASKA

In 2004, a record-breaking 10,156 sq miles (26,304 sq km) of Alaskan forest was destroyed by wildfires. Fires burning every 80 to 200 years are a necessary part of forest development, as they consume dead vegetation and recycle vital nutrients without destroying the soil's organic matter, so fires that do not threaten populated areas are allowed to burn. After the fire, vegetation returns in a well-defined succession. As the forest matures, leaf litter collect on the forest floor, until a lightning strike restarts the cycle.

Administrative office of the Yukon-Charley Rivers National Preserve in Eagle

Chicken ⓯

71 miles (114 km) N of Tok. **Road Map** F3. 🏃 40. 🚌 *tour bus from Tok to Eagle.* 🚗 🅿️

Chicken reputedly got its unusual name when early gold miners were unable to spell the chosen name, Ptarmigan, which is a bird that somewhat resembles a chicken. Today, the chicken theme is rather pronounced, with chicken T-shirts, stuffed chickens, a cutout of a chicken-pulled dogsled, and even a set of Chicken Poop outhouses.

Modern Chicken, south of the Taylor Highway, is divided into three main communities, Chicken Center, Beautiful Downtown Chicken, and Chicken Gold Camp. The Pedro Creek Dredge, which operated on Chicken Creek in the 1960s, lies on the grounds of Chicken Gold Camp and can be viewed on a guided tour. The historic town lies north of the highway. The Goldpanner in Chicken Center arranges guided tours of the area, including the schoolhouse made famous in Anne Purdy's 1976 book, *Tisha*.

Jack Wade Dredge No. 1 ⓰

Mile 86, Taylor Highway. **Road Map** F3. 🚌 *tour bus from Tok to Eagle.* 🚗

Gold mining in the Alaskan Interior began as early as 1881 with the discovery of

gold on the North Fork of the Fortymile River. It proved to be one of the richest veins in Alaska, with its ore assaying $20,000 per ton (900 kg). The remnants of both historic and active mining claims are strewn along the graveled Taylor Highway between Chicken and Eagle.

One of the most prominent claims is the Jack Wade Dredge No. 1 at Mile 86. Such mining dredges *(see p178)* were used throughout Interior Alaska and in the Nome area from 1910 to the 1950s and even later. Dating from 1934, Jack Wade Dredge No. 1 is now in such an unsafe condition that it is possible to view it only from the exterior. Visitors should note that streams in this area are lined with active gold claims that are off limits to the public. Bureau of Land Management (BLM) sites along the Taylor Highway are also closed to recreational panning.

The derelict Jack Wade Dredge No. 1, off the Taylor Highway

Yukon-Charley Rivers National Preserve ⓱

12 miles (20 km) N of Eagle. **Road Map** E2. 🚢 *Dawson–Eagle cruise.* 🛈 *Chamberlain St, Eagle; 547-2233.* 🖥️ **www.nps.gov/yuch**

Administered by the US National Park Service, the Yukon-Charley Rivers National Preserve spreads over 3,906 sq miles (10,117 sq km), protecting 115 miles (185 km) of the Yukon River and the entire Charley River basin. This New Jersey-sized preserve, with only 30 year-round residents, is one of the wildest places in the US.

During the Klondike Gold Rush, the rivers in the area served as the main highways for prospectors trying to reach their claims along smaller gold-bearing streams. Today, most visitors to the preserve are kayakers and rafters, who use the rivers for recreational trips through this vast wilderness floodplain. Most people begin in Dawson City, in Canada's Yukon Territory, or in Eagle and float down the Yukon to Eagle or Circle, respectively. To raft the more challenging Charley River requires good whitewater skills and a chartered bush flight to the Finger-Charley or Golvins airstrips within the park, with a take-out at Circle. The preserve's visitor center in Eagle provides maps, and canoes can be hired in either Dawson City or Eagle.

Eagle ⑱

166 miles (267 km) NE of Tok. **Road Map** E2. 🏔 *300.* 🚢 *Dawson–Eagle cruise.* ℹ️ *3rd & Chamberlain, 547-2325.* www.eagleak.org

The historical town of Eagle sits beside the Yukon River *(see pp198–9)* at the end of the Taylor Highway. Started as the Belle Isle Trading Post, just 12 miles (19 km) west of the Canadian border, the town was founded in 1897 by unsuccessful Klondike Gold Rush prospectors. They named it Eagle after the birds nesting on the bluff.

As the Gold Rush boomed, the founders staked 400 town lots and sold them to settlers for a $5 recording fee. By 1898, the settlement had grown into the military, judicial, and commercial heart of the region. New settlers set up gambling halls, saloons, restaurants, and businesses. Fort Egbert was established in 1899, and a year later the legendary Judge Wickersham *(see p143)* chose Eagle as the site of the Interior's first federal courthouse. In 1905, Norwegian explorer Roald Amundsen mushed a dog team from the Beaufort Sea to Eagle to announce that his ship, the *Gjoa*, had successfully negotiated the Northwest Passage.

Yukon Queen II moored on the Yukon River at Eagle

Welcome sign at Eagle Village

This apparent boom ended when the Gold Rush waned, but there is still much to explore in Eagle today. A popular town tour takes in the historical sights, the stroll to the BLM campground is pleasant, and the summit of Eagle Bluff offers great views. Other excellent options include canoeing on the Yukon River and sailing to Dawson on the *Yukon Queen II.*

🏛 Fort Egbert

4th St Extension. ☐ *late May–early Sep: 9am–5pm daily.*
Fort Egbert was established by the US Army in 1899 and five of its 46 original buildings at the fort were restored by the BLM between 1974 and 1979. Open to the public as a National Historic Landmark, the buildings include the **Mule Barn**, built in 1900 to house the army's horses and

mules. It now holds tools used in early mining, woodcutting, trapping, agriculture, and transportation. The distinctive **Waterwagon Shed** was used in the winter to prevent the fort's water supply from freezing. Sliding doors admitted the horsedrawn wagons and sleds that delivered water. The building now houses transportation exhibits and vintage vehicles. The Scandinavian-style **Non-Commissioned Officers Quarters**, built in 1901, is now set up as a military residence, complete with period furnishings. There is also an 1899 **Quartermaster Storehouse** and a 1903 **Storehouse**, which now features an interpretive display on the restoration.

🏛 Eagle Historical Society Museum Tour

Wickersham Courthouse. **Tel** *547-2325.* ☐ *late May–early Sep: 9am–noon daily.* 📷 🎫 📷
Many of Eagle's finest historic buildings are still in place, and in the summer, the Historical Society conducts a walking tour of the prominent sights. Built by Judge James Wickersham, the 1901 **Wickersham Courthouse** still contains his original courtroom, and also houses a museum of town history. The old **Customs House**, part of Fort Egbert, contains a period residence. The tour also covers the 1904 **Improved Order of Redmen Lodge** (now the home of the Historical Society), and the town icon, the 1903 **Wellhouse**. A massive flood in 2009 damaged many buildings along the Yukon River. Fortunately, most of Eagle's historic structures escaped the floods.

Log cabin gift shop decorated with moose and caribou antlers, Eagle

The Yukon River ⑲

Rising in the high peaks of northwestern British Columbia in Canada and flowing 2,300 miles (3,680 km) across the Yukon Territory and Alaska to the Bering Sea, the Yukon River provides a vital transport route for the people who live along it. Only four bridges cross the river – at Tagish, Whitehorse, and Carmacks in Canada, and at Mile 56 of Alaska's Dalton Highway. In the winter, the frozen river is a venue for a part of the Yukon Quest International Sled Dog Race, while in the summer, it offers adventure activities ranging from afternoon paddles and catamaran cruises to longer expeditions from the river's headwaters to the Bering Sea.

KEY

☐ Area illustrated

Circle, a village on the Yukon River *(see p179)*, offers beautiful wilderness views across braided river channels.

★ **Alaska Pipeline Crossing**
The E. L. Patton Bridge spans the river at Mile 56 of the Dalton Highway (see pp222–3), providing a crossing for both the highway and the Trans-Alaska Pipeline (see p186).

★ **Yukon-Charley Rivers National Preserve**
This vast swathe of wilderness floodplain (see p196) offers a range of activities, including biking, skiing, and rafting on the Yukon and the more challenging Charley River.

0 km 100
0 miles 100

KEY

━━ Alaska Highway

═══ Highway

━ ━ International border

‐ ‐ Park boundary

••• Trans-Alaska Pipeline

STAR SIGHTS

★ Alaska Pipeline Crossing

★ Yukon-Charley Rivers National Preserve

★ Canoe Trips

Eagle

Founded by unsuccessful Gold Rush prospectors, Eagle (see p197) is one of Alaska's most interesting towns with numerous old artifact-filled buildings. Downstream, the river passes through some of Alaska's wildest country.

VISITORS' CHECKLIST

From Whitehorse, Canada to the Dalton Highway. **Road Map** E2. ✈ *charter plane to Eagle.* 🚌 *tour bus to Dawson City, Canada.* ⛺ *Dawson City RV Park and Campground, Eagle Campground, Yukon River Camp* **www**.touryukon.com **Yukon Queen II** Dawson City, Canada. *Tel* (867) 993-5599, (888) 452-1737. **www**.grayline ofalaska.com **Eagle Canoe Rentals** Eagle, AK. *Tel* 547-2203. **www**.eaglecanoerentals.com

The catamaran *Yukon Queen II* connects Dawson City with Eagle, allowing visitors the opportunity to experience the Yukon River in comfort.

CANADA

agle

E WORLD HWY

Dawson City

Yukon

Carmacks

Whitehorse

Dawson City, Canada

One of the main centers of the Klondike Gold Rush, Dawson City (see pp200–1) has preserved its architectural legacy and makes a lovely stop on a Yukon River trip.

Whitehorse, Canada

Located in a valley, the town was at the head of the river's navigable waters during the Gold Rush. Today, Whitehorse is the capital of the Yukon Territory and a major stop on the Alaska Highway.

★ Canoe Trips

The Yukon offers exciting adventures for canoeists, kayakers, and rafters. The most popular routes are the four-day float between Dawson and Eagle and the five-day trip from Eagle to Circle. Fly-in options and vehicle shuttles are available at Eagle, Dawson, and Circle.

Dawson City ㉚

Over the international border in the Yukon Territory of Canada, Dawson City is a worthwhile side trip for visitors to Interior Alaska. Once an Athabaskan fishing camp at the confluence of the Yukon and Klondike Rivers, the area boomed in 1896 when gold was discovered in Rabbit Creek. In 1898, when the Yukon became a Canadian Territory, Dawson was designated its capital. Along with government agencies, the thriving town was packed with saloons, brothels, and dance and gambling halls. Designated a Parks Canada National Historic Site in the 1960s, Dawson City is now a living museum. Although gold mining continues, the town's most reliable source of income is tourism.

The Yukon River curving past the Gold Rush town of Dawson City

🏛 Tr'ondëk Hwëch'in Dänojà Zho Cultural Center

Front St & York St. *Tel* (867) 993-5385. ◯ Jun–Sep: 10am–6pm daily. ● 🖼 🎦 2pm & 3pm daily. ⚊ 🛈 www.trondek.ca

The center provides an insight into the cultural history and traditions of the Tr'ondëk Hwëch'in, who were the original inhabitants of the region. During the Klondike Gold Rush, many members of this Native group moved away to Moosehide, about 4 miles (6 km) down the Yukon River. Some of the people returned in the 1950s, eventually setting up the center in an effort to preserve their traditions.

The center's award-winning modern architecture reflects the traditional housing and fish drying racks that were so prominent in the indigenous way of life. Inside are displays of archeological artifacts, reproductions of traditional tools, historical photographs, and costumes. The center also hosts cultural events such as traditional dance performances.

🎭 Palace Grand Theatre

King St between 2nd & 3rd. *Tel* (867) 993-6217. ◯ late May–early Sep: 9am–5pm daily. ● 🖼 for tours and shows. 🎦 ⚊ limited.

Built from the remnants of two wrecked sternwheelers in 1899 by the Wild West showman and notorious gunslinger "Arizona Charlie" Meadows, the Palace Grand Theatre was at Dawson's cultural heart during the Gold Rush. Everything from Wild West shows to opera was staged in its opulent auditorium. After gold was discovered in Nome

Historic Palace Grand Theater, which now hosts the *Gaslight Follies*

(*see pp233–5*), Dawson began to decline, and in 1901, the theater was sold. Saved from destruction and restored in the 1960s, it is now open for tours. A vaudeville show, *Gaslight Follies*, is staged nightly in the summer.

🎭 Diamond Tooth Gertie's

4th Ave & Queen St. *Tel* (867) 993-5525. ◯ early May–mid-Sep: 7pm–2am Sun–Wed, 2pm–2am Fri & Sat. 🖼 ⚊ 🍴 ▭ 🛈

Constructed in 1910, the building was used for the town's most important social gatherings. In the 1970s, it was transformed into a casino and named after a popular dance hall queen. Diamond Tooth Gertie's is currently the only legalized gambling hall in the Yukon Territory. It is run by the non-profit Klondike Visitors' Association, who use the proceeds to promote tourism in Dawson City. Slot machines and all the major games are on offer for gaming enthusiasts. Nightly shows of garter-wearing, high-kicking dance hall girls attempt to re-create the bawdy atmosphere of the Gold Rush days.

🎭 Robert Service Cabin

8th Ave & Hanson St. ◯ May–Sep: 9am–5pm daily. 🖼 ◯ 11am, 3pm, & 8pm daily.

One of Dawson City's most popular attractions is the humble two-room cabin once owned by "the Bard of the Yukon," Robert Service (1874–1958). Nestled amid willows and alders at the edge of town, the cabin is typical of the era. Built of logs and chinked with moss, it was originally heated with a wood stove and illuminated with coal oil lamps.

Although Service spent only three years in Dawson, between 1909 and 1912, he absorbed the essence of this wild region. His seminal works, "The Cremation of Sam McGee," "The Shooting of Dan McGrew," "The Call of the Wild," and "The Spell of the Yukon" have long defined the Gold Rush era and the magic of the North. Today, Service's poetry is brought to life through the

Exterior of the original log cabin of Gold Rush poet Robert Service

interpretations of engaging Park Service actors, who tell his story and recite his most popular works.

Jack London Cabin

8th Ave & Grant St. ☐ mid-May– mid-Sep: 11am–3pm daily. 🖾 ☑ noon & 2.30pm. 🖾 🖸

The renowned author Jack London (1876–1916) first came to the Yukon in search of gold, but instead found a wealth of material for the tales of adventure he spun about frontier life. The cabin he lived in was located on the North Fork of Henderson Creek, 72 miles (120 km) south of Dawson City. Local trappers rediscovered his

cabin in 1936, and it was dismantled and shipped to Dawson in 1965 by Yukon author Dick North. Two replicas were made from the original logs, one of which is on view in Oakland, London's California home-town. The other remains in Dawson and houses relics, photographs, documents, and newspaper articles from the Gold Rush days. Every summer, Dick North interprets the site for visitors.

Situated across the road from Jack London Cabin, the 1920s **Frank Berton Cabin** is worth a visit. The building now houses the Berton House Writer's Retreat Program.

VISITORS' CHECKLIST

328 miles (525 km) N of White-horse. **Road Map** F3. 🏠 1,900. ✈ from Whitehorse, Canada & Fairbanks. 🚌 from Whitehorse. 🏢 🖸 🚹 Front & King St, (867) 993-5566. www.dawsoncity.ca

The Goldfields

10 miles (16 km) SE of Dawson City on Bonanza Creek Rd. 🚗 🚲 only for tours. 🕐 May–Sep: 10am–4pm daily on the hour at Dredge No. 4. Book at the visitors' center in town.

Although numerous Gold Rush prospectors worked gravel for alluvial gold, the real environmental impact of mining came after 1910 with the introduction of dredges. For a close look at the effects of large-scale gold extraction, it is worth making a trip to Dredge No. 4. This enormous wooden-hulled dredge func-tioned from 1912 to 1966, when it was turned into a Parks Canada Historic Site. Down the road at Discovery Claim, a monument marks the spot where George Carmack found ore in 1896, launching the Gold Rush that changed the area forever. Nearby, Claim No. 6 is open to visitors for panning free of charge.

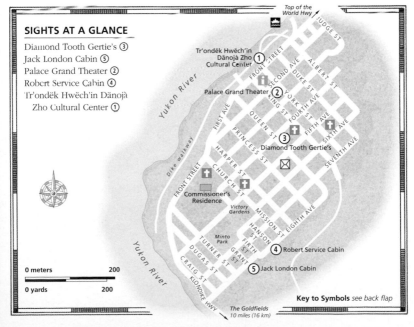

SIGHTS AT A GLANCE

Diamond Tooth Gertie's ③
Jack London Cabin ⑤
Palace Grand Theater ②
Robert Service Cabin ④
Tr'ondëk Hwëch'in Dänojà Zho Cultural Center ①

Top of the World Hwy

Tr'ondëk Hwëch'in Dänojà Zho Cultural Center ①

Palace Grand Theater ②

Diamond Tooth Gertie's ③

Commissioner's Residence

Victory Gardens

Minto Park

④ Robert Service Cabin

⑤ Jack London Cabin

Yukon River

Dike walkway

JUDGE ST
FRONT STREET
SECOND AVE
DUKE ST
ALBERT ST
KING STREET
YORK ST
FOURTH AVE
FIFTH AVE
SIXTH AVE
SEVENTH AVE
FIRST AVE
QUEEN ST
PRINCESS ST
HARPER ST
CHURCH ST
MISSION ST
EIGHTH AVE
HANSON ST
FIFTH ST
TURNER ST
GRANT ST
DUGAS ST
CRAIG ST
KLONDIKE HWY

0 meters 200
0 yards 200

Key to Symbols see back flap

The Goldfields
10 miles (16 km)

SOUTHWEST ALASKA

The arc of volcanoes that form the Alaska Peninsula and Aleutian Islands stretches through the Southwest like a fiery necklace. Lying across the fault line where the North American and Pacific tectonic plates collide, flanked by the North Pacific and the Bering Sea, and almost continuously battered by the forces of the wind and sea, this is a land of great extremes.

The original inhabitants of the region were the Aleut islanders and the Alutiiq of the Alaska Peninsula. Over the millennia, they wrested a living from the stormy seas and managed to thrive despite the forbidding climate and volcanic activity.

The first outsiders to arrive were the Russians in the mid-1700s. As the first point of contact for the Russians in Alaska, the Southwest experienced tempestuous cultural clashes. The newcomers' quest for the valuable pelts of seals and sea otters led them to first employ the locals for their hunting expertise and to later forcibly exploit them for their labor.

Today, visitors to the region come for both the culture and the incredible wealth of natural beauty.

The opulent churches that dominate nearly every town and village are a lasting legacy of the Russian era. Kodiak, the second-largest island in the US, was once the capital of Russian America and is the heart of the Alutiiq culture today.

While the national parks of the Alaska Peninsula are among the most remote in the US National Park System, they attract growing numbers of visitors with opportunities to hike through stark volcanic landscapes. Enthusiastic naturalists head to the remote Pribilof Islands, where cliffs are packed with thousands of nesting birds and basking seals. The ride down the stormy Aleutian chain on the ferry *Tustumena* makes an adventure-filled excursion.

The lovely Church of the Holy Ascension overlooking Illiuliuk Bay, Dutch Harbor/Unalaska

◁ Brown bears fishing for salmon at Brooks Falls, Katmai National Park

Exploring Southwest Alaska

Lying on the Pacific Ring of Fire and beset by stormy weather, this region is among the most difficult to access, but visitors who manage to get this far off the beaten track marvel at the region's history, abundant wildlife, and ethereal beauty. Aniakchak National Monument features the striking Surprise Lake, while Wood-Tikchik State Park's river systems are popular with boaters. Wildlife enthusiasts will enjoy Katmai National Park, which has the world's largest population of brown bears, and the Pribilofs, world-renowned for their bird and fur seal populations. Kodiak, part of a beautiful, rainy archipelago, has the area's largest town, while Dutch Harbor/Unalaska, Dillingham, and Sand Point are busy fishing ports.

Horned puffins on St. Paul Island

SEE ALSO

- *Where to Stay* pp250–51
- *Where to Eat* p263

13 PRIBILOF ISLANDS
St. Paul

St. George

KEY

—— Minor road

- - Ferry route

△ Peak

SIGHTS AT A GLANCE

Towns and Cities

Cold Bay and Izembek
National Wildlife Refuge ⑪
Dillingham ③
Dutch Harbor/Unalaska ⑫
King Cove ⑩
King Salmon ②
Kodiak ①
Sand Point ⑨

National and State Parks

Aniakchak National
Monument ⑧
Katmai National Park
pp210–11 ⑦
Lake Clark National Park ⑥
Walrus Islands State Game
Sanctuary ④
Wood-Tikchik State
Park ⑤

Area of Natural Beauty

Pribilof Islands pp216–17 ⑬

Hooper

Haze

Mekoryuk
*Nunivak
Island*
*Roberts
Mountain
1,668 ft*

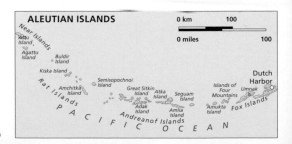

Pogromni Volcano
6,547 ft
Makushin Volcano
6,658 ft Akutan *Unimak*
Pass
DUTCH HARBOR/
UNALASKA ⑫
Fox Islands

0 km   100

0 miles   100

ALEUTIAN ISLANDS

0 km   100

0 miles   100

Near Islands
*Attu
Island*
*Agattu
Island* ○ *Buldir
Island*
Kiska Island
Rat Islands   Semisopochnoi
Island   Great Sitkin Atka Seguam
Amchitka   Island   Island   Island
Island   Adak   Amlia
Island   Island
Andreanof Islands
*Islands of
Four
Mountains* Umnak
*Amukta
Island* Fox Islands

Dutch
Harbor

P A C I F I C   O C E A N

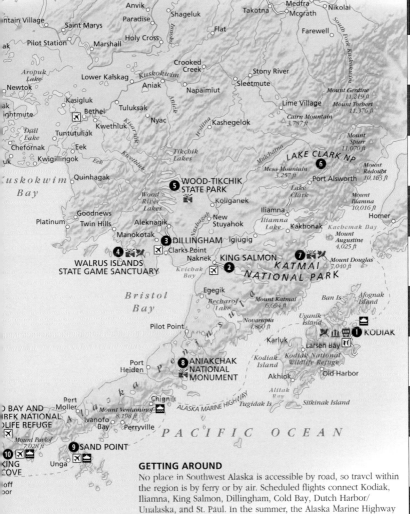

GETTING AROUND

No place in Southwest Alaska is accessible by road, so travel within the region is by ferry or by air. Scheduled flights connect Kodiak, Iliamna, King Salmon, Dillingham, Cold Bay, Dutch Harbor/Unalaska, and St. Paul. In the summer, the Alaska Marine Highway ferry *Tustumena* does a twice-monthly run between Homer and Dutch Harbor/Unalaska, stopping at otherwise hard-to-reach Alaska Peninsula ports of call. Other towns and national parks – Aniakchak, Lake Clark, and Katmai – are accessible by chartered floatplane.

Russian Orthodox church overlooking Karluk Lagoon, Kodiak Island

Looking down on Kodiak town from Pillar Mountain

Kodiak ●

150 miles (241 km) SW of Homer.
Road Map D4. 🏔 14,000. ✈ ⛴
from Homer. 🚏 100 Marine Way
(Marine Hwy Terminal building), 486-
4782. 🏌 Pillar Mountain Golf Classic
(late Mar), Crab Festival (Memorial
Day weekend, State Fair & Rodeo (1st
weekend in Sep). **www**.kodiak.org

Known as Alaska's Emerald
Isle, Kodiak Island and its surroundings are famous for rain,
bears, and fishing. Kodiak was
settled by Alutiiq hunters and
fishermen as many as 7,000
years ago. Its name, in fact,
comes from the Alutiiq word
Qiq'rtaq, which simply means
"island" and was corrupted by
the Russians to Kodiak. The
first Russian explorer landed
here in 1763, and a town was
built by 1784. About a decade
later, Alexander Baranov set up
a trading post, designating it
the capital of Russian America.
Kodiak suffered two major
natural disasters in the last
century: the 1912 explosion of
Novarupta (see p211) and the
1964 earthquake (see p25). The
island was once largely treeless, but spruce seeds and pol-
len blowing across from the
mainland have taken hold of
the northern end of the archipelago and the forests are
slowly spreading southward.

🏛 Holy Resurrection Russian Orthodox Church

Mission Road. **Tel** 486-3854. 📷 late
May–early Sep: 1–2pm daily. 🚫
🏛 6:30pm Thu, 9:30am Sun.
Following Russian colonists to
Alaska in the 18th and 19th
centuries, Orthodox priests
converted large numbers of
Natives, whose descendants

still follow the faith. The
present Holy Resurrection
Russian Orthodox Church
is, in fact, the third on this
site. A scale replica of the
original 1794 church is
kept at St. Herman's
Theological Seminary
next door. The second
church, built in 1874,
was destroyed by fire
in 1943. The current
building, with blue
onion domes and
gold-flecked win-
dows, contains an
original 1790s Russian
icon, ornate candlestands,
and the reliquary of the
18th-century Russian monk,
St. Herman, canonized here
in 1970. The neighboring
chapel houses a collection
of 17th-century manuscripts
and a hand-carved chandelier.
Each August, some 300 boats
join a pilgrimage to nearby
Spruce Island, the saint's
retreat in his later years.

🏛 Baranov Museum

101 Marine Way. **Tel** 486-5920. ◯
10am–4pm Mon–Sat, noon–4pm Sun.
📷 🏛 **www**.baranovmuseum.org
The Kodiak Historical
Society's Baranov Museum
occupies the white weather-
board Erskine House, built
by Alexander Baranov in
1808 as a warehouse for otter
pelts, and named after one
of its later owners. Although
minor changes have been
made, this is the oldest existing building on the US West
Coast. The museum features
such oddities as an unusual
three-seat *baidarka* (skin
boat) and a Russian sealskin
bank note. It also holds
Alutiiq and Aleut artifacts
such as woven grass
baskets, seal gut bags,
and bone carvings. The
Russian era is reflected
in a beautiful collection
of brass samovars and
icons, and the 1912
Novarupta eruption is
chronicled in a photo-
graphic display. The
archives and exten-
sive library are open
to the public.

Samovar at the Baranov Museum

🏛 Alutiiq Museum

215 Mission Road. **Tel** 486-7004.
◯ Jun–Aug: 9am–5pm Mon–Fri,
10am–5pm Sat; winter: 9am–5pm
Tue–Fri, 10:30am–4:30pm Sat. 📷
♿ 🏛 **www**.alutiiqmuseum.com
With the arrival of the Russians
in Alaska in the late 18th century, many aspects of Alutiiq
culture on Kodiak and on the
Alaska and Kenai Peninsulas
were lost, but over
1,000 archeological
sites around the region
reveal the original
ways of the Alutiiq.
This museum has put
together an archive
and collection of his-
torical artifacts, including Alutiiq ornaments,
a replica of an 1883
ground squirrel parka,
and a fabulous
awirnaq (spruce root
hat), shared between
this museum and the
Anchorage Museum
(see pp6–9) in
alternating years. The
renowned Alutiiq
Dancers occasionally
perform here.

Holy Resurrection Russian Orthodox Church

Clouds hanging over the peaks of Afognak Island, north of Kodiak

🏯 Fort Abercrombie State Historical Park

Miller Point Road, 5 miles (8 km) E of Kodiak. **Tel** 486 6339. 🚗 🅿 park: 24 hrs; visitors' center; 8:30am–noon, 1–5pm Mon–Fri. 🅰 **www** dnr. alaska.gov/parks/units/kodiak

The lovely Fort Abercrombie State Historical Park lies on Miller Point along Rezanof Road. In June 1941, fearing a Japanese attack on Alaska, President Franklin D. Roosevelt authorized the establishment of a 780-acre (312-ha) military post at Miller Point. After the attack on Pearl Harbor, coastal defense gun emplacements were installed on the site. Although the garrisons were removed some time ago, remnants of the searchlight bunkers, pillbox bunkers, ammunition dumps, and gun emplacements can still be seen around the lovely wooded site. The **Kodiak Military History Museum**, with a wealth of military artifacts, is housed in the Ready Ammunition Bunker on the Miller Point Headland.

The park, crisscrossed by numerous short hiking trails, is accessed on a forest road that leads past the picnic site at Lake Gertrude, where anglers can fish for stocked rainbow trout and grayling. Beyond is a campground in lush, mossy spruce forest.

🏛 Kodiak Military History Museum

Tel 486-7015. 🅾 May–Sep: 1–4pm Fri–Mon. 🈺 **www**.kadiak.org

🦌 Kodiak National Wildlife Refuge

SW of Kodiak. ✈ chartered float-plane from Kodiak. 🚤 from Kodiak. ℹ 420 Center St, 487-2626. 🅰 🅰 www.kodiakwildliferefuge.org

Established in 1941 to protect the Kodiak bear and sea mammals, the Kodiak National Wildlife Refuge covers most of the southwestern end of Kodiak Island, as well as Uganik and Ban Islands and much of the Red Peaks area on Afognak Island. This wild area sprawls over 3,405 sq miles (8,820 sq km) of rugged mountains, lakes, bogs, and meadows, and includes hundreds of miles of

Alaskan wildflower

convoluted shoreline. It is currently home to about 2,300 Kodiak brown bears, as well as 30 million wild salmon, representing all five Alaskan species. There are also 250 bird species and 1.5 million seabirds. The refuge has no roads or trails, so access is limited to floatplane, bush flights, or watercraft from Kodiak town. The most popular activity is taking a half-or one-day flightseeing trip to prime bear-viewing areas such as Frazer Lake and Karluk Lake.

The refuge also offers backcountry camping, rafting, hunting, as well as fishing opportunities at the popular Karluk and Ayakulik Rivers.

KODIAK BEARS

Solitary Kodiak bear on Kodiak Island

The Kodiak archipelago is home to around 3,000 Kodiak brown bears *(Ursos arctos middendorffi)*, the world's largest land carnivores. While sows weigh 400 to 600 lbs (180 to 270 kg), the boars weigh from 800 to 1,500 lbs (360 to 675 kg) and can stand up to 12 ft (4 m) tall on their hind legs. The omnivorous bears stay at sea level during spring, feeding on grasses, but as summer progresses, they move uphill to eat alpine shoots. In mid-July, they begin congregating around streams to partake in a feast of spawning salmon. Pregnant sows enter their winter dens, usually natural rock outcrops, in fall. They bear two to three cubs by late January, who emerge from the den when they are about four months old. Cubs typically stay with their mother for two to three years.

Boats docked at the bustling harbor in Dillingham

King Salmon ❷

285 miles (459 km) SW of Anchorage. **Road Map** D4. 🏃 385. ⊠ ℹ *Airport terminal, 246-4250.*

The rugged little village of King Salmon occupies a lovely setting amid wide open spaces. The town overlooks the banks of the Naknek River, 15 miles (24 km) upstream from the fishing port of Naknek on Bristol Bay. Much of the current population of King Salmon is descended from people who were forced to relocate after the 1912 eruption of the Novarupta volcano, in what is now Katmai National Park *(see pp210–11).*

As the gateway to Katmai National Park, King Salmon features an airstrip and lodging for those without reservations at Brooks Camp inside the national park. The Katmai National Park tourist office at the airport has natural history displays and videos on the park, as well as a gift shop selling maps and books.

Dillingham ❸

481 miles (774 km) SW of Anchorage. **Road Map** C4. 🏃 2,300. ⊠ ℹ *348 D St, 842-5115.* **www**.dillinghamak.com

Founded by Russian fur traders in 1822 as a fort called Alexandrovski Redoubt, Dillingham is the largest community in the Bristol Bay region, as a result of its commercial fishing industry. In 1884, after the US took possession of Alaska, enormous runs of salmon in the Wood and Nushagak Rivers made Dillingham a logical fish processing and canning site. Today, up to 10,000 tons (9 million kg) of fish is processed every year from the Bristol Bay salmon fishery.

The chief attraction here is the **Sam Fox Museum**, which outlines the history of the Bristol Bay region, and features a gillnetter fishing boat with a sail, built around 1936. The town is a staging point for visits to Togiak National Wildlife Refuge, Walrus Islands State Game Sanctuary, and Wood-Tikchik State Park.

🏛 **Sam Fox Museum**
Tel 842-5610. ◯ *summer: 10am–5pm Mon–Fri.* ♿ 📷

Walrus Islands State Game Sanctuary ❹

100 miles (160 km) W of Dillingham. **Road Map** C4. ⊠ *Dillingham, then by charter boat.* ℹ *842-2334.* ◯ *May–mid-Aug.* 🎫 **Permits** 10 available for each 5-day period from Alaska Department of Fish and Game. **www**.wildlife.alaska.gov

Located in the northwestern reaches of Bristol Bay, the Walrus Islands State Game Sanctuary is an archipelago of seven rocky islands. The most popular destination in the sanctuary is **Round Island**, where lounging walruses cover the beaches.

After the northern pack ice recedes in the spring, male walruses – as many as 14,000 a day – haul out onto the rocky, exposed beaches between feeding excursions at sea. In the summer, the surrounding seas abound with harbor seals, as well as gray, orca, and humpback whales. The beaches of Round Island and the neighboring islands also attract several hundred breeding Steller sea lions, and the cliffs above bustle with nearly 400,000 nesting sea birds. Red foxes roam the beaches to feed on seabird eggs and fallen chicks.

Access to Round Island is by permit only. Visitors need to be self-sufficient with gear that will accommodate a range of climatic conditions.

Closely packed walruses lying on Round Island

THE TUSKY PINNIPED

The Pacific walrus *(Odobenus rosmarus divergens)*, a resident of the western Gulf of Alaska, Bristol Bay, the Bering Sea, and the Chukchi Sea, is a large, brown pinniped covered with coarse hair. Its most distinctive features are its shaggy "old man" moustache and its two ivory tusks, which are actually enlarged canine teeth. While breeding, males use the tusks to vanquish competitors for females. They also use the tusks to anchor themselves to the sea bottom while digging for mollusks. Male walruses can grow up to 12 ft (4 m) in length and weigh in at 3,700 lbs (1,480 kg). Only Alaska Natives are permitted to hunt walruses for food and for ivory, which they turn into their renowned scrimshaw carvings.

Red fox in Wood-Tikchik State Park

Wood-Tikchik State Park ❺

25 miles (40 km) N of Dillingham. **Road Map** C4. *Tel* 842-2641. ✈ Dillingham, then by floatplane or bus. 🛈 Ranger Station, Dillingham 🌐 www.dnr.alaska.gov/parks/units/woodtik.htm

America's largest state park, the 2,345 sq mile (6,070-sq km) Wood-Tikchik State Park is a vast landscape of two interconnected lake systems, that of the Wood River in the south and the Tikchik River in the north. The park is situated in a biological transition zone between coniferous forest and tundra, with willow and alder thickets as well as spruce and birch forests. Its eastern side consists of low, boggy wetlands studded with lakes and streams, while to the west rise the wild and untracked Wood River Mountains.

The remoteness of the park makes it especially good wildlife habitat. Brown bears, caribou, and moose are abundant, as are porcupines, wolverines, marmots, beavers, land otters, and foxes. Throughout the park, well appointed fly-in lodges serve as staging points for canoeing and fishing trips. Anglers will find all five Alaskan salmon species, especially sockeyes (reds), plus trout, Arctic char, Arctic grayling, and northern pike.

The most usual access for independent groups is to fly in to one of the lakes on the Wood River system, and then canoe downstream to Aleknagik on Lake Aleknagik, accessible via a gravel road. On the Tikchik system, most people fly into one of the lakes and then float downstream along the Nuyakuk and Nushagak Rivers, to be picked up at the airstrips at Ekwok or New Stuyahok.

Visitors who are considering an expedition but not planning to stay in one of the fly-in lodges should keep in mind that well-honed survival skills are essential for trips into the park's wilderness.

Lake Clark National Park ❻

200 miles (320 km) SW of Anchorage. **Road Map** D4. *Tel* 781-2218. ✈ Iliamna, then charter plane to Port Alsworth. 🚌 only in Port Alsworth. www.nps.gov/lacl

When ANILCA was passed in 1980 *(see p57)*, the 6,250-sq mile (16,187-sq km) Lake Clark National Park came into being to protect the 50-mile (80-km) long Lake Clark and its surrounding ecosystems. These include the shores of Cook Inlet, which is prime bear territory, and the glaciated heights of the Chigmit Mountains and the Aleutian Range. The twin volcanoes, Mount Iliamna and Mount Redoubt, are also included. The park boasts an array of wildlife, most prominently brown bears and migrating herds of caribou. Activities include canoeing, kayaking, fishing, and hiking, but the only marked hiking trail leads from Port Alsworth to Tanalian Falls.

The park's headquarters are at the tiny village of Port Alsworth on Lake Clark's southern shore. While Port Alsworth has several small lodges, there are no shops or services anywhere in the park, so non-lodge visitors will need to carry camping and cooking gear. Access to remote parts of the park is by chartered bush flight only.

Fishing in Crescent Lake, surrounded by the Chigmit Mountains in Lake Clark National Park

Katmai National Park ❼

Katmai was proclaimed a National Monument in 1918 to preserve the unique geological features that were formed after the eruption of Novarupta in 1912. Designated a National Park when ANILCA was passed in 1980 *(see p57)*, it now encompasses 5,500 sq miles (15,000 sq km) of cold lakes, scenic valleys, volcanic landscapes, and wild seacoasts. Lakes and marshes serve as nesting sites for waterfowl, including swans, ducks, grebes, loons, and Arctic terns. The Brooks River, which flows past Brooks Camp, and the McNeil River to the northeast draw large numbers of visitors to view bears feeding at the salmon runs.

Fishing at Naknek Lake
Anglers flock to the park's rivers and lakes to fish for salmon, trout, and Arctic char.

★ **Brooks Camp**
This prime bear-viewing spot lies on the shores of Naknek Lake. It consists of a campground, ranger station, lodge, and elevated viewing platforms overlooking the Riffles and Brooks River Falls.

EXPLORING THE PARK

A rough 23-mile (37-km) road accesses the Valley of 10,000 Smokes. A steep trail descends into the valley, from where trails lead to Ukak Falls and the confluence of River Lethe and Windy River. A chartered bush plane is necessary to access remote areas of the park, while hiking to Mount Katmai or Novarupta is challenging and needs good backcountry skills. Camping is allowed throughout the park, but a permit is needed for backcountry camping.

Map labels:
Kukaklek
Alagnak
Nonvian Lake
Lake Coville
King Salmon
KING SALMON–NAKNEK RD
Naknek Lake
Gros
Brooks Camp
Moun La Go △ 3,183
Brooks Lake
Iliuk Arm
Mount Kelez 3,250 ft
Three Forks
Windy
Mount Martin 6,050 ft

★ **Valley of 10,000 Smokes**
After the 1912 Novarupta eruption, thousands of fumaroles steamed from this bleak landscape of ash deposits, which is now slashed by deep river canyons.

STAR SIGHTS

★ Brooks Camp

★ Valley of 10,000 Smokes

★ Mount Katmai and Novarupta

Brown bear with yearlings at McNeil River State Game Sanctuary

MCNEIL RIVER STATE GAME SANCTUARY

The McNeil River State Game Sanctuary, at the northeast boundary of Katmai, provides the most reliable summer bear viewing. Often, a big group of brown bears congregates at the falls to feast on salmon, offering good opportunities for photographs. Access is by lottery permit only.

VISITORS' CHECKLIST

290 miles SW of Anchorage. **Road Map** D4. **Tel** 246-3305, 365-2267. ☒ charter floatplane to Brooks Camp. 🚌 🚶 daily guided bus tour from Brooks Lodge to Valley of 10,000 Smokes. Ⓐ **Permits** for backcountry camping available at Brooks Camp Visitor Center & Park HQ, King Salmon. **www.** nps.gov/katm **McNeil River State Game Sanctuary** N of Katmai National Park. **Tel** 267-2182. ☒ from King Salmon. **www.**wildlife.alaska.gov

Map showing the region with McNeil River State Game Sanctuary, Ilik Lodge, Spotted Glacier, Mount Douglas 7,065 ft, Fourpeaked Mountain 7,903 ft, Mount Griggs, Novarupta, Snowy Mountain 7,090 ft, Mount Katmai 6,715 ft, Serpent Tongue Glacier, Trident Volcano. Scale 0 km 10, 0 miles 10.

Mount Douglas

At the summit of this 7,000-ft (2,100-m) volcano is an active fumarole field and a warm, highly acidic crater lake. The park contains at least 14 active volcanoes.

KEY

☒	Airstrip
Ⓐ	Campground
ℹ	Visitor information
═	Minor road
‑‑	Trail
‑ ‑	Park boundary
△	Peak

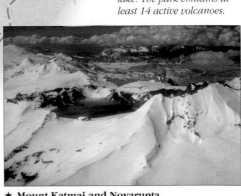

★ Mount Katmai and Novarupta

In June 1912, severe earthquakes around Mount Katmai led to a cataclysmic eruption that covered the surrounding tundra with volcanic debris. It was initially thought that Mount Katmai had erupted, but Novarupta proved to be the source. As Novarupta's explosion emptied Mount Katmai's magma chamber, Katmai's summit collapsed, leaving a caldera with a crater lake.

Colorful iron springs at Surprise Lake in the Aniakchak Caldera

Aniakchak National Monument ❽

100 miles (160 km) SW of Kodiak.
Road Map C5. ✈ *King Salmon, then chartered floatplane to Surprise Lake.* 🛈 *King Salmon airport terminal, 246-3305.* **www**.nps.gov/ania

With the unofficial distinction of being the least visited unit in the US National Park System, Aniakchak National Monument is tucked away in a remote corner of the Alaska Peninsula. The park's most striking feature is the 2,000-ft (600-m) deep, 6-mile (10-km) wide **Aniakchak Caldera**, an ash-filled bowl formed 3,500 years ago when Aniakchak Volcano collapsed into its own empty magma chamber. Over the millennia, minor eruptions,

including one in 1931, have added several small cinder cones and lava flows to the crater.

Located within the caldera, Surprise Lake is the remnant of a larger lake that once existed here. After a weakness developed in the caldera's southeastern wall, the lake drained. The resulting white-water Aniakchak River created the canyon known as The Gates and flowed 27 miles (43 km) to the Gulf of Alaska. Fed by brilliant red iron springs, Surprise Lake provides floatplane access to the park and is the put-in point for whitewater rafting trips. The park has excellent hiking opportunities, but hikers and rafters need to be self-sufficient and prepared for long weather-related delays.

Sand Point ❾

440 miles (710 km) SW of Kodiak.
Road Map C5. 🚶 950. ✈ 🛥

Situated on the northwest coast of Popof Island, the town of Sand Point was settled in the late 19th century by the Russians. Like nearby King Cove, it has Aleut and Scandinavian heritage, and these two groups still constitute the majority of its population. As with the rest of the region, the area's economy has always been based on the fishing industry. In 1898, a trading post and cod fishing station were set up by a San Francisco seafood company, and by the 1930s, fish processing had become the dominant activity. Today, Sand Point is home to one of the largest fishing fleets in the Aleutian region.

Visitors can view the large flocks of bald eagles that gather near the shore, ride the popular 14-mile (23-km) bike trail, and visit the 1933 Russian Orthodox Church, which is listed on the National Register of Historic Places.

To visit Sand Point, travelers will most likely take the Marine Highway ferry *(see pp290–91)* from Kodiak. The first stop on the journey is the tiny, beautifully situated village of **Chignik**, which is flanked by snow-capped peaks. Farther south is Perryville, founded by villagers from Katmai who migrated after their homes

Magnificent lagoon at the mouth of the Aniakchak River in Aniakchak National Monument

For hotels and restaurants in this region see pp250–51 and p263

The active Shishaldin Volcano, best viewed from the Izembek National Wildlife Refuge

were destroyed in the 1912 eruption of Novarupta *(see pp210–11).* The ferry arrives at Sand Point nine hours after leaving Chignik.

King Cove ⓰

551 miles (887 km) SW of Kodiak. **Road Map** C5. 🕍 *750.* ✈ 🚌 🛈 *497-2340.* **www.**cityofkingcove.com

Founded in 1911, King Cove developed around a salmon cannery belonging to the Pacific American Fisheries. The first settlers in the village were Scandinavian, Aleut, and Anglo fishermen who either hauled in the fish or worked in the processing plant. The plant operated until 1976, when it was damaged by fire and replaced by the Peter Pan Seafood Cannery.

Today, half the residents are of Native descent, while the rest are descended primarily from the early Scandinavian settlers. They continue to fish commercially or work for the cannery, which has grown into one of Alaska's most successful commercial operations. Locals also engage in subsistence fishing and hunting for geese, caribou, and ptarmigan.

Most visitors arrive on the Alaska Marine Highway's twice-monthly ferry between Homer and Dutch Harbor/Unalaska, which stops long enough for a visit to the Russian Orthodox Church. The church's bells

and interior icons were brought here in the 1980s by residents who moved from the abandoned town of Belkofski, 12 miles (19 km) to the southeast.

Visitors should be wary of the unusually large numbers of bears that invade town, chasing dogs, tipping over trash cans, and trying to break into homes and buildings.

Cold Bay and Izembek National Wildlife Refuge ⓱

579 miles (930 km) SW of Kodiak. **Road Map** C5. 🕍 *100.* ✈ 🚌 **Izembek National Wildlife Refuge** 🛈 *Izembek St, 532-2445.* **http://**izembek.fws.gov

The small town of Cold Bay, within view of the dramatic 9,370-ft (2,850-m) Shishaldin Volcano, officially came into existence in August 1941 as a covert US military base to ward off Japanese attacks. Its construction was classified and its military contractor, General William Buckner, assumed a civilian name and claimed to have built a salmon cannery.

Even after Fort Randall was constructed here in 1942, the Japanese failed to realize its military significance. In 1945, the US and Russia forged an alliance and made Fort Randall a training site for over 12,000 Russian troops. During the Vietnam War in the 1960s,

Cold Bay sprang back to life as a freight hauling base and the headquarters of the famed Flying Tigers squadron. Cold Bay is today the air hub for the Aleutians.

The main attraction is the beautiful 650-sq mile (1,700-sq km) **Izembek National Wildlife Refuge**, partly accessible via gravel roads from Cold Bay. The refuge protects the habitat of brown bears, caribou, seals, sea lions, and whales. At the 150-sq mile (390-sq km) brackish Izembek Lagoon, 10 miles (16 km) from Cold Bay, vast beds of eelgrass provide food for migrating birds. These include 98 percent of the world's population of Pacific black brant, a small dark goose. Visitors can watch the wildlife from a viewing hide at the lagoon.

Caribou grazing in Izembek National Wildlife Refuge

Dutch Harbor/Unalaska ⑫

For thousands of years, Dutch Harbor and its sister town Unalaska have provided shelter from stormy seas. The Aleuts, or the Unangan, have lived here for centuries, fishing and hunting sea mammals from *iqax* (skin boats). The first outsiders to arrive were the Russians. Settling on Iliuliuk Bay, the site of Unalaska, in 1759, they conscripted the Aleuts to hunt fur seals and sea otters. After buying Alaska, the US also used the islands as a seal hunting base and, during World War II, as a military outpost. The king crab boom of the 1970s and the growth of the fishing industry have made this ice-free port the largest in the US in terms of the weight and value of the catch.

Fishermen repairing crab pots at Dutch Harbor

SIGHTS AT A GLANCE

Aleutian World War II National
  Historical Park ③
Church of the Holy Ascension ①
Mount Ballyhoo ④
Museum of the Aleutians ②

Key to Symbols
see back flap

0 meters   500

0 yards   500

🏠 Church of the Holy Ascension

Broadway Rd. **Tel** 581-3790.
📷 groups by appt. 🚫 ⛪ 6:30pm Sat & 9:30am Sun.

The focal point of Unalaska, the cruciform Church of the Holy Ascension stands on a small spit at the western end of the village. In 1808, it was the site of Alaska's first Russian Orthodox church, a basic structure that Bishop Veniaminov *(see p74)* reconstructed in a more opulent style in 1827. A third structure was built in 1858 by Aleut priest Innokenti Shaishnikov. The present building, dating from 1896, had suffered so much damage from Aleutian storms that by 1990 it needed repairs. The renovated church was rededicated in 1996, in time for its

centenary. Its interior is filled with a rich collection of icons from abandoned villages around Unalaska Islands, as well as an ornate candelabra, bronze bells, and paintings. The adjacent 1882 Bishop's House reflects a style characteristic of 1880s San Francisco.

Church of the Holy Ascension in Unalaska

🏛 Museum of the Aleutians

314 Salmon Way. **Tel** 581-5150.
🕐 Jun–Aug: 11am–5pm Tue–Sun; Sep–May: 11am–5pm Tue–Sat. 🍴
♿ 📷 www.aleutians.org

Opened in 1999 on the site of an old World War II warehouse, the museum is one of the finest attractions in the area. The modern building, with lovely terrazzo tiles in the entryway, has an extensive collection that includes historic photographs, drawings, and relics from the Russian era, as well as objects salvaged from the World War II defense of the islands and a 1920s herring fishery.

Also on display are Aleut artifacts uncovered in several archeological digs around Unalaska, Amaknak, and other Aleutian Islands, including many of the 100,000 items recovered from the adjacent Margaret Bay village site. Once a flourishing fish camp, this village is thought to have thrived about 2,000 years ago.

For hotels and restaurants in this region see pp250–51 and p263

Summer Bay Road winding across the tundra toward Ugadaga Pass

VISITORS' CHECKLIST

850 miles (1,368 km) SW of Kodiak. **Road Map** B5. 🚶 *4,000.* ✈ *from Anchorage.* ⛴ *from Homer & Kodiak.* ℹ **Unalaska** *Broadway & 5th St, 581-2612, (877) 581-2612.* **Permits** *needed to camp or hike on Unalaska and Amaknak Islands, which are available from the Ounalashka Native Corporation in Dutch Harbor.* **www**.unalaska.info

Volunteers and students are welcome to apply to participate in the ongoing museum-sponsored digs around the Aleutian Islands.

⚜ Aleutian World War II National Historical Park
Dutch Harbor Airport. *Tel* 581-9944. ⏰ *May–Sep: 11am–8pm daily; Oct–Apr: 11am–6pm Tue–Sat.* 🅿 ♿ www.nps.gov/aleu

Known as Unangax Tenganis, which means "Our Islands" in Aleut, the Aleutian World War II National Historical Park was designated by the US Congress in 1996. It aims to showcase the little known war history of the state, focusing on the culture and role of the Aleuts and their islands in the defense of the US.

The visitor center, at the airport in Dutch Harbor, occupies the renovated Naval Air Transport Service's Aerology Building. Its displays include a 1940s-era radio room and exhibits on the mass evacuation of the Aleuts. The area's remaining World War II structures and ruins convey the grand scale of the war effort mounted in the islands.

⚜ Mount Ballyhoo
During World War II, Mount Ballyhoo was the site of Fort Schwatka, one of Dutch Harbor's four coastal defense posts. It was named for Lt. Frederick Schwatka, who was responsible for surveying the Aleutians in the 1880s.

At this strategic location, 897 ft (269 m) above the harbor, engineers built over 100 buildings designed to withstand nature's fury. Today, the fort is a part of the Aleutian

World War II National Historical Park. A stroll across the site reveals concrete bunkers, observation posts, and gun emplacements from the 1940s. The site also offers views across the sea and toward the Makushin Volcano. While it is possible to negotiate the steep, twisting road with a hardy vehicle, a pleasant day hike is also an option.

🚣 Summer Bay
Heading east from Unalaska, a gravel road along the scenic coastline of Iliuliuk Bay turns north to reach the beautiful inlet known as Summer Bay. Behind coastal sand dunes that attract picnickers, the

pristine freshwater Summer Bay Lake reflects the surrounding green hills and magical Aleutian light. At the head of the lake, the road winds uphill across the tundra to Ugadaga Pass. From here, a relatively easy hiking trail leads down to Ugadaga Bay on the east coast of Unalaska Island. In fine weather, this makes an excellent day hike.

Just northeast of Ugadaga Bay at Ugadaga Head, it is possible to see remnants of another of the island's coastal defense posts. The last mile (2 km) or so is rough, so park your vehicle and walk. Local companies provide guided birding and historical tours.

MV *Tustumena* sailing in Kachemak Bay

THE TRUSTY TUSTY

Built in 1964, the 296-ft (89-m) long ferry MV *Tustumena*, affectionately known as the "Trusty Tusty," plies some of the roughest waters on earth. Once a month from April to September, this sturdy vessel – the oldest ship in the fleet of the Alaska Marine Highway *(see p290–91)* – does the difficult, stormy four-day run from Homer to Dutch Harbor/Unalaska. This spectacular trip attracts adventurous visitors hoping to see one of the most remote corners of the world. Be forewarned though that the amenities are basic. Deck-class passengers have access to a solarium where they can stake out a warm spot to roll out their sleeping bags.

Pribilof Islands

In 1786, Gerassim Pribilof claimed the Pribilof Islands for Russia, and set up Russian trade interests based on the large fur seal colonies he found there. These five islands in the middle of the Bering Sea have been dubbed the "Northern Galapagos" due to their dense concentrations of breeding pinnipeds and nesting birds. While the larger islands of St. Paul and St. George have small Aleut communities, Otter Island, Walrus Island, and Sea Lion Rock are inhabited only by wildlife. Bird-watching groups dominate island tourism, but an increasing number of visitors also come to appreciate the local Aleut culture, the profusion of summer wildflowers across the volcanic landscapes, and the stark beauty of the islands.

Bering Sea

Village houses and the Russian Orthodox church, St. Paul Island

KEY

☒ Airstrip

= Minor road

St. Paul Island

🏛 670. ☒ ⛴ 🛈 *Tanadgusix Corporation, PO Box 88, St. Paul; 546-2312.* 🎣 🍴 🛏 🎿 *St. Peter and Paul Feast Day (Jul 12).* 🐚 **Permits** *needed to camp on the island; issued by the Tanadgusix Corporation.* **St. Paul Island Tours** *Tel 278-2318, (877) 424-5637.* **www**.alaskabirding.com

St. Paul Island, with an area of just over 40 sq miles (104 sq km), lies in the Bering Sea, 375 miles (600 km) west of the mainland. The island's only village, also called St. Paul, has the state's largest Aleut community, with 86 percent of the population consisting of indigenous people.

Life in the community revolves around the St. Peter and Paul Russian Orthodox Church, which is the only church on the island. For visitors, highlights include forays to the island's spectacular bird cliffs and northern fur seal rookeries, as well as the opportunity to hike through the wild interior to see reindeer herds, volcanic formations, numerous small lakes,

and a changing tableau of wildflowers. While it is possible to visit the island independently, tours are available only through St. Paul Island Tours, operated by the Native Tanadgusix Corporation.

St. George Island

🏛 150. ☒ ⛴ 🛈 *St. George Tanaq Corporation, PO Box 939, St. George, 859-2255 or 2600 Denali St #300, Anchorage, 272-9886.* 🎣 🛏 🐚 **Permits** *needed to camp on the island; issued by the St. George Tanaq Corporation.* **www**.stgeorgetanaq.com

Lying 47 miles (75 km) south of St. Paul, St. George Island is less visited, but is considered to be even more spectacular than its more easily accessed neighbor. Much wilder than St. Paul Island, it has six fur seal rookeries, harboring up to 250,000 animals, and the highest and most prolific bird cliffs in the Pribilofs.

About 90 percent of the islanders are Aleut or belong to other indigenous groups. As with St. Paul Island, the beautiful Russian Orthodox

church of St. George the Martyr dominates the local social scene and is one of the island's main attractions. Hiking around St. George or camping are other interesting options, but it is worth noting that there are few roads or trails, and in places, the going can be quite rough. Visits are organized by the St. George Tanaq Corporation, which is headquartered in Anchorage.

Towering cliffs with St. George village in the distance

For hotels and restaurants in this region see pp250–51 and p263

Wildlife of the Pribilof Islands

The biodiversity of the Pribilof Islands is largely due to the Bering Sea, which is rich in fish, shellfish, seaweed, and plankton, as well as to the island's range of habitats, which include sand dunes, tundra, beaches, lagoons, and towering cliffs. Half of the world population of northern fur seals breeds on St. Paul and St. George, while Steller sea lions breed on Walrus Island and harbor seals on Otter Island. In the summer, the spectacular cliffs that gird the islands hum with millions of nesting birds. Sea ice that once reached this far south from the Arctic brought a substantial population of Arctic foxes to the Pribilofs, while a reindeer herd that was introduced to the St. Paul in the early 20th century still inhabits the interior of the island.

Bird cliffs are alive with thousands of nesting birds such as murres, a type of auk.

Horned puffins *are awkward fliers, but can dive up to 20 ft (6 m) and swim underwater while retrieving the small fish that form their main diet.*

The crested auklet *sports a distinctive plume of dark feathers during the breeding season.*

BIRDS

The towering cliffs of these tundra-covered, treeless islands annually attract over two million birds of at least 200 species, including Asian migrants that are blown off course by strong westerly winds.

Red-legged kittiwakes *are similar in size and shape to black-legged kittiwakes (see p117), but have red legs and darker wings undersides.*

ANIMALS

The abundance of wildlife attracts visitors to the Pribilofs, who come to view the world's largest colony of northern fur seals. Arctic foxes, reindeer, and harbor seals are easily spotted, while Steller sea lions are seen occasionally.

Arctic foxes *den in grassy bluffs, foraging for sea bird eggs and chicks. They have both blue and white phases, when their coats change color, but the blue phase is most common in the Pribilofs.*

Northern fur seals *are "eared" seals, with a waxy coating in their ears and nostrils that prevents water from entering during dives. Their large bare flippers regulate body temperature by shedding heat while on land. Hunting them is now restricted to Alaska Natives, who take around 2,000 animals a year.*

The reindeer herd *on St. Paul Island, introduced in 1911, was originally of Russian stock. These domesticated caribou are shorter and stockier than their wild counterparts.*

ARCTIC AND WESTERN ALASKA

*C*overing *nearly two-thirds of Alaska, the vast coastal plain stretching from the Canadian border to Norton Sound is a quintessentially Arctic region. While this pristine wilderness is home to only a few thousand people, Arctic wildlife is abundant: great herds of caribou live on the tundra, musk oxen inhabit the North Slope, and millions of migrating birds flock to the region's lakes in summer.*

Although the winters along the lonely coastline are not as harsh as those of the Alaskan Interior, the early Athabaskans chose to continue onward to the forested lands to the south, leaving the coast to the Inupiat and Yup'ik peoples who arrived later. Remarkably, these groups, collectively known as Inuit, thrived in this barren region. They subsisted mainly on fish and sea mammals such as seals, sea lions, walrus, and whales, using their skins to make clothing and their fat to provide heat and light. While Native traditions are still followed to some extent, the Inuit now lead an increasingly modern way of life.

The Inuit were the last Native people to be contacted by Europeans, mainly because their lands offered few natural resources. However, in the early 20th century, the Nome area experienced a surge of outside interest as prospectors stampeded in to mine the gold-bearing beach sands. Today, while the attractions of the region are undeniably spectacular, they are also universally difficult and expensive to access. This relative inaccessibility has resulted in swathes of untouched wilderness in parks such as the Arctic National Wildlife Refuge and Gates of the Arctic National Park. Several designated Wild Rivers offer rafting and fishing, and excellent bird-watching is available around Nome and Gambell. Adventure-seekers will enjoy driving the spectacular Dalton Highway to Deadhorse.

Caribou swimming across the Alatna River, Gates of the Arctic National Park

◁ Truck on a lonely stretch of the Dalton Highway, also known as the Haul Road

Exploring Arctic and Western Alaska

Most visitors to the region want to experience its fierce, desolate beauty and venture north of the Arctic Circle. Of the three major towns, historical Nome has roads leading into spectacular country, Barrow is the largest Inupiat community in Alaska, and commercial Kotzebue is a gateway to four remote national parks. The rewarding Arctic National Wildlife Refuge is one of America's last true wildernesses and Prudhoe Bay displays the harsh conditions involved in Arctic oil extraction. Gambell and Nome are world-renowned bird-watching venues, and the Kobuk, Noatak, John, Kongukut, and Hulahula Rivers provide excellent kayaking, rafting, fishing, and access to wildlife viewing.

Kayaking on Walker Lake in the Brooks Range

SIGHTS AT A GLANCE

Towns and Cities
Barrow **5**
Gambell **12**
Kotzebue **6**
Nome **10**
Prudhoe Bay **2**

Tour
*Dalton Highway Tour
pp222–3* **1**

National and State Parks
Arctic National Wildlife Refuge **3**
Bering Land Bridge National Preserve **11**
Cape Krusenstern National Monument **9**
Gates of the Arctic National Park **4**
Kobuk Valley National Park **7**
Noatak National Preserve **8**

Atigun River flowing along the Dalton Highway

KEY

══	Minor road
▬▬	International border
△	Peak
)(	Pass

Wainwri
Point Lay
Utukok

Wevok

Point Hope   *Kukpuk*   *Kokolik*   B

CHUKCHI SEA   Kivalina   NOATAK NATIO PRESERV **8**
    Noatak   Tututal Mounte 4,460 f
    Noatak   KOBUK VAL
9   NATIONAL P **7**
CAPE KRUSENSTERN NATIONAL MONUMENT
Kotzebue Sound   KOTZEBUE **6** ✕   An
    Kiana   Sel
Shishmaref   *Goodhope Bay*   Selaw Lak
11   BERING LAND BRIDGE NATIONAL PRESERVE   Kiwalik   Buckland
Wales   Kougarok
Port Clarence   Teller   *Kuzitrin*   *Koyuk*
    Council   Koyuk
✕   Elim   Nu
Bering Strait   NOME **10**   Solomon   *Norton Bay*   Shaktoolik
GAMBELL **12**   Savoonga   Nu
    Norton Sound   Kalta
St. Lawrence Island   Unalakleet
Camp Kulowiye   Stebbins
    Pastol Bay
BERING SEA   Kotlik
Emmonak   Grayling
Sheldon Point   *Yukon*

Native whalers launching an *umiaq* (skin boat) into the Arctic Ocean near Barrow

SEE ALSO

• *Where to Stay* p251

• *Where to Eat* p263

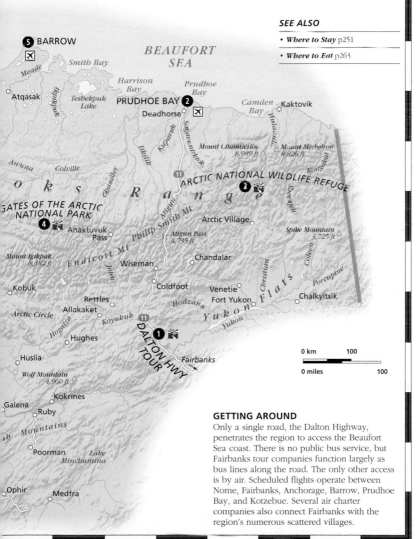

GETTING AROUND

Only a single road, the Dalton Highway, penetrates the region to access the Beaufort Sea coast. There is no public bus service, but Fairbanks tour companies function largely as bus lines along the road. The only other access is by air. Scheduled flights operate between Nome, Fairbanks, Anchorage, Barrow, Prudhoe Bay, and Kotzebue. Several air charter companies also connect Fairbanks with the region's numerous scattered villages.

Dalton Highway Tour ⓵

Originally built in the 1970s to supply equipment to the Prudhoe Bay oilfields and provide a service corridor for the Trans-Alaska Pipeline, the Dalton Highway is the only road in Alaska that crosses the Arctic Circle. Also known as the Haul Road, it was initially accessible only to supply trucks, but in the 1990s, the full route was opened to private drivers. While astoundingly scenic, much of the highway is a bone-jarring gravel route that should not be taken lightly. Services are available only in a handful of places, and drivers should travel with essentials such as food, water, a first aid kit, and spare tires.

Sukakpak Mountain ⓺
This dramatic 4,460-ft (1,360-m) peak was once a limestone deposit before heat and pressure metamorphosed it into marble.

Wiseman ⓹
The village of Wiseman was founded in 1907 as a camp to service the gold strike at nearby Nolan. Today, the site resembles an open-air museum, with equipment and several historic buildings still standing.

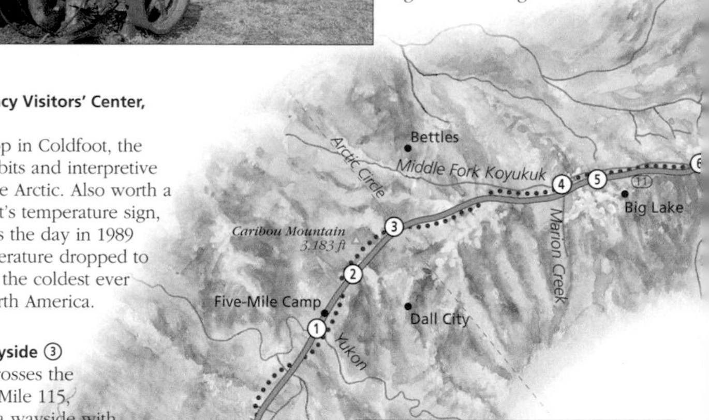

Arctic Interagency Visitors' Center, Coldfoot ⓸
An essential stop in Coldfoot, the center has exhibits and interpretive programs on the Arctic. Also worth a look is Coldfoot's temperature sign, which describes the day in 1989 when the temperature dropped to -63° C (-82° F), the coldest ever recorded in North America.

Arctic Circle Wayside ⓷
The highway crosses the Arctic Circle at Mile 115, where there is a wayside with a picnic area, a basic campsite, and interpretive signs.

Bettles

Middle Fork Koyukuk

Arctic Circle

Caribou Mountain
3,183 ft

Five-Mile Camp

Dall City

Big Lake

Marion Creek

Yukon

MANLEY HOT SPRINGS

ELLIOTT HWY

DALTON HIGHWAY

Trans-Alaska Pipeline

Livengood

E. L. Patton Yukon Bridge ⓵
This 2,295-ft (688-m) long bridge carries both the Dalton Highway and the Alaska Pipeline. Built in 1975, this is the only US bridge across the Yukon (see pp198–9).

FAIRBANKS

Finger Mountain ⓶
Distant views from the Finger Mountain wayside take in the lovely tor-studded landscape and Caribou Mountain.

TIPS FOR DRIVERS

Starting point: Livengood on the Elliot Highway, 73 miles (117 km) N of Fairbanks.
Length: 414 miles (662 km).
Accommodation: Coldfoot at Mile 175 has a hotel and café. There is a campground at Marion Creek, and Wiseman at Mile 188.6 has lodging and a general store. The Prudhoe Bay Hotel in Deadhorse serves meals.
Note: there are only four gas stations on the Dalton Highway – at Yukon Crossing, Five-Mile Camp, Coldfoot, and Deadhorse.

Atigun Pass ⑦

The highway crosses the Brooks Range at the 4,800-ft (1,440-m) high Atigun Pass, the highest point on Alaska's road system. Its steep grades should be driven with great caution.

Kuparuk

Deadhorse

Prudhoe Bay

⑨

Toolik

Happy Valley Camp

⑧

Sagavanirktok

⑪

Galbraith Lake

Innaviat Mountain 3,680 ft

Sag River Overlook

B r o o k s   R a n g e

⑦

...rich Camp

| 0 km | 20 |
| 0 miles | 20 |

KEY

━━ Tour route

━━ Highway

••• Trans-Alaska Pipeline

✲ Viewpoint

△ Peak

Trans-Alaska Pipeline ⑧

Near the northern end of the highway, the gleaming pipeline winds across a vast tundra landscape along the western edge of the Arctic National Wildlife Refuge.

Franklin Bluffs ⑨

The iron-rich soil on the east bank of the Sagavanirktok River on the plains of the North Slope gives Franklin Bluffs their striking yellow, tan, and orange color.

Pipelines crisscrossing the oilfields at Prudhoe Bay on the North Slope

Prudhoe Bay ❷

487 miles (784 km) N of Fairbanks.
Road Map E1. 🚶 25. ✈ from
Anchorage. 🚌 tour bus from
Fairbanks. ℹ Prudhoe Bay Hotel,
659-2449.

The North Slope oilfields,
often collectively called
Prudhoe Bay, make up the
largest oil producing field in
North America. While geo-
logic surveys took place in
the 1950s, the first major
discovery was made only in
1968. The Alyeska Pipeline
Service Company was formed
a year later to construct a
pipeline (see p186) across the
state to the ice-free port of
Valdez. Today, the vast
oilfields use the latest technology to minimize their
impact on the delicate tundra.
   Deadhorse, the oilfields'
service center, has a shop, a
gas station, a hotel, and restaurants. Prudhoe Bay and the
Arctic Ocean coast, which lie
beyond a checkpoint, can
only be accessed on tours run
by the Prudhoe Bay Hotel.

Arctic National Wildlife Refuge ❸

200 miles (320 km) N of Fairbanks.
Road Map E1. ✈ air taxi to Fort
Yukon, Arctic Village, Deadhorse,
or Kaktovik, then bush plane.
🚌 tour bus to Galbraith Lake, then
hike. ℹ 101 12th Ave, Fairbanks;
456-0250, (800) 362-4546. 🕐 year-
round. **http://**arctic.fws.gov

The 30,000-sq mile (78,000-sq
km) Arctic National Wildlife
Refuge (ANWR, pronounced
AN-wahr) was established in
1960 to protect the region's

abundant wildlife, flocks of
migratory birds and its range
of ecosystems.
   However, studies of the
ANWR coastal plain east of
Prudhoe Bay have determined
that the northwestern corner
of the refuge holds vast
amounts of natural gas and oil.
Political forces have long
tussled over ANWR, with pro-
development organizations
and many Republicans
lobbying to allow oil drilling,
while environmental groups
and most Democrats oppose
opening the wildlife refuge to
industrial development.
   Scenically stunning, ANWR
is bisected by the Brooks
Range and crossed by the
Sheenjek, Kongukut, Hulahula,
and other Wild Rivers (see
p274) that are popular for rafting trips. Wildlife enthusiasts
may have the chance to spot
all of Alaska's bear species, as
well as musk oxen, bowhead
whales, and over 140 species
of birds. ANWR has no trails
or facilities, and visitors need
to be self-sufficient.

Gates of the Arctic National Park ❹

200 miles (320 km) NW of
Fairbanks. **Road Map** D1. ✈ to
Anaktuvuk Pass, Bettles, Coldfoot, or
Kotzebue, then bush plane. 🚌 tour
bus to Coldfoot, then bush plane.
ℹ Bettles Visitors' Center, 692-5494.
Also Anaktuvuk Pass Ranger Station
& Arctic Interagency Visitors' Center
(Coldfoot). **Note** no roads or facilities
in refuge. **www.**nps.gov/gaar

The second-largest national
park in the US after Wrangell-
St. Elias (see pp192–3), Gates
of the Arctic National Park
encompasses 12,500 sq miles
(32,000 sq km). The park got
its name in the 1930s when
wilderness advocate Bob
Marshall described Frigid Crags
and the Boreal Mountains as
the "gates" to the Arctic Slope.
   The heart of the park is the
Brooks Range, the northernmost extent of the Rocky
Mountains. The abundant
wildlife includes all three bear
species, caribou, moose, and
migratory birds, and the vegetation away from the bare,
glaciated peaks ranges from
boreal forest of spruce, birch,
and aspen to alder thickets,
taiga, and muskeg.
   Most visitors fly in for hiking
or rafting on National Wild and
Scenic Rivers (see p274) such
as the Kobuk, John, and Noatak. Commercial trips are available, but lone travelers usually
take an air taxi to Bettles, and
then a bush plane to a drop-off
point. Lodges at Bettles provide
accommodation and meals.

The mighty Brooks Range, Gates of the Arctic National Park

The Arctic Tundra

Lying north of the Brooks Range, Alaska's North Slope encompasses 88,000 sq miles (227,920 sq km) of largely flat, open Arctic tundra. Derived from the Finnish *tunturia*, meaning "treeless land," this circumpolar environment is characterized by low temperatures and thin topsoil that supports only ground-hugging vegetation such as reindeer mosses, sedges, lichens, liverworts, berries, dwarf birch, and miniature wildflowers. This thin surface is underlain by permanently frozen ground known as permafrost. Tundra areas typically have little precipitation, a growing season of less than 60 days, and average temperatures of 12° C (54° F) during the summer and around -34° C (-30° F) in the harsh winter.

Vibrant miniature wildflowers *carpet the tundra during the short flowering season in summer. Alaska has about 400 species of wildflowers.*

LANDSCAPE
Underlying the thin tundra surface is permafrost. This permanently frozen ground cannot absorb surface water, resulting in numerous small shallow ponds and bogs.

Crater lakes *are sometimes found in* pingos, *domed ice-cored mounds of earth. The expanding ice may cause the summit of the pingo to crack. This exposes the ice core and allows part of it to melt, forming the crater lake.*

WILDLIFE
The tundra teems with wildlife, including Arctic hares, caribou, Arctic foxes, polar bears, and wolves, species that are well-adapted to the severe climatic conditions.

The Arctic ground squirrel *digs burrows in the ground and hibernates through the long, cold winter.*

Musk oxen *live year-round on the open tundra, protected from the extreme cold by a soft insulating layer of hair known as* qiviut. *Musk oxen eat a wide variety of plants, including grasses, sedges, and woody plants.*

Caribou *have broad hooves that provide support in soft tundra and snow, function as paddles when the animal swims, and, in winter, help to scrape away snow to expose the limited grazing below. Unlike moose, both bulls and cows grow antlers.*

Barrow ⑤

The northernmost town in the US and seat of the vast North Slope Borough, Barrow sits on the tundra beside the Beaufort Sea. Its Inupiat name, Utqiagvik, means "the place to hunt snowy owls." Offshore ice huddles close to the shore almost all year round, retreating for just a few weeks in July and August. This isolated community experiences the midnight sun for 84 days in the summer; conversely, the sun does not rise at all for the same period in the winter. At 300 miles (480 km) north of the Arctic Circle, the people of this Inupiat outpost continue to live on subsistence fishing and hunting, as they have always done.

Whalers towing a whale out of the sea, Barrow

🪦 Ukkuqsi Archeological Site
Stevenson St.
Along the coast at the western end of town, a series of sod ruins and remnants of archeological digs sit on the bluffs overlooking a lonely stretch of beach. While contact between Europeans and indigenous peoples began around 1825, trade was not common until the 1870s. For that reason, the types of items unearthed – ivory points, weapons, tools, and artwork – are still familiar to the older residents of the town, who usually participate in the excavations. This grassy bluff makes a pleasant place to stroll and enjoy the views out over the Arctic Ocean.

🪦 Will Rogers and Wiley Post Monument
Akhovak & Momegana Sts. 🚻
This memorial honors the renowned pilot Wiley Post and his friend, Cherokee humorist Will Rogers. Post, famous for setting 1920s distance records in his Lockheed Vega, decided to survey an air route from California to Russia in 1935. Funded by interested airlines, he built a low-wing monoplane. In July 1935, Post and Rogers left Seattle for Alaska. Near Barrow they encountered bad weather and made an emergency landing. However, soon after they took off again, the engine failed and the plane plunged into a lagoon, killing both men. Visitors can hire ATVs or hike to the crash site 15 miles (24 km) to the south.

🏛 Inupiat Heritage Center
5421 North Star St. *Tel* 852-4594.
◯ 8:30am–5pm Mon–Fri. ⬤ public holidays. 🖼 📷 ♿ 🛍
www.nps.gov/inup
The town's main attraction, the Inupiat Heritage Center was set up in recognition of Inuit contribution to whaling. For hundreds of years, the Inuit hunted whales from their *umiaqs*, and in the 19th and 20th centuries, crewed on whaling ships and provided shelter for shipwrecked sailors.

In addition to the whaling connection, the center celebrates Inupiat culture, displaying diverse facets of local life, such as a whale baleen sled, spirit masks, and ivory implements. A large performance area hosts singing, drumming, and dance performances.

🪦 Whalebone Arch and Brower's Café
Stevenson St.
This lonely spot on the coast of the Arctic Ocean is the historic site from where generations of Inuit whalers have set out across the icy seas in

Prominent whalebone arch on the Arctic Ocean coast

For hotels and restaurants in this region see p251 and p263

POLAR BEARS

Polar bear in Alaska's Arctic regions

Polar bears *(Ursus maritimus)* are marine mammals that wander across the Arctic ice in search of walruses and seals. Rivaling Kodiak bears as the world's largest four-footed carnivores, these bears keep warm due to their hollow tube- like hairs which seem white in the sunlight. Currently, about 3,000 to 5,000 polar bears live in Alaska, and one of the best places to see them is around Barrow's rubbish dump or on the nearby sea ice and gravel beaches. Sadly, global warming is starting to impact the bears as less ice makes it difficult for them to hunt.

VISITORS' CHECKLIST

580 miles (928 km) N of Fairbanks. **Road Map** D1.
4,400. Momegana & Ahkovak St, 852-5211. Kivqiq Midwinter Festival (late Jan), Piuraagiaqta Spring Festival (Apr), Nalukataq (late Jun).
www.cityofbarrow.org

hopes of killing a whale to feed the community through the winter. An arch made from the massive jawbone of a bowhead whale commemorates this indigenous tradition.

Next to the arch is Brower's Café, located in the former trading post of the first European settler, Charles Dewitt Brower, who arrived in Barrow in 1884. He was married twice to Inupiat women and acted as postmaster, census taker, military recruiter, and unofficial surgeon. Brower's grave, marked by whalebones, is located beside the nearby lagoon.

Point Barrow

12 miles (19 km) N of Barrow.
North of Barrow, a coastal gravel road leads to the lonely cape, Point Barrow, which is the northernmost point of land in the US and divides the Chukchi Sea in the west from the Beaufort Sea in the east. At about 71 degrees N, it is roughly at the same latitude as North Cape in Norway, but without the warming waters of the Gulf Stream, it experiences considerably harsher climatic conditions. In the winter and spring, polar bears den in the area. Any sort of food will attract their attention so visitors should ensure they leave no waste on the beach.

Along the route to Point Barrow is the local Ilisagvik College, which works with the Barrow Arctic Science Consortium to research the Arctic environment.

Stress test being conducted on Arctic sea pack ice, Point Barrow

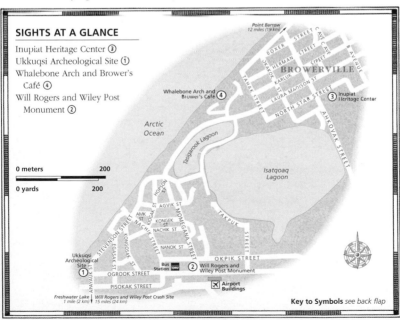

SIGHTS AT A GLANCE

Inupiat Heritage Center ③
Ukkuqsi Archeological Site ①
Whalebone Arch and Brower's Café ④
Will Rogers and Wiley Post Monument ②

Point Barrow
12 miles (19 km)

BROWERVILLE

Whalebone Arch and Brower's Café ④

③ Inupiat Heritage Center

Arctic Ocean

Tasigarook Lagoon

Isatqoaq Lagoon

0 meters 200
0 yards 200

Ukkuqsi Archeological Site ①

Bus Station

② Will Rogers and Wiley Post Monument

OKPIK STREET

Airport Buildings

Freshwater Lake
1 mile (2 km)
Will Rogers and Wiley Post Crash Site
15 miles (24 km)

Key to Symbols see back flap

Barrow, America's northernmost settlement, snow-bound in the winter ▷

Kotzebue ❻

550 miles (880 km) NW of
Anchorage. **Road Map** C2.
🏔 3,200. ✈ ℹ 258A 3rd Ave, 442-
3401. **www**.cityofkotzebue.com

The commercial, economic,
and political center of the
Northwest Arctic Borough,
Kotzebue – with a 75 percent
Inuit population – is a settlement on the Chukchi Sea. The
site, which has been occupied
since at least the 15th century,
lies 26 miles (43 km) north of
the Arctic Circle on a 3-mile
(5-km) long sandspit at the
end of the Baldwin Peninsula.
Kikiktagruk, its Inupiat name,
simply means "the peninsula,"
and its modern one honors
Otto von Kotzebue, a German
who arrived in 1816.

The economy of modern
Kotzebue depends largely
on the Red Dog Mine, a lead
and zinc mine 100 miles (160
km) north of town, which
employs hundreds of workers
and provides a good income
for the Northwest Arctic
Native Association (NANA).
Kotzebue also has Alaska's
only power grid that is
supplemented by electricity
generated by windmills.

Kotzebue is not a major
tourist destination, but visitors
will get a taste of life in this
harsh place where the winters
are long and summers brief
and intense. Walk along the
shore south of town to view
local fish camps where fish,
seal, and walrus meat are

**Bear sculpture on Ootukahkuktuvik
Museum roof, Kotzebue**

smoked and dried. In the heart
of town, the cemetery is worth
a visit for its beautifully decorated graves, or head out the
dirt road east from Kotzebue
to explore the rolling tundra
stretching to the horizon. Be
sure to pack head nets and
mosquito repellent, as well as
a good supply of water.

The National Park Service's
**Northwest Arctic Heritage
Center** has a wealth of exhibits
on Kobuk Valley National
Park, Cape Krusenstern
National Monument, Noatak
National Preserve, and Bering
Land Bridge. The facility also
provides an introduction to
Inupiat culture. The parks
themselves are very remote,
requiring bush flights and
total self-sufficiency for the
duration of the trip.

The local **Ootukahkuktuvik
Museum**, which translates

from the Inupiat language as
"the place having old things,"
is open only sporadically, and
requires a trip to the town
hall to find someone to open
it up. The collection of Arctic
artifacts of Kotzebue history
makes for an unusual visit.

🏛 **Northwest Arctic Heritage
Center**
Tel 442-3890, (800) 478-7252.
⟳ late May–Aug: 8am–5pm Mon–
Sat. ♿ 📷
www.nps.gov/noaa

🏛 **Ootukahkuktuvik
Museum**
2nd Ave. ℹ 442-3401 (town hall).
⟳ by appt.

Kobuk Valley
National Park ❼

125 miles (200 km) E of Kotzebue.
Road Map D2. ✈ charter plane
from Kotzebue. ⛴ charter boat from
Ambler. ℹ 154 2nd Ave, Kotzebue;
442-3890, (800) 478-7252.
www.nps.gov/kova

Situated between the Baird
and Waring Mountains, Kobuk
Valley National Park is a
sanctuary for the area's range
of Arctic wildlife, including
caribou, moose, and wolves.

The park's most unique
sight are the Great Kobuk
Sand Dunes which lie along
Kavel Creek, a tributary of the
Kobuk. Covering over 25 sq
miles (65 sq km), the dunes,
which rise as high as 250 ft

Fall migration of caribou through Kobuk Valley National Park

DeLong Mountains rising from the tundra in Noatak National Preserve

headwaters in the Brooks Range inside Gates of the Arctic National Park *(see p224)*, is the preserve's main highway. River runners regard the wild 350-mile (550-km) descent of the Noatak as one of Alaska's best river trips. The trips, which can take up to three weeks, involve a bush flight into the Noatak headwaters from either Kotzebue or Bettles, with a pickup in Noatak village.

Cape Krusenstern National Monument **9**

50 miles (80 km) NW of Kotzebue. **Road Map** C2. ✈ *charter bush plane from Kotzebue.* ⓘ *154 2nd Ave, Kotzebue; 442-3890, (800) 478-7252.* **www**.nps.gov/cakr

The broad coastal plain of the haunting Cape Krusenstern National Monument is made up of 114 parallel limestone bluffs and ridges that create the Chukchi Sea coastline. In the autumn, this changing landscape of alternating lagoons and beaches attracts migrating waterfowl with its swarms of protein-rich insects. There is also rewarding bird-watching, hiking, and wildlife viewing.

However, the only facility here is a lonely summer ranger station at Anigaaq, near the beach ridges. There are no roads, trails, cabins, or campsites, and visits must be carefully planned.

(75 m), were created when glacier-ground rock was deposited and built up in an area where vegetation could not take hold.

The park is popular with river runners, who fly to Walker Lake and raft, canoe, or kayak 260 miles (416 km) down the Kobuk River over three weeks to the village of Kiana. Those who prefer a tamer adventure fly to Ambler, just east of the park entrance, and float the relatively mild 85-mile (136-km), six-day section to Kiana.

Noatak National Preserve **8**

200 miles (320 km) NE of Kotzebue. **Road Map** C1. ✈ *charter bush plane from Kotzebue.* ⓘ *154 2nd Ave, Kotzebue; 442-3890, (800) 478-7252.* **www**.nps.gov/noat

The wonderfully wild Noatak National Preserve, between the DeLong and Baird Mountain Ranges, encompasses some of the loneliest landscapes in the country and protects an array of plants and wildlife. The Noatak River, with its

---

THE INUIT BLANKET TOSS

The blanket toss, in its most traditional form, is performed using a large walrus hide blanket held by a dozen or more people. The jumper stands in the middle of the blanket and while those holding the sides count to three, he or she makes increasingly higher jumps, as on a trampoline. Once a bit of altitude and momentum are gained, those holding the fringes provide a serious boost, and the jumper is propelled high into the air. Historically, the toss was used to allow lookouts to gain a bit of elevation over the largely flat coastline and determine whether whales, seals, walrus, or polar bears were visible on the ice or out at sea. Today, it is used mostly in celebration of a successful whaling season, hence the Inupiat name of Barrow's main festival, Nalukataq, which means "blanket toss." Blanket tosses are also staged for visitors in Barrow. Although they will not have a chance to be tossed in the air, they can participate as blanket holders.

Propelling a jumper skyward at a blanket toss, Kotzebue

Alaskan Wildflowers and Berries

Beginning in the spring and through the short northern summer, a series of wildflowers splash color across the Alaskan landscape. Plants of the same species may bloom as much as six weeks apart, depending on their location. Perhaps the finest show is in the Pribilof Islands, where the summer-long sequence of wildflower displays is renowned. From mid- to late summer, the edible berries emerge, many developing from the flowers of the early summer. In the late summer, after the salmon runs, this rich harvest provides sugar for the bears, to fatten them before they take to their winter dens.

Lowbush cranberries *are tart fruits that grow in both muskeg and tundra.*

Salmonberries can be either red or yellow in color.

Wild blueberries are popularly used in pies and desserts.

BERRIES

Wild strawberries grow in southern and central Alaska in late June, followed by the cloudberries and blueberries that carpet many parts of the state. Rose hips and lowbush cranberries ripen in late summer.

Labrador tea grows mainly in muskeg.

The aromatic leaves can be used as tea.

The chocolate lily, *also called skunk lily due to its smell, is found in damp woodlands and open meadows.*

Lupines, *found in a range of elevations, bloom in June.*

WILDFLOWERS

During Alaska's short flowering season in the summer, the forests, bogs, and meadows are alive with the brilliant colors of blooming wildflowers. Tiny northern anemones and delicate pasqueflowers appear first, often just after the snow melts. At the height of summer, bright fireweed, lemon yellow Arctic poppies, skunk cabbage, and other flowers carpet the landscape.

The alpine forget-me-not, *Alaska's state flower, blossoms between May and August.*

Fireweed in full bloom

FIREWEED

Every summer, large swathes of the landscape turn purple as fireweed blooms. The young stems and leaves are rich in vitamins A and C, and Athabaskans have long eaten them either boiled or raw, and used raw cut stems to draw infection from boils. When the blooms go to seed and turn to cotton fluff, Alaskans say that the winter is only six weeks away.

Villous cinquefoil, *one of the first to flower, grows in cracks in boulders and cliff faces.*

Nome ❿

650 miles (1,050 km) W of
Fairbanks. **Road Map** C2.
🏠 3,500. ℹ️ 301 Front St, 443-
6624. 🎿 Iditarod Finish, Bering Sea
Ice Classic Golf Tournament, Miner's
& Musher's Ball (all after the Iditarod,
mid-Mar), Midnight Sun Festival
(Jun 21). www.visitnomealaska.com

Nome's curious name
probably dates from the
1850s, when a British officer
scrawled "?Name" across a
naval chart. It is said that a
draughtsman later misread
this as "Nome." Attractively
situated on the shores of
Norton Sound, this mixed
Inupiat and Anglo community
is the commercial and transport hub for northwest Alaska.

A former Gold Rush town,
Nome is today less busy than
it was in its heyday in the late
1890s, when Jafet Lindberg,
Erik Lindblom, and John
Brynteson discovered gold in
nearby Anvil Creek. In 1899,
gold was also found in the
beach sands (see pp52–3).
Over 30,000 people staked
claims, sparking a boom that
lasted until 1906, when Nome
quickly slipped into obscurity.

However, gold fever has
not entirely faded in modern
Nome. The public beach,
from the end of the seawall
to the roadhouse, is open for
recreational mining and in the

**Semipalmated sandpiper in the
meadows around Nome**

summer, a motley colony of
hopeful prospectors camps
here. Clad in wet suits, they
brave the freezing, ice-choked
waters of Norton Sound,
using diesel-powered dredges
to process the sands and collect what remains of the gold.

Nome is also famous for its
superb bird-watching and as
the finish line of the Iditarod.
Visitors in January can see
the whimsical Nome National
Forest, created each year
when residents plant their
old Christmas trees in the
sea ice just outside town.

🏛️ The Burled Arch
Front St. 🚻 www.iditarod.com
Each March, the official finish
line, called the Red "Fox"
Olson Trail Monument and
better known as the Burled
Arch, becomes the ultimate

destination of all Iditarod
mushers (see pp38–9). The
original arch, with the inscrip-
tion "End of the Iditarod Dog
Race," was erected for the
first Iditarod in 1975. It suc-
cumbed to dry rot after 26
years and was replaced with a
large burled spruce log, which
rests outside the Town Hall in
the summer. During the race,
a kerosene lantern hangs
from the arch until the last
competitor crosses the finish
line and retrieves it, winning
the Red Lantern Award. This
tradition recalls the early days
of transport in Alaska, when
mushers carrying goods or
mail would look for the
lanterns hanging outside
roadhouses along the route.

🏛️ Carrie M. McLain Museum
223 Front St. **Tel** 443-6630. 🕐 Jun–
early Sep: 9am–5:30pm daily; early
Sep–May: noon–6pm Tue–Fri.
🎿 donations accepted. 🚻
www.nomealaska.org/museum
The city-owned Carrie M.
McLain Memorial Museum
reveals Nome's colorful
history with original displays
on its Gold Rush days. Other
exhibits focus on modern
Nome, as well as on historic
aviation, the arts and culture
of the Bering Strait Inuit, the
world-famous Iditarod, and
the original Nome Kennel
Club and its All Alaska
Sweepstakes sled dog race.

🏛️ Old St. Joseph's Catholic Church
279 King Place, Anvil City Square.
Tel 443-5527. 🕐 late May–early
Sep: 10am–2pm Mon–Fri. 🚻
Nome's oldest building, the
1901 St. Joseph's Catholic
Church, was built on the
waterfront as a counterpoint
to the rollicking Gold Rush
atmosphere of the time. On
its steeple, a cross lit by electric lights served as a beacon
to guide mushers and miners
into town. Eventually, the
building fell into decay and a
new one was built. In 1996,
the old church was moved to
its present site, restored, and
given a new steeple. The
church now serves as a community hall. In front of it are
statues of Lindberg, Lindblom,
and Brynteson.

Dog team finishing the Iditarod in Nome

For hotels and restaurants in this region see p251 and p263

Exploring Beyond Nome

Located on the Seward Peninsula, Nome may be remote, but it is the hub of an extensive wilderness road system. Most visitors rent a vehicle or join a tour to explore the area's wild hinterlands. The drive east along the coast to Council includes fine bird-watching and the remains of a failed railroad, while the Kougarok Road accesses remote hot springs. The Teller Road leads through spectacular scenery to the end-of-the-world village of Teller on the windswept coast of the Bering Sea.

SIGHTS AT A GLANCE

Council Road ①
Kougarok Road ②
Teller Road ③

KEY

☒ Airstrip

═══ Minor road

--- Trail

🚉 Council Road

72 miles (115 km) to Council.
The causeway-like Council Road follows the coastline east of Nome past campsites of wildcat prospectors, who mine the beach sands with gas-powered dredges. Passing superb bird-watching sites at the marshes of **Safety Sound**, it arrives at the photogenic **Last Train to Nowhere**, three locomotives and several decrepit railcars of the 1881 Council City and Solomon River Railroad that stand rusting on the tundra at Mile 33. The railway was envisioned as part of a link between Nome and the Lower 48, but the plans were abandoned in 1907 due to a lack of funds. At this point, the road turns inland, through the tiny village of **Solomon**, now virtually abandoned. After crossing scenic Skookum Pass, the road reaches its end at the Niukluk River. There is a ford into the Gold Rush village of Council, but the village is best accessed with the help of local boat owners.

🚉 Kougarok Road

89 miles (143 km) to Kougarok Bridge. **Pilgrim Hot Springs** Turn-off at Mile 62. *Tel 443-5583.*
Also known as the Taylor Road, the wonderfully scenic Kougarok Road passes through the Kigluaik Mountains, paralleling the Wild Goose Pipeline, which was built in 1909 to transport water to Nome but never used. North of the mountains, a graveled spur road leads to an oasis of cottonwood trees at **Pilgrim Hot Springs**. The site has a simple wooden hot tank, which visitors can use after getting the owner's permission. Beyond the springs, the road passes through wetlands and tundra to its end at **Kougarok Bridge**. From here, a rough track leads to Taylor.

🚉 Teller Road

66 miles (110 km) to Teller.
Leaving Nome, this beautiful, lonely road follows clearwater streams, grasslands, and steep climbs on its way to **Teller**. Passing through the Kigluaik Mountains, it reaches rolling tundra, where there is a good chance of seeing wild musk oxen and domestic reindeer. Teller, at the westernmost tip of this westernmost road in North America, lies on a gray gravel spit at Port Clarence on the Bering Sea. It is known as the site where Norwegian explorer Roald Amundsen landed after his legendary 70-hour airship flight over the North Pole in 1926.

Rusting engines and railcars of The Last Train to Nowhere, on the tundra east of Nome

For hotels and restaurants in this region see p251 and p263

Granite tors at the Bering Land Bridge National Preserve

Bering Land Bridge National Preserve ⑪

100 miles (160 km) N of Nome.
Road Map C2. ✈ *charter bush plane from Nome.* 🛈 *1/9 Front St, Nome; 443-2522.* ⬡ *year-round.* ⛺
www.nps.gov/bela

Designated a National Monument in 1978, Bering Land Bridge received National Preserve status when ANILCA was passed in 1980 *(see p57)*. Encompassing 4,200 sq miles (10,900 sq km), the preserve commemorates the 55-mile (88-km) long and 1,000-mile (1,600-km) wide land bridge that once connected North America and Asia *(see p49)*. It is believed that during the last major Ice Age, this bridge allowed the passage of both prehistoric wildlife and early human settlers from Asia into North America. Around 15,000 years ago, the melting of the ice caused a gradual rise in sea level, and the land bridge disappeared beneath the waves of the newly formed Bering Strait.

The broad Arctic landscape of the preserve includes wide expanses of tundra, as well as scenic granite tors that bear testament to the area's distant volcanic past. The 6 public use cabins scattered around the preserve, and the 20-bed bunkhouse and hot tub at the preserve's main attraction, **Serpentine Hot Springs**, may be used free of charge and require no reservations, although users may have to share the space with other parties. The preserve's visitor center in Nome has exhibits, maps, and videos showcasing the cultural and natural history of the preserve.

Access into the preserve is almost exclusively by bush plane in the summer and snowmachine in the winter, although a few people do hike the 40 miles (64 km) to Serpentine Hot Springs from Kougarok Bridge.

Gambell ⑫

230 miles (370 km) E of Nome.
Road Map B3. ⛽ *650.* ✈ *from Nome.* **Permits** *needed to access lagoons and other areas.*

The small Yup'ik village of Gambell sits on beach gravel at the northwestern corner of St. Lawrence Island, which measures 70 miles (112 km) in length and includes the even more isolated village of **Savoonga**. Lying near the Siberian coast, the island is one of Alaska's most remote outposts.

When ANCSA was passed in 1971 *(see p56)*, Gambell and Savoonga decided not to participate, and thus gained title to about 1,780 sq miles (4,600 sq km) of land. The villagers are therefore able to charge an "outsider tax" from non-residents wishing to access the lagoons and areas around the village and farther afield.

Getting around the island requires an ATV, and visitors can usually get rides from the villagers for a small fee. Most visitors to the island come to view birds not seen elsewhere in North America, including several incidental Eurasian species such as Lapland longspurs. Summer visitors can also spot flocks of eider ducks, murres, kittiwakes, puffins, and auklets either nesting or heading north.

In addition to the birdlife, the island's main attractions include the unique boneyards south of the village and at the base of Sivaquaq Mountain, where waste from Native hunts – mainly whalebones – is tossed. Walrus ivory from the yards is now carved and sold to visitors.

The remote Yup'ik village of Gambell on St. Lawrence Island

TRAVELERS' NEEDS

WHERE TO STAY 238–251

WHERE TO EAT 252–263

CRUISING IN ALASKA 264–271

OUTDOOR ACTIVITIES 272–275

WHERE TO STAY

The extensive range of accommodation in Alaska ranges from informal campsites along remote hiking trails to business-class hotel rooms in Anchorage, Fairbanks, and Juneau. Those who prefer to experience local flavor can choose from a plethora of bed-and-breakfast accommodation ranging from simple lodges to well-appointed houses with home-grown

Hotel sign, Cordova

vegetables and gourmet cuisine. Budget travelers will find a selection of low-priced hostels accessible by public transport, while those with a vehicle can stay in one of the traditional roadhouses. In the bush, a number of hunting, fishing, and wildlife viewing lodges offer wilderness luxury far from the well-trodden routes. For more information, refer to the detailed listings on pages 242–51.

Hotel Captain Cook in downtown Anchorage *(see p242)*

SEASONAL PRICING

While the summer months of June, July, and August offer the year's finest weather, summer prices in most parts of Alaska can be almost two to three times the off-season rates. In the winter off-season between October and April, many of the hostels, hotels, and bed-and-breakfasts (B&Bs) located away from urban areas are closed, as are most federal and state campsites. At this time, hotel rates are often less than half of the high season prices, and luxury rooms may be available for the cost of a budget motel room. The obvious exceptions are the Alyeska Ski Resort and those hotels in the Interior that cater to visitors wishing to see the aurora borealis. Here high season can last all winter. During the Fur Rondy and the Iditarod Trail Sled Dog Race *(see p45)* in February and March, prices in Anchorage and some other

places along the race route may be higher than the usual winter discount rates.

Generally, Alaska has two shoulder seasons, in May and September. Hoteliers may offer discounts of up to 25 percent during these months, which fall between the high season, when the crowds and prices are highest, and the off-season, when many facilities are closed and the weather is at its worst.

CHOOSING A HOTEL AND GETTING THERE

In Alaska, hotels range from very basic to four-star luxury. In nearly every town, hotels compete for business travelers with convention facilities and wireless Internet connections. Fairbanks, Juneau, Ketchikan, and Anchorage have the most expensive business hotels. Most towns also have comfortable motels providing decent, relatively inexpensive accommodation, as well as historic

and independent hotels filled with period furnishings and run with meticulous attention to detail. While most historic hotels are non-smoking, guests may be permitted to light up on patios and terraces. In addition, a selection of mid-range and bottom-end choices offer travelers a simple bed, a hot shower, and basic amenities.

Some of the better hotels have free telephone links in the baggage claim areas at Anchorage, Fairbanks, and Juneau airports, as well as at many Alaska Marine Highway terminals. Travelers can use these to arrange rooms or free shuttle transport from the airport or ferry terminal to the hotel. Most cruise ship passengers will have pre-booked rooms in finer establishments near tourist sites.

Most bed-and-breakfasts within a few minutes' drive of a ferry terminal or airport are happy to provide transport for booked guests. Hikers and backpackers hoping to stay in hostels or campsites will have to rely on rental cars or taxis.

HOSTELS

Alaska has a network of more than 30 official **Alaska Hostel Association** hostels scattered around the state. Largely offering no-frills amenities, these inexpensive options provide a basic place to sleep, most often in a shared dormitory setting with toilets and showers down the hall, as well as communal cooking facilities. Dorms are usually single sex, although, if requested, a private room may occasionally be arranged for couples traveling together.

While hostels usually provide basic bedding and linen, travelers often bring their own sheets or sleeping bags. Most hostels offer lockers where luggage or valuables can be stored, as well as a games or television room and laundry facilities. In several places, as a general rule, guests are locked out between 9am and 5pm. For this inconvenience, hostelers can expect to pay less than 50 percent of the price of a bed in an inexpensive hotel.

RV PARKS

Driving through Alaska in a Recreational Vehicle or RV (see pp296–7) is an extremely popular way of seeing the state. While most RVs can be accommodated at "pull-through" sites in public campgrounds, only private RV parks offer such amenities as hook-ups and dump stations. The better RV parks usually provide water and electric hook-ups, dump stations, hot showers, bathrooms, and laundromats. Some even have cable TV and Wi-Fi access. Full hook-up facilities can cost up to $75 per night. Normally, even those not staying at the site can use the showers for a small fee. RV parks are found in most cities and towns along the highway system, as well as in most Marine Highway

Kenai Princess Lodge in Cooper Landing on the Kenai Peninsula

ports in Southeast and Southcentral Alaska. This guide lists eight of the best-appointed and most convenient RV parks across Alaska (see pp242–51).

HOTEL CHAINS

Anchorage and other large Alaskan cities have many hotel chains, including **Sheraton Hotels**, **Hilton**, **Hawthorn Suites**, **Embassy Suites**, **Extended Stay**, **Hampton Inn**, **Super 8 Hotels**, **Best Western**, **Marriott Inns**, and **Holiday Inn**. There is little to differentiate one from the other, apart from desired price and location. Many of the newer hotels have large rooms, Wi-Fi access, buffet breakfasts, small fridges and microwaves, and king-size beds. Shuttle services to and from the airport are often available. For cruise ship passengers and visitors looking for a lavish wilderness

experience, **Princess Lodges** offer interesting architecture and comfortable accommodation in and around major tourist sites.

BED-AND-BREAKFASTS

While the bed-and-breakfast idea is relatively new to Alaska, it has rapidly become popular. B&Bs come in many shapes and sizes, but unlike their European counterparts, they are not a budget option. Guests should be prepared to pay at least what they would for an average mid-range hotel room.

The advantage offered by B&Bs is the chance to meet friendly locals and fellow guests while staying in cozy, comfortable homes rather than in impersonal hotels. Many of these places are lovingly tended by people who take pride in their gardening and culinary skills, and who treat their guests not only to excellent breakfasts but often to memorable experiences. Some of the best B&Bs are in quiet neighborhoods or idyllic rural areas, while the more convenient ones in town centers tend to be functional places.

For those who have not pre-booked, a good way to find a B&B is via the brochures stacked in every airport, ferry terminal, and tourist office. Many, but not all B&Bs, are members of the **Bed and Breakfast Association of Alaska**, which can help in finding and booking a room. Some of the best choices are included in the listings.

Stores at the entrance to Denali Rainbow Village RV Park (see p247)

Carlo Creek Lodge and Campground, on the Parks Highway south of Denali National Park

CAMPGROUNDS

Alaska has two main types of campgrounds – public and private. Generally, public campgrounds occupy scenic sites in national and state parks, wildlife refuges, forests, recreation areas, and game sanctuaries. The **Alaska Public Lands Information Centers (APLIC)** provide details on public campgrounds, most of which are not reservable. **Lifetime Adventures** makes reservations for some **Alaska State Park** campgrounds. **Reserve Denali** takes bookings for that popular park. It is worth arriving early on summer weekends to find a good camping spot.

While public campgrounds offer few amenities, they do provide spacious individual campsites and easy access to scenic outdoor attractions. Sites in government campgrounds along the road system offer parking spaces, picnic tables, and a basic barbecue pit. Communal facilities usually include outhouses and public water pumps.

A few of the campgrounds administered by the **Chugach National Forest** or **Tongass National Forest** may be used free of charge. However, most of the state and nationally administered sites charge between $8 and $20 for pitching a tent or parking an RV.

Some campgrounds include pre-cut firewood in the price of the site. Most of these places are open from mid- or late May to early September. Those that stay open through the winter generally shut down the water supply in early September.

Private campgrounds (also called RV parks) are found near popular tourist areas and are often within walking distance of town centers. They charge from $20 to $50 per site.

PUBLIC USE CABINS

In the Chugach and Tongass National Forests, as well as in several state parks and recreation areas, over 200 cabins are available to individuals and groups for overnight use. Most of these public use cabins are in remote areas or along hiking trails. Access to these isolated cabins is almost always on foot, by boat, or by floatplane.

Many cabins have wood stoves and ranger-provided firewood. They usually contain bunks for eight or more people. Mattresses are not provided and travelers need to bring their own ground pads

and sleeping bags. Alaskan public use cabins require pre-booking, and with few exceptions, are available to only one party at a time. Because they get booked up quickly between June and August, reserve in advance, especially in popular locations such as Chugach State Park, Nancy Lake State Recreation Area, and in the Chugach National Forest. National forest cabins may be booked up to six months in advance at **www.recreation.gov**, while state park cabins can be booked with **Alaska State Parks Public Use Cabins**.

Private cabin, Kachemak Bay State Park

ALASKAN ROADHOUSES

For those who would like a taste of rustic accommodation without the expense of flying in to a wilderness lodge, Alaskan roadhouses offer a good option. Scattered along the road system, they range from simple log-built complexes with a basic eatery, bar, and simple cabin accommodation to historic traditional roadhouses with all those amenities as well as inn-style rooms with period furnishings. Some of the best choices, including some fine historic options, can be found in the listings *(see pp242–51)*.

WILDERNESS LODGES

Dotted around the wildest parts of Alaska, wilderness lodges offer accommodation in remote areas off the road system. Usually accessed by boat or bush plane, most have their own dock, airstrip, or floatplane landing facility. While many are hunting or angling lodges, several cater to visitors interested in photography, wildlife viewing,

King Salmondeaux Lodge, near Soldotna on the Kenai Peninsula *(see p244)*

and hiking. Their prices reflect not only the undeniable beauty of the sites, but also the exclusivity of the lodge, the quality of the experience, and the difficulties of accessing and supplying such remote locations. In the most expensive places, prices can range from $500 to $1,400 per person per night, and include accommodation, meals, activities, guides, and local boat or plane transport. Many fishing lodges also provide fishing equipment and freezer space.

In the mid-priced lodges, guests can expect to pay a set rate for accommodation, as well as a substantial charge for a bush flight or boat transport and additional charges for meals and activities. While those willing to share rooms or cabins with other guests may be able to get a discount, the tariff will still be two or three times what a traveler would usually pay at a hotel in town. Details on some of the best lodges are included in the listings *(see pp242–51)*,

DIRECTORY

HOSTELS

Alaska Hostel Association
www.alaskahostel
association.org

HOTEL CHAINS

Best Western
Tel (800) 780-7234.
www.bestwestern.com

Embassy Suites
Tel (800) 362-2779.
www.embassysuites.com

Extended Stay
Tel (800) 804-3724. www.
extendedstaydeluxe.com

Hampton Inn
Tel (800) 426-7866.
www.hamptoninn.com

Hawthorn Suites
Tel (888) 469-6575.
www.hawthorn.com

Hilton
Tel (800) 445-8667.
www.hilton.com

Holiday Inn
Tel (888) 465-4329.
www.holiday-inn.com

Marriott Inns
Tel (800) 627-7468.
www.marriott.com

Princess Lodges
Tel (800) 426-0500.
www.princesslodges.com

Sheraton Hotels
Tel (800) 598-1753.
www.sheraton.com

Super 8 Hotels
Tel (800) 800-8000.
www.super8.com

BED-AND-BREAKFASTS

Bed and Breakfast Association of Alaska
www.alaskabba.com

CAMPGROUNDS

Alaska Public Lands Information Center

Anchorage
605 W 4th Ave, Suite 105.
Tel 644-3661.
www.alaskacenters.gov

Fairbanks
101 Dunkel St.
Tel 456-0527.
www.alaskacenters.gov

Ketchikan
50 Main St. *Tel* 228-6220.

Tok
Mile 1314 Alaska Hwy.
Tel 883-5667.
www.alaskacenters.gov

Alaska State Parks
Tel 269-8400.
www.alaskastateparks.org

Chugach National Forest
3301 C St, Anchorage.
Tel 743-9500. www.fs.
fed.us/r10/chugach

Lifetime Adventures
www.lifetime
adventures.net

Reserve Denali
241 West Ship Creek Ave,
Anchorage.
Tel (800) 622-7275.
www.reservedenali.com

Tongass National Forest
648 Mission St, Ketchikan.
Tel 225-3101.
www.fs.fed.us/r10/
tongass

PUBLIC USE CABINS

Alaska State Parks Public Use Cabins
550 W 7th Ave, Suite
1260, Anchorage.
Tel 289-8400. www.
alaskastateparks.org

Recreation.gov
Tel (877) 444-6777.
www.recreation.gov

Choosing a Hotel

Most of the hotels and lodges in this guide have been selected across a wide price range for facilities, good value, and location. The prices listed are those charged by the hotel, although discounts may be available through agencies. The hotels are listed by area. For map references for Anchorage, see pages 64–5.

PRICE CATEGORIES
The price ranges are for a standard double room and taxes per night during the high season. Breakfast is not included, unless specified.

ⓢ $10–$50
ⓢⓢ $50–$100
ⓢⓢⓢ $100–$175
ⓢⓢⓢⓢ $175–$240
ⓢⓢⓢⓢⓢ Over $240

ANCHORAGE

ANCHORAGE Anchorage Ship Creek Landing RV Park
150 N Ingra St, Anchorage, AK 99501 **Tel** *277-0877, (888) 778-7700* **Rooms** *119 sites*

Conveniently located just a few blocks from downtown Anchorage, this rather crowded RV park is open from May until September. It has full hook-ups and pull-through sites, as well as restrooms, showers, laundry facilities, a gift shop, a tour reservations desk, and Wi-Fi access. Tent sites are also available, and pets are allowed. **www.alaskarv.com**

ANCHORAGE Spenard Hostel International
2845 W 42nd Ave, Anchorage, AK 99517 **Tel** *248-5036* **Fax** *248-5036* **Rooms** *8*   **Map** *E1*

Located about a mile (2 km) away from the international airport on a main bus route, this friendly hostel with laundry and cooking facilities is the best low-budget accommodation in Anchorage. There are bike trails nearby and bicycles are available to rent for a small daily charge. The hostel has no lockout. **www.alaskahostel.org**

ANCHORAGE Oscar Gill House B&B
1344 W 10th Ave, Anchorage, AK 99501 **Tel** *279-1344* **Fax** *279-1344* **Rooms** *3*   **Map** *E1*

Originally built at Knik Arm by a former Anchorage mayor, this charming 1913 B&B was moved to the Park Strip immediately south of downtown Anchorage. Guests have free use of bicycles and limited freezer space can be arranged for anglers who wish to store their catch. Breakfast is included in the room rate. **www.oscargill.com**

ANCHORAGE Puffin Inn
4400 Spenard Rd, Anchorage, AK 99517 **Tel** *243-4044, (866) 494-4841* **Rooms** *86*   **Map** *E1*

This popular motel-style place near the international airport offers simple but comfortable accommodation in the heart of the quirky district of Spenard. Anglers have access to freezer space and a free 24-hour shuttle transports guests to and from the airport. **www.puffininn.net**

ANCHORAGE Extended Stay Deluxe
108 E 8th Ave, Anchorage, AK 99501 **Tel** *868-1605, (866) 506-7848* **Fax** *868-3520* **Rooms** *89*   **Map** *E1*

This modern hotel, which caters to both tourists and business travelers, is located within walking distance of most downtown sights of interest. The hotel has a small swimming pool and Jacuzzi. Airport and Alaska Railroad shuttles are available for visitors. Breakfast is included in the room rate. **www.extendedstaydeluxe.com**

ANCHORAGE Inlet Tower Hotel and Suites
1200 L St, Anchorage, AK 99501 **Tel** *276-0110, (800) 544-0786* **Fax** *258-4914* **Rooms** *180*   **Map** *E1*

Rooms at the hotel boast wonderful views – the Chugach Range to the east, Mount Susitna and Cook Inlet to the west, and Mount McKinley to the north. The restaurant, Mixx Grill *(see p257)*, is well-known for its game meat and seafood dishes. The hotel is a short walk from the Tony Knowles Coastal Trail. **www.inlettower.com**

ANCHORAGE Voyager Hotel
501 K St, Anchorage, AK 99501 **Tel** *277-9501, (800) 247-9070* **Fax** *274-0333* **Rooms** *40*   **Map** *C5*

Built in 1965, this downtown hotel is probably the most acclaimed small hotel in Anchorage. The hotel's claim to fame is their attention to detail and few visitors will dispute that. Each room features a microwave, a refrigerator, and a small bar. **www.voyagerhotel.com**

ANCHORAGE Dimond Center Hotel
700 E Diamond Blvd, Anchorage, AK 99515 **Tel** *770-5000, (866) 770-5002* **Fax** *770-5001* **Rooms** *109*

The location is a bit odd (sandwiched between Dimond Mall and Wal-Mart) but this Native-owned hotel is one of Alaska's finest. Amenities include plush bedding, large soaking tubs, flat-screen televisions, Belgian waffle breakfasts, a stylish lobby and free airport and train station shuttles. **www.dimondcenterhotel.com**

ANCHORAGE Hotel Captain Cook
4th & K St, Anchorage, AK 99501 **Tel** *276-6000, (800) 843-1950* **Rooms** *547*   **Map** *C4*

One of Anchorage's oldest and classiest hotels, this yellow high-rise landmark in downtown boasts a dozen shops, both men's and women's athletic clubs (free to guests), and three restaurants, including a gourmet coffee and wine bar. Nearly every room has a great view of Cook Inlet or the Chugach Range. **www.captaincook.com**

Key to Symbols *see back cover flap*

GIRDWOOD Alyeska Hostel $

Alta Dr, PO Box 953, Girdwood, AK 99587 Tel 783-2222 Rooms 4

This affordable no-frills hostel offers mixed dormitories, one private double room, and basic cabins. Cooking facilities are available, and it lies within reasonable walking distance of the ski slopes. The hostel is also a good staging point to use for hiking the Crow Pass Crossing into Chugach State Park. **www.alyeskahostel.com**

GIRDWOOD Hotel Alyeska $$$$$

1000 Arlberg Ave, Girdwood, AK 99587 Tel 754-1111, (800) 880-3880 Fax 754-2200 Rooms 307

This large four-diamond hotel set in stunning, forested surroundings is renowned as an elegant resort. It boasts a fine-dining restaurant *(see p257)*, three eateries, two bars, and easy access to the Alyeska ski slopes and appealing hiking routes. The hotel also has an indoor swimming pool and a large hot tub. **www.alyeskaresort.com**

WASILLA Lake Lucille Inn $$$

1300 W Lake Lucille Dr, Wasilla, AK 99654 Tel 373-1776, (800) 897-1776 Fax 352-0410 Rooms 54   Map B1

Part of the Best Western chain, this comfortable and well-decorated hotel on the shores of Lake Lucille near central Wasilla is a popular place for pilots to fly in for dinner. Several good restaurants are nearby, and the deck provides views of distant mountains and floatplanes on the lake. **www.bestwestern.com/lakelucilleinn**

THE KENAI PENINSULA

COOPER LANDING Kenai Riverside Campground & RV Park $$

Mile 49.7 Sterling Hwy, Cooper Landing, AK 99572 Tel (888) 536-2478 Rooms 18 sites

Located right on the banks of the Kenai River, this RV park has electric and water hook-ups, tent sites, and several simple B&B-style rooms. Centrally located for exploring the Kenai Peninsula, it is especially well-placed for fishing and hiking in the Chugach National Forest. **www.kenairv.com**

COOPER LANDING Inn at Tenn Lake $$$

Mile 36, Seward Highway, Moose Pass, AK 99572 Tel 288-3667 Fax 288-3667 Rooms 5

Popular for summer weddings, this lovely modern lodge sits along the shore of picturesque Tenn Lake (look for the terns and gulls), 6 miles (10 km) north of Moose Pass. Five guest suites are available, each with private bath, balcony, fireplace, and Wi-Fi. A big breakfast is included, but children are not allowed. **www.tennlake.com**

HOMER Homer Hostel $

304 W Pioneer Ave, Homer, AK 99603 Tel 235-1463 Rooms 5

The relaxed and conveniently located Homer Hostel, housed in the 1939 Pratt House, provides simple budget accommodation in private rooms or dorms with good views across Kachemak Bay and renovated facilities with a guest computer, outdoor grill, and bike rentals. **www.homerhostel.com**

HOMER Old Town Bed & Breakfast $$$

106 W Bunnell St, Homer, AK 99603 Tel 235-7558 Rooms 3

Owned by artist Asia Freeman, this little three-room B&B is located above the acclaimed Bunnell Street Arts Center. One room has a private bath and the others share a bath, and rooms are decorated with antique pieces. It's just a block to Bishops Beach, a wonderful place for an evening stroll. **www.oldtownbedandbreakfast.com**

HOMER Bear Creek Winery and Lodging $$$$

PO Box 164, Homer, AK 99603 Tel 235 8484 Fax 235-3491 Rooms 2

Located 3 miles (5 km) from downtown Homer, the winery offers two elegant suites. In addition to comfortable lodgings with excellent views and surroundings, guests can enjoy the outdoor firepit and cedar hot tub, and sample the establishment's own blueberry, raspberry, rhubarb, and fireweed wines. **www.bearcreekwinery.com**

HOMER Land's End Resort $$$$

4786 Homer Spit Road, Homer, AK 99603 Tel 235-0400, (800) 478-0400 Fax 235-0420 Rooms 84

Located at the end of Homer Spit, this lodge is surrounded on three sides by the waters of Kachemak Bay. In addition to the excellent views of the bay and the Kenai Mountains, the resort offers a small indoor lap pool, a sauna, and an outdoor hot tub facing the bay. **www.lands-end-resort.com**

SELDOVIA Alaska Tree Tops Fishing Lodge $$$$$

PO Box 135, Seldovia, AK 99663 Tel 234-6200 Fax 234-6202 Rooms 5

This beautiful waterfront fishing lodge is the finest accommodation available in tiny Seldovia, with views of whales and sea otters right off the deck. Guests can book deep-sea fishing on the owners' fishing catamaran. Access is by floatplane or water taxi from Homer. Three gourmet meals served daily are included in the rate. **www.alaskatreetops.com**

SEWARD Ballaine House B&B $$

437 3rd Ave, PO Box 2051, Seward, AK 99664 Tel 224-2362 Rooms 5

For good, homey accommodation within walking distance of popular Seward sights, this well-appointed historic B&B is one of the best. The host is happy to help guests organize their local sightseeing and Kenai Fjords trips. Breakfast is included in the room rate. Open summer only. **www.superpage.com/ballaine**

SEWARD Van Gilder Hotel 🛜 📺 ⑤⑤⑤

308 Adams St, PO Box 609, Seward, AK 99664 **Tel** *224-3079, (800) 204-6835* **Rooms** *31*

Listed on the National Register of Historic Places, this small 1916 hotel is Seward's most atmospheric option, and features an array of period furnishings. Boasting an excellent location in downtown Seward, it is just a few minutes walk from the Alaska SeaLife Center and the Seward Historical Society Museum. **www.vangilderhotel.com**

SEWARD Seward Windsong Lodge 🍽 ♿ 🛜 📺 @ ⑤⑤⑤⑤⑤

Mile 0.5 Herman Leirer/Exit Glacier Rd, Seward, AK 99664 **Tel** *224-7116, (877) 777-4079* **Fax** *224-7118* **Rooms** *108*

Surrounded by high peaks in the Resurrection River Valley, this beautifully situated and well-appointed lodge caters especially to package visitors heading for Kenai Fjords National Park. It is several miles from the town center, but is very well-placed for visits to Exit Glacier. **www.sewardwindsong.com**

SOLDOTNA King Salmondeaux Lodge 🛜 📺 ⑤⑤⑤

33126 Johnson Dr, Soldotna, AK 99669 **Tel** *360-3474, (866) 651-3474* **Fax** *762-1855* **Rooms** *5*

Owned by anglers and boasting about 1,400 ft (425 m) of Kenai River frontage, the emphasis here is definitely on fishing, which is a fabulous draw in the summer. However, even non-fishermen will appreciate the comfortable cabins, all of which have full kitchens. Open summer only. **www.kingsalmondeauxlodge.com**

PRINCE WILLIAM SOUND

CORDOVA Orca Adventure Lodge 🍽 ♿ 🛜 @ ⑤⑤⑤

2500 Orca Rd, PO Box 2105, Cordova, AK 99574 **Tel** *424-7249, (866) 424-6722* **Fax** *424-3579* **Rooms** *27*

Outdoor adventure is the focus of this amenable lodge, which is sited in an old cannery bunkhouse approximately 2 miles (3 km) north of town. Guests can rent equipment or join guided fishing, hiking, cycling, rafting, and sea kayaking trips, along with wintertime heli-skiing. Closed Oct–Feb. **www.orcaadventurelodge.com**

CORDOVA Reluctant Fisherman Inn 🍽 ♿ 🛜 📺 @ ⑤⑤⑤

407 Railroad Ave, Cordova, AK 99574 **Tel** *424-3272, (877) 770-3272* **Fax** *424-7465* **Rooms** *44*

This traditional single-story hotel along the waterfront enjoys great harbor views, as well as a fine restaurant that is a favorite with both locals and visitors *(see p259)*. Copper figures prominently in the decor, and the hotel makes a convenient base for drives along the wonderful Copper River Highway. **www.reluctantfisherman.com**

VALDEZ Brookside Inn B&B 🛜 @ ⑤⑤⑤

1465 Richardson Hwy, PO Box 753, Valdez, AK 99686 **Tel** *835-9130, (866) 316-9130* **Fax** *835-9029* **Rooms** *6*

This beautiful house, located about 2 miles (3 km) from town, was built by the army in the late 1890s and moved to its present site in 1968. Pickup services from the ferry terminal or airport are provided. A hot tub is available and the owners loan guests mountain bikes. Breakfast is included in the room rate. **www.brooksideinnbb.com**

VALDEZ Valdez Harbor Inn 🍽 ♿ 📺 @ ⑤⑤⑤

100 Fidalgo Dr, Valdez, AK 99686 **Tel** *835-3434, (888) 222-3440* **Fax** *835-2308* **Rooms** *88*

The finest hotel in town, the Valdez Harbor Inn does everything possible to accommodate business travelers. Amenities include a business center and fitness room, and some rooms have hot tubs. Rooms with views of the harbor cost extra. **www.valdezharborinn.com**

VALDEZ Wild Roses by the Sea B&B 🛜 📺 @ ⑤⑤⑤

PO Box 3396, Valdez, AK 99686 **Tel** *835-2930* **Fax** *835-4966* **Rooms** *3*

Set on 25 acres (10 ha) overlooking Valdez, this lovely bed and breakfast has two comfortable guest rooms with en suite bathrooms (one with jacuzzi) and good views. The separate Ocean View Guest House is a self-contained unit with kitchen and private entrance. A single foldout bed is available in each room. **www.alaskabytheseabnb.com**

SOUTHEAST ALASKA

ANGOON Whaler's Cove Lodge and Favorite Bay Inn 🍽 ♿ 🛜 ⑤⑤⑤⑤

Mile 1 Killisnoo Rd, PO Box 101, Angoon, AK 99820 **Tel** *788-3123, (800) 423-3123* **Fax** *788-3104* **Rooms** *26*

Situated on Admiralty Island near Angoon Native village, the B&B and sportfishing lodge sit beside forested waterways. Rates for the lodge are much higher than the B&B and include transport from Juneau, accommodation, meals, guides, fishing gear, and boat transport. The lodge offers disabled access. **www.whalerscovelodge.com**

CRAIG Dreamcatcher B&B 🛜 📺 @ ⑤⑤⑤

1405 Hamilton Dr, PO Box 702, Craig, AK 99921 **Tel** *826-2238* **Rooms** *3*

Although located within walking distance of Craig businesses, this friendly B&B feels like an out-of-town lodge. The beautiful waterfront structure offers views of the lagoon through its large windows. All the rooms have outside entrances and private bathrooms. Breakfast is included in the room rate. **www.dreamcatcherbedandbreakfast.com**

CRAIG Ruth Ann's Hotel 🛏️ ♿ 📺 $$$

Front St, Craig, AK 99921 Tel 826-3378 Fax 826-3293 Rooms 15

Housed in three historic buildings, Ruth Ann's Hotel is the best-appointed option in Craig. Overlooking the waterfront is the attached four-star restaurant *(see p259)*, which offers the finest dining, including local seafood, on Prince of Wales Island.

GLACIER BAY NATIONAL PARK Glacier Bay Lodge 🛏️ ♿ 📶 $$$$

199 Bartlett Cove Rd, Bartlett Cove, Gustavus, AK 99826 Tel 264-4600, (888) 229-8687 Fax 258-3668 Rooms 55

Surrounded by large rainforest trees on the shores of Bartlett Cove, Glacier Bay Lodge offers the only accommodation located within Glacier Bay National Park. The lodge's sitting area, with a roaring fire in the large stone fireplace, is inviting after a day of cruising past glaciers. Basic, small rooms. Open summer only. **www.visitglacierbay.com**

GUSTAVUS Annie Mae Lodge 🛏️ ♿ 📶 $$$$

PO Box 55, #2 Grandpa's Farm Rd, Gustavus, AK 99826 Tel 697-2346, (800) 478-2346 Fax 697-2211 Rooms 11

This attractive lodge stands on the banks of the Good River in Gustavus, surrounded by Glacier Bay National Park. Room rates include bicycle hire and ground transportation. The lodge will organize day trips or multi-day fishing and Glacier Bay cruising packages in conjuction with accommodation. Open summer only. **www.anniemae.com**

GUSTAVUS Bear Track Inn 🛏️ 📶 $$$$$

255 Rink Creek Rd, Gustavus, AK 99826 Tel 697-3017, (888) 697-2284 Fax 697-2284 Rooms 14

In the tradition of the big National Park lodges of the Lower 48, this chunky log-built place near the entrance of Glacier Bay National Park has a wildlife theme with moosehorn chandeliers in the lobby. All rooms boast two queen-sized beds. The rates include all meals and flights to and from Juneau. Open summer only. **www.beartrackinn.com**

GUSTAVUS Gustavus Inn 🛏️ 📶 @ $$$$$

PO Box 60, Gustavus, AK 99826 Tel 697-2254, (800) 649-5220 Fax 697-2255 Rooms 14

Built in 1928 on an old homestead, this historic home is now one of Alaska's most famous inns. It features comfortable rooms and a peaceful country setting. Most guests book multi-night stays that include activities such as fishing and whale-watching. Gourmet dinners are made using vegetables from the garden. Open summer only. **www.gustavusinn.com**

HAINES Bear Creek Cabins and Hostel 📶 $

Mile 1 Small Tracts Rd, PO Box 908, Haines, AK 99827 Tel 766-2259 Rooms 9

Popular with backpackers and families, this pleasant complex in the forest about a mile (2 km) from the center of Haines has double and family cabins, as well as hostel bunks and tent camping. Laundry and kitchen facilities are available to guests, and there is no lockout or curfew. Open summer only. **www.bearcreekcabinsalaska.com**

HAINES Captain's Choice Motel 📺 📶 $$$

108 2nd Ave N, PO Box 392, Haines, AK 99827 Tel 766-3111, (800) 478-2345 Fax 766-3332 Rooms 40

Overlooking the harbor just two blocks from the main street, this inexpensive motel style option is a favorite with Alaskans. Many of the rooms offer pleasant views of Lynn Canal and Fort Seward. There is a complimentary Continental breakfast, and free transport is available from the airport or ferry terminal. **www.capchoice.com**

HAINES Hotel Halsingland 🛏️ ♿ 📶 📺 $$$

PO Box 1649, 13 Ft Seward Dr, Haines, AK 99827 Tel 766-2000, (800) 542-6363 Fax 766-2060 Rooms 18

This tasteful Victorian-era hotel in Fort Seward boasts period furnishings and brings a hint of charm and elegance to Haines. The restaurant not only uses fresh herbs from its own kitchen garden, but is also renowned for its wine list. The hotel also manages an adjacent RV park. **www.hotelhalsingland.com**

JUNEAU Juneau International Hostel ♿ 📶 @ $

614 Harris St, Juneau, AK 99801 Tel 586-9559 Rooms 46 dorm beds, 1 room

This hostel, high on the hill above downtown Juneau, provides friendly and very inexpensive dormitory accommodation with the use of cooking and laundry facilities as well as free Internet access. There is limited parking on the steep street outside. The only notable drawback is the daytime lockout. **www.juneauhostel.org**

JUNEAU RV Park – Spruce Meadow 📺 @ $

10200 Mendenhall Loop Road, Juneau, AK 99801 Tel 789-1990 Fax 790-7231 Rooms 47 sites

Located at the border of the Tongass National Forest, 3 miles (5 km) from Mendenhall Glacier and 4 miles (6 km) from the ferry terminal, this leafy RV park offers full hook-ups, including cable TV, plus a laundromat and dump station. Tent sites are adjacent to a communal sink and picnic area. **www.juneaurv.com**

JUNEAU Historic Silverbow Inn 📶 📺 @ $$$

120 2nd St, Juneau, AK 99801 Tel 586-4146, (800) 586-4146 Fax 586-4242 Rooms 11

Right in the heart of historic downtown Juneau, this friendly little boutique hotel also operates the adjacent bakery, reputedly haunted by the benign ghost of the original owner, Austrian baker Gus Messerschmitt. Guests can relax in the lounge or try the games and puzzles on offer. Breakfast is included in the room rate. **www.silverbowinn.com**

JUNEAU Super 8 📶 ♿ 📺 @ $$$

2295 Trout St, Juneau, AK 99801 Tel 789-4858, (800) 800-8000 Fax 789-5819 Rooms 75

This bargain-priced hotel near Juneau Airport has a free shuttle bus to the airport, ferry terminal, and downtown Juneau. The rooms are of a decent standard and many travelers consider it the best value in town. The main disadvantage is the distance to good eateries, but breakfast is included in the room rate. **www.super8.com**

JUNEAU Alaska's Capital Inn   📶 📺 @ $$$$$$

113 W 5th St, Juneau, AK 99801 **Tel** *586-6507, (888) 588-6507* **Fax** *588-6508* **Rooms** *6*

Located right next to the State Capitol, this 1906 hotel has a friendly, casual ambience and period furnishings. Some rooms feature lovely stained glass windows. In the evening, guests can relax in the outdoor hot tub in a pleasant leafy setting. Breakfast is included in the room rate. **www.alaskacapitalinn.com**

JUNEAU Pearson's Pond Luxury Inn and Garden Spa   📶 📺 @ $$$$$$

4541 Sawa Circle, Juneau, AK 99801 **Tel** *789-3772, (888) 658-6328* **Rooms** *5*

This small inn sits by a small pond within Mendenhall Valley, 12 miles (19 km) north of Juneau. Grounds are filled with flowers, and guests appreciate hot tubs, decks, and sumptuously furnished rooms, some including large spa tubs, rain showers, and canopy beds. There's a two night minimum and a separate condo for families. **www.pearsonspond.com**

KETCHIKAN Gilmore Hotel   🍴 📺 @ $$$

326 Front St, Ketchikan, AK 99901 **Tel** *225-9423, (800) 275-9423* **Fax** *275-7442* **Rooms** *38*

The historic Gilmore Hotel, built in 1927, rounds out its retro ambience with puffy feather beds and pillows. It has pleasant views of Tongass Narrows and the attached restaurant, Annabelle's, is a Ketchikan favorite *(see p260)*. There is free Wi-Fi access. Drivers must secure an on-street parking permit. **www.gilmorehotel.com**

KETCHIKAN Cape Fox Lodge   📶 🍴 ♿ 📺 @ $$$$

800 Venetia Way, Ketchikan, AK 99901 **Tel** *225-8001, (866) 225-8001* **Fax** *225-8286* **Rooms** *72*

Perched on a rocky outcrop overlooking the town, the lodge offers beautiful views. Its interior reflects the area's heritage with Native Alaskan cultural motifs, and the large Heen Kahidi *(see p260)* restaurant offers fine dining. The lodge is accessed via a funicular railway, which is free for guests. **www.capefoxlodge.com**

KETCHIKAN New York Hotel   🍴 📶 📺 $$$$

207 Stedman St, Ketchikan, AK 99901 **Tel** *225-0246, (866) 225-0246* **Fax** *225-1803* **Rooms** *12*

This scenic corner of Ketchikan enjoys pleasant harbor views and is walking distance to the town center. In addition to the standard rooms, suites on nearby Creek Street offer Jacuzzi tubs and views of spawning salmon in Ketchikan Creek. On sunny days, the lively café serves guests on the boardwalk deck. **www.thenewyorkhotel.com**

PETERSBURG Alaska Island Hostel   📶 @ $

805 Gjoa St, PO Box 892, Petersburg, AK 99833 **Tel** *772-3632, (877) 772-3632* **Rooms** *9 beds*

Located only 2 miles (3 km) from the ferry terminal and half a mile (1 km) from the airport, this downtown hostel offers single-sex dorms with linen, kitchen facilities, and a library of books, videos, and maps. The second-floor living room overlooks Petersburg and the mountains and muskeg of Mitkof Island. **www.alaskaislandhostel.com**

PETERSBURG Tides Inn   ♿ 📶 @ $$$

307 N 1st St, PO Box 1048, Petersburg, AK 99833 **Tel** *772-4288, (800) 665-8433* **Fax** *772-4286* **Rooms** *46*

The simple, family-run Tides Inn has long been a standard option within convenient walking distance of most sights of interest in Petersburg. All rooms enjoy good harbor and mountain views, and some are equipped with kitchenettes and dining tables. **www.tidesinnalaska.com**

PRINCE OF WALES ISLAND Clover Bay Lodge   🍴 $$$$$

PO Box 8944, Ketchikan, AK 99901 **Tel** *247-8555, (800) 354-0137* **Fax** *247-0724* **Rooms** *12*

Strategically located in the prime fishing area of Clarence Strait, this floating lodge offers excellent salmon and halibut fishing opportunities. Rates include all meals, use of fishing gear, guided fishing trips, and round-trip floatplane access from Ketchikan. **www.cloverbay.com**

SITKA Sitka Hotel   📶 🍴 ♿ 📶 📺 @ $$

118 Lincoln St, Sitka, AK 99835 **Tel** *747-3288* **Fax** *747-8499* **Rooms** *50*

Be sure to request a remodeled room at this charming and historic downtown hotel. Amenities include Wi-Fi, laundry services, and off-street parking. Victoria's Restaurant offers fresh local seafood, as well as soups, salads, and sandwiches. **www.sitkahotel.net**

SITKA Sitka Seaside Lodge   📶 @ $$$$

1404 Sawmill Creek Rd, PO Box 2135, Sitka, AK 99835 **Tel** *747-8113, (866) 747-8113* **Fax** *747-3337* **Rooms** *8*

With a hot tub and large deck overlooking the water, and large windows offering excellent views of the sea, this modern lodge is well-situated just a mile (2 km) from downtown Sitka. Breakfast and world-class fishing charters are included in the room rate. **www.sitkaseaside.com**

SKAGWAY RV Park – Pullen Creek   @ $

The Harbor, PO Box 324, Skagway, AK 99840 **Tel** *983-2768, (800) 936-3731* **Fax** *983-2668* **Rooms** *46 sites*

This is the most convenient RV park for historic downtown Skagway, the White Pass and Yukon Route Railroad Depot, and the ferry terminal. It offers electric and water hook-ups, a dump station, several tent sites, and a dozen RV sites with views of Lynn Canal. Even the largest RVs can be accommodated. **www.pullencreekrv.com**

SKAGWAY Skagway Home Hostel   📶 @ $

456 3rd Ave, PO Box 231, Skagway, AK 99840 **Tel** *983-2131* **Rooms** *3 dorms*

This cozy hostel, which was built during the Gold Rush era, caters mainly to hikers on the Chilkoot Trail. It is run by a bush pilot and a former Chilkoot Trail backcountry ranger, so there is plenty of wilderness advice available. Communal meals are sometimes served. **www.skagwayhostel.com**

Key to Price Guide *see p242* **Key to Symbols** *see back cover flap*

SKAGWAY Sergeant Preston's Lodge
🔥 📺 @ $$$

370 6th Ave, PO Box 538, Skagway, AK 99840 **Tel** *983-2521, (866) 983-2521* **Fax** *983-3500* **Rooms** *35*

This motel was named for Skagway's historic Northwest Mounted Police (now the RCMP) staging post, the only one ever established outside Canada. All rooms have private baths. The lodge is located just a block from the business district. **www.sgt-prestonslodgeskagway.com**

SKAGWAY Skagway Inn B&B
🍴 🔥 @ $$$

7th & Broadway, Skagway, AK 99840 **Tel** *983-2289, (888) 752-4929* **Fax** *983-2713* **Rooms** *12*

Built in 1897, the Skagway Inn was first a brothel, then a residence, and later a boarding house. The Victorian-style inn now features period furnishings and a fabulous garden, which supplies the house restaurant (open for cooking tours only), with organic produce. Breakfast is included in the room rate. Open summer only. **www.skagwayinn.com**

WRANGELL Rooney's Roost B&B
🔥 📺 $$

206 McKinnon St, PO Box 552, Wrangell, AK 99929 **Tel** *874-2026* **Rooms** *5*

With its early 20th century decor, this centrally located B&B provides a cozy, home-like ambience. Each of the five rooms has a different theme, and some have private baths. The B&B is within easy walking distance of the ferry terminal, and transfers are available for booked guests. Breakfast is included in the room rate. **www.rooneysroost.com**

WRANGELL Stikine Inn
🍴 🔥 📺 @ $$$

102 Stikine Ave, PO Box 990, Wrangell, AK 99929 **Tel** *874-3388, (888) 874-3388* **Rooms** *33*

This in-town waterfront hotel, located next to the cruise ship dock and two blocks from the ferry terminal, makes a convenient spot to stage trips up the Stikine River. All rooms have been remodeled, and the Stikine Inn restaurant is the finest dining option in town. **www.stikineinn.com**

WESTERN INTERIOR ALASKA

CHATANIKA Chatanika Gold Camp Lodge
🍴 🔥 $$

Mile 27.5, 5550 Steese Hwy, Chatanika, AK 99712 **Tel** *389-2414* **Fax** *457-6463* **Rooms** *12*

The lodge offers comfortable accommodation in a quiet, historic setting. Guests can choose between a rustic main lodge, or rooms in two log cabins on the ridge, which have Jacuzzi tubs and wraparound decks for viewing the scenic, wooded surroundings. Bar and restaurant on the premises.

CHENA HOT SPRINGS Chena Hot Springs Resort
🍴 🔥 📺 @ $$$$

Mile 56, Chena Hot Springs Rd, Fairbanks, AK 99711 **Tel** *451-8104* **Fax** *451-8151* **Rooms** *87*

Sprawled over about half a square mile (2 sq km) of wild land, the resort revolves around a hot spring spa and aurora viewing, as well as summer and winter outdoor activities. It also boasts an ice museum and ice bar. Budget options include yurts, RV camping, and tent camping *(see p177)*. **www.chenahotsprings.com**

DENALI STATE PARK Mount McKinley Princess
🏞 🍴 📶 🔥 🔥 📺 @ $$$$

Mile 133 Parks Hwy, Trapper Creek, AK 99683 **Tel** *733-2900, (800) 426-0500* **Rooms** *334*

Although it is a good distance away from Denali National Park, this lodge at Chulitna Crossing off the Parks Highway lies just around the corner from the finest views of Mount McKinley that are available outside the park itself. The enormous lobby and fine restaurant complete the air of opulence. **www.princesslodges.com**

DENALI VILLAGE Denali Mountain Morning Hostel
🔥 @ $$

Mile 224.5 Parks Hwy, PO Box 208, Denali Park, AK 99755 **Tel** *683-7503* **Rooms** *8*

With a lovely, quiet location on the banks of Carlo Creek, this is certainly one of the world's most beautiful hostels. Guests sleep in dorms or cabins of varying prices. The hotel rents backpacking gear and offers free luggage storage. A free shuttle operates to and from the Denali National Park Visitors' Center. Open summer only. **www.hostelalaska.com**

DENALI VILLAGE RV Park – Denali Rainbow Village
📺 @ $

Mile 238.6 Parks Hwy, Denali, AK 99753 **Tel** *683-7777* **Fax** *683-7275* **Rooms** *77 sites*

Just a mile (2 km) north of the Denali National Park entrance, this park provides full RV hook-ups and tent sites. On offer are potable water, a laundry, Wi-Fi, and satellite TV. The sites are compact, but the park is within walking distance of shops and restaurants and is the closest option to the national park. Open summer only. **www.denalirv.com**

DENALI VILLAGE Denali Grizzly Bear Resort
$$

Mile 231.1, Parks Hwy, Denali, AK 99755 **Tel** *683-2696, (866) 583-2696* **Rooms** *28 cabins and 83 sites*

This complex has a hotel, pleasant Nenana riverside campsites and RV sites, and well-appointed cabins, each in its own wooded setting. Some cabins date from the Gold Rush and have been restored and relocated here. An on-site shop sells basic supplies, ice cream, and liquor. **www.denaligrizzlybear.com**

DENALI VILLAGE Denali Crow's Nest
🍴 🔥 🔥 $$$

Mile 238.5 Parks Hwy, AK 99755 **Tel** *(888) 917-8130* **Fax** *683-2323* **Rooms** *39*

Offering a spectacular view, this collection of cozy log cabins clings to the hillside above Glitter Gulch. In the evening, guests can relax in the soothing outdoor hot tub farther up the hill or in the precariously perched bar and restaurant *(see p261)*, which enjoys a good reputation. **www.denalicrowsnest.com**

DENALI VILLAGE Grande Denali Lodge

⬜ 💰💰💰💰💰

Grande St, Mile 238.5 Parks Hwy, AK 99755 **Tel** *683-8500, (866) 683-8500* **Fax** *683-8599* **Rooms** *154*

Set high on a steep hill overlooking Glitter Gulch, this imposing hotel enjoys unparalleled panoramic views of the Nenana River Canyon and Alaska Range. The Alpenglow Restaurant is open through the day, while the Peak Experience Theater shows films on the national park. Open summer only. **www.denalialaska.com**

DENALI VILLAGE McKinley Chalet Resort

💰💰💰💰💰

Mile 238.9 Parks Hwy, Denali, AK 99755 **Tel** *276-7234, (800) 276-7234* **Fax** *683-8211* **Rooms** *345*

Thanks to its size, a large number of tour groups wind up in this sprawling complex in the heart of Glitter Gulch. The resort is architecturally quite pleasant, with chalet-style cedar lodges and rooms set on the banks of the Nenana River. Fine dining is on offer at the Nenana View Bar and Grill. Open summer only. **www.denaliparkresorts.com**

FAIRBANKS RV Park – River's Edge Resort

💰

4140 Boat St, Fairbanks, AK 99709 **Tel** *474-0286, (800) 770-3343* **Fax** *474-3665* **Rooms** *180 sites and 94 cottages*

Situated beside the Chena River, this RV park and resort offers sites with full hook-ups and tent camping, as well as fully-equipped cottages and lodge-style accommodation. The RV park and the executive suites offer Internet access. Extras include a restaurant, laundry, and tour-booking services. Open summer only. **www.riversedge.net**

FAIRBANKS Aurora Express

💰💰💰

Box 80128, Fairbanks, AK 99708 **Tel** *474-0949, (800) 221-0073* **Rooms** *8*

Located on a wooded hillside overlooking Fairbanks, Aurora Express consists of five beautifully refurbished railcars from the Alaska railroad. Each is uniquely decorated, and includes very comfortable furnishings and a private bath. The Pullman sleeper is popular with families. Breakfast is included. Open in summer only. **www.aurora-express.com**

FAIRBANKS RV Park – Minnie Street Bed and Breakfast Inn

💰💰💰

345 Minnie St, Fairbanks, AK 99701 **Tel** *456-1802, (888) 456-1849* **Rooms** *13*

This B&B is one of the nicest in Fairbanks, and is located just a few blocks from the heart of downtown and the Chena River. Guests enjoy the outdoor hot tub, Wi-Fi, and quiet setting, plus big breakfasts. Deluxe suites include full kitchens, fireplaces, and jetted tubs, and a small house has room for up to six people. **www.minniestreetbandb.com**

FAIRBANKS Fairbanks Princess Riverside Lodge

💰💰💰💰

4477 Pikes Landing Rd, Fairbanks, AK 99709 **Tel** *455-4477, (800) 426-0500* **Fax** *455-4476* **Rooms** *326*

This enormous and well-appointed hotel, well-located beside the Chena River and near the international airport, features two restaurants, a gift shop, and fitness and steam rooms. Reservations are essential because it is often booked out by Princess Cruises. **www.princesslodges.com**

FAIRBANKS Pike's Waterfront Lodge

💰💰💰💰

1850 Hoselton Rd, Fairbanks, AK 99702 **Tel** *456-4500, (877) 774-2400* **Fax** *456-4515* **Rooms** *208*

This expansive complex offers guests three restaurants, a sauna, a steam room, and a gym, along with a boat launch and adjacent restaurant. Accommodation is in standard or deluxe rooms, of which 70 have views of the Chena River, or in riverfront cabins. **www.pikeslodge.com**

FAIRBANKS Sophie Station

💰💰💰💰

1717 University Ave, Fairbanks, AK 99709 **Tel** *479-3650, (800) 528-4916* **Fax** *451-6376* **Rooms** *148*

All rooms in this long-standing business travelers' favorite include a sitting room, dining area, and full kitchen suite. Business amenities include high-speed Internet, in-room data ports, health club discounts, and free airport transfers. The hotel is well-located midway between the airport and business district. **www.fountainheadhotels.com**

KANTISHNA Camp Denali and North Face Lodge

💰💰💰💰💰

Mile 89 Denali Park Road, PO Box 67, Denali Village, AK 99755 **Tel** *683-2290* **Fax** *683-1568* **Rooms** *32*

With fabulous views of Mount McKinley, this wonderful wilderness retreat has both a lodge and cabin complex. Rates include buses from the park entrance, lodging, meals, guided outdoor and cultural activities, natural history programs, and the use of canoes, mountain bikes, and fishing gear. Open summer only. **www.campdenali.com**

KANTISHNA Kantishna Roadhouse

💰💰💰💰💰

Mile 93 Denali Park Rd, Kantishna, AK 99701 **Tel** *683-8003, (800) 942-7420* **Fax** *459-2160* **Rooms** *32*

Guests at the historic Kantishna Roadhouse, in an inholding inside Denali National Park, will be surrounded by wilderness hiking opportunities, and can also try gold panning, watch mushing demonstrations, and enjoy great views of Mount McKinley. Access from the park entrance is by lodge bus only. Open summer only. **www.kantishnaroadhouse.com**

MANLEY HOT SPRINGS Manley Roadhouse

💰💰💰

100 Front St, Manley Hot Springs, AK 99756 **Tel** *672-3161* **Fax** *672-3221* **Rooms** *20*

Alaska doesn't get more rustic than the 1903 Manley Roadhouse, also known as the Manley Hot Springs Lodge, which comes complete with a cozy old-time saloon *(see p262)*. History buffs can opt for the original rooms, while more modern rooms and cabins are also available. Open summer only. **www.manleyroadhouse.com**

TALKEETNA Talkeetna Hostel International

💰

PO Box 952, I St, Talkeetna, AK 99676 **Tel** *733-4678* **Rooms** *5*

For an easy-going atmosphere and inexpensive accommodation in rooms and dorms, this is the best option in Talkeetna. There is a full kitchen, free Internet, and no lockout. It is within easy walking distance of all the town sites, and the staff is happy to assist with adventure activity bookings. Open summer only. **www.talkeetnahostel.com**

Key to Price Guide *see p242* **Key to Symbols** *see back cover flap*

TALKEETNA Talkeetna Roadhouse ⬛🔳@ $$

PO Box 604, Talkeetna, AK 99676 **Tel** *733-1351* **Fax** *733-1353* **Rooms** *7*

Built in 1917, the Talkeetna Roadhouse may well transport visitors back to the days of prospectors, trappers, and steamboats on the nearby rivers. It makes an excellent budget option with lots of local flavor and an attached café that serves up healthy, hearty fare. **www.talkeetnaroadhouse.com**

TALKEETNA Talkeetna Alaskan Lodge 🔲⬛🔳🔳📺@ $$$$$

PO Box 727, Mile 12.5 Talkeetna Spur Rd, Talkeetna, AK 99676 **Tel** *733-9500, (888) 959-9590* **Fax** *733-9545* **Rooms** *212*

This well-appointed hotel, which is rather incongruous in the rustic atmosphere that prevails in Talkeetna, is the main destination for tour groups overnighting in town. In fine weather, it may be worth paying the higher room rates for one of the Mount McKinley view rooms. Open summer only. **www.talkeetnalodge.com**

WILLOW Gigglewood Lakeside Inn 🔳📺 $$$

Rainbow Ridge Rd, Caswell Lakes, HC89 Box 1601, Willow, AK 99688 **Tel** *495-1014, (800) 574-2555* **Rooms** *4*

Conveniently located between Anchorage and Denali National Park, the Gigglewood Inn is an atmospheric lakeside B&B that offers both private suite and cabin accommodation. The inn takes its name from the twisted birch used on the handrails of the stairs. **www.gigglewood.com**

EASTERN INTERIOR ALASKA

CHITINA Hotel Chitina ⬛🔳🔳@ $$$

Corner of Fairbank and Main Streets, Chitina, AK 99686 **Tel** *823-2244* **Rooms** *16*

First opened in 1914, this historic hotel fills a two-storey building in the heart of Chitina. Tastefully remodeled and refurbished, the hotel has 16 guest rooms, all with private baths and queen beds. There are no in-room phones or TVs, but Wi-Fi is available, and one unit is handicap-accessible. The downstairs restaurant is popular. **www.hotelchitina.com**

COPPER CENTER Copper Center Lodge ⬛📺@ $$$

Drawer J, Copper Center Loop Road, Copper Center, AK 99573 **Tel** *822-3245, (866) 330-3245* **Fax** *822-3948* **Rooms** *19*

A historic hotel in tiny Copper Center, this first served as a roadhouse during the late 1890s, when it was called the Blix Roadhouse. The simple rooms recall the Gold Rush era, while the lodge's staircase, made from twisty local dimond willow, is a work of art. The restaurant is the town's best eatery *(see p262)*. **www.coppercenterlodge.com**

COPPER CENTER Copper River Princess Wilderness Lodge 🔲⬛🔳🔳📺@ $$$$

Brenwick Craig Rd, Mile 101 Richardson Hwy, Copper Center, AK 99573 **Tel** *(800) 425-0500* **Rooms** *85*

This well-appointed and architecturally pleasant lodge caters mainly to cruise ship and organized bus tour visitors on tours to Wrangell-St. Elias National Park. Guests love its fine dining room, spacious lobby, and superb views. The lodge is open only from mid-May to mid-September. **www.princesslodges.com**

DAWSON CITY, YUKON TERRITORY Downtown Hotel ⬛🔳 $$$

2nd & Queen St, Dawson City, YT, Canada Y0B 1G0 **Tel** *(867) 993-5346, (800) 661-0514* **Fax** *(867) 993-5076* **Rooms** *59*

This reconstructed historic hotel in the heart of Dawson brings a touch of modernity to a quintessential Gold Rush theme. The annex has spa rooms and a lovely glass-roofed atrium, while the main building has queen bed suites and standard rooms. There is an airport limousine service for guests. **www.downtownhotel.ca**

DELTA JUNCTION Kelly's Alaska Country Inn 🔳📺 $$$

1616 Richardson Hwy, PO Box 849, Delta Junction, AK 99737 **Tel** *895-4667* **Fax** *895-4481* **Rooms** *21*

Run by three generations of the Kelly family, who are proud of their Alaska pioneer history, this simple motel-style place lies within walking distance of most tourist amenities. It makes a convenient stop for Alaska Highway travelers between the Canadian border and Fairbanks. **www.kellysalaskacountryinn.com**

EAGLE Falcon Inn B&B 🔳🔳 $$$

220 Front St, PO Box 136, Eagle, AK 99738 **Tel** *547-2254* **Rooms** *5*

This log B&B on the banks of the Yukon offers cozy rooms and common areas with river views, and is a great place to relax after a canoe trip or a tour in the historic town of Eagle. The friendly owners are happy to suggest other local activities. Breakfast is included in the room rate. **http://falconinn.mystarband.net**

GLENN HIGHWAY Sheep Mountain Lodge ⬛🔳 $$$

17701 W Glenn Hwy, Mile 113, Sutton, AK 99674 **Tel** *745-5121, (877) 645-5121* **Fax** *745-5120* **Rooms** *10*

Situated along a wild stretch of the Glenn Highway, this lodge enjoys spectacular views of both the Chugach peaks and Sheep Mountain. Accommodation is in individual cabins. It is popular during the summer with hikers and rafters, and with Nordic skiers and snowmachiners during the winter. **www.sheepmountain.com**

GLENNALLEN Lake Louise Lodge ⬛🔳📺 $$

HC01 Box 1716, Glennallen, AK 99588 **Tel** *822-3311, (877) 878-3311* **Rooms** *7*

Once a rustic hunting cabin, this lakeside lodge is known to Alaskans who appreciate the fine fishing, canoeing, snowmachining, and boating on the area's large system of lakes and streams. Visitors have access to the hot tub, sauna, and free boat launch. Breakfast is included in the room rate. **www.lakelouiselodge.com**

GLENNALLEN Caribou Hotel
Mile 186.5 Glenn Hwy, PO Box 329, Glennallen, AK 99588 **Tel** *822-3302, (800) 478-3302* **Fax** *822-3711* **Rooms** *100*

Close to St. Elias National Park and the Copper River Valley, this convenient stop for highway travelers offers a range of options, from budget rooms in the annex to standard rooms and cabins. The hotel restaurant is the local favorite for meals out. **www.caribouhotel.com**

KENNICOTT Kennicott Glacier Lodge
Lot 15, Millsite Subdivision, Kennicott, AK 99588 **Tel** *258-2350, (800) 582-5128* **Fax** *248-7975* **Rooms** *35*

Right in the heart of Wrangell-St. Elias National Park, this lodge enjoys one of Alaska's finest views, taking in the ghost town at Kennicott as well as glaciers and distant peaks. It also has a fine-dining restaurant *(see p263)*. Access is on foot or by shuttle bus from road's end at McCarthy, 5 miles (8 km) away. Open summer only. **www.kennicottlodge.com**

MCCARTHY Lancaster's Backpacker Hotel
Barrett Way, PO Box MXY, McCarthy, AK 99588 **Tel** *554-4402* **Fax** *554-4404* **Rooms** *11*

This comfy no-frills little place is the only budget accommodation east of the Kennicott River footbridge. It is a worthwhile option just for the opportunity to stay in the heart of historic McCarthy. The hotel is affiliated with McCarthy Lodge and Ma Johnson's Hotel, located literally a few feet away. Open summer only. **www.mccarthylodge.com**

MCCARTHY Kennicott River Lodge and Hostel
Mile 59 McCarthy Road, PO Box MXY, McCarthy, AK 99588 **Tel** *554-4441, 590-8753* **Rooms** *7*

Next to the Kennicott River at the end of the McCarthy Road is this convenient lodge, where options include three rooms in the main building, two cabins, and a dozen dorm beds. It also has a sauna, kitchen, and a bathhouse. Open summer only. **www.kennicottriverlodge.com**

MCCARTHY McCarthy Lodge and Ma Johnson's Hotel
PO Box MXY, McCarthy, AK 99588 **Tel** *554-4402* **Fax** *554-4404* **Rooms** *20*

The historic McCarthy Lodge and museum-like Ma Johnson's Hotel offer wonderfully anachronistic accommodation. Room amenities in this upmarket hotel include custom bathrobes and handmade soap. The dining room *(see p263)* is well-regarded and the staff are happy to help plan trips in the park. Open summer only. **www.mccarthylodge.com**

TOK RV Park – Tok RV Village
Mile 1313.4 Alaska Hwy, PO Box 739, Tok, AK 99780 **Tel** *883-5877, (800) 478-5878* **Rooms** *164 sites*

For RV drivers, this is the first RV park west of the international border with Canada. Located at the entrance to Tok, this wooded site offers full hook-ups, including satellite TV, as well as a laundromat, hot showers, and Wi-Fi. It can even accommodate rigs up to 70 feet (21 m). Open summer only. **www.tokrv.net**

SOUTHWEST ALASKA

DUTCH HARBOR/UNALASKA Unisea Inn
188 Gilman Way, PO Box 921169, Dutch Harbor, AK 99692 **Tel** *581-1325, (866) 581-3844* **Fax** *581-7150* **Rooms** *25*

Located in an industrial area near the small boat harbor, this simple inn offers a pleasant budget alternative in Dutch Harbor. Rooms are small and simple, and the adjacent restaurant and no-smoking bar are great places to meet locals. **www.grandaleutian.com**

DUTCH HARBOR/UNALASKA Grand Aleutian Hotel
498 Salmon Way, PO Box 921169, Dutch Harbor, AK 99692 **Tel** *581-1325, (866) 581-3844* **Fax** *581-7150* **Rooms** *112*

Billing itself as a European chalet-style hotel, this agreeable establishment overlooking Margaret Bay comes as a surprise in industrial Dutch Harbor. With comfortable rooms and a wonderful restaurant, it is a fine choice in the Aleutian Islands. Airport transport is available for booked guests. **www.grandaleutian.com**

KATMAI NATIONAL PARK Brooks Lodge
Katmailand, 2145 Aircraft Dr, Anchorage, AK 99502 **Tel** *243-5448, (800) 544-0551* **Fax** *243-0649* **Rooms** *16*

Rustic Brooks Lodge, at Katmai's Brooks Camp, lies within a few minutes' walk of excellent fishing and Alaska's finest brown bear viewing area. Book well in advance for the peak season in June and July. Rates include cabin accommodation and flights from Anchorage. Open in summer only. Meals are extra. **www.katmailand.com**

KODIAK A Smiling Bear B&B
2046 Three Sisters Way, Kodiak, AK 99615 **Tel** *481-6390* **Fax** *486-6390* **Rooms** *2*

With a Kodiak bear theme and a fabulous garden, this lovely place near the Monashka Bay shore offers personable home accommodation and attention to detail. Breakfast, which is included in the room rate, often consists of items grown in the extensive attached forest garden. **www.asmilingbear.com**

KODIAK Best Western Kodiak Inn
236 W Rezanof Dr, Kodiak, AK 99615 **Tel** *486-5712, (888) 563-4254* **Fax** *486-3430* **Rooms** *80*

Part of the Best Western chain, this centrally-located hotel caters largely to business travelers and anglers. The vaulted lobby displays a stuffed mountain goat and an enormous Kodiak bear. Freezers are available for visitors' fish catches, and the hotel also provides shuttle services from the ferry dock and airport. **www.kodiakinn.com**

KODIAK Comfort Inn 🖼 🅗 ♿ 📺 @ $$$$
1395 Airport Way, Kodiak, AK 99615 **Tel** *487-2700, (800) 544-2202* **Fax** *487-4447* **Rooms** *50*

Well-situated for the airport, this scenically located hotel is also close to the Buskin River State Recreation Area, with some excellent fishing opportunities. It is open all year round, with significant discounts in winter. Breakfast and free Wi-Fi are included in the room rate. **www.choicehotels.com**

KODIAK Afognak Wilderness Lodge 🅗 🏊 @ $$$$$
7 Happy Lane, Seal Bay, Kodiak, AK 99697 **Tel** *486-6442, (800) 478-6442* **Fax** *(206) 260-9390* **Rooms** *6*

Located on Afognak Island north of Kodiak, this remote lodge is the only one within Afognak Island State Park. Accommodation is in spacious log cabins that provide all creature comforts. Rates include all meals and guided boat travel for fishing, photography, wildlife viewing, and hiking **www.afognaklodge.com**

ST. PAUL King Eider Hotel 🅗 🏊 $$$
TDX, PO Box 88, St Paul, AK 99660 **Tel** *546-2477, (877) 424-5637* **Fax** *278-2316* **Rooms** *16*

This simple and basic Native-owned hotel is the headquarters for birding and wildlife tours on St. Paul Island in the Pribilofs, and accommodation is almost always sold in conjunction with tours. Bookings are organized through the TDX Native Corporation. **www.alaskabirding.com**

ARCTIC AND WESTERN ALASKA

BARROW Top of the World Hotel 🅗 📺 $$$$
1200 Angvik St, PO Box 189, Barrow, AK 99723 **Tel** *852-3900, (800) 478-8520* **Fax** *852-6752* **Rooms** *50*

This renowned hotel adjoining the popular Pepe's North of the Border restaurant *(see p263)* provides a warm spot in a normally harsh environment. For a slightly higher charge, guests can opt for an ocean view room overlooking the usually frozen Arctic Ocean. **www.tundratoursinc.com**

BARROW King Eider Inn ♿ 🏊 📺 $$$$$
1752 Ahkovak St, Barrow, AK 99723 **Tel** *852-4700, (888) 303-4337* **Fax** *852-2025* **Rooms** *19*

Barrow's finest hotel, this place is beautifully furnished and amazingly tidy, with a wood-mantled stone fireplace and a unique chess set in the lobby. Some rooms have kitchenettes and the guest sauna can warm the soul even on the coldest days. It is conveniently located near the airport. **www.kingeider.net**

COLDFOOT Slate Creek Inn 🅗 $$$$
Coldfoot, Mile 175, Dalton Hwy, AK 99701 **Tel** *474-3500, (866) 474-3400* **Fax** *670-5202* **Rooms** *76*

Housed in a former pipeline construction camp, this simple but comfortable place is the only accommodation in Coldfoot. All rooms have private baths, but no phone, TVs, or Internet access. The complex also has a restaurant *(see p263)*. **www.coldfootcamp.com**

DEADHORSE Prudhoe Bay Hotel 🅗 🏊 $$$$
Spine & Sag River Road, Deadhorse, AK 99734 **Tel** *659-2449* **Rooms** *20*

This hotel, the best-value option in the oilfields, has decent rooms, a buffet restaurant, and a laundry, and serves as the designated Deadhorse campsite for RV travelers, but there are no hook-ups. It also boasts a repair facility for vehicles and heavy equipment. Room rates cover all meals, including breakfast. **www.prudhoebayhotel.com**

KOTZEBUE Nullagvik Hotel 🅗 ♿ 📺 $$$$
PO Box 336, Kotzebue, AK 99752 **Tel** *442-3331* **Fax** *442-3340* **Rooms** *72*

This well-appointed hotel in the Inupiat town of Kotzebue is popular with business travelers and visitors who are there for more than a day tour. The pleasantly decorated restaurant, which features local Arctic fish on the menu, is essentially the only option in town. **www.nullagvik.com**

NOME Aurora Inn & Suites 🏊 📺 @ $$$
302 E. Front St, Nome, AK 99762 **Tel** *443-3838, (800) 354-4606* **Fax** *443-6380* **Rooms** *68*

Located in the heart of town and right across from the beach, the Aurora Inn & Suites is one of Nome's nicest lodging place. Rooms are spacious and some have kitchenettes. A guest sauna and car rentals are also available. **www.aurorainnnome.com**

NOME Nome Nugget Inn 🅗 ♿ 📺 $$$
Front St, PO Box 1470, Nome, AK 99762 **Tel** *443-2323, (877) 443-2323* **Fax** *443-5966* **Rooms** *47*

Located along the waterfront, this simple and rustic hotel aims for an authentic Gold Rush atmosphere with Iditarod memorabilia and artifacts scattered around. The attached Fat Freddie's Restaurant and Gold Dust Saloon are popular local gathering places. **www.nomenuggetinnhotel.com**

WISEMAN Boreal Lodge 🍴 🏊 📺 $$$
1 Timberwolf Trail, Wiseman, AK 99790 **Tel** *678-4566* **Fax** *678-4566* **Rooms** *3*

Set in a historic mining village, this place allows visitors to experience the closest thing to a frontier lifestyle that is available on Alaska's road system. Rooms have shared facilities and access to a communal kitchen and laundry. There is also a cabin with a private bath. **www.boreallodge.com**

WHERE TO EAT

Most of the larger cities in Alaska have a variety of eateries serving better than average fare that spans a range of diverse cuisines reflecting the many immigrant communities that are part of the Alaskan population. Quality can vary, but in general, Anchorage provides the widest selection, including Indian, Japanese, Vietnamese, and Greek restaurants. Fairbanks, Juneau, Homer, and some of the smaller towns also present a surprising number of fine choices.

Nearly all mid-sized communities have Chinese, Mexican, and fast food restaurants, and even the smallest bush community will usually have a basic eatery, a coffee shop, supermarket food stalls, or a cannery canteen. Alaskan cuisine includes hearty and filling dishes *(see pp254–5)*, featuring well-prepared steak and a range of seafood. Portions are generous and may be accompanied by large starters, and as many baskets of bread or tortilla chips as requested by diners.

TYPES OF RESTAURANTS

As with elsewhere in the US, Alaska has several categories of restaurants. The most expensive options are the true gourmet restaurants, which are found only around Anchorage or in larger towns, but most mid-range restaurants offer some imaginative chef's specials that approximate gourmet standards.

The majority of Alaskan restaurants are individual- and family-run and range from satisfying to superb. In small highway towns and along the road system, a large number of roadhouses provide excellent breakfasts, lunches with a choice of home-made soup, and a variety of filling dinners. The larger hotels usually have their own restaurants, which in wilderness areas may be the only places to eat in the

Sign at a seafood restaurant in Seward *(see p258)*

vicinity. The larger towns have chain restaurants that offer decent food at good prices and in very generous portions that few people can finish. The assumption is that most diners will pack up the leftovers in a doggy bag to eat later. Box stores and supermarkets often have bakeries, delis, noodle bars, sushi bars, and cafés that rustle up quick and filling fare.

Fast food is an economical option, and towns of all sizes have at least one of the major chains, such as McDonald's, Taco Bell, and Subway,

serving up the usual gamut of burgers, fried chicken, sub sandwiches, pizzas, and tacos.

As anywhere, reputations come and go, and the best way to find a decent meal is to ask locals, who are usually pleased to promote their favorite places. Tourist offices can only provide listings and are not permitted to offer recommendations, but hotel staff and taxi drivers are happy to offer suggestions. This guide provides a comprehensive listing of recommended restaurants *(see pp256–63)*.

RESERVATIONS AND DRESS CODES

Dinner reservations are recommended for most upscale places, but in the case of popular restaurants that don't accept bookings, it pays to arrive as early as possible. When it comes to

Roadside bakery and pizzeria at Carlo Creek on the Parks Highway near Denali National Park

Pleasant outdoor seating at a restaurant on Homer Spit

dress, Alaska is possibly the most relaxed state in the country, and only a few of the finest restaurants request more formal attire.

MEALS

In Alaska, breakfast can be anything from fruit, toast, and coffee to a hearty spread that includes juice, eggs done any way the diner requests, ham, steak, bacon, or sausage. Fried potatoes, biscuits and gravy, pancakes, and several Mexican possibilities involving beans, vegetables, salsa, tortillas, and cheese may also be on the menu. Many Alaskan hotels, lodges, restaurants, and roadhouses offer all of these choices, but anyone not planning on a full day of exercise may want to order a lighter meal. Lunch staples usually include appetizing soups – often halibut chowder – and salads, and burgers, or sandwiches.

In the US, dinner is the main meal of the day, and is usually eaten between 5 and 9pm. In the long daylight hours of summer, Alaskans tend to eat late, after recreational activities are finished for the day, and outdoor evening barbecues are very popular. Dinner usually includes some sort of meat – beef, pork, chicken, fish, and occasionally moose – as well as a vegetable dish, a salad, and potatoes. In urban restaurants, meals range from the usual Alaskan meat-and-potatoes fare to international options such as Italian, Greek, Mexican, Thai, Chinese, Korean, and Japanese food.

Alaska has access to some of the world's best seafood, from plump, cold-water Kachemak Bay oysters and Alaska king crab to halibut and, of course, wild Alaska salmon, one of the most popular products of the state. In the summer, restaurants and tourist-oriented businesses in many towns organize salmon bakes – often served in an all-you-can-eat style – with freshly caught wild salmon.

PRICES AND TIPPING

Despite the fact that shipping distances dictate higher prices than those found in the Lower 48, visitors will find that restaurant meals in Alaska generally represent good value. In fact, in hotels, locally-run places, and sit-down chain restaurants, generous portions of tasty, filling food will cost only a bit more than if you prepared them yourself. What the food might lack in sophistication, it amply makes up for in quantity and taste. Even fine-dining restaurants are reasonably priced and provide value for money.

As with any restaurant in the country, tipping is essential. Restaurant employees are typically paid low wages under the assumption that customers will liberally tip the servers and bus staff. Tips are usually determined by the quality of the service received, with the average being around 15–20 percent. A tip of 10 percent will make it clear that the service was lacking, while 20 percent will indicate an appreciation of exceptional service.

VEGETARIANS

Despite the local fondness for meals based on fish and game, vegetarians will be happy to find that most Alaskan restaurants cater to a wide variety of preferences, and that Anchorage, Juneau, and Fairbanks have some excellent places specializing in vegetarian cuisine. Nearly every fast food, national chain, and private restaurant offers vegetarian options, although these may be no more interesting than bean burritos or a noodle dish.

In bush towns, Chinese or Korean places always offer several substantial vegetarian options, and wilderness lodges serve buffet meals that allow diners to choose between vegetarian and meat-oriented selections. Visitors on cruises or organized tours will also find that their culinary preferences, whether vegetarian, kosher, or diabetic, are almost universally accommodated.

CHILDREN

Most Alaskan restaurants cater to children with simple meals that include hot dogs, French fries (chips), burgers, and other items that appeal to the younger set. These will typically cost around half the price of an adult meal. In addition, many places provide high chairs, play areas, coloring books, and crayons to keep kids busy as they wait for their meals.

Ketchikan's popular Bar Harbor restaurant (see p260)

The Flavors of Alaska

From Alaska's cold waters, commercial deep-sea fishermen harvest some of the world's best wild salmon, halibut, and cod, as well as three species of crab and other shellfish. Seafood is served grilled, baked, or broiled, or preserved by smoking, drying, or canning. Hunters bring in game meat such as Dall sheep, moose, caribou, and black-tailed deer, which are prepared in a variety of creative ways. A range of local produce, including potatoes, carrots, and other "winter" vegetables, is grown commercially in the Mat-Su Valley; some of these grow to gargantuan proportions in the long daylight hours of the Alaskan summer *(see p84).*

Alaskan crowberries and lowbush cranberries

Commercial crab fisherman off Juneau in Southeast Alaska

ALASKAN FOOD

Alaska's cuisine reflects the variety of people who have come to the state from all over the US and other parts of the world. However, most ethnic foods have been adapted to local tastes. Local specialties include pizzas made with reindeer sausage, bolognaise sauces made with moose meat, and taco fillings that include carrots and halibut. Fresh vegetables play less of a role than they do in the Lower 48. Instead, most Alaskans favor hearty fare that is heavy on meat and fish. In the summer, barbecued meat or grilled fish is accompanied by sourdough bread, salads, light soups, and local vegetables, while in the winter, a typical meal would include a bowl of warming chili or beef, game, or chicken stew, along with potato dishes and vegetable casseroles topped with cheese and breadcrumbs.

The most reliable places to find authentic Alaskan "home cooking" are wilderness lodges and roadhouses along the highway system, which serve up hearty, filling fare that usually features meat, potatoes, and cold-weather vegetables.

Salmon filet

Salmon steak

Halibut filet

Trout

Shrimp

Scallops

A selection of fresh seafood available in Alaska

ALASKAN DISHES AND SPECIALTIES

Alaskan sourdough

Most fine Alaskan restaurants serve local seafood using various creative recipes for wild salmon and halibut, as well as king, Dungeness, and snow crab. Available in season, these are most often served as a pile of legs and claws, accompanied by a selection of dipping sauces. Game meat is also a staple and a few restaurants offer options such as reindeer sausage. Potatoes figure prominently in most meals, and the most popular vegetables used are hardy varieties that can be grown in cold climates. Meals may also feature Alaskan sourdough bread, which was popularized during the Gold Rush. It is made with a starter, which contains a yeast that causes the dough to rise. The periodic addition of sugar keeps the yeast growing and some starters in use today date from the early 1900s. Desserts include pies, tarts, or cobblers made from local wild berries.

Salmon, *an iconic Alaskan dish, is served grilled, baked, or alder-smoked with lemon, dill, and melted butter. Alaska has five species of Pacific salmon.*

Sampling beer at the Alaskan Brewing Company *(see p144)* in Juneau

VEGETABLES AND FRUITS

Alaska's main agricultural area, the Matanuska Valley, produces a wide range of cold-climate vegetables such as carrots, squash, zucchini, potatoes, kohlrabi, rutabagas (swedes), and turnips. These are usually used in stews, baked into casseroles, or eaten as stand alone dishes after being baked, boiled, or mashed. The climate of Anchorage, the Kenai Peninsula, and the Mat-Su is also suitable for growing orchard fruits such as apples and cherries, although not in commercial quantities. Rhubarb and a wide variety of berries grow well through much of the southern half of the state. Most are cultivated in private gardens and canned, made into jams and jellies, or baked into delicious pies.

BEER AND WINE

A recent development in the state is the growth of microbreweries in the larger towns. Alaska's only fully fledged brewery is the Alaskan Brewing Company in Juneau. Its range of award-winning beers include stout, amber, pale ale, and both summer and winter ales, which are available all over Alaska, as well as in the western states.

Alaska's climate is too cold for growing wine grapes, but that does not stop a couple of local wineries from producing delicious and refreshing wines from local flowers, fruits, and other produce. Haines' Great Land Winery creates very respectable wines from berries, fireweed, birch sap, honey, and even potatoes, onions, and carrots. A similar operation in Homer, Bear Creek Winery produces rhubarb, blueberry and raspberry wines. Anchorage's Denali Winery imports grapes to produce palatable vintages.

NATIVE FOODS

Akutaq "Eskimo ice cream" is made by the Inuit from seal oil, whipped berries, and snow.

Caribou, moose, black-tailed deer Hunted by Alaska Natives in Southeast, Interior, and Arctic Alaska, wild game meat is dried, frozen, or eaten in any meat-based recipe.

Dried fish Fish are preserved by drying them on large racks.

Smoked fish Fish are smoked in a wood-fired smoker, usually using alder wood, which adds a fine flavor.

Whale This beef-like meat is a favored part of the local diet. Inupiat villages are allowed to catch small numbers of whales.

Muktuk Whale blubber, the fatty layer beneath the outer skin, is chewed raw or softened by boiling or pickling.

Berries Historically, berries such as salmonberries, elderberries, and blueberries were the main source of sugar in the Native diet.

Crab legs and claws *are steamed or boiled and served with a variety of sauces. Diners need a crab-cracker to extract the meat from the shell.*

Reindeer sausage pizza *is a thick crust pizza spread with marinara sauce and cheese, topped with reindeer sausage, roasted peppers, and onions.*

Wild blueberry pies *are made by baking berries with sugar, cornstarch, and lemon juice in a pie shell. They are served with whipped cream.*

Choosing a Restaurant

The restaurants in this guide have been selected, as far as possible, for the quality of the food and atmosphere. However, in some parts of Alaska there are few restaurants that can be recommended. In such cases, places have been suggested that offer good value. For map references for Anchorage, see pages 64–5.

PRICE CATEGORIES
The price ranges include a main dish, taxes, and service charges, but exclude wine.

$ under $12
$$ $12–$25
$$$ $25–$40
$$$$ $40–$50
$$$$$ Over $50

ANCHORAGE

ANCHORAGE Arctic Roadrunner
$

5300 Old Seward Hwy, Anchorage, AK 99518 **Tel** *279-7311*   **Map** *E1*

Established in the 1960s and located in a delightfully rustic creekside setting, this Alaskan institution serves up the best range of burgers in town, including salmon and halibut burgers. Extra-thick milkshakes and crunchy onion rings are other favorites with the locals. Closed Sunday.

ANCHORAGE Middle Way Café
$

1200 W Northern Lights Blvd, Anchorage, AK 99503 **Tel** *272-6433*   **Map** *E1*

This small café caters to vegetarians and health-conscious diners. The menu features whole-grain wraps, a choice of home-made soups, sandwiches, fruit smoothies, coffee specialties, and a great variety of teas. Reservations are not accepted. Open Monday to Saturday for lunch. Serves light snacks on Sunday.

ANCHORAGE Bombay Deluxe
$$

555 W Northern Lights Blvd, Anchorage, AK 99503 **Tel** *272-1200*   **Map** *E1*

This unassuming Indian restaurant does wonders with North Indian food. It has a good value lunch buffet on weekdays, which provides a sampling of Indian favorites, including a variety of vegetarian dishes. Open from Sunday to Friday for lunch and dinner. No lunch service on Saturday.

ANCHORAGE Café Amsterdam
$$

530 E Benson, Anchorage, AK 99503 **Tel** *274-0074*   **Map** *F1*

A café, bakery, and beer garden with a bit of old world flavor, Café Amsterdam does indulgent breakfasts and bistro-style lunches. The café also dishes out Continental cuisine every evening from Tuesday to Saturday. In the "grotto," diners can sample 16 beers on tap, including a range of excellent Belgian brews.

ANCHORAGE Fu Do
$$

2600 E Tudor Rd, Anchorage, AK 99507 **Tel** *561-6610*   **Map** *F1*

Known for its enthusiastic and attentive staff, this excellent Chinese eatery serves up standard Mandarin, Szechwan, Cantonese, and Mongolian dishes in a lavishly decorated interior. The family menu is especially good value. Fu Do is open for lunch and dinner; closed Monday.

ANCHORAGE Gwennie's Old Alaska Restaurant
$$

4333 Spenard Rd, Anchorage, AK 99517 **Tel** *243-2090*   **Map** *E1*

There is a pronounced Alaskan theme here with stuffed wildlife and Alaskan memorabilia decorating the interiors of this Anchorage institution. Known for its hearty fare and huge portions, its renowned breakfasts include king crab omelets, sourdough pancakes, and reindeer sausage.

ANCHORAGE Moose's Tooth
$$

3300 Old Seward Hwy, Anchorage, AK 99503 **Tel** *258-2537*   **Map** *F1*

The pizzas here, from blackened halibut and Thai chicken to chipotle steak supreme and Greek gyro, are thought to be the best in the state, as evidenced by the long queues. Diners waiting for entry can sample the Moose's Tooth microbrewery's own range of beers.

ANCHORAGE Organic Oasis
$$

2610 Spenard Rd, Anchorage, AK 99503 **Tel** *277-7882*   **Map** *E1*

For a healthy meal in a leafy environment, this is the best option in town. Whole-grain bread and all manner of fresh organic vegetarian ingredients feature on the diverse lunch and dinner menu. Fresh juices, wine, and organic beer are available.

ANCHORAGE Thai Kitchen
$$

3405 E Tudor Rd, Anchorage, AK 99507 **Tel** *561-0082*   **Map** *F1*

The spartan appearance of this eclectic eatery belies the fact that it frequently wins awards as the best Thai restaurant in Anchorage. This is the place for the most authentic Thai cuisine. Highlights include *pad thai*, garlic chicken, *tom kha kai*, and Popeye chicken. Closed for lunch on the weekend.

Key to Symbols *see back cover flap*

ANCHORAGE Benihana
$$$ Map E1

1100 W 8th Ave, Anchorage, AK 99501 **Tel** *222-5212*

Skilled entertainers, the teppanyaki chefs put on a great show preparing hibachi steak, seafood, and vegetables at the tables. While the process is not strictly Japanese, it's always fun to watch. There is also an appetizer lounge, a sushi bar, and ice sculpture display. Benihana is open all days of the week.

ANCHORAGE Club Paris
$$$ Map D5

417 W 5th Ave, Anchorage, AK 99501 **Tel** *277-6332*

Dating from 1957, the cozy and unpretentious Club Paris has consistently been voted the city's best steakhouse. Salad and clam chowder make excellent starters, followed by prime rib, top sirloin, or 4 inch (9 cm) thick filet mignon as a main dish. Reservations are advised. Closed for lunch on Sunday.

ANCHORAGE Glacier Brewhouse
$$$ Map C5

737 W 5th Ave, Anchorage, AK 99501 **Tel** *274-2739*

With wonderful, spacious interiors, a range of home-brewed beers, and consistently great food, this place could serve as a template for the brewhouse genre. Their wood-grilled seafood, pan seared salmon, herb-crusted halibut, and wood-fired pizzas are highly recommended.

ANCHORAGE Snow Goose
$$$ Map D4

717 W 3rd Ave, Anchorage, AK 99501 **Tel** *277-7727*

With wonderful views across Cook Inlet to Mount Susitna, a succulent menu, and home-made beers from the adjacent Sleeping Lady brewery, the Snow Goose offers a unique dining experience. Signature seafood options range from blackened mango rockfish to teriyaki salmon. Closed for lunch on Sunday.

ANCHORAGE Sourdough Mining Company
$$$ Map F1

5200 Juneau St, Anchorage, AK 99518 **Tel** *563-2272*

Housed in a replica of an old mill house, this restaurant caters to travelers seeking a historic Alaskan fantasy. Meals of Alaskan seafood and corn fritters with whipped honey butter are followed by a gold panning demonstration and a Gold Rush show. Open for lunch and dinner Monday to Saturday, and for Sunday brunch.

ANCHORAGE Jens' Restaurant
$$$$ Map L1

Olympic Center, 701 W 36th Ave, Anchorage, AK 99503 **Tel** *561-5367*

The Danish chef in this fantastic but unassuming restaurant and wine bar takes traditional Danish and Alaskan dishes and prepares them in a variety of imaginative ways, depending on what ingredients are in season. One of the city's finest dining options, Jens' is closed Sunday, plus Saturday lunch, and for dinner on Monday.

ANCHORAGE Sacks Café
$$$$ Map C4

328 G Street, Anchorage, AK 99501 **Tel** *276-3546*

Just a block from the Log Cabin Visitor Center, this delightful upscale café has trendy decor, friendly staff, and a pleasant wine bar. The menu changes often, but is always inspired, with a range of meat and vegetarian specials. Dinner reservations are recommended. Weekend brunches are also popular.

ANCHORAGE Marx Bros Café
$$$$$ Map D4

627 W 3rd Ave, Anchorage, AK 99501 **Tel** *278-2133*

In the business since 1979, this tiny café is famous for an innovative menu that changes with the seasons. Fresh Alaskan seafood is always on the menu, along with a delicious made-at-your-table Caesar salad and a notable wine list, but save room for the luscious desserts. Reservations are essential.

ANCHORAGE Mixx Grill
$$$$$ Map E1

1200 L St, Anchorage, AK 99501 **Tel** *222-8787*

It is claimed that every plate served at Mixx is a work of art. This fine restaurant in the Inlet Tower Hotel and Suites *(see p242)* is an excellent choice for a special occasion or a romantic night out. Specialties include a variety of creative dishes of Alaskan seafood, game meat, and handmade pasta.

GIRDWOOD Double Musky Inn
$$$

Mile 0.3 Crow Creek Rd, Girdwood, AK 99587 **Tel** *783-2822*

The Deep South combines with Alaska's northern seas to provide a fine dining experience. Specialties include New Orleans dishes created using Alaskan seafood, as well as lobster kebabs and blackened pepper steaks. The inn takes no reservations and it is advisable to arrive early. Closed on Mondays in summer; only open on weekends in winter.

GIRDWOOD Seven Glaciers Restaurant
$$$$$

Mount Alyeska, Girdwood, AK 99587 **Tel** *754-2237*

A part of the same resort complex as the Hotel Alyeska *(see p243)*, Seven Glaciers is set at an altitude of 2,300 ft (700 m) and offers quality – and prices – to match its lofty setting. The menu includes Alaskan salmon, buffalo steak, and king crab. Access is via a complimentary gondola ride to the restaurant.

PALMER Vagabond Blues
$ Map C1

642 S Alaska St, Palmer, AK 99645 **Tel** *745-2233*

While this vibrant bohemian-style café may seem somewhat out of place in down-to-earth Palmer, it is popular with locals, who sit around the chunky tables, play chess, sip coffee, and enjoy healthy soups, salads, quiche, and cakes. Music enthusiasts can look forward to some live entertainment. Closes at 6pm on Sunday and all day Monday.

WASILLA The Grape Tap
322 N Boundary St, Wasilla, AK 99654 **Tel** *376-8466*

Map *B1*

One of the few notable restaurants in the Mat-Su Valley, this quiet little spot is a haven from the surrounding developments. The menu includes a range of small tapas-style dishes, but don't come here if you're in a hurry. Open for dinners Tuesday to Saturday, closed Sunday and Monday.

THE KENAI PENINSULA

COOPER LANDING Gwin's Lodge
14865 Sterling Hwy, Cooper Landing, AK 99572 **Tel** *595-1266*

This 1940s log roadhouse represents a slice of old Alaska and is a popular highway stop between Anchorage and the western Kenai Peninsula. Expect hearty breakfasts and Alaska-sized portions of well-prepared chili, chowder, steak, and seafood. Open 24 hours in the summer. Closed winter.

HALIBUT COVE The Saltry
9 W Ismailof, Halibut Cove, AK 99603 **Tel** *296-2223, (800) 478-7847*

Everything in this renowned eatery is handmade, from the hand-sawn lumber to the ceramic plates. Specialties include fresh seafood, local vegetables, home-made bread, and organic buffalo meat. Cheesecakes and fine wines are also on the menu. Bookings are essential. Access is aboard the *Danny J* water taxi from Homer across the bay. Open summer only.

HOMER Fresh Sourdough Express
1316 Ocean Dr, Homer, AK 99603 **Tel** *235-7571*

Originally housed in a bakery wagon parked on Homer Spit, this popular little place has expanded and now serves three healthy, organic meals every day. In addition to excellent breakfasts, fresh salmon and halibut, steak, pasta, and organic chicken dishes are served.

HOMER The Homestead Restaurant
Mile 8.2 East End Rd, Homer, AK 99603 **Tel** *235-8723*

Despite its reputation as a fine dining restaurant, the Homestead's ambience tends toward Alaskan rustic. While it is renowned for its local seafood, it also does an excellent prime rib. It is open daily for dinner from May to September, and from Wednesday to Saturday during the rest of the year. Reservations are advised.

HOMER Wasabis
52917 East End Rd, Homer, AK 99603 **Tel** *226-3663*

Located 5 miles (8 km) out of Homer, with big windows facing Kachemak Bay, this Alaska-Asian fusion restaurant is known for its sushi, grilled tuna, ribs, and other fare. The wraparound bar serves infused vodkas, and downstairs is a popular nightclub. Wasabis is open year-round for dinner, but closed Sunday through Tuesday in winter.

HOPE Seaview Café and Bar
PO Box 110, Hope, AK 99605 **Tel** *782-3300*

Operating in this historic little town since 1896, the Seaview Café displays lots of Gold Rush paraphernalia. The café serves simple home-made fare against the stunning backdrop of the Kenai Mountains and Turnagain Arm. It is open daily from noon to midnight between May and September.

MOOSE PASS Summit Lake Lodge
Mile 45.5 Seward Hwy, Moose Pass, AK 99631 **Tel** *244-2031*

Once a rustic roadhouse beside beautiful Summit Lake, the upgraded Summit Lake Lodge is a standard travelers' stop on the Seward Highway between Anchorage and Seward. The food includes excellent halibut, steak, and prime rib. The lodge is open seasonally for three meals a day.

NIKOLAEVSK Samovar Café
PO Box 5050, Nikolaevsk, AK 99556 **Tel** *235-6867*

At this unique eating place in Alaska's Russian Old Believer community, the engaging owner serves Russian treats such as borscht, *pelmeni* (meat dumplings), *pirozhki* (little pies or dumplings), cream puffs, and *chai*. After their meal, guests can dress in traditional Russian costumes for souvenir photographs.

SELDOVIA The Mad Fish
221 Main St, Seldovia, AK 99663 **Tel** *234-7676*

Dating from 1976, this tranquil restaurant overlooking Seldovia Bay has become a town landmark. In addition to a choice of king salmon and Kachemak Bay halibut dishes, it serves home-made bread and desserts. A selection of fine wines and Alaskan microbrews are also on offer. Open summer only.

SEWARD Christo's Palace
133 4th Ave, Seward, AK 99664 **Tel** *224-5255*

This spacious and elegant restaurant introduces a hint of the Mediterranean to the usual New York steaks and Alaskan seafood. True to Seward style, it also does a good range of salads, burgers, Mexican specialties, and pizzas. Christo's Place is open all week for lunch and dinner.

Key to Price Guide *see p256* **Key to Symbols** *see back cover flap*

SEWARD Ray's Waterfront   🔤🔤🔤🔤 $$$
Small Boat Harbor, Seward, AK 99664 **Tel** *224-5632*

With wide views across Seward's scenic small boat harbor, this seasonal restaurant is a good place to savor delicious local fish. House specials include cedar-planked salmon and nut-encrusted halibut. In the summer, it becomes busy and can get noisy with tourist traffic. Open for lunch and dinner from mid-April to September.

SOLDOTNA Mykel's   🔤🔤🔤🔤 $$$
35051 Kenai Spur Hwy, Soldotna, AK 99669 **Tel** *262-4305*

This fine restaurant specializes in Alaskan seafood. It serves delightful walnut-crusted salmon with raspberry butter and wild mushrooms in brandy cream sauce, as well as steak, scallops, chicken, and pasta dishes. The restaurant is open daily for lunch and dinner.

PRINCE WILLIAM SOUND

CORDOVA Reluctant Fisherman   🔤🔤🔤 $$
407 Railroad Ave, Cordova, AK 99574 **Tel** *424-7445*

Located in the eponymous inn *(see p244)* overlooking the small boat harbor, the Reluctant Fisherman is where the residents go to celebrate special occasions. Specialties include the seafood sandwich, halibut and chips, and locally caught salmon. Lunch and dinner served daily.

VALDEZ Magpies   🔤🔤🔤 $
224 Galena Street, Valdez, AK 99686 **Tel** *461-3092*

Very popular with locals, Magpies has espressos, cinnamon rolls, bear claws (Americanized Danish pastry), scones, daily breads, pies, and a variety of light breakfast treats. Lunches include sandwiches, soups, and quiche. The building was one of the few to survive the 1964 earthquake. Closed Sunday and Monday, plus Saturdays in winter.

WHITTIER Varly's Swiftwater Seafood   🔤🔤🔤 $$
The Triangle, Whittier, AK 99693 **Tel** *472-2550*

A wonderful little place with a cheerful atmosphere, this restaurant serves excellent shrimp, halibut, and rockfish straight from the icy waters of Prince William Sound. The fresh halibut and chips are truly special. They also do clam chowder and stock a range of Alaskan beers. Open for lunch and dinner in summer.

SOUTHEAST ALASKA

CRAIG Ruth Ann's   🔤🔤🔤 $$$
Main & Water St, Craig, AK 99921 **Tel** *826-3377*

Located in Ruth Ann's Hotel *(see p245)*, this small but superb restaurant offers seafood specialties, including crab, salmon, halibut, scallops, shrimp, and bacon-topped oysters on the half shell. The back room overlooks the harbor, with splendid views to distant green islands.

HAINES Mountain Market and Café   🔤🔤 $
151 3rd Ave, Haines, AK 99827 **Tel** *766-3340*

An excellent option for a healthy breakfast or light lunch, the Mountain Market and Café offers up a dozen excellent wraps, as well as croissants, deli sandwiches, home-made soups, and a variety of seasonal specialties. Behind the café is a complete health food shop.

HAINES Bamboo Room   🔤 $$
2nd Ave & Dalton St, Haines, AK 99827 **Tel** *766-2800*

Taking its name not from an Oriental reference but from the bamboo curtain that once separated the restaurant from its sports bar, this no-frills local favorite serves filling breakfasts, as well as steaks, seafood, pasta, salads, fish and chips.

HAINES Chilkat Restaurant and Bakery   🔤🔤 $$
5th Ave & Dalton St, Haines, AK 99827 **Tel** *766-3653*

This friendly, good-value restaurant and bakery prides itself on its fresh bread and locally grown produce. For breakfast, they serve up their own bread and pastries, while lunch options include burgers, sandwiches, soups, and salads. Open Monday to Saturday from 7am to 3pm and until 8pm Friday and Saturday. Closed Sunday.

HAINES Fireweed Restaurant   🔤🔤🔤 $$
Bldg 37, Blacksmith Rd, Haines, AK 99827 **Tel** *766-3838*

The tastefully stark decor in this historic old building perfectly mirrors the simple, healthy fare on offer, from home-made bagels, organic pesto, and marinara pizzas to delicious soups, salads, and halibut. The restaurant is open only during the summer months from Tuesday to Saturday.

JUNEAU Red Dog Saloon
278 Franklin St, Juneau, AK 99801 **Tel** 463-3658

With its sawdust floor and flag-draped ceiling, the historic Red Dog Saloon (see p143) is a tourist standard in town. The menu lists bar snacks, soups, sandwiches, and wraps, which make for an appetizing lunch. The saloon can get extremely crowded, especially when cruise ships are in port.

JUNEAU Chan's Thai Kitchen
11820 Glacier Highway, Juneau, AK 99801 **Tel** 789-9777

North of town and across from the Auke Bay Boat Harbor, this is Juneau's favorite Asian restaurant. The unpretentious setting attracts locals who come for dependably great Thai lunches and dinners. Chan's closes at 8:30pm so come early (especially on weekends) and expect to wait. No reservations.

JUNEAU El Sombrero
157 S Franklin St, Juneau, AK 99801 **Tel** 586-6770

Juneau's best Mexican-style restaurant, well located in downtown, is a short walk from the cruise ship docks. It attracts visitors, cruise passengers, politicians, and businesspeople with its tasty options, which include fajitas and a range of inexpensive combination platters.

JUNEAU Thane Ore House
4400 Thane Rd, Juneau, AK 99801 **Tel** 586-3442

This popular buffet-style salmon and halibut bake, housed in a historic building with rough-hewn doors and tables, lies on the shore about 5 miles (7 km) south of Juneau. The fresh and well-prepared halibut and chips are highly recommended. The eatery is open only between May and September.

JUNEAU The Hangar
2 Marine Way, Juneau, AK 99801 **Tel** 586-5018

This boisterous downtown bar and restaurant is housed within the historic Merchant's Wharf building. Dining options include halibut fish and chips, salads, fresh seafood, ribs, and even jambalaya. Order a Juneau-made Alaskan Amber or one of more than 20 other brews on tap.

JUNEAU Twisted Fish
2 Marine Way, #106, Juneau, AK 99801 **Tel** 463-5033

Conveniently located near the tramway and cruise ship docks, this upbeat place is popular with summer visitors. The specialty is wild salmon, but it also serves halibut, crab, and pizzas, as well as fish, buffalo, and chicken burgers. Open daily for lunch and dinner from May to September.

KETCHIKAN Bar Harbor
2813 Tongass Ave, Ketchikan, AK 99901 **Tel** 225-2813

This very popular spot is ideal on a rare sunny day when diners can sit on the deck overlooking Tongass Narrows and munch salads, wraps, sandwiches, burgers, and wonderful halibut tacos. The dinner menu has delicious fettuccine, steaks, ribs, seafood, and chicken. Open for lunch daily, and dinner Sunday to Thursday.

KETCHIKAN Ocean View
3159 Tongass Ave, Ketchikan, AK 99901 **Tel** 225-7566

With a clean, tiled Mediterranean decor, a view that takes in Tongass Narrows and Gravina Island, and a range of cuisines on the menu, this restaurant offers good value for money. It serves up mainly Mexican fare, but also does Greek and Italian food, including a range of pizzas.

KETCHIKAN Annabelle's Keg and Chowder House
326 Front St, Ketchikan, AK 99901 **Tel** 225-6009

Located in the Gilmore Hotel (see p246), Annabelle's features "New York style dining circa 1927," and has a pub and an elegant parlor. It offers an extensive menu, ranging from local seafood and pasta to salads, sandwiches, and desserts. It is open for breakfast, lunch, and dinner daily year round.

KETCHIKAN Heen Kahidi Restaurant
800 Venetia Way, Ketchikan, AK 99901 **Tel** 225-8001, (866) 225-8001

Located in the Cape Fox Lodge (see p246) which is nestled amid cedar and spruce trees on a hill overlooking the town, the Heen Kahidi – Tlingit for Creek House – is the ultimate in Ketchikan dining. Its dinner specialties include salmon, halibut, steak, and teriyaki chicken, but it also features sweet treats like Belgian waffles and cheese blintzes.

KETCHIKAN The Landing
3434 Tongass Ave, Ketchikan, AK 99501 **Tel** 225-5166

With an all-day breakfast, acclaimed steaks, and Alaskan seafood, this eatery in the Landing Hotel is a popular local venue. Jeremiah's, the bullfrog-themed bar upstairs, features Italian fare and has splendid views over Tongass Narrows and the Marine Highway docks.

KETCHIKAN Steamers at the Dock
76 Front St, Ketchikan, AK 99901 **Tel** 225-1600

On the cruise ship dock with a lovely water view, this seafood restaurant has a long wooden bar and a raucous atmosphere. The restaurant gets its name from their signature dish – steamer clams in butter sauce. They also dish up excellent regional oysters. Open summer only.

Key to Price Guide see p256 **Key to Symbols** see back cover flap

PETERSBURG Rooney's Northern Lights

⟨⟩⟨⟩ ⑤⑤

203 Sing Lee Alley, Petersburg, AK 99833 **Tel** *772-2900*

In this restaurant, which sits on pilings overlooking the harbor, diners can choose from a large number of breakfast options, as well as from the range of fresh Alaskan seafood – grilled halibut, shrimp, and seafood combos – and Mexican specialties, including a wonderful cilantro and lime fajita wrap.

SITKA Larkspur Café

⟨⟩⟨⟩ ⑤

2 Lincoln St, Sitka, AK 99835 **Tel** *966-2326*

A favorite Sitka hangout, this little café serves homemade soups, chowders, and paninis for lunch, along with morning espressos and local seafood dinners. It's located on the floor below the public Raven Radio station, with live music some evenings. Closed Mondays and Tuesdays.

SITKA Ludvig's Bistro

⟨⟩⟨⟩ ⑤⑤⑤

256 Katlian St, Sitka, AK 99835 **Tel** *966-3663*

Named for the owner's dog, this cozy bistro is well-regarded for its superb Spanish tapas, served in the afternoon. The dinner menu includes Spanish and Cuban specialties, seafood, unique home-baked breads, and gourmet desserts. Reservations are recommended. Open summer only.

SKAGWAY Red Onion Saloon

⟨⟩⟨⟩ ⑤

2nd & Broadway, Skagway, AK 99840 **Tel** *983-2222*

Once Skagway's exclusive bordello, this historic site is a lively drinking establishment serving bar meals. In addition to snacks, they do excellent salads, a range of fresh sandwiches, and creative pizzas. There is great locally brewed beer on tap and live entertainment on weekends. Open summer only.

SKAGWAY Sweet Tooth Café

⟨⟩⟨⟩ ⑤

3rd & Broadway, Skagway, AK 99840 **Tel** *983-2405*

Mainly a breakfast venue, complete with coffee, American breakfasts, and home-made pastries, this pleasant local favorite in a historic Skagway building also does hearty lunches, including home-made soups and Mexican specials. Open until 3pm daily.

SKAGWAY Stowaway Café

⟨⟩⟨⟩ ⑤⑤

205 Congress Way, Skagway, AK 99840 **Tel** *983-3643*

A funky little place with clapboard siding, a great harbor view, and just a few indoor tables, this is a Skagway favorite. The menu consists of excellent fish, steak, pasta, and Cajun-style seafood dishes. Open for lunch and dinner in summer only.

WESTERN INTERIOR ALASKA

CHATANIKA Chatanika Lodge

⟨⟩ ⑤⑤

5760 Steese Hwy, Chatanika, AK 99712 **Tel** *389-2164*

This roadhouse is known mainly for its disparate collection of items including an outhouse used for annual outhouse races. Travelers on the Steese Highway stop at the attached lodge, which dates from 1925. Meals range from huge traditional Alaskan breakfasts to equally generous lunches and dinners. Bar smoke can be a problem.

DENALI VILLAGE Overlook Bar and Grill

⟨⟩⟨⟩ ⑤⑤

Crows Nest Rd, Mile 238.5 Parks Hwy, Denali Village, AK 99755 **Tel** *683-2723*

Meals in the acclaimed bar and grill of the Denali Crow's Nest *(see p247)* are enhanced by spectacular panoramic views over the village. In addition to the excellent salmon, halibut, and steak, they serve pasta, fresh bread, and imaginative salads, sandwiches, and burgers. Open in the summer only.

DENALI VILLAGE Denali Salmon Bake

⟨⟩⟨⟩ ⑤⑤⑤

Mile 238.5 Parks Hwy, Denali Village, AK 99755 **Tel** *683-2733*

This spacious no-frills restaurant is a favorite for coconut salmon, Thai fresh rolls, burgers, steaks, chicken, halibut and chips, and halibut tacos. They also do a full breakfast and all-you-can-eat pancakes or French toast. Open in the summer only, with live music or DJs nightly.

DENALI VILLAGE The Perch

⟨⟩⟨⟩ ⑤⑤⑤

Mile 224 Parks Hwy, Denali Village, AK 99755 **Tel** *683-2523, (888) 322-2523*

A superb restaurant with a view to match, the Perch provides a welcome break in this remote location on a hilltop overlooking Carlo Creek. Visitors can dine on fresh Alaskan seafood, Angus beef, vegetarian dishes, or even caribou medallions with portobello mushrooms, all accompanied by home-baked bread.

DENALI VILLAGE 229 Parks

⟨⟩⟨⟩ ⑤⑤⑤⑤

Mile 229 Parks Hwy, Denali Village, AK 99755 **Tel** *683-2567*

The finest restaurant in the Denali National Park area, this hidden gem is named for its milepost location along the Parks Highway. The menu changes often, with an emphasis on local and organic produce, along with Alaskan seafood. Service is slow, but worth the wait. Open for dinner and brunch; closed Mondays.

FAIRBANKS Lavelle's Bistro

575 1st Ave, Fairbanks, AK 99701 **Tel** *450-0555*

Housed within the Marriott Spring Hill Suites Hotel in the heart of town, this is Fairbank's finest restaurant, with a diverse choice of cuisine, from potato-crusted salmon to an amazing meatloaf. The restaurant features Wednesday wine tasting paired with a light menu. Open for dinner year round, plus lunch in the summer.

FAIRBANKS Thai House Restaurant

412 5th Ave, Fairbanks, AK 99701 **Tel** *452-6123*

Fairbanks is home to several Thai restaurants, but this family-run spot, two blocks from the Chena River, is one of the best. Delicious spicy meals are served in ample portions and the Pad-ped sam-sahai (prawns, squid, and fish in a hot chili sauce) is a house specialty. You can ask for a mild version if necessary. Open all year round; closed Sundays.

FAIRBANKS Two Rivers Lodge

Mile 16, Chena Hot Springs Road, Fairbanks, AK 99701 **Tel** *488-6815*

Located 16 miles (16 km) out of Fairbanks, this homey spot is a favorite nightspot for locals. The menu includes pasta, chicken, seafood, and all-you-can-eat Dungeness crab. The restaurant sits along a small lake, with a solarium and an adjacent lounge that serves a lighter menu. The big deck is popular on long summer afternoons.

FAIRBANKS Alaska Salmon Bake

Peger Rd & Airport Way, Fairbanks, AK 99707 **Tel** *452-7274, (800) 354-7274*

This popular venue in Pioneer Park attracts tour participants craving such Alaskan treats as salmon, halibut, cod, and prime rib. Dinner also includes a salad bar and other trimmings. After a meal, diners can opt to watch the musical comedy, *The Golden Heart Revue*. Open for dinner only between late May and early September.

FAIRBANKS The Pump House

Mile 1.3 Chena Pump Rd, Fairbanks, AK 99708 **Tel** *479-8452*

On perpetually daylit summer evenings, this sprawling place, which hugs the banks of the Chena River, is probably the busiest place in town. Diners can enjoy well-prepared Alaskan seafood, steaks, chicken, and even musk ox or caribou meat. Bookings are recommended.

FAIRBANKS The Turtle Club

Mile 10 Old Steese Hwy, Fox, AK 99707 **Tel** *457-3883*

Some of the finest dining in the Fairbanks area is found at the Turtle Club, located 10 miles (16 km) from town in Fox village. The delicious appetizers include shrimp cocktail or escargots in butter and wine. Their specialty is prime rib, but they also do seafood, including halibut, prawns, crab, and lobsters, augmented with a generous salad bar.

MANLEY HOT SPRINGS Manley Roadhouse

Manley Hot Springs, AK 99756 **Tel** *672-3161*

This classic 1903 roadhouse, attached to the lodge (*see p248*), is the only dining option in town. It serves hearty, filling fare, including chicken or steak with potatoes and well-made burgers and fries. It serves as a gathering place for local trappers, mushers, and itinerants, who drop by for local news and gossip. Open summer only.

NENANA Skinny Dick's Halfway Inn

Mile 328 Parks Hwy, Ester, AK 99725 **Tel** *388-5770*

The name alone is reason to check out this famously quirky place midway between Fairbanks and Nenana – hence the "halfway" in the name – which really is run by Skinny Dick. The focus is the bar, but its lunches are locally popular with travelers along the Parks Highway.

TALKEETNA Café Michele

Mile 13.75 Talkeetna Spur Rd, Talkeetna, AK 99676 **Tel** *733-5300*

This acclaimed café with a tropical twist offers creative organic salads, halibut, salmon, steak, venison, pasta, curry, and Asian rice dishes. For a treat, try the Cornish game hens, Madras coconut curry, or the Serious Caesar Salad. Open for lunch and dinner in the summer only.

EASTERN INTERIOR ALASKA

CHITINA Hotel Chitina

Corner of Fairbank and Main Streets, Chitina, AK 99686 **Tel** *823-2244*

Housed within one of Chitina's many historic buildings, this fine restaurant is open daily from morning to late evening throughout summer. The atmosphere is cozy and relaxed, with big windows and a lively mix of locals and tourists. The evening menu always includes Alaskan seafood, steaks, and Cajun chicken.

COPPER CENTER Copper Center Lodge

Copper Center Loop Road, Copper Center, AK 99573 **Tel** *822-3245, (866) 330-3245*

Housed in the historic Copper Center Lodge (*see p249*), whose current building dates back to the 1930s, this is the town's premier eatery. Breakfasts include pancakes made from century-old sourdough starter (*see p254*), while lunches and dinners feature steak, seafood, chicken, and pasta.

Key to Price Guide *see p256* **Key to Symbols** *see back cover flap*

DELTA JUNCTION Buffalo Center Drive In ♿ ♨ $$

1680 Richardson Hwy, Delta Junction, AK 99737 **Tel** 895-5089

It may look unassuming, but this relaxed little place, named after the original moniker of Delta Junction, is the town's favorite family eatery. It features beef, chicken, salmon, halibut, and crab, and is one of the only places in Alaska to serve buffalo burgers and steaks from a local herd. Open daily for breakfast, lunch, and dinner.

KENNICOTT Kennicott Glacier Lodge Restaurant 🏠 ♨ $$$

Lot 15 Millsite Subdivision, Kennicott, AK 99588 **Tel** 258-2350, (800) 582-5128

Housed in a lodge *(see p250)* in one of the most spectacular settings possible, overlooking Kennicott Glacier with views to Mount Blackburn, this self-proclaimed "wilderness gourmet" restaurant offers buffet breakfasts and à la carte lunches, while set *table d'hôte* dinners are served at 7pm nightly in the summer only.

MCCARTHY The Potato 📋 🏠 $

Shushanna Ave, McCarthy, AK 99588 **Tel** 554-1100

This small funky place, housed in a stationary trailer surrounded by a permanent wooden frame, is a great place for a quick lunch of burritos, burgers, hot dogs, grilled chicken, or a variety of potato dishes, such as spudniks doused in sausage gravy. Open from 10am to 7pm in the summer only.

MCCARTHY McCarthy Lodge Bistro/Golden Saloon ♿ 🎵 🏠 🍸 ♨ $$$

Kennicott Ave, PO Box MXY, McCarthy, AK 99588 **Tel** 554-4402

McCarthy's finest dining is found at the historic McCarthy Lodge *(see p250)* and Golden Saloon. In addition to breakfasts and an array of sandwiches, burgers, wraps, and salads, they do creative appetizers and bar snacks as well as pasta dishes, halibut, and steak. Open for breakfast, lunch, and dinner in the summer.

TOK Fast Eddy's ♿ ♨ $$

Mile 1313 Alaska Hwy, Tok, AK 99780 **Tel** 883-4411

Fast Eddy's comes as a pleasant surprise to Alaska Highway travelers when they arrive in tiny Tok. It's a standard stopping-off point for both Alaskans and visitors. With a large salad bar and extensive breakfast, lunch, and dinner menus, it offers good value for money. Open all year round.

SOUTHWEST ALASKA

KING SALMON Eddie's Fireplace Inn ♿ 🍸 $$

1 Main St, King Salmon, AK 99613 **Tel** 246-3435

Diagonally opposite the airport terminal, this cozy restaurant and sports bar is a favorite local gathering place. Belying the casual atmosphere, the menu features decent local fish as well as hearty chicken, beef, and burger dishes. Open all year round.

KODIAK The Old Power House Restaurant ♿ 🏠 ♨ $$

516 E Marine Way, Kodiak, AK 99615 **Tel** 481-1088

Under the bridge on the waterfront, this place offers the best dining in Kodiak. With a sushi bar and various other Japanese choices, they also do fish, pork, beef, chicken, pasta, and vegetarian dishes with an Oriental twist. It is open from Tuesday to Saturday for lunch and dinner. No lunch service on Sunday.

ARCTIC AND WESTERN ALASKA

BARROW East Coast Pizza ♨ $$

507 Kingosak St, Barrow, AK 99723 **Tel** 852-2100

Open until midnight on weekends, this little takeout-only place serves surprisingly good pizzas, sub sandwiches, *gyros* (pita bread wrap with meat, tomatoes, onions, and cucumber yogurt), and burgers, which are great for a quick bite or midnight snack. There is no seating, but local taxi companies will deliver.

BARROW Pepe's North of the Border 🍸 ♨ $$

PO Box 403, Barrow, AK 99723 **Tel** 852-8200

Run by Barrow's most well-known resident, the indefatigable Fran Tate, this renowned Mexican restaurant next to the Top of the World Hotel *(see p251)* is a must-visit in Barrow. Here, visitors can warm to a tropical decor and fiery cuisine while the ice beats at the Arctic Ocean shore just outside the door.

COLDFOOT Truker's Café 🎵 🏠 🍸 $$

Coldfoot, Mile 175, Dalton Highway, AK 99701 **Tel** 678-3500

Part of the Coldfoot Camp complex *(see p251)* on the Dalton Highway, this saloon and truck stop is the only eatery for hundreds of miles in any direction but it offers surprisingly good value. In addition to a trucker's breakfast, they have a bar and offer burgers, fish and chips, sandwiches, and buffet breakfasts and dinners in the summer.

CRUISING IN ALASKA

Logo, Princess Cruise Line

Wildlife sightings on land and sea, tide-water glaciers and snowcapped peaks, and the cultural heritage of Alaska's indigenous peoples provide the big draw for cruising the Inside Passage *(see pp34–5)* and the Gulf of Alaska *(see pp36–7)*. For many travelers, an Alaskan cruise is a once-in-a-lifetime experience, providing a luxurious way to see some of the wildest places on earth. Rates vary greatly depending upon the cruise line, the season and national economic conditions. Cruise lines like to appeal to as wide a market as possible, offering numerous itineraries on various classes of ship, resort-style amenities, and a range of shore excursions. Travelers need to be prepared for Alaska's unpredictable weather. While the parkas may end up packed away the entire time, so may the swimsuit and sandals.

BEST TIMES TO GO

While weekly cruises to tropical islands operate all year round, the Alaska cruise season lasts less than five months, typically from mid-May to mid-September. Sun worshipers can aim for cruises that depart at the end of June and through July. With a decrease in the likelihood of storms, this is considered peak season, and cruise lines charge accordingly. Also, as the summer solstice nears, the northern latitudes make for exceptionally long days. This translates into late evenings and technicolor sunsets almost at midnight.

If price matters more than the weather, it is best to hunt for deals in the September and May shoulder seasons *(see p278)*. Generally, the later in the season that travelers depart, the greater the likelihood of damp weather. However, passengers need to be prepared at all times for Alaska's erratic weather.

CHOOSING A CRUISE LINE AND SHIP

The budget may be the most important factor in influencing the choice of a cruise. Also, it is essential to decide which is more important – the ship or the itinerary. For some, cruising is all about low fares, fresh air, and the destination itself. For others, imaginative itineraries and creature comforts matter more.

Cruise lines rate themselves according to a star system that is, however, fast losing definition. Six-star lines offer smaller, more intimate ships, the best cuisine, superior accommodation, and services to match. Naturally, such luxury comes at a price, but travelers may be able to find fares that include round trip air travel, onboard expenses, and excursions. Mass market ships advertise the lowest rates. No line with less than four or five stars will mention their rating, while others may exaggerate their status. Be sure to research the ship's age and when it began to sail under its current name. Lastly, do not judge a ship by the cruise line. Even mass market cruise lines offer new ships with design features and amenities that approach luxury.

CHOOSING AN ITINERARY

Consult cruise route maps *(see pp34–7)* to get your bearings. The Inside Passage has the largest concentration of accessible towns, glaciers, fjords, and forests. Popular stops include Glacier Bay, Haines, Bloonah, Juneau, Skagway, Sitka, Ketchikan, and Misty Fiords. The Gulf of Alaska has fewer ports of call, but benefits include the glaciers, deep fjords, and marine life of Hubbard Glacier and Prince William Sound.

Week-long round trip cruises between Juneau and Seattle, San Francisco, and Vancouver in Canada take in the Inside

Multi-level cruise ship moored in Juneau's Gastineau Channel

Cruise ship with a large decktop swimming pool

Passage and are especially popular. As the route heads north from Canada or the US to Juneau, Seward or Whittier, signs of modern civilization recede gradually with each passing day. Another popular itinerary goes across the Gulf of Alaska between Seward or Whittier and Juneau, and includes points of interest both in the Gulf and in the Inside Passage as far south as Misty Fiords National Monument.

PLANNING AND RESEARCH

To ensure a great vacation, it would be wise to devote some time to planning and research. The Internet offers extensive information on cruise lines and is a fast and efficient way to compare the best deals. **Alaska Cruising Report**, **Cruise Critic**, **Vancouver-Alaska Cruise Watch**, **Cruise Reviews**, **Cruise Mates**, and **Cruise-Chat** have websites with comprehensive, insightful reviews and information on how to book a cruise. For proprietary cruise information, browse through the websites of cruise companies. Travel bookstores are an invaluable resource, as are travel-related websites such as **Expedia Travel**. For

the latest deals, consult the travel sections of leading newspapers in early spring.

MAJOR CRUISE LINES

Most major cruise lines have in their fleet at least two or more ships that are large enough to carry hundreds or even thousands of passengers. Common facilities on board include restaurants and buffets, health spas and salons, theaters, themed lounges, bars, dance clubs, swimming pools and hot tubs, and children's clubs.

Large and midsized cruise ships are offered by **Regent Seven Seas Cruises**, **Celebrity Cruises**, **Holland America Line**, **Princess Cruise Line**, **Royal Caribbean Line**, **Norwegian Cruise Line**, **Disney Cruise Line**, **Silversea Cruises,** and **Carnival Cruise Lines**. Silversea offers vessels that are among the best in Alaskan waters, while Holland America and Princess Cruises, among others, have tied up with Alaska Railroad to offer train tours (*see pp292–5*).

SMALL SHIPS

The only way to sail into secluded villages and hidden coves that large ships cannot approach is to book a

cruise with luxury yacht operators or adventure outfitters, who may occasionally deviate from their fixed itinerary to cater to well-heeled travelers. One such operator, **American Safari Cruises**, pulls into Elfin Cove, a small village on Chichagof Island, and allows passengers to step ashore and experience the local culture. **CruiseWest**, **Discovery Voyages**, and **Lindblad Expeditions** are other excellent choices for visitors looking for small ship or expedition cruising.

WHAT'S INCLUDED

Fares on all mass market cruise ships include meals, snacks, shows, and complimentary drinks at a "Captain's Meet and Greet" cocktail party. Passengers have some control over the amount of gratuities, but more and more lines include a nominal fee for wait staff and room stewards on the final bill. Luxury ships may offer complimentary alcoholic beverages or wine during meals, while other upscale lines stock cabins with bottles of liquor. Economy ships charge for everything at every turn. All purchases made on board are added to the final bill.

SPECIAL DEALS

Promotional fares are easily available in the weeks just before the peak season. The first and last weeks of the season have the cheapest fares. All major lines also offer air add-ons and hotel stays, and in Alaska, that can mean extended rail tours to Denali and other points of interest in the Interior.

Look out for special deals on the websites of cruise lines and travel agencies. Travel clubs, academic societies and other membership associations organize charters to take advantage of group rates. Large cruise lines sponsor themed cruises and these might occasionally offer a good bargain.

TRAVELING SOLO

Fares are always based on double occupancy unless stated otherwise. However, a single traveler can find deals that waive or reduce what is called the single supplement – an additional fee added on to single fares that can sometimes equal another full fare. When such deals are not available travel agents can help book cabins to be shared by single travelers of the same gender. Most large cruise lines also arrange onboard events and parties meant for singles.

CABIN TYPES

Experienced cruisers have two opposing views on how to choose cabins. One opinion holds that as most passengers merely sleep, bathe, and dress in their cabins, it makes little sense to reserve a deluxe stateroom with all possible amenities. However, under certain conditions, comfortable cabins can make all the difference. Travelers should consider booking either an inexpensive inside cabin or an outside one with portholes (or windows that increase in size with every category upgrade). Cabins with balconies are ideal for romantic and restful settings and usually sell first, despite being considerably more expensive. However, many cruisers argue that the same views are available for free from the public decks.

Deluxe cabins may include mini-suites with sitting areas or apartment-style penthouses with separate rooms that can sleep four. Some modern ships have taken this category to new heights, creating opulent spaces for six people, complete with conference facilities, butlers, private hot tubs, and large secluded patios on the ship's top deck.

CABIN FACILITIES

While all standard cabins include a bathroom, beds for two, sufficient storage, a room safe, television, cabin phone, toiletries, and most importantly, lifejackets, all facilities improve with higher fares.

Atrium bar offering a chic sitting area on a cruise ship

Amenities can include a refrigerator, wider and thicker mattresses, softer pillows, and plush comforters. Bathrooms in high priced cabins offer superior quality toiletries.

LOCATION WITHIN THE SHIP

The websites of all cruise lines provide the deck plans of each ship and a layout showing cabin locations. Cabins can be situated aft, forward, or amidships. Depending on the quality of the ship, lower aft cabins can be subject to muted engine noise, vibrations, and heat. In rough seas, lower forward cabins experience the maximum vibrations from wave impact. Even so, if wind and wave height create heavy sway, those subject to seasickness would do well to book a lower cabin amidships, as motion intensifies the higher one goes. However, for some, watching waves splash against their portholes can cause anxiety – such travelers may prefer an upper cabin. It is wise to select a cabin near an elevator if the ship has over a dozen decks. With an upper outside cabin, check that a lifeboat does not obstruct the view.

Restaurants and bars can be located anywhere on the ship, while buffets are generally higher up near the pools.

PUBLIC AREAS

Framed art and sculpture line the stairways and hallways of virtually every ship. While the art can range from sedate to postmodern and whimsical, travelers will almost always find some vestiges of the classic Art Deco era – the glory era of cruise ships – whether in the details of the handrail design or in themed restaurants. Towering atriums are *de rigueur*, and passengers with vertigo should steer

Ship library providing a quiet retreat

clear of the overlooks. Most include comfortable bars and lounges on the periphery, or generic sitting areas with splendid views out to sea.

Large ships stage Vegas and Broadway themed shows in plush theaters, full of glitz and glamor. More sophisti cated ship theaters come complete with multiple stage lifts, large orchestras, and a huge revue staff of singers and dancers. Other cruise lines, while well funded, choose to economize by investing little or nothing in stage musicians, using pre recorded soundtracks instead.

Quiet libraries and card rooms are common, especially in cruise lines popular with the retired set. Most lines have Internet facilities, and some offer Wi-Fi to those with their own laptop computers.

SPA, FITNESS, AND BEAUTY SALONS

Every large or midsized ship boasts a spa and salon with trained staff who pamper passengers with spa treatments and massages. Onboard spas reduce their rates when the ship is in port and as the

The luxurious lobby of an onboard spa and salon

cruise proceeds, but only for more expensive packages.

To maintain your at-home fitness regimen, exercise rooms of large ships have a range of equipment, including climbers and treadmills. They almost always offer hot tubs, some provide saunas, and a few offer steam baths. Fitness centers often remain open round the clock, while salons keep long hours. Fitness programs can include yoga, Pilates, and personal training.

On formal nights, salons generally offer passengers total makeovers, as well as hair styling and facials.

MEDICAL FACILITIES

All cruise ships have a licensed medical professional on board to deal with illness, emergencies, and patient evacuations. If travelers have special needs or require specific medical equipment, it is best to check before making reservations. While no cruise ship pretends to be a floating hospital, some do advertise such equipment as dialysis machines. Costs can vary from ship to ship, but in general the fee for visits and medication is significantly higher than on land.

DIRECTORY

PLANNING AND RESEARCH

Alaska Cruising Report
www. alaskacruising
report.com

Cruise-Chat
www.cruise-chat.com

Cruise Critic
www.cruisecritic.com

Cruise Mates
www.cruisemates.com

Cruise Reviews
www.cruisereviews.com

Expedia Travel
www.expedia.com

Vancouver-Alaska Cruise Watch
www3.telus.net/cruise_
watch

MAJOR CRUISE LINES

Carnival Cruise Lines
Tel (888) 227-6482.
www.carnival.com

Celebrity Cruises
Tel (800) 647-2251.
www.celebrity.com

Disney Cruise Line
Tel (888) 352-2500.
www.disneycruise.com

Holland America Line
Tel (877) 724-5425.
www.hollandamerica.
com

Norwegian Cruise Line
Tel (800) 327-7030.
www.ncl.com

Princess Cruise Line
Tel (800) 774-6237.
www.princess.com

Regent Seven Seas Cruises
Tel (800) 505-5370.
www.rssc.com

Royal Caribbean Line
Tel (866) 562-7625.
www.royalcaribbean.
com

Silversea Cruises
Tel (877) 215-9986.
www.silversea.com

SMALL SHIPS

American Safari Cruises
Tel (888) 862-8881.
www.amsafari.com

CruiseWest
Tel (888) 851-8133.
www.cruisewest.com

Discovery Voyages
Tel (907) 472-2558,
(800) 324-7602. www.
discoveryvoyages.com

Lindblad Expeditions
Tel (800) 397-3348.
www.lindblad.com

Life On Board

The day-to-day goings on of a cruise to Alaska mirror life on board any other cruise, but with a few major exceptions – there is unlikely to be a white sand beach for tanning, and there may be more hiking boots than sandals on deck. Likewise, ship staff never try to re-create tropical themes, leaving the grandeur of Alaska to speak for itself with every passing seascape, fjord, and glacier-topped peak. However, it is still a cruise, and passengers can expect levity, dancing, late-night parties, theater productions, and casino action as on a cruise anywhere in the world.

Enjoying sunshine and a wide-ranging view from the deck

ENTERTAINMENT AND ACTIVITIES

Ship theaters on the larger lines boast professionally lit stages with state-of-the-art audio, and draw full-house crowds for events on each night of the cruise. Talent and musicianship vary among cruise lines, and the Vegas- and Broadway-style productions alternate with stand-up comics. Some of the latter have content older than the ocean, while others present risqué humor. Bigger ships often maintain a separate venue for game shows hosted by cruise directors who urge audiences to participate.

A good ship will also have country singers, jazz crooners, string trios and quartets, and classical pianists to entertain lounge patrons, atrium visitors, and strollers on the ship's interior promenades.

Art shows represent an outlet for buyers interested in originals or numbered prints signed by the artist.

Onboard art auctions usually manage to bring in a large crowd of cruisers.

Given the variable climate, Alaskan lines make none of the promises that tropical operators do. Ships shy away from planning too many outdoor activities that could suffer cancellations due to bad weather. However, deck parties do take place, along with midnight fiestas, usually with a Mexican theme.

Glitzy stage show providing live onboard entertainment

CASINOS

After shopping and sunning on deck, spending time and money in the casino is one of the popular cruise pastimes, despite poor odds of winning.

Gambling options depend on the cruise line and the class of the ship and can range from craps, roulette, and simple slot machines to blackjack, poker, and baccarat. Most ship casinos also offer video poker machines. Ship casinos have a vested interest in educating their clients, so the house often offers classes on how to play some of the more esoteric games.

A shipboard casino is more or less like a land-based one, but with a few differences. It is open only while the ship is actually sailing in inter-national waters. Only passengers over 21 years of age are allowed to play, although anyone may pass through when it is closed to take pictures. It would be considered unusual, and possibly an infringement of casino rules, to photograph ongoing games or people gambling. While every ship has a bar that exclusively serves the casino, patrons are usually not offered free drinks, except at occasional promotional events, such as when the casino first opens.

SHOPPING

Those interested in buying luxury items such as tobacco, spirits, designer clothing and cosmetics, digital cameras, and jewelry will find them at excellent prices, all tax- and duty-free. Usually designed to resemble upscale shopping malls, onboard arcades can sprawl over two decks, or simply consist of a string of interconnected shops. All through the cruise, selected merchandise is also sold at slashed prices in hallways or outside on the upper deck, and liquor tastings are also common. Passengers should note that they cannot take possession of their alcohol purchases until their last night on board the ship.

Crew members preparing a buffet barbecue

MEALS

For many travelers, cruising is all about the cuisine. In addition to three heavy meals a day, served in the main dining rooms, hot and cold buffets, snack bars, cafés, and deckside grills cater to the huge demand.

Large ships manage the rush by establishing at least two main seatings for dinner and assigning tables for the duration of the cruise. Dinner typically begins at 6pm and 8:30pm. Passengers dissatisfied with their seating or table may consult the ship's *maître d'* after the first night to ask for a change, but there is no guarantee of one. Tables for two may not be easy to find, even if passengers make the request prior to booking. Many ships now have more flexible dining programs and a range of onboard restaurants that require no bookings.

The tradition of dining with the captain is mostly historical, and not a common practice. A good alternative is attending the captain's cocktail party to meet him and his senior officers.

EXPENSES

Costs mount rapidly during a cruise. Onboard purchases, beverages, and casino expenses reach unimaginable heights. The need for ready cash almost disappears on a ship, as passengers have the convenience of paying with a swipe of a key card. Many generous passengers do dole out bills as tips to room stewards and other crew members. Note that all cruise lines assert that tipping is optional while stating clearly their policy of adding a basic rate of gratuity for services rendered during the cruise. Passengers are free to accept, raise, or lower that amount at the Purser's Desk.

DRESS CODE

Check the ticket packet for details of the ship's dress code for the main dining room. Most disallow jeans, sleeveless T-shirts, shorts, or tennis shoes for dinner, but relax the rules for other meals and buffet restaurants. Dress rules and styles change all the time, but even aboard luxury ships the trend towards casual lifestyles has prevailed. Still, the classic cruise tradition of formal nights persists for at least one night of the week. Black tie dinners are solely in the province of six-star ships.

For formal nights, men can wear suits; tuxedos are in the minority on most ships. Women wear cocktail dresses or gowns. Semi-formal nights require sports coats and tie and slacks for men, and cocktail dresses for women. Resort casuals such as cotton dresses for women and khaki pants and button-up shirts for men apply on other nights. Except on the most sophisticated ships, restaurant staff rarely turn away inappropriately dressed passengers.

TRAVELING WITH CHILDREN

Virtually all ships have relaxed their restrictions in recent years and allow children of all ages. Most cruise ships come equipped with facilities exclusively for children. Activities range from crafts and treasure hunts for young kids, to teen discos, talent shows, and karaoke events for older children. Baby-sitting fees are incurred for child care when the formal programs end, usually after 10pm. Many programs do not accept children under two or three years of age unless accompanied by a parent. Famous for its family cruises, Disney Cruise Line now visits Alaska's Inside Passage.

WHAT TO PACK

On average, cruise lines provide four baggage tags per person. To carry anything beyond that, passengers must check with the cruise line. Essentials for an Alaskan cruise include:

Hiking boots for excursions

- Cell phone
- Portable music player
- Books and magazines
- Rain shell, hat, and warm sweater
- Comfortable walking or hiking boots
- Toiletries and cosmetics
- Medication and first aid, including sunscreen
- Passport, travel insurance, cruise documents
- Camera, memory card, and batteries
- Formal, semi-formal, and resort casual wear
- Shorts, swimwear, and sandals
- Laptop computer
- Spare luggage for purchased items

Shore Excursions

While not all the tourists who flock to Alaska each year travel via cruise ships, the ones who do often consider shore excursions to be the main event. Tours emphasize Alaska's geological wonders such as tidewater glaciers and vast temperate rainforests, while nature sightseeing focuses on wildlife. Historical tours, on the other hand, offer engaging presentations of human history from the earliest Native American settlements to the first Europeans. No cruise passenger has the time or opportunity to try each tour, but with careful planning, visitors can return home with a deeper understanding of what makes Alaska magical.

Small pleasure craft moored next to a giant cruise ship in Whittier

WHAT'S INCLUDED

Ticket packets, cruise line websites, and flyers placed at the shore excursion desk on board the ship give brief descriptions of each excursion along with the duration and degree of physical stamina required. Usually, all that passengers need are sun or rain protection, water if none is provided, and a willingness to share the experience with fellow passengers. It always helps to ask a few questions before signing up about the chances of cancellation, how large the group will be, and whether food or water will be provided during the excursion.

BOOKING

More and more cruise lines allow online bookings for the dozens of shore excursions offered during week-long cruises. Online booking saves passengers the trouble of filling out forms soon after boarding, which is the recommended time to make choices before tours fill up.

Most ships also have drop boxes for filled out registration forms, to eliminate waiting in line. However, most travelers still prefer to sign up in person, which ensures a face to face meeting with shore tour staffers.

Sometimes a shore operator may cancel the tour if too few people register, or the weather is unfavorable. Always check for postings that identify cancellations, and conversely, if any new tours have been added to the inventory.

EXCURSION PRICES

The fee per person per tour varies widely from one cruise line to another. A walking tour around historic neighborhoods may cost less than $40, and kayaking less than $100. Tours that involve dogsledding, glacier travel, flightseeing by floatplane to remote areas, or heli-skiing can cost hundreds of dollars per person. Depending on the location, luxury cruise lines offer upscale tour programs that can cost over $10,000.

Cancellation policies vary, but in general, there is a 24-hour window before the tour in which visitors can change their minds. After the excursion, refunds are rare, although shore tour staff can reduce or waive the entire fee if a passenger can justify being completely dissatisfied.

Grizzly bear with cubs at Denali National Park

Creek Street, part of a Ketchikan walking tour, a popular shore excursion

GOING ASHORE

Information printed on tour tickets tells passengers where and when to meet, either on the ship or the pier. Private shore tour operators usually hold up boards clearly marked with the tour's name making it easy for passengers to spot where they need to be. Passengers taking tours enjoy priority status once the gangway opens. Some ports cannot handle large ships at the pier, so small launches bring dozens of cruisers ashore, starting with the passengers taking tours.

INDEPENDENT TRAVEL

Cruise lines have made it easier for passengers to book tours with the introduction of online billing systems, among other innovations, and tend to mark up tour costs because tourists usually pay willingly for the convenience.

However, some travelers prefer to arrange hotel stays, rail journeys, and tours entirely on their own. Before taking such matters into your own hands, it is wise to consider all the factors. Research the company and find out about the level of experience of the staff and how long the operator has been in business, and if it

makes customer testimonials available. Remember also that you will be without a tour representative, and will have to get to the tour start point alone. No matter how you book, additional expenses will arise, gratuities, food, and drink among them.

Getting back to the ship after a tour poses other challenges. While ships usually depart promptly at a well-publicized time, they will wait a few minutes for stray passengers after courteous public announcements. The only exception to this rule, and one that will certainly delay a departure, is if a shore excursion group booked via the shore desk is delayed.

Being completely alone may appeal to the adventurous, but travelers need to plan very carefully and stay well-informed.

SAFETY ON SHORE

Alaskan life in small seaside towns is slow and steady, with few residents and not much bustle. Even in the larger cities along the coast, personal safety poses no real concern. However, while most locals will be glad to help you navigate to where you want to go, as with any travel away from home, keep your valuables protected.

BEST SHORE EXCURSIONS

Providing shore excursions for their passengers has become a gigantic industry for cruise lines. Holland America Line and Princess Cruise Line, for example, offer hundreds of tours in Alaska and are specialists in the field. Among the interesting shore excursions visitors can expect to find are:
• Halibut and salmon fishing charters from Ninilchik and Deep Creek (see p108)
• Walking Creek Street in Ketchikan (see pp128–9)
• Visiting Saxman Totem Park near Ketchikan (see p129)
• Flightseeing in Misty Fiords National Monument (see p130)
• Riding the Mount Roberts tramway above Juneau (see pp142–3)
• Helicopter tours to the Juneau Icefield (see p145)
• Riding the White Pass and Yukon Route Railroad in Skagway (see pp150–53)
• Brown bear watching in Denali National Park (see pp166–9)
• Alaska Railroad trips to Denali (see pp166–9) or Seward (see pp98–9)

Helicopter readying for a flight at Skagway's heliport

Floatplane taking off from the serene waters of a lake

OUTDOOR ACTIVITIES

Known around the world as a premier wilderness and adventure holiday destination, Alaska offers visitors a diverse range of outdoor activities. In the summer, visitors can go sportfishing *(see pp40–41)*, hiking, mountaineering, canoeing, and whitewater rafting, while the winter brings opportunities for snowmachining, dogsledding *(see pp38–9)*, and skiing. The daring can even try heli-skiing. Operators usually organize transport, food, and equipment, and even provide guides. For those with the proper equipment, camping, hiking, backpacking, canoeing, and Nordic skiing can be inexpensive and spectacular. However, anything that involves bush travel or motorized vehicles such as snowmachines and ATVs will require extensive planning and cost considerably more. For a price, operators will provide equipment and handle all the logistics.

Hikers on a trail in Girdwood on the outskirts of Anchorage

HIKING

Alaska is a hiker's paradise, and Southcentral, Southeast, and Interior Alaska boast numerous picturesque hiking and trekking trails. The possibilities range from short 2-mile (3-km) strolls to all-day hikes, multi-day backpacking trips, and cross-country wilderness expeditions.

In Southeast Alaska, nearly every city and town lies within easy reach of scenic hiking trails that lead up through lush forest and muskeg to points offering great views. The most popular long-distance route here is the historic Chilkoot Trail *(see pp152–3)*, which requires stamina as well as preparation. **Gastineau Guiding** offers the best excursions around the Juneau area.

Most of the popular trails in Interior Alaska, such as those in Denali State Park *(see p164)* and Wrangell-St. Elias National Park *(see pp192–3)*, are longer, often unmarked routes that demand at least some hiking

experience. Even in popular Denali National Park *(see pp166–9)*, there are few marked trails. Here, most hiking is cross-country, and needs backcountry permits, orientation skills, and the ability to ford unbridged rivers. **Denali Trekking Company** organizes customized trips for visitors.

Even on the outskirts of Anchorage, it is possible to hike one of the many trails in Chugach State Park or around Girdwood. On the Kenai Peninsula, many routes through the spectacular state parks and the Chugach National Forest, including the popular Resurrection Pass Trail *(see p97)*, make excellent introductions to multi-day hiking. **Arctic Wild** adventure guide service offers a range of specialty ecotours.

In Southwest, Arctic, and Western Alaska, hiking is limited to cross-country wilderness routes that can be accessed only by bush plane. **Kodiak Treks** conducts low-impact bear-viewing trips.

BUSH TRAVEL

Due to Alaska's limited road and ferry systems, transport around the state is quite different from other parts of the US. Access to the bush – any place off the highway or Marine Highway systems – requires a helicopter, a boat or water taxi, or a bush plane on wheels, floats, or skis.

Bush flights, which carry residents and supplies to remote homesteads and fly anglers and rafters to uncrowded streams also provide access to rural villages and bush lodges. **Rust's Flying Service**, **Wrangell Mountain Air** and **Brooks Range Aviation** are some of the better operators that arrange trips for tourists. Clients must pay not only for the flight out, but also for the pilot's return trip. The rates differ according to the type of plane, the number of passengers, and the duration of the flight. Client luggage is always limited to the amount of gear that the plane

Floatplane taking off for the bush, Lake Hood, Anchorage

Cross-country skiing in an Anchorage park, against the backdrop of the Chugach Mountains

can safely carry. Anyone who wants to haul a boat or camping gear and supplies for the length of the trip may have to pay for more than one run to the drop-off location.

Usually, a pre-arranged pick-up is scheduled, but travelers need to be flexible, and it is always necessary to carry extra supplies. Note that once the water taxi or bush plane has dropped off its passengers and is out of view, people are on their own until the pick-up date. Remote areas are ruled by the weather, and clouds, wildfires, storms, snow, and wind can make travel impossible, so it is important not to embark on a bush trip without a fair amount of cushion time.

SNOWMACHINING

In the winter, rivers and lakes in the Interior freeze, becoming transport routes and opening up much of the state to relatively easy access. These routes were historically negotiated by dogsled, but today, sleds have been replaced by snowmachines (or snowmobiles). They not only provide access to places off the road system, but also serve as recreational vehicles that allow adrenaline-pumping runs. Snowmachines range from 550cc to 700cc models, and only those who are confident of their riding and navigation skills should consider renting one. Rentals require a hefty

security deposit, and tax and fuel may be extra. **Alaska Snow Safaris** and **Glacier City Snowmobile Tours** offer rentals and a range of guided trips, including short introductory runs, half-day backcountry trips, and full- and multi-day tours.

MOUNTAINEERING

Mountaineering is extremely popular in Alaska and Mount McKinley is the destination of most climbers. While it can be scaled without a guide, guided expeditions must use one of the six accredited outfits listed on the **Denali National Park** website, including the recommended **Alaska Mountaineering School**. All climbers, guided or not, must register with the **Talkeetna Ranger Station** *(see p162)* 60 days before the trip and pay a Mountaineering Special Use Fee of $200.

Alaska is one of the few places in the world that still offers summits that are as yet unclimbed and even unnamed. Most serious climbers arrive either with a pre-organized expedition or come months in advance to seek out appealing peaks and prepare for the ascent. Guiding companies such as **St. Elias Alpine Guides**, **Alaska Mountain Guides and Climbing School**, and **Kennicott Wilderness Guides** accept prospective mountaineers of all levels.

SKIING

Alaska's only world class downhill ski resort is Alyeska, at Girdwood, 40 miles (60 km) south of Anchorage. There are also smaller resorts at Alpenglow and Hilltop in Anchorage, Eaglecrest in Juneau, Cleary Summit near Fairbanks, and Mount Eyak near Cordova.

Heli-skiing – downhill skiing on mountains and glaciers accessed by helicopter – is rapidly gaining in popularity, especially around Valdez and Haines. **Valdez Heli-Ski Guides** offers coaching and individual packages, and **Valdez Heli Camps** organizes luxury and adventure trips. In the summer, Ruth Glacier, in Denali National Park, and the Juneau and Harding Icefields become ski fields. Note, however, that glacier skiing is only for experienced skiers with safety training and equipment.

Nordic or cross-country skiing is widely available, and snowmachine tracks all over the state double as ski trails. Cross-country skiing and noisy snowmachines are not fully compatible, but the fine groomed trails around Anchorage and Fairbanks are reserved for skiing. In the Mat-Su, Hatcher Pass *(see p87)* offers excellent wilderness trails. The Fairbanks area has good trails both in town and at Chena Hot Springs *(see p177)*.

CYCLING AND MOUNTAIN BIKING

In the summer, cycling and mountain biking are popular activities, but cyclists must be prepared to encounter animals, traffic, and narrow shoulders on most paved highways. The Copper River Highway *(see p123)*, the Denali Highway *(see p165)*, the extensive routes on Prince of Wales Island *(see pp132–3)*, and the Edgerton Highway/ McCarthy Road *(see p187)* are among the best, most scenic routes. Biking is allowed on most trails in the Chugach and Tongass National Forests and on limited routes in the state parks. **Alaskabike** and **Alaska Backcountry Bike Tours** offer guided cycling tours all over Alaska. Anchorage's **Downtown Bicycle Rentals** and **Pablo's Bicycle Rentals** hire out bicycles. The **Arctic Bicycle Club** offers information on cycling, mountain biking, and organized rides.

RAFTING AND CANOEING

For most people, the appeal of a whitewater trip lies in running the rapids. Rapids are graded Class I to V, but anything above Class III will need good whitewater skills, while Class V will need an expert guide. The most popular rivers, and the easiest to access, include the Nenana River *(see p172)* and the Chulitna River near Denali National Park, the upper Kenai River *(see p96)*, the Matanuska River, the Eagle River near Anchorage, and the Gulkana River near the Richardson Highway. **Nova**

Rafting on the Chilkoot River near Skagway

River Rafters and **Chilkat Guides** are among Alaska's oldest adventure companies, offering statewide packages. **Talkeetna River Guides** rafts rivers in the Interior, while **Arctic Wild** runs rivers in the Brooks Range.

For a more contemplative, secluded experience, canoe trips of a day or more are possible on many of Alaska's lake and river systems, such as the Lynx Lake Loop *(see p160)* north of Anchorage and the Kenai Peninsula's Swan Lakes Loop *(see p107)*.

OCEAN KAYAKING

One of the best ways to see Alaska's sheltered coastal areas is by kayak, providing easy access to remote beaches in Southeast Alaska, Prince William Sound, the Kenai Fjords, and other well-sheltered waterways. On fine days, the scenery is spectacular, and there is a chance of spotting marine wildlife. Thorough preparation is essential, and a

number of companies hire out gear and offer instruction, kayak transport, and guides. **Anadyr Adventures** and **Prince William Sound Kayak Center** offer trips around Prince William Sound, while **Alaska Canoe and Campground** and **True North Kayak Adventures** operate on the Kenai Peninsula. The Southeast has several good agencies offering comparable packages. These include **Glacier Bay Sea Kayaks** in Gustavus, **Sitka Sound Ocean Adventures**, and **Southeast Sea Kayaks** in Ketchikan.

TOURS

Visitors who prefer organized activities can select from a range of operators. In the Southeast, **Alaska Waters** organizes a variety of tours, **Breakaway Adventures** offers jet boat rides, **Allen Marine Tours** and **Orca Enterprises** arrange whale-watching tours, **Coastal Helicopters** sets up glacier tours, and **Chilkoot Charters and Tours** runs fishing trips. **Phillips Cruises and Tours** *(see p116)* and **Glacier Wildlife Cruises** offer tours in Prince William Sound, while **Glacier Bay Tours** explores Glacier Bay National Park. **Katmailand** runs freshwater sportfishing trips and **Kenai Fjords Tours** offers wildlife cruises. **K2 Aviation** offers flightseeing tours to McKinley, and the **Northern Alaska Tour Company** offers visits to the Arctic. **St Paul Island Tours** and **Wilderness Birding Adventures** offer wildlife viewing in western Alaska.

Kayakers preparing to set off, Whittier

DIRECTORY

HIKING

Arctic Wild
Fairbanks. *Tel 479-8203, (888) 577-8203.*
www.arcticwild.com

Denali Trekking Company
PO Box 93, Talkeetna.
Tel 733-2566.
www.alaskahiking.com

Gastineau Guiding
Juneau. *Tel 586-2666.*
www.stepintoalaska.com

Kodiak Treks
11754 S Russian Creek Rd,
Kodiak. *Tel 487-2122.*
www.kodiaktreks.com

BUSH TRAVEL

Brooks Range Aviation
PO Box 10, Bettles.
Tel 692-5444.
www.brooksrange.com

Rust's Flying Service
Anchorage. *Tel 243-1595.*
www.flyrusts.com

Wrangell Mountain Air
McCarthy. *Tel 554-4411,
(800) 478-1160.* www.
wrangellmountainair.com

SNOWMACHINING

Alaska Snow Safaris
6543 Brayton Dr #A,
Anchorage. *Tel 868-7669.*
www.snowmobile-
alaska.com

Glacier City Snowmobile Tours
Box 1018, Girdwood.
Tel 783-5566.
www.snowtours.net

MOUNTAINEERING

Alaska Mountain-eering School
PO Box 566, 3rd St,
Talkeetna. *Tel 733-1016.*
www.climbalaska.org

Alaska Mountain Guides and Climbing School
PO Box 1081, Haines. *Tel
766-3396.* www.alaska
mountainguides.com

Denali National Park
www.nps.gov/dena

Kennicott Wilderness Guides
PO Box 1 MXY, Glennallen.
Tel 554-4444. www.
kennicottguides.com

National Outdoor Leadership School (N.O.L.S)
Tel 745-4047.
www.nols.edu

St. Elias Alpine Guides
Tel 554-4445.
www.steliasguides.com

SKIING

Valdez Heli Camps
PO Box 2495, Valdez.
Tel 783-3243. www.
valdezhelicamps.com

Valdez Heli-Ski Guides
PO Box 57, Girdwood.
Tel 835-4528. www.
valdezheliskiguides.com

CYCLING AND MOUNTAIN BIKING

Alaska Backcountry Bike Tours
HC 05 Box 6754-JA,
Palmer. *Tel (866) 354-
2453.* www.
mountainbikealaska.com

Alaskabike
2720 Lexington Circle,
Anchorage. *Tel 245-2175.*
www.alaskabike.com

Arctic Bicycle Club
www.arcticbike.org

Downtown Bicycle Rentals
333 W 4th Ave, Anchorage.
Tel 279-3334. www.
alaska-bike-rentals.com

Pablo's Bicycle Rentals
440 L St, Anchorage.
Tel 250-2871. www.
pablobicyclerentals.com

RAFTING AND CANOEING

Arctic Wild
PO Box 80562, Fairbanks.
Tel 479-8203. www.
arcticwild.com

Chilkat Guides
PO Box 170, Haines.
Tel 766-2491.
www.raftalaska.com

Nova River Rafters
Chickaloon. *Tel 745-5753.*
www.novalaska.com

Talkeetna River Guides
Main St, Talkeetna. *Tel
(800) 353-2677.* www.
talkeetnariverguides.com

OCEAN KAYAKING

Alaska Canoe and Campground
35292 Sterling Hwy.
Tel 262-2331. www.
alaskacanoetrips.com

Anadyr Adventures
Valdez. *Tel 835-2814.*
www.anadyradventures.
com

Glacier Bay Sea Kayaks
PO Box 26, Gustavus.
Tel 697-2257. www.
glacierbayseakayaks.com

Prince William Sound Kayak Center
PO Box 622, Whittier.
Tel 472-2452. www.
pwskayakcenter.com

Sitka Sound Ocean Adventures
PO Box 1242, Sitka.
Tel 752-0660. www.
ssoceanadventures.com

Southeast Sea Kayaks
1007 Water St, Ketchikan.
Tel 225-1258. www.
kayakketchikan.com

True North Kayak Adventures
Homer Spit, Homer. *Tel
235-0708.* www.
truenorthkayak.com

TOURS

Alaska Waters
PO Box 1978, Wrangell.
Tel (800) 347-4462.
www.alaskawaters.com

Allen Marine Tours
Sitka. *Tel (888) 747-8101.*
www.allenmarinetours.
com

Breakaway Adventures
PO Box 2107, Wrangell.
Tel 874-2488. www.
breakawayadventures.
com

Chilkoot Charters and Tours
PO Box 1336, Skagway.
Tel (877) 983-3400.
www.chilkootcharters.
com

Coastal Helicopters
8995 Yandukin Dr, Juneau
Airport, Juneau.
Tel 789-5600. www.
coastalhelicopters.com

Glacier Bay Tours
241 W Ship Creek Ave,
Anchorage.
Tel (888) 229-8687.
www.visitglacierbay.com

Glacier Wildlife Cruises
PO Box 1832, Valdez.
Tel 835-5141. www.
lulubelletours.com

K2 Aviation
Box 545B, Talkeetna.
Tel 733-2291.
www.flyk2.com

Katmailand
4125 Aircraft Dr,
Anchorage.
Tel 243-5448.
www.katmailand.com

Kenai Fjords Tours
Seward Waterfront,
Seward. *Tel 224-8068.*
www.kenaifjords.com

Northern Alaska Tour Company
PO Box 82991, Fairbanks.
Tel 474-8600. www.
northernalaska.com

Orca Enterprises
495 S Franklin St, Juneau.
Tel 789-6801. www.
orcaenterprises.com

St. Paul Island Tours
Tel (877) 424-5637.
www.alaskabirding.com

Wilderness Birding Adventures
5515 Wild Mountain Rd,
Eagle River. *Tel 694-7442.*
www.wildernessbirding.
com

SURVIVAL
GUIDE

PRACTICAL INFORMATION 278–287

TRAVEL INFORMATION 288–299

PRACTICAL INFORMATION

Alaska State Parks sign

Thanks to its unparalleled natural beauty, abundant wildlife, and rich cultural history, Alaska attracts a growing number of visitors from all over the world each year. The state's tourist infrastructure is fairly well-developed, offering a range of accommodation and restaurant options. A large number of local tour operators can also organize just about any sort of adventure a visitor may want to undertake. Road and rail systems link numerous sites of interest, but even places away from the highways can be readily accessed via the extensive air transport and ferry routes. Visitor information centers, even in small towns, are plentiful and go out of their way to provide information and assistance. The following pages include tips on a range of practical matters that will assist visitors in getting the most out of their visit to this sprawling, majestic state.

WHEN TO GO

The finest weather in Alaska usually occurs from mid-May to mid-July, when most of the state, except for the Southeast and the Aleutians, experiences almost perpetual daylight. This is the time when all parks and services are open and the state is geared up for visitors.

Rainfall is common all year round in Southeast Alaska, while the Arctic receives little rain. In most parts of Alaska, however, the annual "rainy season" begins in mid-July, ending in early September, when most national park facilities close. However, there are plenty of reasons to visit in the off-season. As nights become colder, the chances of seeing the aurora borealis increase. From December to April, there are outdoor activities *(see pp272–5)* and the entertaining winter festivals *(see pp44–5)* to enjoy. The May and September shoulder seasons are also pleasant, avoiding the bad weather and minimal facilities of the off-season, and the prices and crowds of the high season.

VISA REGULATIONS

Citizens of Australia, New Zealand, the UK, and most European Union nations can visit the US without a visa, but need a passport that is valid for at least six months after their trip, an onward or return ticket, and a completed Electronic System for Travel Authorization (ESTA) form, available online. Note that from September 2010 the ESTA will cost $14. Canadians need to show their passport to enter the US. Visitors from nations that require visas must apply to a US embassy and may be asked for proof of financial solvency and intention to return home.

VISITOR INFORMATION

Most tourist offices in Alaska are known for the quality of their information. All offer free maps, brochures, and hotel and restaurant listings, and local staff answer most travel-related queries. The **Alaska Public Lands Information Centers** and the **Alaska Travel Industry Association** are also good information sources. National parks have their own visitors' centers, with rangers and volunteer staff who help with planning and organizing the necessary permits. The **Alaska Department of Fish and Game** issues hunting and fishing licenses. Most visitor centers are open long hours in the summer, but winter hours are limited. Throughout this guide, details of visitor information centers in major towns are provided.

Rainforest around Ward Lake, Ketchikan

◁ **A floatplane flying over the beautiful wetlands of Denali National Park**

TAXES AND TIPPING

While Alaska does not have a state sales tax, most cities and boroughs impose local sales taxes. These can be up to 8 percent of the purchase price, added to the total at the checkout. A host of taxes are imposed on goods and services that apply mainly to tourists. A bed tax applies to B&Bs, hotels, hostels, lodges, and some campsites. A statewide $50 per head tax is applied to all cruise ship passengers. Rental cars are also subject to tax, and drivers renting vehicles from airport rental desks may have to pay up to 29 percent extra to cover airport maintenance.

Service is not included on restaurant checks, and the tip is usually 15 percent (see pp252–3). Taxi drivers expect $2–5, depending on the fare. At hotels, tip $2 per bag and $1 per day for the room maid. In wilderness lodges, the tip is given to the desk clerk, to be divided among the staff. While tour guides get about $10 per day, depending on the service, fishing guides often get a sum commensurate with the success of the trip.

SMOKING

As in the rest of America, Alaska's attitude toward smoking has changed dramatically and more and more towns are moving to restrict where smoking is permitted. Smoking is banned in all public buildings, shops, and public transport vehicles. Most accommodation options are also smoke-free, although a few may offer specific rooms where smoking is allowed

In Anchorage and Juneau, a local ordinance stipulates that all restaurants and bars are smoke-free.

DIRECTORY

VISITOR INFORMATION

Alaska Department of Fish and Game
Tel 465-4100.
www.adfg.state.ak.us

Alaska Public Lands Information Centers
605 W 4th Ave,
Anchorage. Tel 644-3661
www.alaskacenters.org

Alaska Travel Industry Association
2600 Cordova St,
Suite 201, Anchorage.
Tel 929-2200.
www.travelalaska.com

ANCHORAGE

Anchorage Convention and Visitors' Bureau
524 W 4th Ave,
Anchorage. Tel 274-3531.
www.anchorage.net

Chugach State Park Eagle River Nature Center
Tel 694-2108.
www.ernc.org

Mat-Su Convention and Visitors' Bureau
Tel 746-5000.
www.alaskavisit.com

Palmer Chamber of Commerce
Tel 745-2880. www.
palmerchamber.org

THE KENAI PENINSULA

Alaska Maritime National Wildlife Refuge
95 Sterling Hwy, Homer.
Tel 235-6961. www.
islandsandocean.org

Homer Chamber of Commerce Visitors' Center
Tel 235-7740.
www.homeralaska.org

Kenai Fjords National Park Visitors' Center
Tel 224-2125.
www.nps.gov/kefj

Seward Convention and Visitors Bureau
Tel 224-8051.
www.seward.com

PRINCE WILLIAM SOUND

Cordova Chamber of Commerce
Tel 424-7260. www.
cordovachamber.com

Valdez Convention and Visitors' Bureau
Tel 835-4636.
www.valdezalaska.org

SOUTHEAST ALASKA

Haines Convention and Visitors' Bureau
Tel 766-2234.
www.haines.ak.us

Juneau Convention and Visitors' Bureau
Tel 586-2201.
www.traveljuneau.com

Ketchikan Visitor Information Center
Tel 225-6166.
www.visit-ketchikan.com

Petersburg Visitor Information Center
Tel 772-4636.
www.petersburg.org

Sitka Convention and Visitors' Bureau
Tel 747-5940.
www.sitka.org

Skagway Convention and Visitors' Bureau
Tel 983-2854.
www.skagway.com

WESTERN INTERIOR ALASKA

Denali National Park Visitor Access Center
Tel 683-2294.
www.nps.gov/dena

Fairbanks Convention and Visitors' Bureau
Tel 456-5774. www.
explorefairbanks.com

EASTERN INTERIOR ALASKA

Dawson City Visitors' Center
Tel (867) 993-5575.
www.dawsoncity.ca

Eagle Historical Society
Tel 547-2325.
www.eagleak.org

Wrangell-St. Elias National Park Visitors' Center
Tel 822-7440.
www.nps.gov/wrst

SOUTHWEST ALASKA

Kodiak Island Convention and Visitors' Bureau
Tel 486-4782.
www.kodiak.org

Unalaska/Dutch Harbor Convention and Visitors' Bureau
Tel 581-2612
www.unalaska.info

ARCTIC AND WESTERN ALASKA

Inupiat Heritage Center
Barrow.
Tel 852-4594.
www.nps.gov/inup

Nome Visitors' Center
Tel 443-6624.
www.nomealaska.org

Northwest Arctic Heritage Center
Kotzebue. Tel 442-3890.
www.nps.gov/noaa

Strolling down Anchorage's
bustling 4th Avenue

TRAVELING WITH CHILDREN

With its great opportunities to
see wildlife and get outdoors,
Alaska is excellent for children.
Many towns, especially
Anchorage, have attractions
that were built with children in
mind, such as the H2Oasis
water park and the Alaska Zoo.
Most museums offer free or
discounted admission for
children, with the cut-off age
ranging from 3 to 17 years.
Many Alaska National Parks
offer Junior Ranger programs
for kids, and the majority of
hotels and restaurants are child-
friendly, with discounted or
free accommodation with the
parents, special menus, play
areas, and changing tables.
　Many tour companies
welcome children, but some

wilderness lodges, upscale
restaurants, and adventure
tours, such as helicopter tours
or kayaking, may have a minimum age limit.
　Anyone organizing a family
driving trip through Alaska
should bear in mind that
distances are long, especially
if the trip starts in the Lower
48. Renting an RV (see pp296–
7) can make the journey
easier. There are plenty of
parks and highway pull-offs
where families can stop for
picnics or where kids can
take a short walk with a
field guide to identify plants,
birds, and animals. **Pamela
Lanier's Family Travel** is a
useful resource for general
information about traveling
with children.

SENIOR TRAVELERS

Although the age defining
a senior citizen is usually 65,
discounts are sometimes
accessible to those over 55
or 60 as well. While many
senior travelers in Alaska opt
for all-inclusive cruises and
package tours, many prefer to
travel independently in
private vehicles, especially
RVs. However, it is worth
noting that most car and
RV rental firms have an
upper age limit.
　Several national institutions
give senior concessions. The
National Park Service offers
Senior Passes that reduce the

cost of entry, camping, and
services in national parks.
Exploritas (formerly Elder-
hostel) has educational trips
for travelers over 55, which
may include inexpensive
accommodation, lectures,
and meals. For around
$10, seniors can join the
**American Association of
Retired Persons (AARP)**,
which issues cards that
make available a host of
travel discounts.

STUDENT TRAVELERS

Students receive few special
considerations in Alaska apart
from discounts on some cultural programs and museum
admissions. However, it never
hurts to ask. Proof of student
status will be needed, such as
a current student body card
from a specific school or
university or an **International
Student Identification Card**
(ISIC). Inexpensive tickets can
be arranged by **Student Travel
Association** (STA) branches.

TRAVELERS WITH DISABILITIES

While the Alaskan back-
country can be quite
challenging for travelers
with limited mobility or
other disabilities or health
problems, the state does
offer them a large number
of accessible options. As in
the rest of the country,

Travelers aboard a tour boat in Rudyard Bay in Misty Fjords National Monument

Alaska has regulations requiring government offices, businesses, public transport, and taxis to be designed to accommodate wheelchairs, while road crossings in cities have dropped curbs to enable easier access. In addition, most car parks, public toilets, hotels, and supermarkets offer special arrangements for the wheelchair-bound. Service animals, such as guide dogs, are allowed on public transport and in public buildings.

Frontcountry areas of most national and state parks often have paved or graded trails and viewing platforms that are wheelchair accessible. The National Park Service also offers an America the Beautiful Access Pass, which grants disabled individuals free entry to all national parks.

Cruise ships, tour buses, and railway cars all cater to disabled travelers, and many adventure tour companies do their best to accommodate clients with disabilities. **Access Alaska** can assist in finding accommodations and services for disabled travelers.

In the winter, the challenges can be greater, as snow renders streets and sidewalks difficult for wheelchair users and absorbs many of the acoustics that assist navigation for the blind. More information, from how to rent a specially adapted car to qualifying for parking permits, is offered by the **Access-Able Travel Source** and the **Society for Accessible Travel and Hospitality**, who promote awareness and accessibility for travelers with special needs.

ETIQUETTE

In general, Alaskans are polite, friendly, and helpful, although they may appear to be a bit more outspoken than other Americans. Visitors from across the world are welcomed, but are also expected to respect local ways, especially when visiting Native villages. It is illegal to bring alcohol into some areas and it is always wise to ask before taking photographs, especially of ceremonies, homes, or dances. Dress-wise, Alaska is one of the most relaxed states in the US. Attire tends to be informal, climate-dependent, and practical. Casual clothes such as jeans, T-shirts, flip-flops, and light woolens can be worn even for public performances or in upscale restaurants. Many Alaskans do not allow smoking in their homes or cars and it is considered courteous to check with your hosts if you may smoke *(see p279)*.

Two-prong US plug

ELECTRICITY

Across the US, the electrical current is 110 volts at 60 Hertz. Visitors from abroad need an adaptor plug for the two-prong sockets and a voltage converter to operate 220-volt appliances, such as hairdryers and rechargers for cell phones and laptop computers (unless they have a built-in adaptor). However, bear in mind that most hotel rooms have hairdryers and dedicated sockets for electric shavers.

CONVERSION CHART

One US pint (0.5 liter) is smaller than one UK pint (0.6 liter). One Imperial gallon is the equivalent of five US quarts. To convert from degrees Celsius to degrees Fahrenheit, multiply by 1.8 and add 32. From degrees Fahrenheit to degrees Celsius, subtract 32 and divide by 1.8.

US Standard to Metric
1 inch = 2.54 centimeters
1 foot = 30 centimeters
1 yard = 0.91 meters
1 mile = 1.6 kilometers
1 ounce = 28 grams
1 pound = 454 grams
1 US quart = 0.947 liters
1 US gallon = 3.79 liters

Metric to US Standard
1 centimeter = 0.4 inches
1 meter = 3 feet 3 inches
1 kilometer = 0.6 miles
1 gram = 0.04 ounces
1 kilogram = 2.2 pounds
1 liter = 1.1 US quarts

DIRECTORY

TRAVELING WITH CHILDREN

Pamela Lanier's Family Travel
www.familytravelguides.com

Junior Ranger Program
www.nps.gov/learn/
juniorranger.htm

SENIOR TRAVELERS

American Association of Retired Persons (AARP)
601 E St NW,
Washington, DC 20049.
Tel (888) 687-2277.
www.aarp.org

Exploritas
11 Avenue de Lafayette,
Boston, MA 02111-1746.
Tel (800) 454-5768.
www.exploritas.org

National Park Service
Tel (888) 467-2757. www.nps.
gov/fees_passes.htm

STUDENT TRAVELERS

International Student Identification Card
www.isic.org

Student Travel Association
www.statravel.com

TRAVELERS WITH DISABILITIES

Access-Able Travel Source
PO Box 1796, Wheat Ridge,
CO 80034.
Tel (303) 232-2979.
www.access-able.com

Access Alaska
121 W Fireweed Lane,
Suite 105, Anchorage.
Tel 248-4777.
www.accessalaska.org

Society for Accessible Travel and Hospitality (SATH)
347 5th Ave, Suite 610,
New York, NY 10016.
Tel (212) 447-7284.
www.sath.org

Personal Security and Health

In contrast to much of the US, Alaska has no really large cities, and while Anchorage has some gang and drug-related violence, it is not usually directed at visitors. On the whole, Alaska is a relatively safe place to visit, but even in small towns, it is wise to be alert and learn which areas are unsafe, especially at night. For visitors on adventure holidays (see pp272–5), safety is paramount in the wilds of Alaska. Carry maps and follow the advice of rangers or visitors' centers – they can offer invaluable information on wilderness survival and basic safety procedures. Those on organized tours or cruises should follow the instructions provided by crew or tour leaders. Before setting out, it is a good idea to check local newspapers and television and radio channels for weather reports.

Police patrol car

PERSONAL SAFETY

Surprisingly, Alaska possesses one of the country's higher crime rates, although most tourist hubs are relatively non-threatening. Nevertheless, visitors should observe a few basic rules. Never carry large amounts of cash. Wallets kept in back pockets will tempt pickpockets. It is best to wear handbags and cameras over the shoulder, strapped firmly across the chest, and to keep passports separate from cash and traveler's checks. Drivers should try to keep valuables locked in the trunk of their car when parked at trailheads, especially those around Anchorage – they are known for break-ins. Large towns can be unsafe at night, so avoid walking around alone and try to stay away from areas that are known to be risky. Avoid panhandlers or anyone visibly intoxicated.

In Alaska, law enforcement in cities, towns, and certain boroughs is handled by local police departments. The **Alaska State Troopers** cover the rest of the state. In national parks, some park rangers are additionally in charge of law enforcement.

LOST PROPERTY

It is necessary to report all lost and stolen property to the police in order to make an insurance claim, even though it is unlikely that small items will be recovered. Victims should telephone the **Police Non-Emergency Line** and report the incident. They will subsequently be issued a police report, which can be used to file the claim.

Stolen and lost credit cards and traveler's checks should be reported to the issuer immediately to avoid misuse. Most card companies have toll-free numbers (see p285). Visitors who have kept a record of the check numbers will find replacement a painless experience – new ones are usually issued within 24 hours.

Foreign visitors who have lost their passport should contact their nearest embassy or consulate, which will probably be in San Francisco or Seattle. Normally, the consulate will issue a temporary replacement. In order to speed up the replacement process, visitors might find it useful to keep photocopies of their driver's license, birth certificate, and passport.

MEDICAL CONCERNS

Hospitals in Alaska's largest cities are very well-equipped, but small towns usually only have health clinics, while rural villages often have just a public health nurse. Bear in mind that a range of drugs, such as codeine-based pain-killers, may need prescriptions in the US. Prescription medication in the US is expensive, so those with prescriptions should carry extra supplies. All pharmacies sell prescription drugs, but only hospital pharmacies are open 24 hours a day. Local brand names can be confusing, so keep a list of the generic names of drugs you think you may need and seek assistance in a drugstore if you are

Denali National Park ranger guiding visitors, Toklat Ranger Station

having difficulty finding the drug. Supermarkets such as Carrs stock non-prescription drugs and are open 24 hours.

Medical care in the US can be expensive. Even with medical insurance, you may still have to pay upfront and claim reimbursement from your insurance company later, so ask for all forms and receipts.

TRAVEL INSURANCE

Partly due to the high cost of medical care in the US, visitors are strongly urged to purchase travel health insurance for the duration of their stay. The package should cover death or dismemberment, dental and medical care, flight delays and cancellations, and lost or stolen baggage.

EMERGENCIES

For emergencies that require medical, fire, or police services, dial 911. Contact numbers of ambulance services, the Coast Guard, Rescue Services for stranded hikers or campers, Fire Departments, and the Poison Control Center are given in telephone directory Blue Pages.

All hospitals in Alaska are equipped with emergency rooms, and their numbers are listed in the telephone book. Although critical emergency cases cannot be turned away by hospitals, evidence of the

ability to pay may be required before treatment in non-emergency cases.

Hotel personnel will usually be able to call a doctor or a dentist and recommend a hospital on request. **Fairbanks Memorial Hospital** in Fairbanks and Anchorage's **Providence Alaska Medical Center** offer general medical care and critical care services. **Alaska Regional Hospital** also offers a Physician Referral Service. **Bartlett Regional Hospital** in Juneau has an acute care and emergency department, while **Central Peninsula General Hospital** in Soldotna has a shock trauma center.

OUTDOOR HAZARDS

Alaska's weather can be extreme and volatile, and without proper clothing and shelter, even in the summer, hypothermia is a risk on wet, windy days. The layering method works best, and must include layers for warmth and insulation, as well as an outer waterproof shell.

At higher elevations, the summer sun can be surprisingly strong. It is wise to use an effective sunscreen, wear a hat, and carry sufficient water. Filtering any water taken from natural sources is vital, as Alaskan streams and lakes harbor the giardia parasite.

In the summer, wildfires and thunderstorms are

Classic Smokey Bear fire prevention sign, Dawson City, Canada

perpetual risks, especially in the Interior. It is important to watch campfires closely and extinguish cigarettes carefully. Visitors who see a developing forest fire, especially near populated areas, should move away and report it to authorities. During lightning storms, avoid ridges or open areas, and do not stand or camp beneath tall trees.

Earthquake and tsunami warnings are issued by the **Alaska Tsunami Warning Center**, but the chances of these occuring during a visit are remote. While most people are concerned about bear encounters, following a few simple guidelines (see p109) will almost eliminate the possibility of harm.

DIRECTORY

EMERGENCY SERVICES

All Emergencies
Tel 911.

Alaska State Troopers
Anchorage **Tel** *248-1410.*
Fairbanks **Tel** *451-5100.*
Juneau **Tel** *465-4000.*
Ketchikan **Tel** *225-5118.*
Kodiak **Tel** *486-4121.*
Mat-Su **Tel** *745-2131.*
Sitka **Tel** *747-3254.*
Soldotna **Tel** *262-4453.*

Alaska Tsunami Warning Center
Tel 745-4212. **http://** wiatwc.arh.noaa.gov

Hospitals

Alaska Regional Hospital
2801 DeBarr Rd, Anchorage.
Tel 276-1131, (888) 254-7884 (physician referral).
www.alaskaregional.com

Bartlett Regional Hospital
3260 Hospital Drive, Juneau. **Tel** *796-8900.*
www.bartletthospital.org

Central Peninsula General Hospital
250 Hospital Place, Soldotna.
Tel 262-4404.
www.cpgh.org

Fairbanks Memorial Hospital
1650 Cowles St, Fairbanks. **Tel** *452-8181.*

Providence Alaska Medical Center
3200 Providence Dr, Anchorage.
Tel 562-2211.

Police Non-Emergency Line
Anchorage **Tel** *786-8500.*
Fairbanks **Tel** *459-6500.*
Juneau **Tel** *586-0600.*
Ketchikan **Tel** *225-6631.*
Kodiak **Tel** *486-8000.*
Sitka **Tel** *747-3245.*
Soldotna **Tel** *262-4455.*
Wasilla **Tel** *352-5401.*

CONSULATES

Australia
575 Market St, Suite 1800, San Francisco, CA 94105.
Tel (415) 536-1970.

Canada
412 Plaza 600, 6th & Stewart, Seattle, WA 98101.
Tel (206) 443-1777.

New Zealand
10649 N Beach Rd, Bow, WA 98232.
Tel (360) 766-8002.

UK
900 4th Ave, Suite 3100, Seattle, WA 98164.
Tel (206) 622-9255.

Banking and Currency

Visitors will generally not encounter any problems with financial transactions in Alaska. Banks are plentiful and foreign currency exchanges are available in larger cities, but it is best to verify opening hours before visiting banks or exchange bureaus. Automated teller machines (ATMs), which enable visitors to make cash withdrawals with debit or credit cards, are available all over Alaska, even in small towns and some villages. Found in most banks, supermarkets, and general stores, these are open 24 hours a day. Some banks even have drive-up ATMs. Credit cards are commonly used for making payments, especially at hotels and car rental companies.

ATMs can dispense cash, enact account transfers, and show bank balances

BANKS AND FOREIGN CURRENCY EXCHANGE

Alaskan banks are generally open from 9 or 10am to 4:30, 5, or 6pm on weekdays, and often on Saturdays from 10am to 2 or 3pm, but these hours can vary across the state. Banks will convert traveler's checks to US dollars, and for a substantial commission, some **Wells Fargo** banks in Anchorage, Fairbanks, and Juneau will also change foreign currency traveler's checks and cash.

TRAVELER'S CHECKS

Traveler's checks are safer than cash as they can be replaced if lost or stolen. It is important to keep the checks separate from the list of check numbers, which are required if checks have to be replaced in case of loss or theft. Foreign currency traveler's checks may be cashed at Wells Fargo banks in Juneau,

Anchorage, and Fairbanks, but they are otherwise of little use in Alaska. To avoid extra charges, it is best to carry **American Express** or **VISA** traveler's checks in US dollars. These are always accepted as cash, without fees, in hotels, restaurants, shops, gas stations, and other businesses across Alaska, except in some of the smallest rural villages. Often, some form of photo ID, such as a passport or driver's license, is required as identification when using traveler's checks.

CREDIT, DEBIT, AND CHARGE CARDS

Credit and charge cards are practically essential when traveling in the US. The cards are usually required as a guarantee when renting a car or RV (see pp296–7), and are used to book tours, airline tickets, and tickets for most forms of entertainment. The most widely used cards are

VISA and **MasterCard**, but most places also accept American Express, **Diner's Club**, and **Discover Card**.

ATMs offer better foreign exchange rates than banks, and all credit, charge, and debit cards can be used to withdraw cash from ATMs, with a bank transaction fee of $2 to $3, in addition to the credit card company's charges. The most common international systems are Cirrus and Plus. Before you leave home, it is best to ask your bank or credit card company which ATM system your card can access.

WIRING MONEY

Money can be wired to Alaska from more than 100 countries. Money transfers can usually be sent and received within 15 minutes, but in some cases, it may take as much as a full day or even up to a week. The fastest and most popular service is **Western Union**, which is found all over Alaska, but banks also offer wire services, albeit slower. Thanks to the number of foreign crew members on cruise ships, other businesses offering wire services can usually be found near the cruise ship docks.

CURRENCY

US currency is based on the decimal system, and the standard unit is the US dollar, divided into 100 cents. Bills, or bank notes, are all of similar size and greenish in color (with the exception of the $20 bill, which has a subtle peach background), so it is wise to always check the denomination and count change carefully. In villages and remote areas, smaller bills are preferred, and in some places, $50 and $100 bills are not accepted at night. Similarly, some liquor stores will not change $50 or $100 bills unless the purchase is over half the amount of the bill. The 25-cent piece is useful for public telephones. It is also best to carry cash for small transactions and tips, and for use on public transport and taxis.

Coins

US coins come in $1, 50-, 25-, 10-, 5 , and 1-cent pieces. Each coin has a popular name: 1-cent coins are pennies, 5-cent coins are nickels, 10-cent coins are dimes, and 25-cent coins are quarters. State quarters are in circulation, as are new goldtone Sacagawea dollars. The Susan B. Anthony and Eisenhower dollars are uncommon, as is the John F. Kennedy 50-cent coin, which is now a collector's item.

25-cent coin
(a quarter)

10-cent coin
(a dime)

5-cent coin
(a nickel)

1-cent coin
(a penny)

1-dollar coin
(a buck)

Bank Notes

US bank notes come in denominations of $1, $2, $5, $10, $20, $50, and $100, but the $2 bill is rare. Paper bills were first issued in 1862 to finance the Civil War, when metal for coins was in short supply. The size and design of the notes was decided in 1929, and in the 1990s, the artwork for all but the $1 bill was re-engraved with anti-counterfeit markings.

1-dollar bill ($1)

5-dollar bill ($5)

10-dollar bill ($10)

20-dollar bill ($20)

50-dollar bill ($50)

100-dollar bill ($100)

DIRECTORY

American Express
Tel (800) 926-9400 (Moneygram US only), (800) 221-7282 (check replacement), (800) 992-3404 (stolen cards).

Diner's Club
Tel (800) 234-6377.

Discover Card
Tel (800) 347-2683.

MasterCard
Tel (800) 622-7747.

Thomas Cook/ MasterCard UK
Tel (800) 223-9920.

VISA
Tel (800) 227-6811 (check replacement), (800) 847-2911 (stolen cards).

Wells Fargo
Anchorage *Tel* 263-2565.
Fairbanks *Tel* 459-4300.
Juneau *Tel* 586-3324.
www.wellsfargo.com

Western Union
Tel (800) 325-6000 (wiring money US), (800) 833000 (wiring money UK).
www.westernunion.com

Communications and Media

The United States has some of the most sophisticated communications systems in the world. Postal, telephone, and Internet services are all widely available, providing fast and efficient services to destinations both in-state and worldwide. Public card phones and pay phones are found in most parts of Alaska in cafés, bars, gas stations, supermarkets, hotels, and public buildings. However, in the more remote regions, pay phones and mailboxes are found only in towns and cell phone coverage is usually quite limited.

TELEPHONES

All local telephone numbers have seven digits. The cost of a local call is 25 to 35 cents, which is usually good for any length of call. Alaska's area code is 907. This is required when calling long-distance, even in-state. Long-distance calls to any number outside the local area (especially in-state calls) cost considerably more, but are cheaper when dialled directly or at off-peak times, usually in the evening and on weekends. Calls made on hotel phones will usually be charged at much higher rates.

Pay phones are fairly common and easy to use, with clearly marked instructions. They can be used for international calls, but callers will need a stack of change to dial direct and will be interrupted

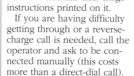

Phone cards for long-distance calls

by an operator when more money is needed. A phone card is easier, but it is advisable to use only reputable companies such as AT&T. Cards can be purchased at supermarkets, convenience stores, and hotels for values between $5 and $50, and operate by providing a series of numbers to punch into the phone, which then accesses the account and announces how much time remains on that card. Each card has clear usage instructions printed on it.

If you are having difficulty getting through or a reverse-charge call is needed, call the operator and ask to be connected manually (this costs more than a direct-dial call).

Toll-free numbers are widely used in the US for contacting hotels, car rental companies, tour operators, and even some tourist offices.

While most toll-free numbers are not accessible when calling from outside the US, in some cases they may occasionally be connected through an operator and charged at the regular toll rate.

CELL PHONES, INTERNET, AND FAX SERVICES

Many travelers bring their own cell (mobile) phones, but service varies among operators, so check if your service provider provides coverage in Alaska. Coverage is usually good in towns, and even, surprisingly, in some remote areas, but may be erratic outside towns.

Internet cafés are common, and an increasing number of establishments offer Wi-Fi access, often free, to patrons with their own laptop computers. Most hotels offer Internet access to their guests. Virtually all libraries also have free Internet access. Faxes can often be sent from larger hotels and copy centers. Many places in rural Alaska have only dial-up Internet or no access at all.

MAIL SERVICES

In the US, all domestic mail is First Class unless otherwise requested, and generally takes between three and five days to arrive. First Class mail costs only about 20 percent more than parcel post (surface mail), which is also available. International mail sent by air takes between five and ten days to arrive, but surface parcels may take over four weeks. Special parcel services are also offered by the **US Postal Service**. Priority Mail delivers faster than normal First Class and costs only marginally more. Express Mail guarantees next day delivery within the Lower 48 states, and a day or two more to Hawaii. International Express Mail

Typical US mailbox

USEFUL DIALING CODES

- To make a direct-dial long-distance call within Alaska, the rest of the US, or Canada, dial **1** (the country code) followed by the area code and local number. Useful area codes: Alaska **907**, Yukon Territory **867**, British Columbia (and Hyder in Alaska) **250**.
- For international direct-dial calls, dial **011** followed by the desired country code. Then dial the area or town code (omitting the first 0 or 1), and the local number.
- To make an international call via the operator, dial **01** and follow the same procedure as detailed above.

- For international operator assistance, dial **01**.
- For local operator assistance, dial **0**.
- For international directory inquiries, dial **00**.
- For local directory inquiries, dial **411**.
- For inquiries in another US or Canadian area code, dial **1** followed by the desired area code and **555-1212**.
- For emergency police, fire, and ambulance services, dial **911**.
- Dial **844** for temperature, weather, and time.
- **1-800**, **866**, **877**, and **888** indicate toll-free numbers.

Newspaper vending machines on 4th Avenue, downtown Anchorage

DIRECTORY

MAIL SERVICES

DHL
Tel (800) 225-5345.
www.dhl.com

Federal Express (FedEx)
Tel (800) 463-3339.
www.fedex.com

UPS
Tel (800) 742-5877.
www.ups.com

US Postal Service
Tel (800) 275-8777.
www.usps.com

guarantees to deliver in five working days. Several private international couriers offer next-day delivery for foreign mail, the best known being **DHL**, **Federal Express**, and **UPS**.

All Alaskan towns have at least one post office. Small packets and letters may be dropped into mailboxes, but all parcels will need to be inspected at the post office counter. Contract post offices in shops and small towns often have shorter queues, but don't accept international parcels.

NEWSPAPERS, RADIO, AND TELEVISION

The major daily newspaper in Alaska is the weekly *Anchorage Daily News*. Other major papers are the *Fairbanks News-Miner*, *Juneau Empire*, and the *Mat-Su Frontiersman*. Bestselling national daily papers such as the *Wall Street Journal*, the *New York Times*, and *USA Today* are also available, although a few days late, at large bookshops and newsstands in major airports. Some visitors' centers and shops offer free papers listing local weather, events, and news. The most popular of these is the *Anchorage Press*.

The Alaska Public Radio Network has stations in all major cities and towns. Anchorage's 91.1 FM is the most popular; 650 and 700 AM have news and talk. In Fairbanks, 970 AM has the news, while 104.7 FM plays rock. 630 AM in Juneau has the news. Most hotels offer a range of cable and satellite TV channels.

ALASKAN LEXICON

Baleen – strips of fibrous tissue from the mouths of baleen whales, used to filter plankton from the sea.
Breakup – wet and muddy period when the ice melts in April.
Bush – the part of Alaska that is off the highway and ferry systems.
Cache – hut built on stilts and used to store items out of reach of animals.
Camai – an Athabaskan greeting (pronounced "cha-MAI") that is the Alaskan equivalent of "Aloha."
Cheechako – a newcomer who has been in Alaska less than about 20 years.
Chinook – warm wind from the Southeast that can melt the snow, even in mid-winter.
Igloo – a variation of the Inupiat word *illu*, which means "house." The ice block variety is used only as an emergency shelter.

Lower 48 – all US states except Alaska and Hawaii.
Mukluks – moosehide or sealskin boots.
Muktuk – whale or seal blubber favored by Native Alaskans
Mushing – driving a dogsled, also Alaska's state sport.
Native – spelled with an uppercase "N," it refers to an indigenous Alaskan. Spelled with a lowercase "n," it refers to anyone born in Alaska.
Outhouse – outdoor toilet consisting of a hole in the ground covered by a shelter.
Permafrost – permanently frozen ground overlain by topsoil or muskeg.
Potlatch – Southeast Alaska Native feast in which the host distributes numerous possessions.
Scrimshaw – Native designs etched onto walrus ivory.
Skookum – anything that's strong, great, or wonderful.
Slough – stagnant backwater formed by old river channels (pronounced "slew").

Snowbirds – older people who live in Alaska but winter in the Lower 48.
Snowmachine – what other North Americans would call a snowmobile or ski-doo.
Sourdough – an old-time prospector or any long time Alaskan, usually those who have been in Alaska for at least two decades. The word is derived from the bread made with sourdough starter (*see p254*).
Taiga – Russian for "little sticks," refering to black spruce. Much of Alaska's muskeg and boreal forest consists of taiga vegetation.
Tundra – derived from the Finnish word for "treeless plain," it refers to areas of miniature plants in Alaska's northern and alpine areas.
Ulu – a crescent-shaped knife used by Natives for cleaning and skinning animal skins and cutting meat.
Xtra Tufs – high-top rubber boots used throughout Alaska.

TRAVEL INFORMATION

The majority of overseas visitors to Alaska land in Anchorage, the state's main gateway. Those coming from the Lower 48 can fly from Seattle directly to Ketchikan or Juneau. Bus services link the Lower 48 and Canada with Anchorage and Fairbanks, but many visitors journey overland by car on the Alaska Highway, or sail on an Alaska Marine Highway vehicle ferry from Bellingham, Washington, through the Inside Passage to Southeast Alaska. There, travelers can transfer to ferries bound for the Kenai Peninsula, Southwest Alaska, and Prince William Sound, where it is possible to connect to the Alaska Railroad. Within Alaska, rental vehicles are a good alternative to the limited public transport systems and provide maximum freedom. Sites off the highways can be accessed by an extensive network of scheduled or chartered flights.

ARRIVING BY AIR

All major cities and towns in Alaska have an airport, while remote towns and villages have airstrips for transport planes and bush traffic. The state's biggest airport – and the one most visitors are likely to see first – is Ted Stevens International Airport in Anchorage, which receives all international flights from Europe and Asia and the greatest number of flights from the Lower 48.

As the only non-stop intercontinental flights to Alaska are from Frankfurt (via Whitehorse in Canada) and East Asia, most overseas visitors arrive via Seattle. There are also non-stop flights from select US cities, including Minneapolis, Salt Lake City, Boston, Chicago, Denver, Newark and Washington, DC.

Alaska's major airline, **Alaska Airlines**, is based in Seattle and connects a host of cities across the US and Mexico to a wide variety of Alaskan destinations such as Anchorage and Fairbanks, several towns in the Southeast including Juneau, Sitka, and Ketchikan, Cordova in Prince William Sound, Nome and Kotzebue in the western Arctic, Barrow in the far north, and Dutch Harbor in the Aleutians.

Scheduled flights into Anchorage are also offered by **Condor**, **Northwest Airlines**, **American Airlines**, **Delta**, **Frontier**, **China Airlines**, and **United Airlines**. They fly to cities around the US, and to various international destinations.

INTERNATIONAL ARRIVALS

Overseas visitors arriving in the US must present a passport and, if necessary, a visa, to immigration officials before claiming their baggage. Those catching connecting flights must collect their luggage at the first point of entry into the US and take it through US Customs before checking it on to their final destination.

Non-resident adults are allowed to bring in a limited amount of duty-free items. These include 0.2 gallons (1 liter) of alcohol, 50 non-Cuban cigars, 200 cigarettes, and up to $100 worth of gifts. There is no legal limit on the amount of money that can be brought into the US, but cash amounts over $10,000 should be declared to US Customs. Completed customs declaration forms must be submitted to a US Customs officer while exiting the Customs hall.

Most major airports offer a wide range of services such as newsstands, car rental companies, shuttle buses, and taxi services. Most terminals also offer facilities for the disabled.

Specially painted Alaska Airlines aircraft underscoring the carrier's role in transporting Alaskan seafood

Floatplane taking off to tour remote corners of Alaska

INTERNAL FLIGHTS

In addition to the numerous Alaska Airlines services, several domestic airlines offer convenient, if occasionally somewhat expensive, services. **Frontier Alaska** flies from Anchorage and Fairbanks to Arctic and Western Alaska, and its subsidiary **Era Aviation** connects Anchorage to Prince William Sound, the Kenai Peninsula, and Kodiak. **PenAir** flies to a host of destinations on the Alaska Peninsula and the Aleutian Islands, including the Pribilof Islands. **Bering Air** accesses tiny places in Western Alaska from Nome and Kotzebue, and also operates charter flights to the Russian Far East. **Grant Aviation** does daily runs between Southwest Alaska, Anchorage, and Bethel. **Wings of Alaska** serves the Southeast, and **Arctic Circle Air** and **Warbelow's Air Ventures** link many far-flung areas of the state.

Alaska also has a host of charter airlines which can take passengers to just about any airport or airstrip in the state, as well as bush airlines *(see p272)* that land fly-in hunters, anglers river runners, or hikers on remote lakes, rivers, glaciers, or gravel bars.

AIR FARES

There is a vast array of fare types and prices available for travel to and around Alaska. Airlines compete with each other, and it pays to compare and book early to get the cheapest fares, especially during the busy summer. Although several websites do offer bargains on last minute bookings, direct flights to the US and Alaska usually need to be booked in advance.

It is usually less expensive to book an APEX (Advance Purchase Excursion) fare, which must be bought no less than seven or 14 days in advance. However, these tickets impose such restrictions as minimum (usually seven days) and maximum (three to six months) lengths of stay. It can be difficult or expensive to alter APEX flight dates after purchase, so it is wise to include compensation for delays or cancellations on a travel insurance policy. A fly-drive deal, where the cost of the ticket includes car rental, is also a lower-priced option that may be worth taking.

Travel agents are useful sources of information on the latest bargains. They may also be able to offer special deals to visitors who book rental cars, accommodation, and domestic flights in addition to their international ticket.

BAGGAGE RESTRICTIONS

Most airlines now charge for checked bags, but allow carry-ons consisting of one piece of hand luggage and a small handbag. On smaller domestic airlines, flightseeing trips, and bush flights, only one piece of hand luggage is accepted and the weight of checked baggage may be limited to as little as 20 lb (9 kg) per person.

Alaska Marine Highway

Often called the "Blue Canoe," the state-run Alaska Marine Highway provides year-round access from Bellingham in Washington state and Prince Rupert in British Columbia, Canada. It also connects the mostly roadless areas of the Southeast, Southwest, and Prince William Sound. The route is so beautiful that it has been officially designated a National Scenic Byway, a term usually reserved for highways. The Marine Highway is also an easy, if expensive, way to transport a vehicle to Alaska, and with advance planning, it is possible to stop off in any of the ports of call along the way. Schedules, however, can often go awry, so it is wise to allow a bit of buffer time.

Alaska Marine
Highway logo

ROUTES

The Alaska Marine Highway has three main routes: Southeast, Southcentral, and Southwest. The Southeast route is the longest one, following the spectacular Inside Passage up the west coast of North America from Bellingham in Washington state to Prince Rupert in Canada, and then northward through Southeast Alaska's islands and channels to Haines and Skagway. Ports of call along the way usually include Ketchikan, Wrangell, Petersburg, and Juneau, with some sailings calling in at Sitka. The MV *Kennicott* does the cross-Gulf run, from Juneau in the Southeast to

Whittier in Prince William Sound via Yakutat, Cordova, and Valdez. The Southcentral route connects Whittier to Cordova, Valdez, and Chenega Bay, and also to Kodiak, Port Lions, Homer, and Seldovia. On the Southwestern route, the MV *Tustumena (see p215)* sails between April and September from Homer to Seldovia, Kodiak, and Port Lions, and down the Alaska Peninsula and the Aleutians to Chignik, Sand Point, King Cove, Cold Bay, and Dutch Harbor.

Access to Hollis on Prince of Wales Island is provided by **Inter-Island Ferries**, while **British Columbia Ferries** sails from the northern tip of Vancouver to Prince Rupert.

FERRIES

Eleven different ferries of various sizes regularly ply the Southeast, Southcentral, and Southwest Alaska routes. Traditionally and legally, the vessels in the fleet are named after Alaskan glaciers. The largest of the ferries, the flagship MV *Columbia* holds 625 passengers and is usually used on runs between Bellingham, WA, and Haines, as is the MV *Malaspina*. Both ships boast a dining room, gift shop, cocktail lounge, solarium, and observation lounge.

The MV *Aurora* and the catamaran MV *Chenega* run shorter routes in the Southeast and also serve Prince William Sound. MVs *Kennicott, Taku, Matanuska, LeConte, Lituya* and the catamaran MV *Fairweather* do a variety of runs in the Southeast. The fleet's oldest, sturdiest ship, the MV *Tustumena*, does the turbulent Aleutian Island run.

FACILITIES

In general, the long-haul ferries are better equipped than the ones doing day runs. Except for the fast catamarans MV *Fairweather* and MV *Chenega*, which have only snack bars, the larger vessels have cafeterias that serve snacks, hot meals, and beverages. The MV *Columbia* and MV *Tustumena* also have full-service dining rooms, where both American and Continental breakfasts are available, and lunch and dinner menus usually offer a daily special or choice of main dishes, featuring seafood, salad, and vegetable dishes. Sandwiches and snacks are always available. Mixed drinks are sold only on the MV *Columbia* and MV *Tustumena*, but beer and wine are available in the snack bars on the fast ferries.

MVs *Columbia, Malaspina, Matanuska, Tustumena,* and *Taku* offer cabins with private bathroom facilities, while the MV *Kennicott* has a few two-berth unserviced rooms without facilities. The five

Marine Highway ferry sailing away from Valdez in Prince William Sound

Under the solarium on the upper deck of a Marine Highway ferry

short-haul ferries do not have cabins. All ferries, however, have public showers.

Deck passengers on overnight trips can sleep in the indoor recliners, or on reclining plastic deck chairs in the heated solariums on the top decks of the ferries. On all overnight sailings, travelers are allowed to pitch tents on the top deck and fix them with waterproof duct tape. These are usually quite close to the smokestack and noisy engines, so it may be useful to carry some earplugs. All ferries have elevators and wheelchair-accessible facilities, and the larger vessels also offer cabins suitable for disabled passengers.

LIFE ON BOARD

There are few things more relaxing than sitting in the observation lounge or warm solarium of a ferry and watching the passing scene. While onboard amenities are spartan

by most standards, there's always plenty to fill up the time. In addition to watching the undeniably spectacular landscapes along most routes, passengers find they have plenty of time to lean back with a book, take a hot shower, sleep or lounge in the fresh air, and meet people from across the world.

TAKING A VEHICLE

Book as far in advance as possible in order to transport a vehicle on the Marine Highway, especially between Bellingham, WA, and Haines in the peak season from June to August. Tariffs depend on the size of the vehicle, measured from the front bumper to the end of the back bumper or trailer. Most vessels on the Southeast and Southcentral routes can take vehicles up to 70-ft (20-m) long, but the maximum length on the MV *Tustumena* is 40 ft (12 m). Except in some small

ports, drivers will usually be required to check in two hours before sailing. The crew will direct them to their parking location, where they must set their hand brake, take any possessions needed onboard, and lock the vehicle. The vehicle deck will not be accessible while sailing. However, escorted trips to the vehicle deck are periodically announced by the purser, and there is vehicle access while the vessel is in port. RV propane tanks and firearms must be reported to the purser upon boarding, so they can be sealed by the crew. Boats under 100 lb (45 kg), bicycles, and kayaks incur an extra charge, while larger boats will be charged as vehicles. Except for guide dogs, transporting pets also incurs an extra charge.

DIRECTORY

FERRIES

Alaska Marine Highway
7559 N Tongass Hwy, Ketchikan.
Tel 465-3941, (800) 642-0066.
www.dot.state.ak.us/amhs
www.ferryalaska.com

Inter-Island Ferries
PO Box 495, Craig.
Tel 826-4848, (866) 308-4848.
www.interislandferry.com

British Columbia Ferries
Tel (250) 386-3431, (888) 223-3779. www.bcferries.com

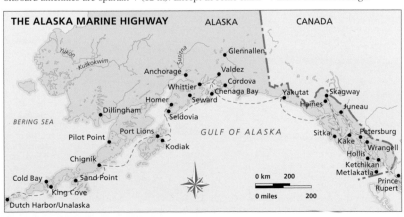

THE ALASKA MARINE HIGHWAY

Traveling by Bus and Train

Although slower than car and plane travel, taking a bus or train in Alaska can be an enjoyable way of exploring the region. Long-distance bus services, however limited, are the least expensive way to travel, although some places are served only by costly tour buses. Within the larger cities, local buses are the only form of public transport. Although these tend to focus on daytime services for local commuters, they are also useful to visitors since most centrally placed attractions lie along or near main bus routes. A good option is to buy an Alaska Pass, which allows unlimited bus, train, and ferry travel for a set period on the Alaska Railroad, Alaska Marine Highway, White Pass and Yukon Route Railroad (WP&YR), and Gray Line buses in Alaska.

Gray Line tour bus

Skagway's popular yellow tourist bus

TRAVELING BY BUS

In Alaska, only a handful of popular routes are served by long-distance buses, and those services that do exist are generally infrequent. Many services are operated only during the summer.

The best-served routes are those between Anchorage, Fairbanks, and the Kenai Peninsula, and points in between. **Alaska Park Connection** runs from Seward to Denali National Park via Anchorage. **Seward Bus Lines** connects Anchorage with Seward while the **Homer Stage Line** runs between Anchorage, Homer, and Seward. **Alaska-Yukon Trails** has a year-round service between Anchorage and Fairbanks, as well as summer services to Dawson City in Canada. **Alaska Direct Bus Line** operates services between Anchorage, Fairbanks, and Whitehorse, in Canada's Yukon Territory.

Backcountry Connection buses run between Glennallen and McCarthy in Wrangell-St. Elias National Park.

To reach Alaska by bus from the Lower 48 states, it is best to take **Greyhound Canada** to Whitehorse, and connect to the Alaska Direct Bus or Alaska/Yukon trails to Anchorage or Fairbanks. Green Tortoise is a unique bus touring company with several 10 or 14 day trips each summer. It's especially popular with young international travelers.

TRAVELING BY TRAIN

Traveling by train in Alaska means riding the **Alaska Railroad** *(see pp294–5)* between Seward and Fairbanks or taking the tourist route on the **White Pass and Yukon Route Railroad** *(see pp152–3)* from Skagway. While rail services are limited and relatively expensive, they're both relaxing and scenic, and most visitors will want to experience at least one rail trip during their stay.

Alaska Railroad train pulling into Denali National Park station

The Alaska Railroad is an extremely popular and convenient way to reach Denali National Park. While there are no overnight trains and, therefore, no sleeper services, all visitor-oriented trains on the main line between Seward and Fairbanks offer onboard dining services. Because so many cruise ships and tour companies use the Alaska Railroad to transport their passengers from Seward and Whittier to Anchorage, Denali National Park, and Fairbanks, many trains have special double-decker domed observation cars owned by Princess Cruise Line and

Park shuttle buses lining up for passengers, Denali National Park

White Pass and Yukon Route Railroad depot, Skagway

buses to Palmer or Wasilla. With a day's notice, **Anchor Rides** provides door-to-door transport for disabled or elderly passengers. **Metropolitan Area Commuter System** (MACS) covers the Fairbanks area. **Capital Transit** in Juneau links the downtown area with the Mendenhall Valley and Douglas Island. **The Bus** in Ketchikan connects the downtown area, the North Tongass Highway, and Saxman village.

TICKETS AND BOOKINGS

One of the best ways to see the state is to buy an **Alaska Pass** for $799 to $979. This allows unlimited travel for a set period on the Alaska Railroad, Alaska Marine Highway, and WP&YR. For other trains and buses, it is advisable to book tickets well in advance as this ensures availability, confirms the place to meet the bus, and provides assurance that the service is operating – small bus lines cancel trips if there is insufficient interest. No Alaskan town has a central bus station, and buses leave from their offices or a centrally located landmark.

Holland America Line (see pp264–7). Accessible only to tour members, these offer onboard guides and other amenities. In addition, the railroad has its own luxurious "Goldstar" railcars with open-air viewing platforms. A number of seasonal day trips are also offered by the **Alaska Railroad** from Anchorage and other cities. Especially popular is the all-day Spencer Glacier float trip. This includes a rail ride to the glacier on the Kenai Peninsula with a gentle raft trip past icebergs on the lake and then down the Placer River.

CITY PUBLIC TRANSPORT

Only Anchorage, Juneau, Fairbanks, and Ketchikan have regular public bus services, but Barrow, Kodiak, the Mat-Su region, Sitka, and Skagway have limited services or shuttles. In Anchorage, **People Mover** covers most parts of the city from the Downtown Transit Center. Services run from 6am to 10pm from Monday to Friday, with limited routes on weekends. People Mover will take passengers as far north as Eagle River, where on weekdays the buses connect with **Mat-Su Community Transit** (MASCOT)

DIRECTORY

BUS COMPANIES

Alaska Direct Bus Line
PO Box 501, Anchorage.
Tel (800) 770-6652 (Anchorage), (867) 668-4833 (Whitehorse, YT).
www.alaskadirectbusline.com

Alaska Park Connection
PO Box 22–1011, Anchorage. *Tel* (800) 266-8625.
www.alaskacoach.com

Alaska-Yukon Trails
PO Box 84608, Fairbanks.
Tel (888) 770-7275.
www.alaskashuttle.com

Backcountry Connection
PO Box 65, Glennallen.
Tel 822-5292.
www.kennicottshuttle.com

Green Tortoise
Tel (415) 956-7500, (800) 867-8647.
www.greentortoise.com

Greyhound Canada
877 Greyhound Way SW, Calgary AB T3C 3V8.
Tel (800) 661-8747.
www.greyhound.ca

Homer Stage Line
PO Box 1912, Homer.
Tel 235-2252.
www.homerstageline.com

Seward Bus Lines
1915 Seward Hwy, Seward. *Tel* (888) 402-7788, 224-3608.
www.sewardbuslines.net

RAIL COMPANIES

Alaska Railroad
PO Box 107500, Anchorage. *Tel* 265-2494, (800) 544-0522.
www.alaskarailroad.com

White Pass and Yukon Route Railroad
231 2nd Ave, Skagway.
Tel (800) 343-7373.
www.whitepassrailroad.com

CITY PUBLIC TRANSPORT

Anchor Rides
3650 A East Tudor Rd, Anchorage.
Tel 562-8444.

Capital Transit
Juneau. *Tel* 789-6901.
www.juneau.org/capitaltransit

Mat-Su Community Transit
Tel 376-5000.
www.matsutransit.com

Metropolitan Area Commuter System
Fairbanks. *Tel* 459-1011.
www.co.fairbanks.ak.us/transportation

People Mover
3650 A East Tudor Rd, Anchorage. *Tel* 343-6543.
www.peoplemover.org

The Bus
Ketchikan. *Tel* 225-8726, 247-5541. www.borough.ketchikan.ak.us

TICKETS AND BOOKINGS

Alaska Pass
Tel (800) 248-7598.
www.alaskapass.com

The Alaska Railroad

The Alaska Railroad may not be that far off the mark when it claims to offer the best rail trips in the world. Few journeys in the country cross such beautiful and wild terrain as this ribbon of steel that stretches across the landscape between Seward and Fairbanks. The trains allow passengers the best views possible, with all seats facing forward in the 1950s railcars. Travelers on the Denali Star can book seats in the domed viewing cars and access outdoor viewing areas from where the best photographs can be taken. Some trains also carry viewing cars owned by cruise companies and meant exclusively for their clients.

HISTORY OF THE RAILROAD

The Alaska Railroad had its beginnings in 1903 when the Alaska Central Railway was built northward from Seward. In 1907, after 50 miles (80 km) of track were laid, the company went bankrupt. After the company was reorganized as the Alaska Northern Railway, another 21 miles (34 km) of track were laid. In 1914, the US Congress sanctioned $35 million for the construction of a complete line between Seward and Fairbanks, and the tent city of Anchorage was designated as a railroad construction camp. The entire 470-mile (756-km) Alaska Railroad line was finally completed in 1917, and was inaugurated by President Warren G. Harding in Nenana in 1923 (see p173).

A branch line to Whittier was laid during World War II by blasting tunnels through the Chugach Range, and the railroad began making a profit by transporting military and civilian supplies. In addition to the $30 million damage caused by the 1964 Good Friday earthquake, the railroad has overcome landslides, heavy snowfalls, derailments, and even chemical spills. The rolling stock was upgraded between 1999 and 2005, and today the scenic lines of the Alaska Railroad rank among the state's most popular tourist attractions.

Baggage tickets issued by the Alaska Railroad

REGULAR SERVICES

While some regular commuter services on the railroad double as tourist services, other trains cater specially to tourists while also accommodating local passengers. Most visitor-oriented trains carry a dining car and railway gift shop, and each summer, guides on the trains interpret the history and wildlife seen along the route.

Between mid-May and mid-September, the daily Coastal Classic runs between Anchorage and Seward. During the same period, the regularly scheduled Glacier Discovery connects Anchorage to Whittier, followed by an optional trip to Spencer Glacier. From the glacier, passengers can either take a raft trip or continue to Grandview Pass for spectacular glacier viewing. The most popular route, however, is the Denali Star, which does the incredibly scenic run between Anchorage and Fairbanks, stopping en route at Denali National Park. The summer Hurricane Turn has Thursday to Sunday services, with extra runs on certain holidays, to serve bush passengers between Talkeetna and Hurricane. This 60-mile (97-km) local route has no food services.

In the winter, the Aurora does a weekend run between Anchorage and Fairbanks, with flag-stop services. From October to May, on the first Thursday of each month, the winter Hurricane Turn does the return day trip between Anchorage and Hurricane, offering wonderful views of the Susitna Valley and the Alaska Range.

Hurricane Turn rolling across Hurricane Gulch, between Talkeetna and Denali National Park

Flag-stop passengers boarding the Alaska Railroad

FLAG-STOP SERVICE

The Alaska Railroad proudly boasts that its summer Hurricane Turn train between Talkeetna and Hurricane is one of the last rail journeys in the world to offer a flag-stop service. Passengers can flag down the train – also called the "Bug Car" due to a profusion of onboard mosquitos in the summer – anywhere along the route, and it will stop to let them board. In the winter, all Alaska Railroad trains offer a flag-stop service. This is important for bush residents who live in remote areas without ready access to the road system. Similarly, travelers can disembark anywhere for a few days of hiking or fishing, and then board the train again wherever they would like to continue with their journey. Note that stove fuel cannot be carried on the train.

EVENT TRAINS

During the off-season, the railroad runs many special services between Anchorage and Portage or Seward. Known as Event Trains, these are, in effect, rolling festivities with specific themes. The Alaska Railroad Blues Train runs in September and features local blues bands, a blues concert, a barbecue, and an overnight stay in Seward. In October, the Great Alaska Beer Train offers Alaskan appetizers and microbrews from Anchorage's Glacier Brewhouse (see p257) while traveling between Anchorage and Portage. The festive Alaska Railroad Holiday Train in December includes carol singers, an onboard Santa Claus, and Christmas storytelling, followed by a visit to the Seward Holiday Festival before returning to Anchorage. For Halloween, the Alyeska Mystery Trail includes a rail trip to "Girdwoodvania" for a haunted murder mystery. The railroad's website has detailed information on tours.

SPECIAL TOURS

The railroad has teamed up with local operators to offer visitors unique rail-based itineraries and peripheral tours. These include a fabulous ten-day trip covering the entire railbelt, taking in Anchorage, Seward, Denali, Fairbanks, and Whittier. Other options take in sections of these routes, including, a

THE ALASKA RAILROAD

Fairbanks
Nenana — Tanana
Clear
Healy
Denali National Park
Denali National Park
Cantwell
Talkeetna
Susitna
Willow
Wasilla — Palmer
Eklutna — Matanuska
Anchorage — Valdez
Girdwood — Portage
Kenai — Grandview — Whittier
Ninilchik — Moose Pass
Homer — Seward
GULF OF ALASKA
0 km 100
0 miles 100

Prince William Sound cruise with **Phillips Cruises and Tours**, a flight to the Arctic Circle offering magnificent views, river trips in Talkeetna with **Mahay's Riverboat Service**, and a Glacier Bay cruise with glacier landings by helicopters. The railroad's website provides timetables and details on special tours.

TICKETS AND BOOKING

In the summer, cruise lines and organized tour companies book up large blocks of seats on the Glacier Discovery, Coastal Classic, and Denali Star. While many clients are accommodated on the companies' special private rail cars, other seats get booked up quickly – especially the Alaska Railroad's own domed cars – so it pays to reserve online or call or mail the railroad as far in advance as possible. For the smaller local trains, such as the summer Hurricane Turn, tickets are available onboard or from railroad reservation counters.

Traveling by Car and RV

Although it is possible, with some effort, to travel around Alaska on public transport, nothing compares to the freedom of the open road that comes with using a private or rental vehicle. For both residents and visitors, driving is a necessary part of life and will also be the only means of reaching many sites of interest. The road system may be limited, but where it is possible to drive, few will be disappointed with what is on offer, as the scenery is spectacular throughout the state. In addition, some fabulously scenic routes, such as the Denali Highway, the Elliott Highway, the Steese Highway, and the back roads of Southeast Alaska are accessible only by car.

RENTING A CAR

Anyone over 20 years of age can rent a vehicle, but some agencies impose a surcharge on people under 25. Overseas visitors need an International Driving License if their home license is not in Roman script. It is also essential to have a credit card to pay rental deposits, as few agencies accept cash. Child seats or cars for disabled drivers must be arranged in advance.

Visitors who rent a car in one city and leave it in another have to pay hefty drop-off fees. Cars must be returned with a full tank of gas.

Collision Damage Waiver (CDW) insurance, covering the car for any visible damage, and state and local taxes can increase the final total by 20 to 30 percent. Discounts may be available for members of the **American Automobile Association** (AAA) or the American Association of Retired Persons *(see p281)*. Most national agencies, such as **Alamo**, **Avis**, **Budget**, **Hertz**, **Thrifty**, and **Enterprise**, have outlets at airports, but charge more than local agencies and may add airport taxes. For inexpensive rentals, try the local **Cheapwheels Rent-a-Car**.

The biggest issue drivers will face is that rental agencies do not allow their non-4WD (four-wheel drive) cars to be taken on unpaved roads or to be driven off-road, and some of Alaska's finest routes are gravelled, including the McCarthy Road and the Taylor, Denali, Elliott, Steese, Dalton, and Top of the World

Highways. Driving any of them in a rental vehicle will invalidate any insurance or maintenance agreements, which means an accident or breakdown could wind up being very costly. However, visitors should be aware that renting a 4WD vehicle will typically double the charge. Only **Denali Car Rental** allows gravel road travel (except on the Dalton Highway north of the Yukon River) in a non-4WD. They require advance booking, especially in the summer peak season.

Gold Rush centenary license plate

RENTING AN RV

Renting a Recreational Vehicle (RV) can be an excellent, if expensive, way of getting around. A small RV, essentially a shell strapped onto a pickup truck, can sleep two

people in crowded comfort and costs around $120 per day. Fully-equipped motor homes usually include a bathroom, kitchen, and hideaway beds, sleeping four to eight people and costing as much as $300 per day. National RV rental agencies such as **Cruise America** and local ones such as **ABC Motorhome Rentals**, **Alaska Motorhome Rentals**, and **Clippership Motorhome Rentals** offer a wide range of RVs and amenities. **Great Alaskan Holidays** also rents larger RVs with expanding "pop-out" living rooms. Private RV campsites usually provide dump stations and water and electricity hookups. Some rental agreements, especially those for over a week, include unlimited mileage, while others may limit drivers to 50 or 100 miles (80 or 160 km) per day, after which an additional per mile charge applies.

RULES OF THE ROAD

Alaska's road systems are not as developed as those in the Lower 48, and there are less than 60 miles (96 km) of freeways. Highway speed limits range from 50 mph (80 kmph) on frost-heaved roads to 65 mph (105 kmph) for open stretches on main roads. The limit on some highways is 65 mph (105 kmph) but most roads are 55 mph (90 kmph). On gravel roads, the

Traffic on Tudor Road, one of Anchorage's main thoroughfares

Recreational vehicle in Alaska

THE GREAT AMERICAN RV

Every summer, people from the Lower 48 head north in motor homes equipped with every imaginable amenity, including televisions, satellite dishes, microwaves, gas cans, showers, bicycles, and rowboats. Many pull trailers carrying the family car or a pair of ATVs (all-terrain vehicle). The snail analogy is enhanced by the fact that the slow, heavily loaded RVs cannot reach speeds acceptable to drivers of smaller cars, and winding or busy roads can rapidly become jammed as traffic backs up behind a string of RVs. RV drivers should note that in Alaska, drivers must pull over by law if over five vehicles are being held up behind their vehicle.

limit varies from 30 mph (50 kmph) to 50 mph (80 kmph). Posted limits vary in towns, and during school hours, limits in school zones drop to 20 mph (30 kmph). Local police and the Alaska State Troopers enforce speed limits with particular vigilance in and around Anchorage, Fairbanks, and Juneau. The blood alcohol content limit in Alaska is 0.08 percent and there are heavy penalties for driving while drunk. Further information on local traffic rules is available from rental agencies or the AAA.

GAS STATIONS

Fuel is much cheaper in the US than in Europe, but prices do vary, and gas is sold by the gallon, not by the liter. In remote areas, drivers may pay a third more than they would in major cities, and prices may double along the Dalton Highway and other gravel roads. All stations are self-service, but some may have a pump attendant who will add at least 20 cents per gallon to the cost of the fuel. At non-automated stations, drivers may have to pay in advance. The cheapest gas is found at stores such as Fred Meyer, Carrs, and Costco. Those traveling on remote routes should carry extra gas as stations can

be few and far between. The longest stretch is the 244-mile (390-km) leg between Coldfoot and Deadhorse on the Dalton Highway.

OFF-ROAD DRIVING

While traveling in remote parts of Alaska it is important to have the latest maps, check the route in advance, and be aware of seasonal dangers. If there is a chance of snowfall, it may be best to change plans, as snow could make an otherwise viable route impassable and few minor roads are maintained in the winter. A 4WD is essential in many areas, especially in the winter and during the spring thaw. Minor routes may have unbridged river crossings that become impassable to low-clearance vehicles after rain, and many forestry roads are little more than parallel ruts meant for logging trucks. Avoid driving off-track, as it damages vegetation and increases the risk of the vehicle bogging.

While information about the weather and routes will be available at tourist offices, local residents should also be able to help. It is wise to inform local tourist offices of your route and return date, and report back to them upon returning. Carry extra water, food, and gas for emergencies.

DIRECTORY

American Automobile Association
1005 E Dimond Blvd, Anchorage. *Tel 344-4310.*
www.aaa.com

CAR RENTAL COMPANIES

Alamo
Tel (877) 222-9075.
www.alamo.com

Avis
Tel (800) 230-4898.
www.avis.com

Budget
Tel (800) 527-0700.
www.budget.com

Cheapwheels Rent-a-Car
Tel 561-8627. www.cheapwheelsrentacar.com

Denali Car Rental
Tel 276-1230, (800) 757-1230.
www.denalicarrentalak.com

Enterprise
Tel (000) 736 8222
www.enterprise.com

Hertz
Tel (800) 654-3131.
www.hertz.com

Thrifty
Tel (800) 367-2277.
www.thrifty.com

RV RENTALS

ABC Motorhome Rentals
3875 W Old International Airport Rd, Anchorage. *Tel 279-2000.*
www.abcmotorhome.com

Alaska Motorhome Rentals
150 N Ingra St, Anchorage.
Tel (800) 357-7368, 258-7109.
www.bestofalaskatravel.com

Clippership Motorhome Rentals
Tel 562-7051, (800) 421-3456.
www.clippershiprv.com

Cruise America
2230 Cinnabar Loop, Anchorage.
Tel 349-0499.
www.cruiseamerica.com

Great Alaskan Holidays
3901 W International Airport Rd, Anchorage. *Tel 248-7777.*
www.greatalaskanholidays.com

The Alaska Highway

For many drivers, the Alaska Highway – formerly called the Alcan, short for the Alaska-Canada Highway – is the adventure of a lifetime. Crossing some of the wildest territory in the world, every stretch of this 1,390-mile (2,224-km) road offers breathtaking sights and experiences. Starting in Dawson Creek in Canada's British Columbia, it crosses remote ranges, running through taiga forests and past crystalline lakes into the Yukon Territory. At Haines Junction, drivers can take the Haines Cut-Off *(see p154)* to Southeast Alaska, or continue northwest through Canada's strikingly lovely Kluane National Park. For the next 200 miles (320 km), it crosses scenic mountain country to the US-Canada border, and continues northwest past the Alaskan gateway town of Tok for its final stretch to Fairbanks.

Truck hauling freight over Tok River Bridge east of Tok

HISTORY OF THE HIGHWAY

Although an overland route to Alaska was being considered as early as 1930, it was not until the December 7, 1941, attack on Pearl Harbor that it became clear how militarily strategic this route would be. In February 1942, President Franklin D. Roosevelt authorized the construction of the Alaska Highway, and soon, an agreement with Canada granted the US right of way and waived taxes, import duties, and immigration requirements.

The first surveyors who marched across the wilderness to locate a route roughly followed a chain of airstrips known as the Northwest Staging Route. Wherever possible, they used existing winter roads, pack trails, and trap lines, often having to divert to avoid muskeg and rough terrain. Construction began in March 1942, with temperatures of -40° C (-40° F), while in the summer, the workers battled mosquitoes, black flies, and the blazing sun.

In June 1942, the Aleutian Islands were invaded by the Japanese army and a sense of urgency arose to complete the road. More than 10,000 troops worked feverishly 16 hours a day, seven days a week, cutting trees, mashing out a road surface, and bridging rivers and streams. The final construction work ended on October 25, 1942. While the military road officially opened in November, civilian traffic was restricted until 1948.

DRIVING THE ALASKA HIGHWAY

The Alaska Highway has long had a reputation for challenging road conditions, but over time, the conditions have improved. The entire two-lane highway is now paved or chip-sealed, and is also shorter than it originally was, with at least 35 miles (56 km) of the historical route having been cut off due to rerouting and straightening. It is still a long trip, however, and the roadside scenery is so fabulous that it is worth allowing extra time for sightseeing.

Despite these improvements, some parts of the highway still suffer from serious cracks, frost heaves, and potholes, and every summer, long stretches of the road undergo extensive construction and repair, which can significantly slow drivers' progress. The roughest, most frost-heaved portion is between Canada's Kluane Lake and the Alaskan border, while the most serious grades and turns are found between Dawson Creek and Watson Lake in Canada. Information on highway conditions can be obtained from **Drive British Columbia**, **Yukon Daily Road Report**, and the **Alaska Road Traveler Information Service**.

As far as safety regulations go, drivers in Canada are required to use their headlights at all times and this is also required on some Alaska highways. Drivers should watch out for wildlife on the road. Moose are common everywhere and a collision can destroy both the animal and the vehicle. There are bison in northern British Columbia and the Yukon Territory, and in the winter, caribou stand on the road to lick salt off the surface.

At the US-Canada border, US and Canadian citizens must present a passport. International visitors must show their passports and, if necessary, their visas *(see p278)*.

Welcome sign, Alaska Highway

Alaska Highway passing through the Yukon Territory, Canada

ALASKA HIGHWAY SERVICES

Between the 1940s and the early 1980s, fuel was available only every 250 miles (400 km) or so, but as the road became more traveled, more businesses sprang up along the route, and now there are gas stations approximately every 50 miles (80 km). There are also plenty of roadhouses and lodges along the way, where drivers can stop for a meal or a night rest. The towns of Watson Lake, Whitehorse, Haines Junction, Beaver Creek, and Tok all have breakdown services and shops selling groceries and other supplies. Whitehorse, which is the capital of the Yukon Territory, has the most amenities and services.

THE CASSIAR HIGHWAY

Coming from the US or the Canadian west coast, many drivers opt to take the Cassiar Highway, which is a shorter but equally beautiful and more rugged alternative to the Alaska Highway. The Cassiar Highway is entirely asphalt surfaced, but the stretch between Iskut and Dease Lake in Canada contains several steep and winding sections.

Beginning at the Skeena River Bridge at Kitwanga in the Canadian province of British Columbia, the Cassiar Highway runs north for 450 miles (720 km) before connecting with the Alaska Highway 13 miles (21 km) west of Watson Lake in the Yukon Territory. The Cassiar

DIRECTORY

HIGHWAY INFORMATION

Alaska Road Traveler Information Service
Tel 511 or (866) 282-7577.
http://511.alaska.gov

Drive British Columbia
Tel (800) 550-4997.
www.drivebc.ca

Yukon Daily Road Report
Tel (877) 456-7623.
www.511yukon.ca

is also the access route to Hyder, Alaska *(see p130)*, 40 miles (64 km) west of Meziadin Junction, and to Telegraph Creek on the upper Stikine River *(see p135)*, 70 miles (112 km) on a gravel road west of Canada's Dease Lake.

There are several highlights along the way. The Kitwanga Fort National Historic Site at Mile 2 is the site of an 18th-century indigenous fortified village and offers excellent views of the Kitwanga River valley. The beautiful Kinaskan Lake Provincial Park at Mile 227 is good for trout fishing. Drivers can see huge jade boulders being cut at Jade City at Mile 375. Boya Lake at Mile 397 is known for its clear aquamarine waters and excellent camping and fishing.

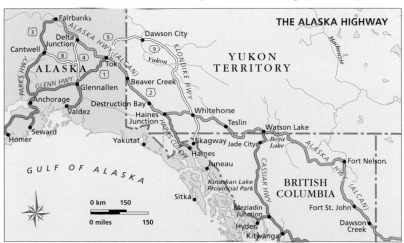

THE ALASKA HIGHWAY

General Index

Page numbers in **bold** refer to
main entries

4th Avenue Theatre 64, 66, **70**

A

AAA (American Automobile
Association) 296, 297
Accommodation *see* Hotels
Admiralty Island National Monument
126, **139**
Adventure holidays *see* Outdoor
activities
Aialik Bay (Kenai Fjords National Park)
57
Air travel **288–9**
Alaska Aviation Heritage Museum
(Anchorage) **75**
Alaska Botanical Garden (Anchorage)
77
Alaska Brewing Company (Juneau) 144
Alaska Highway 10, 55, 194, 195, 181,
298–9
Alaska Islands and Oceans Visitors'
Center (Homer) **110**
Alaska Marine Highway 93, 213, 215,
290–91
Alaska National Interest Land
Conservation Act (ANILCA) **57**, 107,
169, 209, 210, 235
Alaska Native Claims Settlement Act
(ANCSA) **56–7**, 235
rejection by Tsimshian 23, 130
Alaska Native Heritage Center
(Anchorage) 8, 15, 18, 63, **72–3**
Alaska Permanent Fund 56
Alaska Pipeline see Trans-Alaska
Pipeline
Alaska Public Land Information Centers
(APLIC) 66, 194, 240, 241, 278
Alaska Railroad 54, 93, 162, 166, 173,
292, 293, **294–5**
Alaska Range 8, 157, 159, 165
Alaska Raptor Center (Sitka) 141
Alaska SeaLife Center (Seward) 9, 94,
100–1
Alaska State Capitol Building (Juneau)
142
Alaska State Museum (Juneau) 142
Alaska State Parks 240, 241
Alaska State Troopers 70, 282, 283
Alaska State Trooper Museum
(Anchorage) 67, 69, **70**
Alaska Statehood Bill 55, 143
*The Signing of the Alaska Treaty of
Cessation, March 30, 1867* (Emanuel
Gottlieb Leutze) 48
Alaska Wild Berry Products
(Anchorage) **76**, 89
Alaska Zoo (Anchorage) **76**
Alaskan art and antiques 88, 89
Alaskan food *see* Food and drink
Alaskan lexicon 287
Alaskan roadhouses 241, 242–51
Aleut 20, 23, 49, 73, 203, 214, 216
Aleutian Islands 11, 60, 203, 214–15
climate 46
map 13, 204
role in World War II 18, 55, 99
Aleutian Trench 24
Aleutian World War II National
Historical Park (Dutch Harbor/
Unalaska) 215
Alexander, Malcolm 174
The Unknown First Family 174

Alsek River **155**
Alutiiq 11, 23, 49, 73, 203, 206
Alutiiq Museum (Kodiak) 11, 206
Alyeska Ski Resort (Anchorage) 81, 273
Amundsen, Roald 197, 234
Anan Creek Wildlife Observatory 9,
109, 126, **135**
Anchor Point **108**
Anchorage 8, 12, 50, 54, 56, **62–91**
area map 64–5
Alaska Native Heritage Center 8, 15,
18, 63, 72–3
Anchorage Museum at Rasmuson
Center 8, 64, 67, **68–9**
Chugach State Park 8, 63, **78–9**
climate 47
entertainment 90–91
getting around 65
hotels 242–3
Independence Mine State Historical
Park **86–7**
restaurants 256–8
satellite image 13
shopping 88–9
street-by-street map 66–7
Turnagain Arm Tour **80–81**
urban wildlife 71
visitor information centers 279
Wild Salmon on Parade 67
Anchorage Coastal Wildlife Refuge
(Anchorage) 80
Anchorage Museum (Anchorage)
8, 62, 67, **68–9**
Angling *see* Fishing
Aniakchak National Monument 11,
204, **212**
Arctic and Western Alaska 11, **218–35**
area map 220–21
climate 46–7
Dalton Highway **222–3**
getting around 221
hotels 251
restaurants 263
visitor information centers 279
Arctic Brotherhood Hall (Skagway) 150
Arctic foxes 217
Arctic Interagency Visitors' Center,
Coldfoot (Dalton Highway) 222
Arctic Man (Paxson) 182, **185**
Arctic National Wildlife Refuge 219,
220, **224**
prospective oil drilling 16, 57
Arctic Ocean 11
Arctic tundra 29, **225**
Arness, James 163
Wager with the Wind 163
Athabaskans 22, 49, 157, 194, 219
Eklutna Historical Park (Anchorage)
77
Native Village Museum (Pioneer
Park, Fairbanks) 175
Dena'ina 93, 96, 106, 111, 113
village site, Alaska Native Heritage
Center (Anchorage) 72–3
Atigun Pass (Dalton Highway) 223
Atigun River 220
ATMs 284
Aurora borealis 10, 157, **176**
show at Ester 173
Aurora Ice Museum (Chena Hot
Springs) 177

B

Backcountry permits 168
Bald eagles 16, 30, 31, 135, **149**

Bald eagles (cont.)
American Bald Eagle Foundation
Center (Haines) 149
Bald Eagle Protection Act 149
Chilkat Bald Eagle Preserve (Haines)
149
Sand Point 212
Balto's statue (Anchorage) 66
Banking and currency **284–5**
Baranov, Alexander **32**, 50, 206
Baranov Museum (Kodiak) 11, 206
Barrow 11, 60, 220, **226–7**, 228–9
climate 46
bear viewing 109, 227
hotels 251
map 227
restaurants 263
Bartlett Cove (Glacier Bay National
Park) 147
Bears 78, 107, **109**
Black bears 28, 109, 135
Brown bears or grizzlies 60, 109,
130, 135, 139, 167, 169, 202, 210–11
Kodiak bears 109, **207**
Polar bears 109, **227**
See also Bear viewing, Wildlife
Bear safety 109
Bear viewing
Anan Creek Wildlife Observatory 9,
109, 126, 135
Arctic National Wildlife Refuge 224
Barrow 109, 227
Brooks Falls (Katmai National Park)
11, 60, 202, 210
Cook Inlet 209
Denali National Park 109, 169
Frazer Lake (Kodiak National
Wildlife Refuge) 207
Karluk Lake (Kodiak National
Wildlife Refuge) 207
King Cove 213
McNeil River State Game Sanctuary
(Katmai National Park) 11, 211
Stan Price State Wildlife Sanctuary
(Admiralty Island) 139
Wonder Lake (Denali National Park)
169
See also Bears, Tours
Beaver Clan House, Saxman Totem
Park (Ketchikan) 61, 129
Bed-and-breakfasts *see* Hotels
Begich-Boggs Visitors' Center, Portage
Lake (Turnagain Arm) 81
Behm Canal (Misty Fjords National
Monument) 163
Beluga Point (Turnagain Arm Tour) 80
Bennett Lake, Canada (Gold Rush
Routes) 152, 153
Benny Benson Memorial (Seward) 98
Bering Glacier 26, 37
Bering Land Bridge National Preserve
235
Bering Sea 101, 198, 216, 217
Bering Strait 12, 50
Bering, Vitus 50
Fraser, Canada (Gold Rush Routes) 153
Big Lake 160
restaurants 261
Birch Creek Access (Steese Highway)
179
Birds 20–21, 30–1, 105, 107, 113, 117,
141, 174, 204, 210, 217, 235
See also Bald eagles, Bird-watching,
Migratory birds, Seabirds, Trumpeter
swans

Bird-watching
  Alaganik Slough (Copper River
    Road) 9, 114, 115, 123
  Copper River Delta *see* Alaganik
    Slough
  Creamer's Field Migratory Waterfowl
    Refuge (Fairbanks) 10, 31, 174
  Gambell 219, 220, 235
  Glacier Bay 30, 146–7
  Izembek National Wildlife Refuge
    213
  Kenai Flats State Recreation Site
    (Kenai) 107
  Kenai National Wildlife Refuge 107
  Nome 11, 219, 220, 233, 234
  Pribilof Islands 11, 30, 216, 217
  Tetlin National Wildlife Refuge 195
  See also Bald eagles, Birds Migratory
    birds, Seabirds, Trumpeter swans
Blackstone Bay (Prince William
  Sound), 114, 116
Blanket toss *see* Inuit blanket toss
Blockhouse and Russian Cemetery
  (Sitka) 141
Bodenburg Butte (Anchorage) **84**
Bore tides 80
Boreal forest 10, 28, **161**
Boxed text
  Alaskan Dishes and Specialities **254–5**
  Alaskan Lexicon 287
  The Arctic Man 182, **185**
  Bald Eagles 16, 30, 31, 135, **149**
  Beluga Whales 71, **80**
  Best Shore Excursions 271
  Bush Flying in Alaska 75
  Copper River and Northwestern
    Railway 123, 181, **187**, 188
  Dialing Codes 286
  Dredging for Gold 137, **178**
  Exxon Valdez Oil Spill 57, 100, 113,
    119, 122
  Fireweed 232
  Forestry in Southeast Alaska 133
  The Great American RV 280, **296–7**
  Green Giants **84**
  Hubbard Glacier **27**, 136–7, 155
  The Inuit Blanket Toss 20, 230, **231**
  Kittiwakes 31, 105, **117**, 217, 235
  Kodiak Bears 109, **207**
  The Last Great Race on Earth 39
  Little Norway 139
  McNeil River State Game Sanctuary
    11, **211**
  Midnight Sun 47
  Mountaineers and Glacier Pilots 162
  No-See-Ums 164
  Old Believers **32**, 108
  Polar Bears 109, **227**
  Rocky Coastlines 29
  Soapy Smith 151
  Tectonic Activity 24
  Totem Poles 21, 22, **129**
  The Trusty Tusty (MV *Tustumena*)
    203, 205, **215**, 290
  The Tusky Pinniped 29, **208**
  Urban Wildlife in Anchorage 71
  What to Pack 269
  Wildfires in Alaska 195
  Wildlife Viewing at Denali 167
  Wild Salmon on Parade 67
  The Wolves of Denali 169
Brooks Camp (Katmai National Park)
  208, 210
Brooks Falls (Katmai National Park)
  11, 202, 203, 210

Brooks Range 11, 223, 224, 225
Brower's Café (Barrow) **227**
Brushkana River (Denali Highway) 165
Bunnell Street Gallery (Homer) 110
The Buried Arch (Nome) 233
Buses 292, 293
Bush flying **75**, 272, 275, 289
Butcher, Susan 175

C

Caines Head State Recreation Area
  (Seward) 99
The Call of the Wild (Service) 53, 200
Camping *see* Hotels
Canoeing 274, 275
  Cross-Island Canoe Route (Admiralty
    Island) 139
  Honker River Canoe Route (Prince
    of Wales Island) 133
  Lynx Lake Loop (Nancy Lake State
    Recreation Area) 160, 274
  Swan Lakes Loop (Kenai National
    Wildlife Refuge) 107, 274
  Swanson River Canoe Route (Kenai
    National Wildlife Refuge) 107
  Tikchik River system 209
  Wood River system 209
  Yukon River 199
  See also Kayaking, Whitewater rafting
Cantwell **164**
Cape Krusenstern National Monument
  231
Captain Cook State Recreation Area **107**
Caribou 28, 29, 16, 107, 167, 169, 215,
  219, 225, 230
  See also Wildlife
Caribou Mountain (Dalton Highway)
  222
Carl E. Wynn Nature Center (Homer)
  111
Carrie M. McLain Museum (Nome) 233
Cars *see* Tours, Travel information
Cassiar Highway 299
Cell phones 286
Central (Steese Highway) 179
Chaplin, Charlie 53
  The Gold Rush 53
Charlie and the Chocolate Factory
  (Dahl) 76
Chatanika (Steese Highway) 174, 179
  hotels 247
  restaurants 261
Chena Hot Springs (Chena River State
  Recreation Area) 10, 158, 177
  hotels 247
Chena River 156, 157, 174, 175, 177
Chena River State Recreation Area
  (Fairbanks) 10, 177
Chicken 10, 182, **196**
Chief Shakes Island (Wrangell) 134
Children
  restaurants 253
  traveling with 269, 280, 281
  See also Children's entertainment
Children's entertainment **91**
  Alaska SeaLife Center (Seward) 9,
    100–1
  H2Oasis (Anchorage) 76
  Reindeer Farm (Anchorage) 84
Childs Glacier (Copper River Highway)
  123
Chilkat Bald Eagle Preserve (Haines)
  149
Chilkat Pass (Haines Cut-Off) 154
Chilkoot Pass (Gold Rush Routes) 152

Chilkoot Trail 9, 52, 152–3
Chitina (Edgerton Highway/McCarthy
  Road) 187
Chugach National Forest (Seward
  Highway) 16, 80
  campgrounds 240, 241
Chugach Range (Anchorage) 8, 61, 63,
  77
Chugach State Park (Anchorage) 8, 63,
  78–9
  Nordic skiing 77
Churches
  Old St. Joseph's Catholic Church
    (Nome) 233
  St. Mark's Mission Church (Nenana)
    173
  See also Russian Orthodox churches
    and cathedrals
Circle (Steese Highway) 10, 179, 198
Clam Gulch **108**
Clan houses 20–21
Clausen Memorial Museum
  (Petersburg) 138
Clearwater Creek Controlled Use Area,
  Denali Highway 165
Climate **46–7**
  best times to visit 278
  seasonal pricing 238
Cold Bay **213**
Coldfoot (Dalton Highway) 222
  hotels 251
  restaurants 263
College Fjord 9, 36, 114, 116, **117**
  See also Cruising tours
Columbia Glacier 61, 114, 115, **117**,
  118, 120–21
  cruises 114, 117
  See also Cruising
Communications and media **286–7**
Consulates 283
Cook Inlet 50, 63, 71
  beluga whales 80
  climate 46
  oil 56, 93, 107
Cook, Captain James 50, 71, 80, 107,
  108, 113
Cooper Landing **96**
  hotels 243
  restaurants 258
Copper Center 10, **184–5**
  hotels 249
  restaurants 262
Copper River and Northwestern
  Railway 123, 181, 184, **187**, 188
Copper River Delta 113, 114, 123
Copper River Highway 9, 114, 123, 274
Copper River, Chitina 192
Cordova 9, 36, 37 114, 181, **122**
  Copper River and Northwestern
    Railway 113, 118, 122
  hotels 244
  restaurants 259
Cordova Historical Museum (Cordova)
  122
Corrington Museum (Skagway) 151
Council Road (Nome) 11, 234
Craig (Prince of Wales Island) 132
  hotels 244–5
  restaurant 259
Creamer's Field Migratory Waterfowl
  Refuge (Fairbanks) 10, **174**
Credit cards 282, 284, 296
Creek Street (Ketchikan) 126, 128–9
The Cremation of Sam McGee
  (Service) 53, 200

Crevasse *see* Glaciers
Cross-Island Canoe Route (Admiralty Island) 139
Crow Pass Crossing (Chugach State Park) 78
Cruising 15, **34–7**, **264–71**
 Alaskan cruise routes **34–7**, 264–5
 best times to go 264
 cabin types and facilities 266
 casinos 268
 choosing a cruise line 264
 cruise lines 265, 267
 dress codes 269
 entertainment and activities 268
 expenses 269, 270
 medical facilities 267
 planning and research 265, 267
 shopping 268
 shore excursions 270–71
 spas 267
 special deals 265
 tours *see* Cruising tours
 traveling alone 266
 traveling with children 269
 what to pack 269
 what's included 265
 See also Outdoor activities, Tours
Cruising tours
 Blackstone Bay 114, 116
 College Fjord 9, 114, 116, 117
 Columbia Glacier 114, 117
 Glacier Bay National Park 146–7
 Gulf of Alaska 15, **36–7**, 264
 Inside Passage 15, 28, **34–5**, 264
 Kenai Fjords National Park 9, 60, 104–5
 Misty Fjords National Monument 130
 See also Cruising
Crystal Lattice (Pfitzenmeier) 63
Currency **284–5**
Cycling and mountain biking **274**, 275
 Hatcher Pass Road (Hatcher Pass) 87
 Tony Knowles Coastal Trail (Anchorage) 74

D

Dahl, Roald 76
 Charlie and the Chocolate Factory 76
Dall sheep 28, 29, 78, 107, 168
 See also Wildlife
Dalton Highway 11, 198, 218, 219, **222–3**
Dawson City, Canada 10, 81, 183, 196, 199, **200–1**
 hotels 249
 map 201
Deadhorse (Prudhoe Bay) 224
 hotels 251
Delta Junction **185**
 hotels 249
 restaurants 262
Dena'ina Athabaskans 93, 96, 106, 111, 113
Denali Highway 158, 165, 274
 traveling by car 296
Denali Highway Tour **165**, 296
Denali National Park 10, 28, 61, 57, 158, 159, **166–9**, 170–71
 campgrounds 240, 241
Denali National Park Headquarters Area (Denali National Park) 168
Denali National Park Road (Denali National Park) 168
Denali State Park 10, 158, **164**
 hotels 247
Denali Park (Denali National Park) **172**
 hotels 247–8
 restaurants 261

Denver (Gold Rush Routes) 153
Diamond Tooth Gertie's (Dawson City) 200
Dillingham 204, **208**
Discovery Pool, Alaska SeaLife Center (Seward) 101
Dogsled races 39
 Iditarod Trail Sled Dog Race **39**, 45, 85, 91, 160, 233
 World Championship Sled Dog Races 39, 45
 Yukon Quest International Sled Dog Race 39, 45
Dogsledding 15, **38–9**, 45, 145, 168
Dolly's House (Ketchikan) 129
Driving tours *see* Tours
Drowned Forest (Turnagain Arm) 81
Dutch Harbor/Unalaska 11, **214–5**
 climate 46
 hotels 250
 map 214
 Russian settlements 50
Dyea (Gold Rush Routes) 152

E

E. L. Patton Yukon Bridge (Dalton Highway) 198, 222
Eagle 10, 182, **197**, 199
 hotels 249
Eagle Historical Society Museum Tour (Eagle) 197
Eagle River Nature Center (Chugach State Park) 8, 79
Eagle's Hall (Skagway) 151
Earthquakes **24–5**
 1964 Good Friday earthquake 56, 63, 66, 70, 81, 98, 118, 122, 206
Eastern Interior Alaska 10, **180–201**
 area map 182–3
 climate 46–7
 getting around 183
 hotels 249–50
 Kennicott **188–9**
 restaurants 262–3
 visitor information centers 279
 Wrangell-St. Elias National Park **192–3**
 Yukon River **198–9**
Ecological concerns in Alaska 16–17
Economy 17
Edgerton Highway/McCarthy Road 10, 182, **187**, 274, 296
Eisenhower, President Dwight D. 55
Eklutna Historical Park (Anchorage) **77**
Eklutna Lake (Chugach State Park) 79
El Capitan Cave (Prince of Wales Island) 133
El Dorado Gold Mine (Fairbanks) 178
Eldred Rock Lighthouse, Lynn Canal (Haines) 148
Elliott Highway 10, 158, 178, 296
Emergencies 282, 283
Encounter Tours, Alaska Sealife Center (Seward) 100
Endicott Oil Production Island, Prudhoe Bay 56
Erie Mine Bunkhouse (Kennicott) 190–91
Eskimos *see* Inuit
Ester **173**
Etiquette 281
Exit Glacier (Seward) 99, 105
Exxon Valdez oil spill 57, 100, 113, **119**, 122

F

Fairbanks 8, 10, 12, 158, **174–8**
 aurora borealis 176

Fairbanks (cont.)
 climate 47
 headquarters of Trans-Alaska Pipeline 157
 hotels 248
 maps 174–5, 177
 restaurants 262
Fairbanks North Star Borough 177
Fairbanks Ice Museum (Fairbanks) 174
Fairs and festivals **42–5**
Fairview Inn (Talkeetna) 163
Fairweather Range (Glacier Bay National Park) 146
Ferries *see* Alaska Marine Highway
Finger Mountain (Dalton Highway) 222
Fisherman's Memorial (Cordova) 113, 122
Fishing **40–41**
 Alaskan sportfish 41
 charters 40
 combat fishing 41, 94, 96
 commercial 17
 deep-sea fishing 41, 93
 derbies 43, 74, 99
 dipnetting 40
 fly fishing 19, 40
 licenses 41, 74, 108, 278
 best fishing sites 41
 subsistence fishing 19, 23, 213, 226
Fjords 8, **26–7**
 Blackstone Bay 116
 College Fjord 9, 36, 117
 Glacier Bay National Park 146–7
 Kenai Fjords National Park 104–5
 Lynn Canal (Haines) 148
 Misty Fjords National Monument 9, 130
 Russell Fjord (Yakutat) 27, 155
 Tracy Arm (Inside Passage) 34
 Turnagain Arm (Anchorage) 80–81
Flattop Mountain (Chugach State Park) 78
Floatplanes 8, 75, 272, 275, 289
Food and drink
 Alaskan specialities **254–5**
 beer and wine 255
 Native food 255
 shopping 89
 vegetables and fruits 255
 vegetarian food 253
 See also Restaurants
Forests
 boreal 10, 28, **161**
 fires 160, **283**
 forestry **133**
 temperate rainforest 28, **131**
 See also Chugach National Forest, Tongass National Forest
Fort Abercrombie State Historical Park (Kodiak) 207
Fort Egbert (Eagle) 118, 197
Fort Seward (Haines) 148
Fox (Steese Highway) 179
Franklin Bluffs, Sagavanirktok River 223
Frederick Sound (Inside Passage) 35
Fur seals *see* Seals

G

Gambell, St. Lawrence Island **235**
Gastineau Channel 142, 143, 144
Gates of the Arctic National Park 57, 219, **224**
Gathering of the Eagles, Chilkat Bald Eagle Preserve (Haines) 149
Genet, Ray 162, 163
Giant vegetables (Matanuska-Susitna Valley) 8, **84**, 255
Gilahina Trestle 187

Girdwood (Anchorage) 81
  hotels 243
  restaurants 257
Glacier Bay National Park 9, 34, 125, 127, **146–7**, 155
  hotels 245
Glacier Gardens (Juneau) 144
Glacier pilots **162**
Glaciers **26–7**
  Aialik (Kenai Fjords National Park) 26, 105
  Beloit (Blackstone Bay) 116
  Bering Glacier 26, 37
  Blackstone (Blackstone Bay) 116
  Byron (Turnagain Arm) 81
  Childs (Copper River Road) 26, 123
  Columbia (Prince William Sound) 26, 61, 114, 115, 117, 120–21
  crevasse 26
  Eklutna (Chugach State Park) 26, 79
  Exit (Seward) 26, 99
  Grand Pacific (Glacier Bay National Park) 146
  hanging glacier 27, 117
  Holgate (Kenai Fjords National Park) 104, 105
  Hubbard 26, 27, 136–7, 155
  icefield see Icefields
  Kahiltna (Denali National Park) 162
  Kennicott 10, 188
  Knik (Anchorage) 84
  lateral moraine 26
  Malaspina (Yakutat) 26, 37, 155
  map 26
  Margerie (Glacier Bay National Park) 146
  Matanuska 26, 184
  medial moraine 27
  Mendenhall (Juneau) 26, 145
  Miles (Copper River Road) 123
  moulin 27
  Muldrow (Denali National Park) 162, 169
  Northland (Blackstone Bay) 116
  nunatak 27, 104
  outlet glacier 26
  Portage (Turnagain Arm) 8, 26, 81
  Raven (Anchorage) 79, 81
  Salmon (Hyder) 130
  Shakes (Wrangell) 135
  Sheridan (Copper River Road) 123
  Susitna (Denali Highway Tour) 165
  Taku (Juneau Icefield) 145
  tidewater glacier 9, 26, 27, 104, 114, 116, 146–7
  Whittier (Whittier) 116
  Worthington (Valdez) 9, 119
  Yakutat (Yakutat) 155
  valley glacier 27, 117
Glenn Highway 65, 77, 184, 194
  hotels 249
Glennallen **184**, 194
  hotels 249
Gold dredging 157, **178**
  Gold Dredge No. 3 (Steese Highway) 179
  Gold Dredge No. 4 (Dawson City) 201
  Gold Dredge No. 8 (Old Steese Highway) 178, 179
  Jack Wade Dredge No. 1 (Taylor Highway) 196
  Pedro Creek Dredge (Chicken) 196
Gold, discovery of
  Chatanika 174
  Dawson City, Canada 200
  Fortymile River 196
  Hope 93

Gold, discovery of (cont.)
  Juneau 52, 54, 125, 126, 142
  Klondike **52–3**, 54, 150, 181, 196
  Nome 52, 233
  Talkeetna Mountains 86, 160
Gold mining 157, 181, 196
  El Dorado Gold Mine (Fairbanks) 178
  Independence Mine State Historical Park (Anchorage) 86–7
  Klondike see Gold Rush, Klondike
  tools 53
Gold panning 52–3, 178, 196, 201, 233
Gold Rush 8, 16, **52–3**, 54, 96, 150, 181, 196, 197
  discovery of gold see Gold, discovery of
  dredging see Gold dredging
  Klondike 8, **52–3**, 54, 150, 181, 196, 197
  literature 53
  routes 9, 52, **152–3**
  towns see Gold Rush towns
  women travelers 53
  See also Service, Robert
Gold Rush towns 181
  Central (Steese Highway) 179
  Chicken 10, 196
  Cooper Landing 96
  Cordova 122
  Council (Nome) 234
  Dawson City, Canada 10, 181, 200–201
  Dyea (Gold Rush Routes) 152
  Eagle 10, 197
  Ester 173
  Hope 96
  Lindeman (Gold Rush Routes) 152
  Nome 11, 233
  Skagway 150–51
  Whitehorse, Canada 199
  Willow 160
The Gold Rush (Chaplin) 53
Golden Heart Plaza (Fairbanks) 174
The Goldfields (Dawson City) 201
Government and politics 17–18
Great Alaskan Lumberjack Show (Ketchikan) 128
Gulf of Alaska 15, **36–7**, 264
Gustavus (Glacier Bay National Park) 147
  hotels 245

H

H2Oasis (Anchorage) **76**
Haida 21, 22, 49, 125, 129, 132, 133
  See also Totem poles
Haines 34, **148**
  hotels 245
  restaurants 259
Haines Cut-off Tour **154**
Haines Highway see Haines Cut-Off Tour
Haines Junction (Haines Cut-Off) 154
Halibut Cove (Homer) 111
  restaurants 258
Hammer Museum (Haines) 149
Hammer Slough (Petersburg) 138
Hanging glacier see Glaciers
Harbor seals see Seals
Harding Icefield (Kenai Fjords National Park) 27, 94, 99, 105
Harding, President Warren G. 173, 175
Harriman Expedition 113, 117
Harriman Fjord (College Fjord) 117
Hatcher Pass (Anchorage) **87**
Haul Road see Dalton Highway
Hazelwood, Captain Joseph 119

Healy **172–3**
Heli-skiing 273, 275
Hiking **272**, 275
  Alpine Loop Trail (Juneau) 143
  Battery Point Trail (Haines) 149
  Bodenburg Butte (Anchorage) 84
  Chilkoot Trail 9, 152–3
  Devil's Pass Trail 97
  East Glacier Loop, Mendenhall Glacier (Juneau) 145
  Edge Nature Trail (Matanuska Glacier) 184
  Exit Glacier (Seward) 99
  Eyak River Trail (Copper River Road) **123**
  Gold Mint Trail (Hatcher Pass) 87
  Gull Rock Trail (Hope) 96
  Johnson Pass Trail (Moose Pass) 96
  Kincaid Park (Anchorage) 75
  Kupreanof Island (Petersburg) 138
  Lowenfels Family Nature Trail (Alaska Botanical Garden) 77
  Mitkof Island (Petersburg) 138
  Moraine Ecology Trail, Mendenhall Glacier (Juneau) 145
  Mount Riley Trail (Haines) 148, 149
  Mount Ripinsky Trail (Haines) 148, 149
  Mount Roberts (Juneau) 143
  Photo Point Trail, Mendenhall Glacier (Juneau) 145
  Pinnell Mountain Trail (Steese Highway) 179
  Resurrection Pass Trail 9, 94, 96, 97
  Ridge Trail (Valdez) 119
  Sheridan Ridge Trail (Copper River Road) 123
  Thunderbird Falls (Eklutna) 77
  Tony Knowles Coastal Trail (Anchorage) 8, 74–5
  Ugadaga Pass (Dutch Harbor/Unalaska) 215
  West Glacier Trail, Mendenhall Glacier (Juneau) 145
  See also Historical Parks and Historic Sites; National and State Refuges; National Monuments; National Parks; National Preserves; State Parks; State Recreation Areas; State Sanctuaries
Hilltop Ski Area (Anchorage) **76–7**
Historical Parks and Historic Sites
  Aleutian World War II National Historical Park (Dutch Harbor/Unalaska) 215
  Big Delta State Historical Park (Delta Junction) 185
  Eklutna Historical Park (Anchorage) 77
  Fort Abercrombie State Historical Park (Kodiak) 207
  Independence Mine State Historical Park (Anchorage) 86–7
  Klondike Gold Rush National Historical Park (Skagway) 150
  Petroglyph Beach State Historic Site (Wrangell) 135
  Sitka National Historical Park (Sitka) 141
  Totem Bight State Historical Park (Ketchikan) 129
  Wickersham State Historical Site (Juneau) 143
  See also National and State Refuges; National Monuments; National Parks; National Preserves; State Parks; State Recreation Areas; State Sanctuaries

History **48–57**
Gold Rush **52–3**
Hitchcock, Mary
Holy Assumption of the Virgin Mary
Russian Orthodox Church (Kenai)
33, 106, 107
Holy Resurrection Russian Orthodox
Church (Kodiak) 11, 206
Homer 9, 93, 94, **110–11**
climate 47
hotels 243
restaurants 258
Homer Spit (Homer) 110, 111
Hoonah (Inside Passage) 34
Hope **96**, 97
discovery of gold 93
restaurants 258
Horseshoe Lake (Denali National Park)
160
Hospitals 282, 283
Hotels **238–51**
Anchorage 242–3
Arctic and Western Interior Alaska
251
camping 240, 241
Eastern Interior Alaska 249–50
Kenai Peninsula 243–4
Prince William Sound 244
prices, seasonal 238
public use cabins 240, 241
roadhouses 241
RV parks 239
smoking 279
Southeast Alaska 244
Southwest Alaska, 250–51
taxes and tipping 279
types 238–41
Western Interior Alaska 247–9
wilderness lodges 241
Hot springs
Chena Hot Springs (Chena River
State Recreation Area) 10, 158, 177
Chief Shakes Hot Springs (Wrangell)
135
Manley Hot Springs (Elliott
Highway) 10, 178
Pilgrim Hot Springs, Kougarok Road
(Nome) 11, 234
Serpentine Hot Springs (Bering Land
Bridge National Preserve) 235
Tenakee Springs 139
Tolovana Hot Springs (Elliott
Highway) 178
Houston **160**
Hubbard Glacier **27**, 37, 136–7, 155
Hurricane Gulch 164, 294
Hydaburg (Prince of Wales Island) 133
Hyder **130**

I
Icefields 27, 29
Bagley 27
Harding 27, 94, 99, 105
Juneau 27, 126, 145
Icy Bay (Gulf of Alaska) 37
Iditarod Trail Sled Dog Race **39**, 45,
85, 91, 160, 233
Igloo, Parks Highway 164
Ilanka Cultural Center (Cordova)
122
Imaginarium (Anchorage) 66, 91
Independence Mine State Historical
Park (Anchorage) **86–7**
Indigenous peoples of Alaska **22–3**
See also Native Alaskans
Inside Passage 15, 28, **34–5**, 264
Into the Wild (Krakauer) 173
Inuit *see* Aleut, Aluttiq, Inupiat, Yup'ik

Inuit blanket toss 20, 230, **231**
See also Native art, craft, and culture
Inupiat 11, 20, 21, 23, 219, 220, 226
village site, Alaska Native Heritage
Center (Anchorage) 73
Inupiat Heritage Center (Barrow) 226
Isabel Miller Museum (Sitka) 140
Izembek National Wildlife Refuge **213**

J
Jack London Cabin (Dawson City) 201
Jack Wade Dredge No. 1 196
Japan, invasion of Alaska 55, 157
Johnson, President Andrew 51
Juneau 8, 9, 18, 34, 54, **142–5**
climate 47
discovery of gold 52, 54, 125, 126
hotels 245–6
maps 142–3, 144
restaurants 260
Juneau Creek Falls (Resurrection Pass
Trail) 97
Juneau Icefield (Juneau) 27, 126, 145
Juneau, Joe 142

K
Kachemak Bay State Park (Homer) 9,
110, 111
Kantishna (Denali National Park) 169
hotels 248
Kantishna Roadhouse 169
Kasaan (Prince of Wales Island) 133
Kathleen Lake (Haines Cut-Off) 154
Katmai National Park 11, 57, 60, 203,
210–11
hotels 250
Kayaking 9, 274, 275
Blackstone Bay 116
Glacier Bay National Park 146–7
Kenai Fjords National Park (Seward)
60, 104–5
Kenai River 96
Kupreanof Island (Petersburg) 138
Misty Fjords National Monument
130
Mitkof Island (Petersburg) 138
ocean kayaking 9, 274, 275
Prince William Sound 9
Tangle Lakes (Denali Highway) 165
Walker Lake 220
Whittier 116
See also Canoeing, Whitewater
rafting
Kenai 9, 93, 94, **106–7**
Kenai Fjords National Park 9, 57, 60,
93, 94, 99, **104–5**
Information Center (Seward) 98, 105
Kenai Landing (Kenai) 107
Kenai Mountains 93, 102–3, 105
Kenai National Wildlife Refuge **107**,
195
Kenai Peninsula 8, 9, 12, **92–111**
Alaska SeaLife Center (Seward)
100–1
area map 94–5
climate 46–7
getting around 94
hotels 243–4
Kenai Fjords National Park *see* Kenai
Fjords National Park
restaurants 258–9
Resurrection Pass Trail **97**
visitor information centers 279
Kenai River 8, 93, **96**, 106
fishing 19, 44, 94, 96
Kennicott (Wrangell-St. Elias National
Park) 10, 61, 122, 181, 182, **188–9**,
190–91, 193

Kennicott (Wrangell-St. Elias National
Park) (cont.)
hotels 250
restaurants 263
Kent, Rockwell 98
Ketchikan 9, 34, 35, 125, 126, **128–9**
hotels 246
restaurant 260
Keystone Canyon (Valdez) 9, **119**
King Cove 204, **213**
King Salmon **208**
Kittiwakes 31, 105, 113, **117**, 217, 235
Klawock (Prince of Wales Island) 132
Klondike Gold Rush *see* Gold Rush
Klondike Gold Rush NHP Visitors'
Center (Skagway) 150
Klondike Highway 152
Klukshu Village (Haines Cut-Off) 154,
155
Kobuk Valley National Park 230–31
Kodiak 11, 203, 204, **206–7**
hotels 250–51
restaurants 263
Kodiak bears 109, **207**
See also Bears, Bear viewing
Katmai National Park 207, **210–11**
Kodiak National Wildlife Refuge
(Kodiak) 11, 207
Kotzebue 11, 220, **230**
hotels 251
Kougarok Road (Nome) 11, 234
Krakauer, Jon 173
Into the Wild
Kuskulana Bridge 187

L
Lake Clark National Park **209**
Lake Hood (Anchorage) 8, **75**
Lake Louise State Recreation Area **184**
Lake Spenard (Anchorage) 8, **75**
Landscape 16, **28–9**
arctic tundra 29, **225**
boreal forest 10, 28, **161**
icefields 26–7, 29
taiga 28
temperate rainforest 28, **131**
The Last Blue Whale (Princiotta) 71
Last Chance Mining Museum (Juneau)
143
Last Train to Nowhere (Nome) 11, 234
Lateral moraine *see* Glaciers
Laurence, Sydney 68, 122
Mount McKinley 68
Licenses, hunting and fishing 278
Lindeman (Gold Rush Routes) 152
Little Norway **139**
See also Petersburg
Log Cabin Visitor Information Center
(Anchorage) 64, 66, 70
Lynn Canal (Haines) 148

M
Mail service 286
Manley Hot Springs (Elliott Highway)
10, 178
hotels 248
restaurants 262
Manley Roadhouse, Manley Hot
Springs (Elliott Highway) 178
Maps
Alaska at a Glance 60–61
Alaska Highway 299
Alaska Marine Highway 291
Alaska Railroad 295
Aleutian Islands 13, 204
Anchorage 64–5
Anchorage, downtown (street-by-
street) 66–7

Maps (cont.)
  Arctic and Western Alaska 220–21
  Barrow 227
  Fairbanks 174–5
  Fairbanks, beyond 177
  Chugach State Park 78–9
  climate zones 46–7
  Dalton Highway Tour 222–3
  Dawson City 201
  Denali Highway Tour 165
  Denali National Park 166–7
  Dutch Harbor/Unalaska 214
  Eastern Interior Alaska 182–3
  Fairbanks 174–5
  Fairbanks, beyond 177
  Glacier Bay National Park 146–7
  glaciers 26
  Gold Rush Routes 152–3
  Gold Rush territory 52
  Gulf Route 36–7
  Haines Cut-Off Tour 154
  Independence Mine site plan 87
  indigenous peoples 22
  Inside Passage 34–5
  Juneau 142–3
  Juneau, beyond 144
  Katmai National Park 210–11
  Kenai Fjords National Park 104–5
  Kenai Peninsula 94–5
  Kennicott site plan 189
  Nome, beyond 234
  orientation 12–13
  Pribilof Islands 216
  Prince of Wales Island 132
  Prince William Sound 114–15
  Resurrection Pass Trail 97
  Seward 99
  Sitka 140–1
  Skagway (street-by-street) 150–51
  Southeast Alaska 126–7
  Southwest Alaska 204–5
  Steese Highway Tour 179
  Trans-Alaska Pipeline 186
  Transport Map of Alaska inside back cover
  Turnagain Arm Tour 80–81
  volcanoes 24–5
  Western Interior Alaska 158–9
  Wrangell-St. Elias National Park 192–3
  Yukon River 198–9
Margerie Glacier (Glacier Bay National Park) 146
Marine wildlife 9, 28, 29
  See also Seals, Sea otters, Walruses, Whales
Markets 88, 89
Matanuska Colony (Palmer) 54, 84
Matanuska Glacier **184**
Matanuska River 81, 82–3, 84
Matanuska-Susitna Valley 8, 84, 160
  giant vegetables 84, 255
McCandless, Chris 173
McCarthy (Edgerton Highway/ McCarthy Road) 10, 187, 193
  hotels 250
  restaurants 263
McCarthy Road see Edgerton Highway/ McCarthy Road
McCauley Salmon Hatchery (Juneau) 144
McKinley River 169, 170–71
McLaren Summit (Denali Highway) 165
McNeil River State Game Sanctuary 11, **211**
Medial moraine see Glaciers

Mendenhall Glacier (Juneau) 26, 145
Metlakatla 23, **130**
Midnight sun **47**, 226
Migratory birds 9, 30–31
  Copper River Delta 113, 114, 123
  Izembek National Wildlife Refuge 213
  Kenai National Wildlife Refuge 107
  Tetlin National Wildlife Refuge 195
Million Dollar Bridge (Copper River Road) 114, 123
Million Dollar Falls (Haines Cut-Off) 154
Misty Fiords National Monument 9, 35, 126, **130**
Mitkof Highway **138–9**
The Mitre (Chugach State Park) 79
Moore Cabin (Skagway) 151
Moose 28, 75, 167, 298
  See also Wildlife, Wildlife viewing
Moose Pass **96**
  restaurants 258
Mosquito Lake (Haines Cut-Off) 154
Moulin see Glaciers
Mountaineering **273**, 275
Mount Ballyhoo (Dutch Harbor/ Unalaska) 215
Mount Douglas (Katmai National Park) 211
Mount Katmai (Katmai National Park) 211
Mount McKinley (Denali National Park) 10, 61, 157, 158, 166, 169, 170–71
  climbing 162, 273, **275**
  flightseeing 159, 162, 274, 275
Mount McKinley (Laurence) 61
Mount Ripinsky (Haines) 148, 149
Mount Roberts Tramway (Juneau) 143
Mount Wrangell (Wrangell-St. Elias National Park) 192
Muldrow Glacier (Denali National Park) 169
Museum of the Aleutians (Dutch Harbor/Unalaska) 11, 214
Museums
  Alaska Pioneer Museum (Pioneer Park, Fairbanks) 175
  Alaska State Museum (Juneau) 142
  Alaska State Troopers Museum (Anchorage) 67, 70
  Alaska Railroad Museum (Nenana) 173
  Alutiiq Museum (Kodiak) 206
  Anchorage Museum (Anchorage) 8, 64, 67, 68–9
  Aurora Ice Museum (Chena Hot Springs) 177
  Baranov Museum (Kodiak) 206
  Carrie M. McLain Museum (Nome) 233
  Clausen Memorial Museum (Petersburg) 138
  Colony House Museum (Palmer) 84
  Copper Center Museum (Copper Center) 184
  Cordova Historical Museum (Cordova) 122
  Corrington Museum (Skagway) 151
  Dolly's House, Creek Street (Ketchikan) 129
  Dorothy Page Museum (Wasilla) 85
  Duncan Cottage Museum (Metlakatla) 130
  Eagle Historical Society Museum (Eagle) 197
  Fairbanks Ice Museum (Fairbanks) 174

Museums (cont.)
  Hammer Museum (Haines) 149
  Heritage House Museum (Eklutna Historical Park) 77
  Isabel Miller Museum (Sitka) 140
  Knik Museum and Musher's Hall of Fame (Wasilla) 85
  Kodiak Military History Museum (Fort Abercrombie State Historical Park) 207
  Last Chance Mining Museum (Juneau) 143
  McCarthy-Kennicott Museum (McCarthy) 187
  Museum of Alaska Transportation and Industry (Wasilla) 85
  Museum of the Aleutians (Dutch Harbor/Unalaska) 11, 214
  Native Village Museum (Pioneer Park, Fairbanks) 175
  Ootukahkuktuvik Museum (Kotzebue) 230
  Pioneer Park Air Museum (Pioneer Park, Fairbanks) 175
  Pratt Museum (Homer) 110
  Russian Orthodox Museum (Anchorage) 67, 69
  Sam Fox Museum (Dillingham) 208
  Seward Museum (Seward) 98–9
  Sheldon Jackson Museum (Sitka) 140
  Sheldon Museum (Haines) 148
  Skagway Museum (Skagway) 151
  Soldotna Historical Society Museum (Soldotna) 106
  Southeast Alaska Discovery Center (Ketchikan) 128
  Sullivan Roadhouse Museum (Delta Junction) 185
  Talkeetna Historical Society Museum (Talkeetna) 162–3
  University of Alaska Fairbanks Museum of the North (Fairbanks) 10, 175
  Valdez Museum (Valdez) 118
  Village Tribe Museum and Visitors' Center (Seldovia, Homer) 111
  Whitney Museum (Valdez) 118
  Wrangell Museum (Wrangell) 134
Mushing see Dogsledding
Musk ox 6, 11, 29, 85, 219, 225
Musk Ox Farm (Palmer) 85
Muskeg Meadows Golf Course (Wrangell) 135

N

Nabesna Road (Wrangell-St. Elias National Park) 193, 194
Nagley's Store (Talkeetna) 163
Naknek Lake (Katmai National Park) 11, 210
Nancy Lake State Recreation Area 158, **160**
National Forests
  cabin and campground reservations 240, 241
  Chugach 16, 80
  Tongass 126, 128, 131, 132, 133, 139, 144
National and State Refuges
  Anchorage Coastal Wildlife Refuge (Anchorage) 80
  Arctic National Wildlife Refuge 16, 57, 219, 220, 224
  Creamer's Field Migratory Waterfowl Refuge (Fairbanks) 10, 31, 174
  Izembek National Wildlife Refuge 213
  Kenai National Wildlife Refuge 107

National and State Refuges (cont.)
  Kodiak National Wildlife Refuge
    (Kodiak) 11, 207
  Tetlin National Wildlife Refuge 10,
    194, 195
  Togiak National Wildlife Refuge
    208
  See also Historical Parks and Historic
    Sites; National Monuments; National
    Parks; National Preserves; State
    Parks; State Recreation Areas; State
    Sanctuaries
National Monuments
  Admiralty Island National Monument
    126, 139
  Aniakchak National Monument 11,
    204, 212
  Cape Krusenstern National
    Monument 231
  Misty Fjords National Monument 9,
    126, 130
  See also Historical Parks and Historic
    Sites; National and State Refuges;
    National Parks; National Preserves;
    State Parks; State Recreation Areas;
    State Sanctuaries
National Parks
  creation under ANILCA 57
  Denali National Park 10, 61, 157,
    158, 159, **166–9**
  Gates of the Arctic National Park 57,
    219, 224
  Glacier Bay National Park 9, 125,
    126, 127, **146–7**
  Katmai National Park 11, 60,
    210–11
  Kenai Fjords National Park 9, 57, 60,
    93, 94, 99, **104–5**
  Kluane National Park, Canada 154,
    155, 298
  Kobuk Valley National Park 230–31
  Lake Clark National Park 209
  Wrangell-St. Elias National Park 10,
    57, 61, 155, 181, 183, 187, **192–3**
  See also Historical Parks and Historic
    Sites; National and State Refuges;
    National Monuments; National
    Preserves; State Parks; State
    Recreation Areas; State Sanctuaries
National Preserves
  Bering Land Bridge National
    Preserve 235
  Noatak National Preserve 231
  Yukon-Charley Rivers National
    Preserve 10, 196, 198
  See also Historical Parks and Historic
    Sites; National and State Refuges;
    National Monuments; National
    Parks; State Parks; State Recreation
    Areas; State Sanctuaries
Native Alaskans 16, 19, **22–3**, 72–3
  Aleut *see* Aleut
  Alutiiq *see* Alutiiq
  Athabaskan *see* Athabaskans
  compensation through ANCSA 56–7
  Eyak 113, 122
  Haida *see* Haida
  Inuit *see* Aleut, Alutiiq, Inupiat,
    Yup'ik
  Inupiat *see* Inupiat
  Kenaitze 93
  subsistence fishing and hunting 19,
    23, 213, 226
  Tlingit *see* Tlingit
  Tr'ondëk Hwëch'in 200
  Tsimshian *see* Tsimshian
  Yup'ik *see* Yup'ik
  See also Native art, craft, and culture

Native art, craft, and culture **20–21**
  Alaska Native Heritage Center
    (Anchorage) 8, 15, 18, 72–3, 88, 90
  Alaska State Museum (Juneau) 142
  Alutiiq Museum (Kodiak) 11, 206
  Anchorage Museum of History and
    Art (Anchorage) 8, 62, 67, 68–9
  Beaver Clan House, Saxman Totem
    Park (Ketchikan) 61
  blanket toss 20, 230, 231
  clan houses 20–21, 61, 130
  Doyon Building, Golden Heart Plaza
    (Fairbanks) 174
  Eklutna Historical Park (Anchorage)
    77
  Inupiat Heritage Center (Barrow)
    226
  Ilanka Cultural Center (Cordova) 122
  K'Beq Kenaitze Footprints Heritage
    Site (Cooper Landing) 96
  Ketchikan 128–9
  Kotzebue 230
  Museum of the Aleutians (Dutch
    Harbor/Unalaska) 11, 214
  Native art and craft shops 88, 89
  Native Village Museum (Pioneer
    Park, Fairbanks) 175
  Prince of Wales Island 132–3
  Sitka 140–41
  Tr'ondëk Hwëch'in Dänojà Zho
    Cultural Center (Dawson City) 200
  Whitney Museum (Valdez) 118
  See also Native Alaskans, Totem
    poles
Nenana River 10, 158, 167, **172**, 173
Nenana 172, **173**
  restaurant 262
New Archangel Dancers 32, 140
Newspapers 90–91, 287
Nikolaevsk 9, **108**
  restaurants 258
Ninilchik 93, **108**
Noatak National Preserve **231**
Nome 11, 220, **233, 234**
  discovery of gold 52, 54, 200, 219
  hotels 251
  map 234
Nordic skiing 157, 273, 275
  Chena River State Recreation Area
    (Fairbanks) 177
  Chugach State Park (Anchorage) 77
  Hatcher Pass (Anchorage) 87
  Kincaid Park (Anchorage) 75
  Lowenfels Family Nature Trail
    (Alaska Botanical Garden) 77
  Nancy Lake State Recreation Area
    160
  See also Skiing
North Pole (Fairbanks) 177
Northern fur seals *see* Seals
Northern Lights *see* Aurora borealis
Northway **195**
Novarupta (Katmai National Park) 25,
  206, 208, 210, **211**
Nunatak *see* Glaciers

O

Ocean kayaking 9, **274**, 275
  See also Canoeing, Kayaking,
    Whitewater rafting
Oceans and Islands Visitors' Center
  (Homer) 94
Oil
  Arctic National Wildlife Refuge 224
  Cook Inlet 93
  discovery of oil 16, 17, 56
  ecological impact 16, 57
  Kenai 106

Oil (cont.)
  Prudhoe Bay 11, 17, 56, 181, 186,
    224
  See also Trans-Alaska Pipeline
Old Believers **32**, 108
Old St. Joseph's Catholic Church
  (Nome) 233
Oscar Anderson House (Anchorage)
  71
Outdoor activities **272–5**
Outdoor hazards 283
Outlet glaciers *see* Glaciers

P

Page, Dorothy 85
Palace Grand Theater (Dawson City)
  200
Palmer (Anchorage) 54, **84**
  restaurants 257
Paragliding and parasailing
  Bodenburg Butte (Anchorage) 84
  Hatcher Pass (Anchorage) 87
  Mount Alyeska 81
Parks
  Earthquake Park (Anchorage) 74
  Elderberry Park (Anchorage) 74
  Glacier Gardens (Juneau) 144
  H2Oasis (Anchorage) 76
  Kincaid Park (Anchorage) 75
  Resolution Park (Anchorage) 64, 71
  See also Historical Parks; National
    and State Refuges; National
    Monuments; National Parks;
    National Preserves; State Parks; State
    Sanctuaries; Recreation Areas
Parks Highway 85, 160, 162, 165
Paxson 182, **185**
People and society 18–19
Personal security **282**
Petersburg 9, 34, 35, 125, **138**
  hotels 246
  restaurants 260
Petroglyph Beach State Historic Site
  (Wrangell) 135
Pfitzenmeier, Robert 63
  Crystal Lattice 63
Pinnell Mountain Trail (Steese
  Highway) 179
Pioneer Park (Fairbanks) 175
Point Barrow (Barrow) 227
Polar Bears 109, **227**
  See also Bears, Bear viewing
Polychrome Pass (Denali National
  Park) 167, 168
Portage Glacier (Turnagain Arm) 8, 26,
  81
Pratt Museum (Homer) 110
Pribilof Islands 11, 29, 203, 204, **216–7**
Prince of Wales Island (Southeast
  Alaska) 9, 126, **132–3**
  hotels 246
Prince William Sound 9, 36, **112–23**,
  120–21
  area map 114–15
  climate 46–7
  Exxon Valdez oil spill 113
  getting around 114
  hotels 244
  restaurants 259
  visitor information centers 279
Prince William Sound Science Center
  (Cordova) 122
Princiotta, Josef 71
  The Last Blue Whale
Prudhoe Bay (Arctic and Western
  Alaska) 11, 220, **224**
  oilfields 11, 16, 56, 181, 186, 224
  tour 224

Public holidays 45
Public use cabins *see* Hotels
Purdy, Anne 196
  Tisha 196

Q

Qiviut 29, 85, 88

R

Rafting *see* Whitewater rafting
Recreation.gov 240, 241
Red Dog Saloon (Juneau) 143
Red "Fox" Olson Trail Monument *see* Burled Arch (Nome)
Red Onion Saloon (Skagway) 150
Redington, Joe 39, 85
Reindeer Farm (Anchorage) 84
Resolution Park (Anchorage) 64, **71**
Restaurants
  Anchorage 256–8
  Arctic and Western Alaska 263
  children 253
  dress codes 253
  Eastern Interior Alaska 262–3
  Kenai Peninsula 258–9
  meals 253
  Prince William Sound 259
  reservations 252
  smoking 279
  Southeast Alaska 259–61
  Southwest Alaska 263
  tipping and prices 253, 279
  types of restaurants 252
  vegetarian food 253
  Western Interior Alaska 261–62
  See also Food and drink
Resurrection Pass Trail 8–9, 94, 96, **97**
Resurrection River 14, 15
Richardson Highway 119, 181, 184, 187
Rika's Roadhouse (Delta Junction) 185
Riverboat Discovery Cruise (Fairbanks) 10, 156, 175
Robert Service Cabin (Dawson City) 200–1
Roosevelt, President Franklin D. 207
  New Deal 54, 84
Rosemaling 138
Russia 12, 16
  colonization of Alaska 15, 32, 50–51, 106
  demand for seal and sea otter pelts 16, 50, 51, 140, 203, 214
  Dutch Harbor/Unalaska 214
  Kodiak 50, 206
  Pribilof Islands 216
  sale of Alaska 51
  Sitka 140
  Southeast Alaska 125
  Southwest Alaska 203
  Yakutat 155
  Wrangell 13
  See also Russian culture in Alaska, Russian Orthodox Churches and Cathedrals
Russian-American Company 32, 50, 51, 134, 155
Russian Bishop's House (Sitka) 33, 141
Russian culture in Alaska **32–3**
  Anchorage 69, 71, 74
  Kenai Peninsula 92–111
  Nikolaevsk 93, 108
  Ninilchik 93, 108
  Seldovia 93, 111
  Baranov Museum (Kodiak) 11, 206
  Sitka 9, 140–41

Russian culture in Alaska (cont.)
  Russian Orthodox Museum (Anchorage) 67, 69
  See also Russia, Russian Orthodox Churches and Cathedrals
Russian Orthodox Churches and Cathedrals **32–3**, 203
  Church of the Holy Ascension (Dutch Harbor/Unalaska) 203, 214
  Holy Assumption of the Virgin Mary Russian Orthodox Church (Kenai) 33, 106, 107
  Holy Resurrection Russian Orthodox Church (Kodiak) 11, 206
  interiors 33
  Russian Orthodox Church (King Cove) 213
  Russian Orthodox Church (Nikolaevsk) 108
  Russian Orthodox Church (Sand Point) 212
  Russian Orthodox Church, Tatitlek 112
  Russian Orthodox Church of St. George the Martyr (Pribilof Islands) 216
  St. Herman's Theological Seminary (Kodiak) 33, 206
  St. Innocent Russian Orthodox Cathedral (Anchorage) 15, 61, 74
  St. Michael's Russian Orthodox Cathedral (Sitka) 33, 140
  St. Nicholas Russian Orthodox Church (Eklutna, Anchorage) 33, 77
  St. Nicholas Russian Orthodox Church (Juneau) 33
  St. Nicholas Russian Orthodox Church, Seldovia (Homer) 111
  St. Peter and Paul Russian Orthodox Church (Pribilof Islands) 216
  Transfiguration of our Lord Russian Orthodox Church (Ninilchik) 95, 108
Russian Orthodox clergy, arrival in Alaska 15, 77
  See also Old Believers
Russian Orthodox Museum (Anchorage) 67, **69**
Russian heritage gifts 88
RVs 280, **296–7**
  driving the Alaska Highway 298–9
  renting 284, 296, 297
  RV parks 239
  weather and route information 297

S

Salmon 17, 41, 78, 79, 130, 207, 209
  derbies 43, 74, 99
  Ship Creek Salmon Viewing Platform (Anchorage) 74
  See also Salmon fishing, Salmon runs
Salmon canneries
  Dillingham 208
  Ketchikan 128
  King Cove 213
  Klawock 132
Salmon fishing 40, 41
  Anchor River (Anchor Point) 108
  Bristol Bay 41
  Cordova 122
  Deep Creek (Ninilchik) 108
  Kenai River 96
  Ninilchik River (Ninilchik) 108
  Seward 98
  Sterling 106
Salmon runs
  Anan Creek 135
  Blind River Rapids (Mitkof Highway) 139

Salmon runs (cont.)
  Brooks River (Katmai National Park) 60, 210
  Campbell Creek (Anchorage) 76, 77
  Ketchikan Creek (Ketchikan) 129
  McNeil River (McNeil River State Game Sanctuary) 60, 211
  Steep Creek (Mendenhall Glacier) 145
  Tatshenshini River 155
Salty Dawg Saloon lighthouse (Homer Spit) 111
Sand Point 204, **212**
Saxman Totem Park (Ketchikan) 126, 129
  Beaver Clan House 61
Scandinavian settlers 212, 213
Sculptures
  Balto's statue 66
  Baranov's statue 32
  Bojer Wikan's statue 138
  Captain Cook Monument (Freeborn) 71
  The Last Blue Whale (Princiotta) 71
  Pipeline Workers' Monument 118
  The Unknown First Family (Alexander) 174
  Wyland Whale Mural (Wyland) 76
Seabird Habitat, Alaska SeaLife Center (Seward) 101
Seabirds 30, 31
  Chiswell Islands (Kenai Fjords National Park) 105
  Pribilof Islands 217
  Round Island (Walrus Islands State Game Sanctuary) 208
  Whittier 116, 117
Seals 11, 28, 29, 205, 214
  harbor 100, 135, 217
  Northern fur seals 11, 29, 217
  pelts, Russian demand for 16, 51, 203, 214
  Pribilof Islands 216, 217
Sea otters 28, 135
  pelts, Russian demand for 16, 50, 51, 140, 203, 214
Seldovia (Homer) 111
  hotels 243
  restaurants 258
Senior travelers 280, 281
Service, Robert 53, 181, 200–1
Seward (Kenai Peninsula) 9, 36, 80, 92, 93, 94, **98–101**, 102–3
  Alaska SeaLife Center **100–1**
  hotels 243–4
  map 99
  restaurants 258–9
Seward Highway 6, 16, 65, 80, 93
Seward Museum (Seward) 98–9
Seward Peninsula 85, 234
Seward Waterfront (Seward) 98
Seward, William H. 51, 148
Sheldon Jackson Museum (Sitka) 140
Sheldon Museum (Haines) 148
Sheldon, Don 162, 163
Ship Creek Salmon Viewing Platform (Anchorage) **74**
Shishaldin Volcano (Izembek National Wildlife Refuge) 213
The Shooting of Dan McGrew (Service) 200
Shopping
  in Anchorage **88–9**
  on cruises 268
Shrine of St. Therese de Lisieux (Juneau) 145
Sing Lee Alley (Petersburg) 138

Sitka 9, 34, 51, 125, 126, **140–41**
  hotels 246
  map 140–1
  restaurant 260–61
Sitka National Historical Park (Sitka) 141
Skagway 9, 34, 125, **150–51**
  hotels 246–7
  restaurant 261
Skagway Museum (Skagway) 151
Skiing 15, **273**, 275
  Alyeska Resort (Girdwood) 76, 81
  Chena River State Recreation Area 177, 273
  Harding Icefield (Kenai Fjords National Park) 105, 273
  Hatcher Pass (Anchorage) 87, 273
  Hilltop Ski Area (Anchorage) 76–7
  Juneau Icefield (Juneau) 145, 273
  Ruth Glacier (Denali National Park) 273
  See also Nordic skiing
Smoking 279
Snowmachining **273**, 275
Soapy Smith **151**
Soldotna **106**
  hotels 244
  restaurants 259
Soldotna Historical Society Museum (Soldotna) 106
Sons of Norway Hall, Sing Lee Alley (Petersburg) 138
Southeast Alaska 9, 12, **124–55**
  area map 126–7
  climate 46–7
  forestry 133
  getting around 126
  Glacier Bay National Park **146–7**
  Gold Rush Routes Tour 152–3
  Haines Cut-Off Tour 154
  hotels 244–7
  restaurants 259–61
  visitor information centers 279
Southeast Alaska Discovery Center (Ketchikan) 128
Southwest Alaska 11, **202–17**
  area map 204–5
  climate 46–7
  getting around 205
  hotels 250–51
  Katmai National Park **210–11**
  Pribilof Islands **216–17**
  restaurants 263
  visitor information centers 279
The Spell of the Yukon (Service) 53, 200
Spenard (Anchorage) **75**
Spirit houses 33, 77
  See also Russian culture in Alaska
Sportfishing see Fishing
Sports 42–5, **91**, 272–5
State Parks
  Chugach State Park (Anchorage) 8, 78–9
  Denali State Park 10, 158, 164
  Kachemak Bay State Park (Homer) 9, 110, 111
  Kachemak Bay State Wilderness Park (Homer) 111
  Wood-Tikchik State Park 11, 209
  See also Historical Parks and Historic Sites; National Monuments; National Parks; National Preserves; National and State Refuges; State Recreation Areas; State Sanctuaries
State Recreation Areas
  Anchor River State Recreation Area (Anchor Point) 108

State Recreation Areas (cont.)
  Blind Slough Recreational Area (Mitkof Highway) 139
  Blueberry Lake State Recreation Site (Worthington Glacier) 119
  Caines Head State Recreation Area (Seward) 99
  Captain Cook State Recreation Area 107
  Chena River State Recreation Area (Fairbanks) 10, 177
  Deep Creek State Recreation Area (Ninilchik) 108
  Eagle Trail State Recreation Site (Tok) 194
  Kenai Flats State Recreation Site (Kenai) 107
  Lake Louise State Recreation Area 184
  Liberty Falls State Recreation Site (Edgerton Highway/McCarthy Road) 187
  Matanuska Glacier State Recreation Site (Matanuska Glacier) 184
  Mosquito Lake State Recreation Site (Haines Cut-Off) 154
  Nancy Lake State Recreation Area 158, 160
  Stariski State Recreation Area (Anchor Point) 108
  Summit Lake State Recreation Area (Hatcher Pass) 87
  Tok River State Recreation Site 10, 194–5
  Worthington Glacier State Recreation Site (Valdez) 119
  See also Historical Parks and Historic Sites; National Parks and Monuments; National Preserves; National and State Refuges; State Parks; State Sanctuaries
State Sanctuaries
  McNeil River State Game Sanctuary 11, 211
  Stan Price State Wildlife Sanctuary (Admiralty Island National Monument) 139
  Walrus Islands State Game Sanctuary 11, **208**
  See also Historical Parks and Historic Sites; National Monuments; National Parks; National Preserves; National and State Refuges; State Parks; State Recreation Areas
Steese Highway 158, 296
Steese Highway Tour 10, **179**, 296
Sterling **106**
Sterling Highway 9, 96, 97, 106
St. George Island (Pribilof Islands) 216
St. Herman's Theological Seminary (Kodiak) 33, 206
Stikine River (Wrangell) 134, 135
St. Innocent see Veniaminov, Bishop Ioan
St. Innocent Russian Orthodox Church (Anchorage) 15, 61, **74**
St. Michael's Russian Orthodox Cathedral (Sitka) 33, 140
St. Nicholas Russian Orthodox Church (Eklutna, Anchorage) 33, 77
St. Nicholas Russian Orthodox Church (Juneau) 33
St. Paul Island (Pribilof Islands) 204, 216
  hotels 251
Stony Hill Overlook (Denali National Park) 169

Student travelers 280, 281
Subsistence fishing and hunting 19, 23, 213, 226
Sukakpak Mountain (Dalton Highway) 222
Summer Bay (Unalaska) 11, 215
Surprise Lake (Aniakchak National Monument) 204, 212
Susitna River (Denali Highway) 162, 165
Symphony Lake (Chugach State Park) 78–9

T

Taiga 28
Taku Chief (Nenana) 173
Talkeetna (Western Interior Alaska) 158, **162–3**
  hotels 248–9
  restaurants 262
Talkeetna Cemetery (Talkeetna) 163
Talkeetna Historical Society Museum (Talkeetna) 162–3
Talkeetna Mountains 84, 86, 87, 160
Talkeetna Ranger Station 162, 273
Tanana River 172, 173, 175, 194
Tangle Lakes, Denali Highway 165
Tatshenshini River **155**
Taylor Highway 10, 196, 197, 296
Taylor Road see Kougarok Road
Teller Road (Nome) 11
Temperate rainforest 28, 131
Tenakee Springs **139**
Tetlin National Wildlife Refuge 10, 194, **195**
Thorne Bay (Prince of Wales Island) 133
Three Guardsmen Lake and Peaks (Haines Cut-Off) 154
Tidewater glaciers see Glaciers
Tipping 279
Tisha (Purdy) 196
Tlingit 21, 22, 32, 49, 51, 125, 129, 132, 134, 140, 141, 155
  See also Totem poles
Tok **194**
  hotels 250
  restaurants 263
Tok Cut-Off **194**
Tok River State Recreation Site 10, **194–5**
Tongass National Forest 126, 128, 131, 132, 133, 139, 144
  campgrounds 240, 241
Tony Knowles Coastal Trail (Anchorage) 8, **74–5**
Top of the World Highway 10, 296
Totem Bight State Historical Park (Ketchikan) 129
Totem poles 21, 22, **129**
  Chief Shakes Island (Wrangell) 134
  Hydaburg (Prince of Wales Island) 133
  Kasaan (Prince of Wales Island) 132, 133
  Klawock (Prince of Wales Island) 132
  Saxman Totem Park (Ketchikan) 129
  Sitka National Historical Park (Sitka) 141
  Southeast Alaska Discovery Center (Ketchikan) 128
  Totem Bight State Historical Park (Ketchikan) 129
Tours 274, 275
  Alaska Highway 298
  Dalton Highway Tour 222–3

Tours (cont.)
Denali Highway Tour 165
Elliott Highway (Fairbanks) 178
Gold Rush Routes 152–3
Haines Cut-Off Tour 154
Steese Highway Tour 179
Turnagain Arm Tour 80–81
Yukon River 198–9
See also Cruising tours, Outdoor activities, Trains
Town square (Anchorage) 66
Tracy Arm (Inside Passage) 34
Trains 292–3, 294
Alaska Railroad 166, 294–5
event trains 295
flag-stop service 295
tickets and booking 295
tours 292–5
White Pass and Yukon Route Railroad 52, 150, 152–3, 292, 293
Trans-Alaska Pipeline 9, 16, 17, 56, 63, 113, 119, 174, 181, **186**, 222, 223, 224
Alaska Pipeline Crossing, Yukon River 198, 222
Transfiguration of our Lord Russian Orthodox Church (Ninilchik) 95, 108
Travel information **288–99**
air travel 288–9
Alaska Highway *see* Alaska Highway
Alaska Marine Highway *see* Alaska Marine Highway
Alaska Railroad *see* Alaska Railroad
Alaska Travel Industry Association 265, 267, 278, 279
buses 292, 293
bush travel 272, 275
cars and 4WD vehicles 296, 297
cruises *see* Cruising, Cruising tours
disabled travelers 280–81
insurance 283
off-road driving 297
road rules 296
seniors 280, 281
students 280, 281
tickets and booking 293
trains *see* Trains
travelers with disabilities 280–81
RVs *see* RVs
weather information 278, 297
Tr'ondëk Hwëch'in Dänojà Zho Cultural Center (Dawson City) 200
Trumpeter swans 10, 31, 123, 195
Kenai National Wildlife Refuge 107
Swan Observatory 139
Tetlin National Wildlife Refuge 195
Tsimshian 21, 23, 49, 125, 129
See also Totem poles
Turnagain Arm (Anchorage) 8, 63, 80
Turnagain Arm Tour **80–81**
Tustumena 203, 205, **215**, 290

U

Ukkuqsi Archeological Site (Barrow) 226
Umiaq 20, 23, 49, 221, 226
Unalaska *see* Dutch Harbor/Unalaska
UNESCO World Heritage Sites
Glacier Bay National Park 9, 125, 126, 127, **146–7**
Wrangell-St. Elias National Park 10, 57, 61, 155, 181, 183, 187, **192–3**
University of Alaska Fairbanks
Museum of the North (Fairbanks) 10, 175
The Unknown First Family (Alexander) 174

V

Valdez 36, 37, 114, **118–19**, 181, 224
heli-skiing 273, 275
hotels 244
marine terminal of Trans-Alaska Pipeline 9, 113
restaurants 259
Valdez Museum (Valdez) 118
Valhalla (Petersburg) 138, 139
Valley glaciers *see* Glaciers
Valley of 10,000 Smokes (Katmai National Park) 210
Van Buren, Edith 52
Vancouver, Captain George 50, 130, 132
Veniaminov, Bishop Ioan 33, 67, 69, 74, 140, 141
Visas 278
Visitor information centers 278, 279
Volcanoes **24–5**
Aleutian 8, 202–17
Great Sitkin (Great Sitkin Island) 24
Mount Augustine (Cook Inlet) 25
Mount Cleveland (Chuginadak Island) 24
Mount Douglas (Katmai National Park) 211
Mount Iliamna (Lake Clark National Park) 209
Mount Katmai (Katmai National Park) 211
Mount Redoubt (Lake Clark National Park) 209
Mount Spurr (Anchorage) 74, 107
Mount Wrangell (Wrangell-St. Elias National Park) 192
Mount Veniaminof 25
Novarupta (Katmai National Park) 25, 210, 211
Shishaldin Volcano (Izembek National Wildlife Refuge) 213
Skookum (Wrangell-St. Elias National Park) 193
tectonic activity 24

W

Wager with the Wind (Arness) 163
Walker Lake 220, 230
Walruses 29, 208
Walrus Islands State Game Sanctuary 11, **208**
Wasilla **85**, 160
hotels 241
restaurants 258
Western Interior Alaska 10, **156–79**
area map 158–9
climate 46–7
Denali Highway Tour 165
Denali National Park 10, 28, 61, 157, 158, 159, **166–9**, 170–71
getting around 159
hotels 247–9
restaurants 261–2
Steese Highway Tour 179
visitor information centers 279
Whalebone Arch and Brower's Café (Barrow) 226–7
Whales 28
belugas 71, **80**
grays 104
humpbacks 8, 104, 147
minkes 104, 147
orcas 28, 147
whale-watching 104, 125, 146, 147
White Pass (Gold Rush Routes) 153
White Pass and Yukon Route Railroad 52, 150, 152–3, 292, 293

Whitehorse, Canada 199, 299
Whitewater rafting 15, 274, 275
Alsek 155
Aniakchak 212
Charley 196, 198
Chilkoot 152
Chulitna 162, 274
classification of rapids 274
Eagle 274
Gulkana (Paxson) 185, 274
Hulahula 220, 224
John 220, 224
Kenai 94, 96, 274
Kobuk 220, 224, 230, 231
Kongukut 220, 224
Matanuska 82–3, 274
Nenana 10, 158, 167, 172, 173, 274
Noatak 220, 224, 231
Sheenjek 224
Susitna 155
Tatshenshini 155
Yukon 196, 198
See also Canoeing, Kayaking
Whitney Museum (Valdez) 118
Whittier 9, 36, 113, 114, **116**
hotels 244
kittiwake colonies 113, 117
restaurants 259
Whittier, John Greenleaf 116
Wickersham State Historical Site (Juneau) 143
Wickersham, Judge James 143, 197
Wilderness lodges *see* Hotels
Wildfires **195**
Wildflowers 232
Wildlife 16, **28–9**
Willow 87, **160**
hotels 249
Will Rogers and Wiley Post Monument (Barrow) 226
Wiseman (Dalton Highway) 222
hotels 251
Wolves 17, 169
Wonder Lake (Denali National Park) 10, 166, 169
Wood-Tikchik State Park 11, 204, **209**
World Championship Sled Dog Races (Anchorage) 39, 45, 91
Worthington Glacier (Valdez) 9, 119
Wrangell 9, 34, 35, 125, 126, **134–5**
hotels 246
restaurants 261
discovery of copper 118
Wrangell Museum (Wrangell) 134
Wrangell Narrows, Tongass National Forest 131
Wrangell-St. Elias Mountains 10, 182, 184, 192, 194
Wrangell-St. Elias National Park 10, 57, 61, 155, 181, 183, 187, **192–3**
hotels 250
restaurants 263
visitors' center 185
Wyland Whale Mural (Wyland) 67
Wyland, Robert 67
Wyland Whale Mural 67

Y

Yakutat 37, **155**
Yukon Queen II 197, 199
Yukon Quest International Sled Dog Race 39, 45, 198
Yukon River 10, 179, 181, 182, 196, 197, **198–9**, 200
Yukon-Charley Rivers National Preserve 10, **196**, 198
Yup'ik 11, 18, 20, 21, 23, 73, 219

Acknowledgments

Dorling Kindersley would like to thank the following people whose contributions and assistance have made the preparation of this book possible.

Main Contributor

After graduating from university, Deanna Swaney cast around in search of a career befitting a hopeless travel addict and eventually – following a bout of financial systems programming – she stumbled across travel writing and photography. As a result, over the past 20 years, she has researched and written eight first edition Lonely Planet titles, covering Bolivia; Tonga; Samoa; Iceland, Greenland, and the Faroe Islands; Zimbabwe, Botswana, and Namibia; Norway; The Arctic; and Namibia. She has also collaborated on dozens of Lonely Planet updates on six continents and has contributed text and photographs to numerous newspaper, magazine, and web features. Between trips, she finds time to work on construction projects around Big Lake, Alaska, and seeks out additions to her increasingly burdensome collections of rocks and frogs.

Additional Contributor

Eric Amrine is a freelance writer, photo-grapher, and musician living with his wife and two children in Seattle's Fremont district. His favorite travel assignments include hiking, kayaking, and wildlife, and have taken him through Alaska's Inside Passage via luxury yacht, white-water rafting in Oregon's Rogue River wilderness, and expedition cruising to pristine beaches and remote islands of the Sea of Cortez in Mexico. Eric is passionate about the Caribbean, having reviewed the cruise ships that regularly sail there.

Fact Checker Don Pitcher

Proofreader Vandana Bhagra

Indexer Jyoti Dhar

Design and Editorial

Publisher Douglas Amrine
Publishing Managers
Jane Ewart, Scarlett O'Hara
Senior Editor Kathryn Lane
Senior Designer Paul Jackson
Senior Cartographic Editor Casper Morris
Senior DTP Designer Jason Little
DTP Designer Natasha Lu
Picture Researcher Ellen Root

Editorial and Design Revisions
Claire Baranowski, Mariana Evmolpidou, Hayley Maher, Sonal Modha, Marianne Petrou, Don Pitcher, Rada Radojicic, Ellen Root, Conrad Van Dyk

DK Picture Library Romaine Werblow

Production Controller Linda Dare

Additional Photography
Geoff Brightling, Eric Crichton, Peter Gathercole, Frank Greenaway, Andrew Holligan, Ellen Howdon, Dave King, Kim Taylor.

Cartography DK Cartography, London

Special Assistance
Dorling Kindersley would like to thank the following for their kind permission to photograph at their establishments: Alaska Aviation Heritage Museum, Alaska Native Heritage Center, Jason Wettstein and the Alaska SeaLife Center, Alaska State Museum, Alaska State Trooper Museum, Janet Asaro and the Anchorage Museum of History and Art, Baranov Museum, Hammer Museum, Isabel Miller Museum, Petroglyph Beach State Historic Site, Pioneer Park Air Museum, Pratt Museum, Saxman Totem Park, Sheldon Jackson Museum, Sheldon Museum, Sitka National Historical Park, Soldotna Historical Society Museum, Southeast Alaska Discovery Center, Totem Heritage Center, Town Docks Museum, Hull, Valdez Museum, Wrangell Museum.

Picture Credits
t=top; tc=top centre; tr=top right; cla=centre left above; ca=centre above; cra=centre right above; cl=centre left; c=centre; cr=centre right; clb=centre left below; cb=centre below; crb=centre right below; bl=bottom left; bc=bottom centre; br=bottom right.

Every effort has been made to trace the copyright holders and we apologize in advance for any unintentional omissions. We would be pleased to insert the appropriate acknowledgments in any subsequent edition of this publication.

Works of art have been reproduced with the permission of the following copyright holders: *Crystal Lattice*, Front Endpaper tl, 62, 68tr; © Robert Pfitzenmeier; *Raven the Creator*, 72tr; © John Hoover.

The Publishers are grateful to the following individuals, companies, and picture libraries for permission to reproduce their photographs:

Alamy Images: Ace Stock Limited 81br; Alaska Stock LLC 20tr, 20clb, 38tl, 40cla, 40br, 41tl, 78tr, 78clb, 80tr, 182cla, 184t, 217cr, 231br, 270b; Bryan and Cherry Alexander Photography 47tr, 56cb, 224tl; Wally Bauman 161cb; David Boag 117tr; Brand X Pictures 10t; Bill Brooks 37tl, 154clb; Loetscher Chlaus 179cl, 189tl, 219b, 220tr, 224br, 225cr; Gary Cook 183tr, 199cra, 199crb, 199bl; Danita Delimont 44t, 139cl, 166cla, 204cl, 269tl; David Sanger Photography 18t, 23bl, 32-33c; Robert Destefano 34tr; Dennis Frates 254tr; Jeff Greenberg 254cla; Imagebroker 86cl, 87c, 150cra, 153tl; Jon Arnold Images 34br, 36clb, 53crb, 53bl, 75cr, 86tr, 188cla, 193bl; Steve Bloom Images 210cla; Steve Bly 19tr, 40tr; Steven J. Kazlowski 135br; Terrance Klassen 17b; Erich Kuchling 207br; Dennis MacDonald 70tl; Medioimages 26tr, 134t; Ron Niebrugge 2-3, 10bc, 14, 16t, 17tr, 18bl, 19b, 27tl, 34clb, 43b, 44br, 61tr, 104cla, 104clb, 161bl, 165bc, 180, 183cr, 188tr, 190-191, 193tl, 198cla, 220clb, 222cla, 223crb, 223b; Luc Novovitch 33tr; Purcell Team 32c, 32br; DY Riess MD 37cra; Kevin Schafer 203b, 214bc; John Schwieder 147tl, 158cl, 194br; Allen Thorton 165cla; Visions of America, LLC 107crb; Richard Wainscoat 136-137; Doug Wilson 40bl, 41cr; WorldFoto 35bl.

Alaska Airlines: 288b. Alaska Photo Graphics: Patrick J. Endres 8cra, 9t, 9br, 11tr, 11bl, 16bl, 21tl, 30tl, 33crb, 36tr, 36br, 37bl, 38-39c, 39cra, 39bl, 43tc, 45tc, 45br, 84cla, 85bl, 112, 113b, 116bl, 156, 163b, 170-171, 173bl, 176cr, 181b, 188bl, 189cra, 193cr, 197bl, 198bl, 199tl, 210tr, 210bl, 218, 222tr, 222br, 223tl, 227b. Alaska Public Lands Information Centers NPS: 66cla. Alaska Railroad Corporation: 294b, 295tl. Alaska SeaLife Center: Clark James Mischler 100cl; Jason Wettstein 100clb, 101tl, 101cra. Alaska Volcano Observatory: Alaska Division of Geological and Geophysical Surveys 25tl, C. Neal 211br, C. Nye 211cr; Cella B. and the US National Park Service 192cla; Image Analysis Laboratory, NASA Johnson Space Center 24cl, 24cr; U.S. Geological Survey 25bl, M. L. Coombs 57br, Game McGimsey 25tr. Alaska Wild Berry Products: 76tl. Anchorage Convention and Visitors Bureau: 67tr. Anchorage Museum of History and Art: 67cr, 68cla, 69c, 69bc. Autographs and Ogden Photography: © 2005 Doug Ogden 185tr.

Corbis: 13cr; 52br, 54t, 54bc, 59 (inset), 151br; Dave Bartruff 21tr; Tom Bean 22crb, 27cra, 207t, 209tl; Peter Beck 40-41c; Joel Bennett 22cl, 208b; Bettmann 48, 51bc, 53tr, 54cb, 55tr, 56tl; Gary Braasch 119crb; Tom Brakefield 29b; Brandon D. Cole 80br, 131cb; Richard A. Cooke 205b; Roy Corral 211tl; Richard Cummins 265tl; Michael DeYoung 157br, 273t; Kevin Fleming 42cl, 133br, 159br, 276-277; Natalie Fobes 57tl, 202, 214cl; D. Robert and Lorri Franz 30crb; Peter Guttman 23crb; Carol Havens 175b; Historical Picture Archive 50t; Eric and David Hosking 111tr, 240br; Rob Howard 155bl; Chase Jarvis 236-237; Ann Johansson 20br, 235br; Mark A. Johnson 146clb; Wolfgang Kaehler 35cra; Karen Kasmauski 186cla; Steve Kaufman 31cra, 169tr, 195c, 209b; Kit Kittle 139tr; Bob Krist 77br, 85cr, 87tr; Dan Lamont 22bl, 133tl; Danny Lehman 58-59, 166clb; George D. Lepp 232cla; W. Wayne Lockwood, M.D 28cr; Gunter Marx Photography 55crb, 102-103, 299tl; Michael Maslan Historic Photographs 32cla, 49ca; Charles Mauzy 161c; Arthur Morris 233tc; David Muench 26cla; Marc Muench 82-83; Museum of History and Industry 52cla; Pat O'Hara 6-7, 20-21c, 29cl, 38cla, 231tl, 235tl; Charles O'Rear 32bl; Papilio: Bjorn Backe 195clb; Douglas Peebles 35tl, 39cr; PEMCO - Webster and Stevens Collection, Museum of History and Industry, Seattle: 38tr; Greg Probst 27bl, 129tr; Neil Rabinowitz 1; Lynda Richardson 80cla; David Samuel Robbins 255bl; Joel W. Rogers 30tr, 105tl; Galen Rowell 30-31c, 60tr, 84bc, 221t, 226cla, 228cr, 229 230; Progressive Image: Bob Rowan 21cra, 23tr; Richard Hamilton Smith 169crb; Scott T. Smith 29cr; Paul A. Souders 8br, 28cb, 29bl, 38bl, 60bl, 71tl, 85t, 131crb, 162clb, 186bl, 233bl; Stapleton Collection 7 (inset); Vince Streano 35br, 151tl, 174cla, 187crb; Corbis Sygma: Jacques Langevin 32tr, Brenda Tharp 225cra; Tim Thompson 132cl, 147cr, 151cr, 216cl; Allen Thorton 165cla; US Airforce/ZUMA: Joshua Strang 176b; Kennan Ward 31cb, 109cr; Karl Weatherly 135tr; Werner Forman Archive 21bc; Stuart Westmorland 167tl, 217b; Nik Wheeler 230tc; Staffan Widstrand 23cla, 225br; Yogi, Inc.: 168b; Zefa: Frank Krahmer 225bc; Elisabeth Sauer 164bc.

Garote: 21crb.

Getty Images: Digital Vision 176cla; Gerry Ellis 225cl; Image Bank: Kim Heacox 26–27c; National Geographic Image Collection: Joseph Baylor Roberts 213t; Photographer's Choice Collection: Tom Walker 230b.

The Granger Collection, New York: 49bl, 50bl, 52-53c.

Holland America Line: 29cb, 266tr, 266br, 267tr, 268bc.

Juneau Convention and Visitors Bureau: 28tr.

King Salmondeaux Lodge: 241tr.

Mary Evans Picture Library: 51tc, 52bl, 53c, 237 (Inset), 277 (Inset). Masterfile: Andrew Wenzel 38br.

National Oceanic and Atmospheric Administration: 25crb.

National Park Service, Digital Image Archives: 212tl, 212b.

North Wind Picture Archives: 51clb.

Photolibrary.com: Index Stock Collection: Mark Gibson 42bc; Alaska Stock Images: G. Smith Kevin 120–121.

Princess Cruises: 264tc.

Deanna Swaney: 69tr, 78cla, 79cr, 215tl.

US Fish and Wildlife Service, Alaska Image Library: 29crb, 161bc, 232cra; Steve Amstrup 109crb; Lee Forrest B. 29ca; Bob Angell 217bl; Kate Banish 28br; Connie Barclay 228tl; Vernon Byrd 216br; David Cline 29tr; Donna A. Dewhurst 161clb, 161crb, 174tr; Steve Hillebrand 28bl, 109cl; Izembek National Wildlife Refuge: 213br; Dean Kildaw 217cl; John Sarvis 161br; Art Sowls 217cra, 217c, 217crb.

University of Washington Libraries, Special Collections: 53tl (Negative Number – UW9069).

USDA Forest Service, Tongass National Forest: 27crb.

Harry M. Walker: 215cb, 234b.

Front Endpaper: All special photography except Alamy: Ron Niebrugge tr; Alaska Photo Graphics: Patrick J. Endres trc, cb, cr; Corbis: Natalie Fobes tlc.

Cover Picture Credits
Front: Alamy Images: Richard Wainscoat main image; Corbis: Kevin Fleming clb.

Back: Alaska Photo Graphics: Patrick J. Endres tl; Corbis: *Sea Monster and Master Carver Totem Poles* by John Wallace, photograph Greg Probst bl; Courtesy of the Alaska Railroad Corporation: clb; DK Images: Andy Holligan cla.

Spine: Alamy Images: Richard Wainscoat t; DK Images: Frank Greenaway b

All other images © Dorling Kindersley. For more information see www.DKimages.com

Transport Map of Alaska

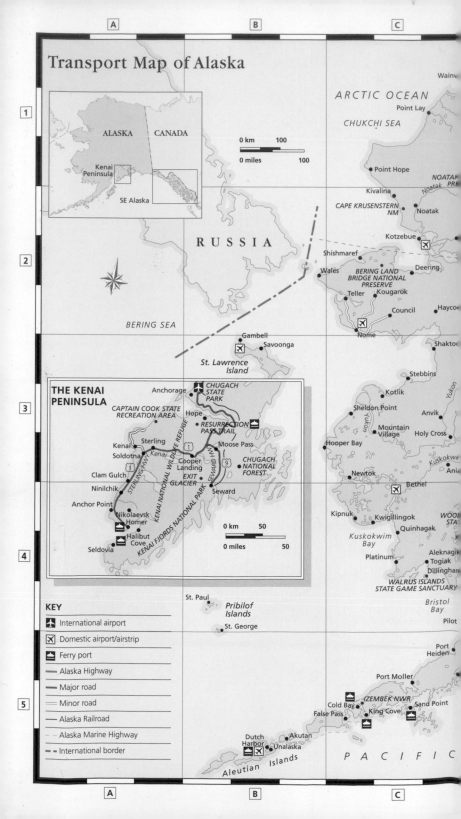

ALASKA CANADA

Kenai
Peninsula

SE Alaska

0 km 100

0 miles 100

ARCTIC OCEAN

Wainw

Point Lay

CHUKCHI SEA

Point Hope

NOATA
PRI

Kivalina

Noatak

CAPE KRUSENSTERN
NM

Noatak

Kotzebue

Shishmaref

BERING LAND
BRIDGE NATIONAL
PRESERVE

Deering

Wales

Teller

Kougarok

RUSSIA

Council

Hayco

Nome

Shakto

BERING SEA

Gambell

Savoonga

St. Lawrence
Island

Stebbins

Kotlik

**THE KENAI
PENINSULA**

Anchorage

CHUGACH
STATE
PARK

Sheldon Point

Anvik

CAPTAIN COOK STATE
RECREATION AREA

Hope

RESURRECTION
PASS TRAIL

Mountain
Village

Holy Cross

Kenai

Sterling

Moose Pass

Hooper Bay

Yukon

Soldotna

Cooper
Landing

CHUGACH
NATIONAL
FOREST

Kuskokwi

Ania

Clam Gulch

EXIT
GLACIER

Ninilchik

Seward

Bethel

Anchor Point

Nikolaevsk
Homer

Newtok

Halibut
Cove

KENAI FIORDS NATIONAL PARK

Kipnuk

Kwigillingok

WOO
STA

Quinhagak

Seldovia

0 km 50

0 miles 50

Kuskokwim
Bay

Platinum

Aleknagi

Togiak

Dillinghan

WALRUS ISLANDS
STATE GAME SANCTUARY

St. Paul

Pribilof
Islands

Bristol
Bay

St. George

Pilot

KEY

✈ International airport

☒ Domestic airport/airstrip

⛴ Ferry port

— Alaska Highway

— Major road

— Minor road

— Alaska Railroad

-- Alaska Marine Highway

-·- International border

Port
Heiden

Port Moller

Cold Bay

IZEMBEK NWR

False Pass

King Cove

Sand Point

Dutch
Harbor

Akutan

Unalaska

Aleutian Islands

PACIFIC